THE JEWS OF PARIS
AND THE FINAL SOLUTION

STUDIES IN JEWISH HISTORY

JEHUDA REINHARZ, GENERAL EDITOR

Other Volumes Are in Preparation

THE JEWS OF PARIS AND THE FINAL SOLUTION

Communal Response and Internal Conflicts, 1940–1944

JACQUES ADLER

New York   Oxford
OXFORD UNIVERSITY PRESS
1987

Oxford University Press

Oxford   New York   Toronto
Delhi   Bombay   Calcutta   Madras   Karachi
Petaling Jaya   Singapore   Hong Kong   Tokyo
Nairobi   Dar es Salaam   Cape Town
Melbourne   Auckland

and associated companies in
Beirut   Berlin   Ibadan   Nicosia

Original title of French Edition
Face à la persécution: les organizations juives à Paris de 1940 á 1944

Copyright © Calmann-Lévy 1985
Copyright © Jacques Adler 1985

Published by Oxford University Press, Inc.,
200 Madison Avenue, New York, New York 10016

Oxford is a registered trademark of Oxford University Press

Library of Congress Cataloging-in-Publication Data
Adler, Jacques, 1927–
The Jews of Paris and the final solution.
(Studies in Jewish history)
Bibliography: p.   Includes index.
1. Jews—France—Paris—Persecutions.
2. Holocaust, Jewish (1939–1945)—France—Paris.
3. Union générale des Israélites de France.
4. World War, 1939–1945—Underground movements, Jewish—France—Paris.
5. Paris (France)—Ethnic relations. I. Title. II. Series.
DS135.F85P243   1987   940.53′15′03924044   86–31302
ISBN 0-19-504305-7

987654321

Printed in the United States of America
on acid-free paper

*To the memory of my father, Szymon Jacob Adlersztejn,
killed at Birkenau.*

To the French who saved my mother and my sister.

*To my comrades of the companie Rayman, battalion 51/22,
1e Régiment de Paris.*

Jacques Adler, July 1942, soon after the introduction of the compulsory wearing of the "Yellow Star."

Preface

I

The choices of areas of research for students of history are often the outcome of accidents in one's personal life. Saul Friëdlander's *Pius XII and the Third Reich* was no doubt influenced by his experience as a Jewish orphan about to enter the Catholic priesthood in Occupied France. Henri Noguères's participation in the French Resistance led him to study both the people involved in the Resistance and the ideas that motivated such a unique group of individuals. My own case is equally affected by accidents of birth and circumstances.

Some weeks before 8 May 1975, I received an invitation to attend a reunion of former members of the Jewish Communist underground movement, which operated in Paris during the Occupation, and to celebrate the thirtieth anniversary of the defeat of Nazi Germany. It was through the emotional turmoil of that reunion, the sight of former comrades, that questions, long dormant in my mind, emerged: Are people powerless when confronted with a state determined to destroy them? Why did not more Jews survive? How did we survive? Did we, the survivors, do all we could at the time to help more people to survive? Were we really helpless?

These questions appeared to me all the more striking when I observed these seemingly ordinary men and women, all middle-aged now, who had once chosen to risk all and defy those who had singled them out as subhumans. Each one was a former immigrant Jew or the son or daughter of an immigrant. Had they, as a group, really represented a threat to the well-armed German soldiers who patrolled the streets of Occupied Paris? In fact they had. All the members of that group could have boastfully recounted feats of courage and heroism wrought from them in response to those who were executing the timetable for the genocide of the Jewish people.

When French armed resistance began in 1941, these people belonged to an organization that represented a major section of that resistance. By 1943 the Jewish Communist underground was among the most prominent forces still fighting in Paris. Neither the Gestapo nor the French police, neither torture nor death, could tame this organization into submission. As each wave of fighters fell, new volunteers emerged from the Jewish population to replace them.

This was a unique group of individuals. Their stubbornness was born of that pain and anger which came from losing loved ones. Their political ideology sustained them even when they faced the threat of starvation and the loneliness of clandestine existence. Their anguish was all the more intense because they belonged to that community of immigrant Jews in Paris which was first selected, and in the greatest numbers, as fodder for the Final Solution.

As the first and only organization in the Paris Jewish community to take up arms, they were perceived by other Jews as provocateurs who were putting the community at risk. But to them, as Jewish Communists, it seemed clear from the outset that the community was facing a life or death confrontation. Therefore they chose to fight rather than be taken without resisting. For this they were misunderstood and isolated. For other Jewish organizations, it took the experience of persecution before they finally accepted the fact that a war was being waged against the Jews.

Within organized group responses one also finds individual responses, based upon personal experience, which, when examined, contribute to the understanding of group motivation. I feel obliged to relate some of my own experiences as examples of what each of those who survived has encountered, one way or another, as well as to present to the reader the personal feelings that led me to undertake this study.

The Jews of Paris I am referring to were the immigrants from Eastern Europe. They are my past, and my family was an integral part of their community. Yiddish was spoken in our home though I addressed my parents in French. As a boy, some of my friends were children of French-born Jews whose families had been living in France for countless generations, and who always referred to themselves as *Israélites,* as they preferred to be called, believing the term to be less pejorative than *Juif,* the term used in reference to the foreign or immigrant Jew. But I always felt more at home in my parents' cultural milieu. It was, somehow, more comfortable, not only because I found more warmth there, which is a personal sentiment, but because it had its own specific way of expressing human relations. I could never understand why my French friends were so implacably nationalistic, why they were always ill at ease whenever I would throw into a sentence a Yiddish word which seemed to me so much more appropriate. Indeed, the immigrants, despite or perhaps because of their own parochial, no less than cosmopolitan, attitudes, lived and acted in a manner that breathed a unique kind of brotherhood. In homes such as ours, which I believe not to have been too different from the large majority of immigrants' homes, what mattered most was not class but rather the notion of belonging to a people.

Inevitably, my past, my personal experiences, have definitively influenced my selection of issues and finally my judgments. I would nonetheless like to believe that I have maintained some objectivity. But what does objectivity consist of when one's moral standards become subjected to the stresses of such extraordinary times? When I compare my personal memories of events and of the countless tragedies I have witnessed with the records of the bureaucratic process of extermination, how can I judge the desperate attempts by Jewish organizations to develop "appropriate" survival responses simply by their results?

I am only too well aware of the limits of my own experiences, and my own inadequacies in the face of the collective experience, to assume for a moment that I am in a position to define precisely the meaning of "collective experience." Yet I was there. I remember a day in June 1941 when I saw my father standing behind rows of barbed wire that seemed to me enormously high and deep. I had gone to the camp where he was interned in the hope of seeing him, and there we tried to catch each other's words above the voices of hundreds of others who had come with the same intention. The French gendarmes were running amuck trying to move us away from the camp perimeter. It was the last time I saw him; I was fourteen years old.

I remember too deciding that the time had come to tell my mother that I was a member of an underground organization. That was early in 1943. She opened her arms to me, and with tears in her eyes told me to "be careful." There was no question why, no attempt to dissuade me, and no probing about what I "did." It was not ignorance that explained her response. Every Parisian and certainly every Jew knew of the terrible reprisals extracted from the would-be resisters and their families. Everyone saw all-too-frequent black-bordered posters on the walls of Paris announcing executions. My mother's silence was a defiant answer made with the full understanding of the risks involved. I later asked some of my underground comrades, the few who still had a living parent, what the reaction had been in their homes and each had met with a similar reaction. Were we an unusual assortment of people? Perhaps.

But of one thing I am certain: though our actions may have been limited to a comparatively small group, the sentiments that motivated us were shared by many more. The blanket of fear which had covered all our lives was tightly woven with the threads of hatred for all those forces that had shattered our families and turned our lives into permanent nightmares. Of the immigrant population of prewar Paris, one half was sent first to Drancy, the central transit camp from which deportation from France took place. From there they were sent for "resettlement" to Eastern Europe in sealed wagons formerly used for horses or goods. Whole families vanished.

In our home only my father had been "caught" and in June 1942 had been sent on his way to Auschwitz. Can the reader visualize what it is like to wait for a word, even a line, or any indication of the fate of the deportee? And then to wait again for a sign of life once the hostilities are over. I remember the weeks following the end of the war; deportees were beginning to return from the camps, and we were walking up our narrow street when my mother suddenly began running toward someone who was walking our way. She was calling out my father's name and I ran with her believing for an instant that it was him. But history usually does not deal with individual emotions.

The three incidents that I have chosen to relate were shared in a multitude of forms by all survivors. Their significance, I believe, is not only psychological but historical in character as well. The experiences I have related point both to the conditions under which Jews lived and to the problems of building new lives once the war was over.

This study is undertaken not only to record and explain the past but also for deep personal reasons. In the first place it is dedicated to the memory of my father who left home at the age of thirty-eight and who died in Birkenau at the age of forty-one. To the memory of my mother who died in Melbourne at the age of sixty, a broken human being, who never recovered from her personal experiences, her sufferings, and the loss of her life's companion. Finally, to the memory of all my underground comrades who were no longer with us when Paris was liberated in August 1944. And particularly to those to whom I owe my life: those who refused to betray their comrades under Gestapo tortures.

In the course of researching the role of Jewish organizations in the survival of the Jews in Paris under the German Occupation, 1940–44, I listened to many heart-breaking testimonies without which no such study can be carried out. One in particular, I feel, needs to be related as it encapsulates the tragedy that befell the Jewish population as well as explains some of their reactions.

A demographer now working in the Institut National d'Etudes Démographiques whom I met in Paris in 1978 told me of an incident he had witnessed. In July 1942 he was a boy of twelve and lived with his parents in a block of apartments in the twelfth arrondissement. On 16 July, a Thursday, and traditionally a school holiday in France, he had been playing in the street. That day the French police had raided that area and were arresting Jews. Since he was not Jewish the raid did not affect him or his family directly. But his play was interrupted when a young Jewish schoolmate, the son of a neighbor, came up to him. The Jewish boy and his parents had been arrested in that day's raid but he was released because he was French-born; his parents were detained because they were foreigners. The boy had returned to the family's apartment only to find the door sealed. He then went to each family in the block begging to be taken in until his parents returned, but all refused him. Now he stood in the street, tears streaming down his face, flourishing a metro ticket. One family had covered their refusal with the price of a train ride. After the war the father of the Jewish boy came back from Auschwitz and returned to his former apartment in search of his son. He never found the boy and a few years later committed suicide.

While this tragedy is not typical of the non-Jewish response to the persecution of the Jews, it must be said that such cases were not rare. It does reflect on the many who turned their heads as these cruel tragedies were taking place before their eyes, and, at the same time, it illustrates the desperate isolation experienced by many Jews. These Jews felt that they were "outsiders" and sensed that only their own resources and those of their own small community could be relied upon. Their responses to Nazi terror were in part motivated by this feeling of abandonment.

II

In any comparative examination of the destruction of the Jews in Europe, those in France, having lost only 25 percent of their number, appear to have fared relatively better than those of almost all the other European countries. This was due to a number of factors, not the least being the help given to them by the French population. But of all the factors that contributed to their survival, the role and actions of the Jewish organizations were of crucial importance.

The task of writing the overall history of the defense of the Jews in France needs to begin with an examination of what the Jews themselves did; what their organizations were able to achieve in order to assist individuals. But in the final analysis, the Jewish population itself, whether French-born or immigrant, depended not only on the personal assistance of non-Jews but also on communal structures that were established long before the war in order to help those to whom no external help was available.

This study is therefore directed at examining the role of the Jewish organizations and their efforts to organize and support the Jews in their search for ways and means that would help them survive. It is a study of responses and of leadership of a community under siege. Although we may never be able to establish, with any degree of certainty, the organizations' material contribution to the survival of the Jews, we are able to show that by their work they not only directly assisted thousands but, perhaps more important, contributed significantly to the survival of the overwhelming majority by alerting the non-Jewish population to the terrible threat faced by every Jewish family. In that sense, therefore, this book contributes to the overall understanding of the conditions that permitted so many Jews to survive in France.

The central problem faced by the Jewish organizations was that the anti-Jewish measures were applied gradually. Such a situation gave rise to conflicting evaluations, so that responses were fragmented. The problems faced by the organizations in Paris in developing a common policy stemmed from the fact that there had never been a unified Jewish community. The native-born and the foreign Jews were separate communal bodies which never joined to form a single representative organization. Even in the late 1930s, when Jewish organizations viewed antisemitism in France as a serious problem and when Nazi racialism had become a source of major concern to world Jewry, no consensus was achieved about either the extent of the problem or what could be done.

The Central Consistory, the body representing French Judaism, which was supported by those French-born Jews who sought to ensure the continued existence of the Jewish religious tradition, viewed the "Jewish Question" at home in terms of closing the French frontiers to Jewish refugees from the east. As for Nazism, that was a question best left to those who determined French foreign policy. In both cases the Central Consistory refused to consider public Jewish initiatives. The immigrants' organizations, in contrast, saw the close relationship between the two issues. The immigrant organizations were firmly convinced that it was imperative to develop a wide public protest. They sought in vain the support of the Central Consistory for a world boycott of German products. They also failed to convince the Central Consistory to give continuing aid to all the Jewish refugees, victims of German racism.

The conflicts between the two distinct groups of organizations in Paris were due not only to serious political differences but also to irreconcilable conceptions of identity. French Judaism defined itself in French national terms. It rejected any notions that would question its place in French society by endowing Judaism with national characteristics. As far as it was concerned Judaism was one of those religions that some Frenchmen practiced and some not. The immigrants, on the other hand, although seriously divided on political solutions that would ensure the future of the Jews as a people, never questioned that they were a national group, albeit without a land. Inevitably such conflicting attitudes about what united or distinguished them were not conducive to a community of views. These attitudes profoundly affected the development of responses when the Germans introduced racist laws into France.

The immigrants' organizations, though in agreement on the danger of German racism and its influence in France, were themselves divided on political lines. Communism and Zionism, the two prewar political currents that had divided the immigrants, continued to influence and reinforce former divisions even when France was occupied. Each of these factors, the major differences between French Jews and immigrants and the conflicts among the immigrants themselves, contributed to perpetuating disparate responses.

One of the central questions facing French Judaism and the immigrants as they developed responses was what stance they should adopt toward "imposed representation." In Paris that problem asserted itself in November 1940 with the German demand that all existing Jewish organizations amalgamate under the occupier's control. The Vichy government extended this move when it decided to establish a nationwide Jewish representation for the whole of France in November 1941. French Judaism, despite its opposition to the principle of being ostracized by the rest of the French people, soon accommodated. But the immigrant organizations saw the Vichy move as a permanent danger to the Jewish population, both as an instrument to isolate them first juridically and then physically from the rest of the population. They therefore viewed "imposed representation" as a legal device to intensify their persecution. As far as the immigrant organizations were concerned the imposition had to be rejected, not only on account of its potential danger but also because it stood in the way of persuading French Judaism that all the Jews were equally threatened.

French Judaism never fully accepted the view that the imposed representation had gained credibility within the Jewish population because it had not unequivocally and practically opposed the idea. The silence of French Judaism had helped deceive the Jewish population about the intended role of the imposed representation. French Judaism never really accepted the fact that French Jews were as exposed as the foreign Jews. Yet as the occupation wore on, a process of realization did take place. The immigrants' organizations were the first to resolve their differences. Later, French Judaism itself began to reassess its own position, and a reconciliation between French and immigrant Jews did take place.

But for most of the war, until the French Jews themselves became equal victims, no common language between French Judaism and the immigrant organizations could be found. French Judaism did materially assist foreign Jews, but only in the same manner as it had in the prewar days; it was the kind of help the rich give to the poor, philanthropy. It was in this division that the drama lay; there was no sense of solidarity. French Judaism refused to accept the fact that its future was inevitably linked to the fate of the foreign Jews. When the schism between them was finally bridged, it was due to the development of the Final Solution which caught up with the French Jews and, more significantly, to the efforts of the immigrant organizations which finally found the arguments necessary to convince them.

My study will show that in the last analysis it was the immigrants who, despite all difficulties and limitations, had been the pacesetters in the work of defense. It was their organizations that prodded and challenged French Judaism into recognizing the immediate danger of Nazi racism and persuaded it to discard its static posture. Only then did French Judaism assume the communal responsibility of representing the French Jews, as it had always claimed it did, within a Jewish body truly recognized by all Jews as theirs.

This book is divided into four parts. In the first part, which comprises three chapters, I will present a broad overview of the impact of the racial legislation upon the Jewish population in France. Chapter 1 will deal with the impact of internments and deportations upon their numbers; Chapter 2 concerns the policy of economic "aryanization" which sought to expropriate and pauperize the Jews before their deportation from France; Chapter 3 synthesizes these two chapters and discusses other administrative measures, which were designed to further isolate Jews, in order to present the conditions under which the organizations set out to assist and defend that population. In Part II, I shall discuss the effects of the gradual imposition of Nazi and Vichy controls over the activities of the Jewish organizations. Chapter 4 addresses the problems and responses of the Jewish organizations resulting from this policy until the end of 1941. Chapter 5 examines the negotiations between the Vichy government and Jewish representatives over the establishment of an official Jewish representation. These negotiations, which began in September 1941 and ended in January 1942, led to the establishment of the Union Générale des Israélites de France led by French Jews. Part III describes the activities of this organization until the Liberation of France in August 1944. Chapter 6 analyzes its organization, role, and function until the end of 1942. Chapter 7 carries the study up to the Liberation of Paris. Part IV concerns the policies and responses of the immigrant organizations during the whole of the Occupation to the specific problems encountered by the immigrant Jews.

Chapter 8 will examine their problems, resulting not only from the deteriorating material conditions, the consequences of the racial legislation, but also from divided perceptions of the nature of the threat from without and from the inability of the immigrants to reach an understanding with the French Jews. This chapter will cover the period up to the eve of the Jews' indiscriminate internment and deportation in July 1942. Chapter 9 will deal with the immigrant organizations' responses engendered from this new and unprecedented situation until Liberation.

III

The problem of sources presented certain difficulties. Although there are extensive records available from the legal organizations, the Comité de Coordination des Oeuvres de Bienfaisance du Grand Paris (Coordination Committee of Relief Organizations from Paris, hereafter referred to as the Coordination Committee), and the Union Générale des Israélites de France (General Union of the Israelites of France—hereafter UGIF), these documents need to be examined with the knowledge that they were at all times subject to control by the authorities, both German and French. Special care is therefore required insofar as we expect them to present real positions. In order to understand the strategy adopted at various times by these organizations, a process of interpolation based upon Nazi and Vichy demands and on what was effectively carried out had to be employed consistently. But even then many questions will remain unanswered until other surviving archival sources become available for consultation. We do know for instance that André Baur, leader of the UGIF in Occupied France, had contacts with Cardinal Suhard. What was discussed will remain privy, however, until the French Catholic Church decides to allow access to its archives. There were also contacts between Georges Edinger, Baur's successor, and the Milice, a national paramilitary police force of French volunteers against the Resistance, in 1944.* Nor do we know all the reasons for the arrests, in July and August 1943, of most of the UGIF leadership in Paris; why were some persons and not others arrested, and why were they kept in France for a number of months before being deported to Auschwitz? Nor do we know the role of the banks in the sordid story of "Aryanization." The answers to all these questions may rest in the French National Archives and the archives of the Ministry of Finance, if at all.

In the case of the immigrant organizations, the quality and availability of sources pose other problems. One group of organizations, which functioned as the Comité Amelot (Amelot Committee—sometimes referred to as Amelot), has left an extensive collection of records. But again these records were

---

* Philippe Henriot, Secretary for Information and Propaganda, was executed by the French Resistance on 28 June 1944. Edinger claimed, after the war, that the Milice threatened the UGIF with a pogrom unless it paid a million francs. The sum would have been paid on 15 July 1944. CRIF, procès-verbal, 16 January 1946.

public documents which did not reflect the fact that Amelot was a conglomerate of organizations. None of the participating organizations' own records have remained which would allow us to evaluate their aims and objectives within the Amelot Committee.

We do have collections of illegal Communist and Bundist publications which are invaluable, but they do not explain the process through which decisions were made or the roles played by individuals. A number of articles and books were written by former immigrant leaders. Although written with hindsight, these works do help us understand the reasons for their actions and the problems they faced.

All these various sources, however abundant, do not provide us with the records of the clandestine meetings and discussions. In order to overcome these gaps I have consulted depositions of former participants collected by institutions such as Yad Vashem Remembrance Authority, Jerusalem; Centre de Documentation Juive Contemporaine, Paris; YIVO Institute for Jewish Research, New York; and Leo Baeck Institute, New York. The depositions were recorded over a period of years and are of uneven quality. The best collections, those made under the direction of trained historians, are held at the Oral History Division of the Institute of Contemporary Jewry, Hebrew University of Jerusalem, Israel, under direction of Dr. Geoffrey Wigoder. These depositions were complemented by extensive interviews of surviving participants. The majority of these people now live in Paris and I include a list of their names in the Bibliography. This last group of sources taken alone is also unsatisfactory, as all who have turned to them know. Participants suffer from the frailty of human memory no less than an inevitable desire to justify their own actions or a reticence to concede their failures.

The archives of the Central Consistory and of the Paris Consistory are not open to researchers; the governing bodies have imposed a fifty-year waiting period on access. This is highly regrettable and raises questions about why such a decision was necessary. Given the availability of evidence, we can only conclude that the guardians of these sources were guided, at best, by a desire to avoid controversies and at worst by fear of political embarrassment. In either case researchers will have to wait until 1994 in order to test today's judgments.

Many individuals and institutions have assisted me in my research and I would like to thank the following. In Israel: the director and staff of the Yad Vashem Remembrance Authority, in particular Bronia Klibansky; Geoffrey Wigoder, director of the Oral History Division of the Institute of Contemporary Jewry, the Hebrew University of Jerusalem; and Michael Heymann of the Central Zionist Archives, Jerusalem. In Paris: the director and staff of the Centre de Documentation Juive Contemporaine, in particular Vidar Jacobsen for his untiring assistance. At the Institut d'Histoire du Temps Present (formerly the Comité d'Histoire de la IIe Guerre Mondiale), I thank the director, François Bédarida, Claude Lévy, and Françoise Mercier. At the Institut de Recherches Marxistes (formerly the Institut Maurice Thorez). I am grateful to David Diamant, for his assistance in making all relevant sources available for consultation and for his readiness to share his experiences as a former member of a Jewish underground organization in Paris. At the *Naie Presse,* I would like to thank the editorial board for granting me access to their collection of books and files. At the Medem Library I would like to thank M. Waiszbrot, the director, for his open-hearted and warm encouragement, and the many unknown Bundists who willingly shared their recollections. I thank Pierre Kaufman, who allowed me to examine the archives of the Conseil Représentatif des Juifs de France. At the Secrétariat d'Etat des Anciens Combattants, I would like to thank A. Grisoni for permission to consult the Drancy and deportation files, as well as the relevant index cards from the various camps in the Parisian region where Jews were interned. The president of the Union des Engagés Volontaires et Anciens Combattants Juifs, 1939–45, Joseph Fridman, and the secretary, Maurice Schuster, have been more than generous with their time. Many other individuals also assisted me; I am especially grateful to Serge and Beate Klarsfeld who helped and directed me to many important sources. In the United States I would like to thank the following: at YIVO Institute for Jewish Research, in particular the archivist Marek Web and his assistant Fruma Mohrer, and the late Zosa Szajkowski; at the Atran Center, the late Hillel Kampinski; at the American Jewish Committee, Ruth Rauch; the staff of the Jewish Theological Seminary; the staff of the Leo Baeck Institute; and the American Jewish Joint Distribution Committee archivist Rose Klepfisz. In Melbourne: I thank the University of Melbourne for its financial support, the Arts Faculty and the History Department for material help, as well as Chips Sowerwine and Frederick Ohles for their encouragements and critical assistance. I would also like to thank my dear friend Wilma Hannah without whose critical reading this book would have suffered much. This book was originally published in an abridged version by Calmann-Lévy (Paris) and I would like to thank Roger Errera, the director of the "Diaspora" Collection in which it appeared for his editorial care based above all upon his remarkable understanding of the issues involved. Finally, I would like to add my thanks to the editors of this series and its publishers.

Melbourne   J.A.
October 1986

Contents

Tables

Abbreviations

ACIP Association Consistoriale des Israélites de Paris. Consistorial Association of the Israelites of Paris.

AIU Alliance Israélite Universelle. Universal Israelite Alliance.

AJ Armée Juive. Jewish Army.

CAR Comité d'Assistance aux Réfugiés. Committee for Assistance to Refugees.

CCOJA Commission Central d'Oeuvres Juives d'Assistance. Central Commission of Jewish Relief Associations.

CDJC Centre de Documentation Juive Contemporaine. Center for Contemporary Jewish Documentation.

CGD Comité Général de Défense des Juifs. General Jewish Defense Committee.

CGQJ Commissariat Général aux Questions Juives. General Commission for Jewish Affairs.

CNR Conseil National de la Résistance. National Resistance Council.

CRIF Conseil Représentatif des Juifs de France. Representative Council of the Jews of France.

EIF Eclaireurs Israélites de France. Jewish Scouts of France.

FSJF Fédération des Societés Juives de France. Federation of the Jewish Societies of France.

HICEM HIAS (Hebrew Immigrant Aid and Sheltering Society); JCA (Jewish Colonization Association); Emigdirect (German Immigration Association)

IMT Institut Maurice Thorez. Maurice Thorez Institute.

Joint American Jewish Joint Distribution Committee.

JO *Journal Officiel.*

JTA Jewish Telegraphic Agency.

JTS Jewish Theological Seminary of America (New York).

LBI Leo Baeck Institute (New York).

MBF Militärbefehlshaber in Frankreich. German Military Command in France.

MNCR Mouvement National Contre le Racisme. National Movement Against Racism.

MOI Main d'Oeuvre Immigré. Foreign Workers.

OJC Organisation Juive de Combat. Jewish Fighting Organization.

ORT Organisation pour la Reconstruction et le Travail. Organization for Rehabilitation and Professional Training.

OS	Organisation Spéciale. Special Organization.
OSE	Oeuvre de Secours aux Enfants. Children's Relief Committee.
PCF	Parti Communiste Français. French Communist party.
PQJ	Police aux Questions Juives. Police for Jewish Affairs.
RSHA	Reichssicherheitshauptamt. Central Security Office of the Reich.
SCAP	Service de Control des Administrateurs Provisoires. Control Organism of the Provisional Administrators.
SD	Sicherheitsdienst. Security Services of the Gestapo.
SEC	Section d'Enquête et de Control. Office of Control and Inquiry.
UGIF	Union Générale des Israélites de France. General Union of the Israelites of France.
UJRE	Union des Juifs pour la Résistance et l'Entr'aide. Union of the Jews for Resistance and Mutual Aid.
VOBIF	*Verordnungsblatt des Militärbefehlshabers in Frankreich.* German Military Command Official Gazette.
WIZO	Women's International Zionist Organization.
YIVO	YIVO Institute for Jewish Research (New York).
YVA	Yad Vashem Archives (Israel).

I
FROM ISOLATION
TO DEPORTATION

1

Population and Survival

No one really knew, until the German Occupation in 1940, how many Jews lived in Paris or in France. Historians and demographers had, of course, attempted to evaluate their numbers but their calculations were never more than estimations. We had to wait until the German census of October 1940 and the census held in the Vichy Zone in June 1941 to establish with a reasonable degree of certainty their numbers. The importance of the question is all the more evident when we consider that close to 80,000 people were in the end killed for no other reason than being Jewish. The question of who was a Jew was of course vital for all those who found themselves so categorized, but we shall not enter into the debate about the criteria by which Jews can be defined; throughout our study we have adopted the criteria of the day, the Germans' and Vichy's own definitions.

The reasons for the German and Vichy censuses might have reflected different policies but they proceeded from a common assumption: the Jews represented a threat to the established order and as a group they needed to be controlled by the authorities.[1] The censuses therefore occupied a central position in the application of anti-Jewish policies: the Jews had to be defined and recorded as a group.

From the point of view of our study of the role of the Jewish organizations in the defense of the Jewish population, these censuses, followed by periodical population controls, reveal much more than the ultimate consequences of Nazi and Vichy's anti-Jewish policies. They provide a basis for understanding whom these organizations purported to represent and why there was a failure on their part to agree on the nature of the danger. Indeed, as we shall see, the Jewish population was not a homogeneous community, but a group of historically evolved entities that had little in common.

The presence of Jews in France dates back to Roman rule. By the time the Jews were expelled from France in 1394, they had already formed sizable communities boasting major centers of Hebraic learning that attracted scholars of renown.[2] After the expulsion, small groups of Jews remained in Avignon, Bordeaux, and Alsace-Lorraine; the first two groups experienced little growth while the communities in eastern France grew rapidly. On the eve of the French Revolution of 1789, there were an estimated 30,000 Jews in the whole of France.[3] When the Emancipation Act of 27 September 1791 was proclaimed, there were thought to be between 500 and 1,000 Jews in Paris itself.[4]

By this Emancipation Act, France became the first country to grant civil rights to the Jews. As a consequence, and with the growth of antisemitism in Central and Eastern Europe, there was a marked increase in migration to France. Republican France attracted Jews seeking to escape persecution; the reputation of Paris as a cosmopolitan center was an incentive, and France's liberal immigration policy made entry possible. The nineteenth century accordingly saw a rapid rise in the number of Jews in France.

The various groups of Jews coming to France had diverse backgrounds, reflected in differences in religious practices as well as in language, education, and occupation. The first major influx of Jews in the nineteenth century was from Belgium and Holland, and it was due to the French Emancipation Act. Predominantly descendants of Spanish Jews who had fled the Inquisition, these Jews were Sephardim. The later immigrants from Eastern Europe, who fled the pogroms and counterrevolutionary repressions, were Ashkenazim, that is, Yiddish-speaking Jews of Polish-German origin. Practicing different religious traditions from the Sephardim and steeped in their own culture, the Ashkenazim were products of tightly knit communities and had become, by the end of the century, the largest group among French Jewry.[5] Indeed, from the assassination of the Russian Czar Alexander II in 1881 and the resulting pogroms, migration from Eastern Europe continued uninterrupted until the eve of World War I.[6] As will be seen later, both the economic and social status of these Ashkenazi Jews in France depended greatly on the length of time that they or their families had either been French citizens or, as in many cases, merely residents in France.

There were other distinctive groups of migrants. One, important both numerically and because of its members' French-born status, consisted of thousands of Jews who moved to Paris from Alsace-Lorraine after the German annexation of that territory in 1871.[7] Seeking to affirm their continuing loyalty to France and avoid the loss of civil rights under German rule, they became an important subgroup of French Jewry. By 1939 they were estimated to represent 18 percent of the French Jews (that is, Jews born in France). These French Jews constituted much of the Jewish upper class and had many distinguished members in the liberal professions, in banking, and in business.[8]

Another distinctive group of Jewish immigrants were atypical for this period in that they were Sephardic, not Ashkenazi Jews. They were immigrants from North Africa and Southern Europe, acquainted with French culture through the Alliance Israélite Universelle[9] (Universal Israelite Alliance [AIU]), but economically inferior to the French Jews and culturally far removed from the Ashkenazim who both outnumbered and ignored them.[10]

By the end of the nineteenth century there were an estimated 90,000 Jews in France, 50,000 of whom lived in Paris.[11] The pressures leading to migration continued into the twentieth century. Although most of the 3,000,000 Jews moving westward out of the Russian Empire and Central Europe, between the assassination of Alexander II and the outbreak of World War I, went to the United States, a steady stream of immigrants made France their home.[12] By 1914 the Jewish population of Paris included 20,000 Eastern European Jews.[13]

If we regard the first influx of Eastern European Jews into France as a result of the counterrevolutionary assertion of authoritarian rule in the mid-nineteenth century, and the second as a consequence of the assassination of Alexander II and its aftermath of pogroms, the third and largest influx of Eastern European Jews into France may be said to have occurred from 1921 onward as a result of the First World War and its consequences, particularly the social upheavals resulting from the Russian Revolution. Because of the enormous losses of manpower France had suffered during the war, she welcomed these migrants. The 90,000 Jews in France at the turn of the century became 260,000 by 1935. The high proportion of Jews among the German and Austrian refugees between that year and 1939 brought the total figure of Jews in France at the outbreak of the Second World War to an estimated total of 300,000. Of that number 200,000 were living in Paris.[14]

The residential pattern of the Jewish population in Paris followed the familiar Parisian one. The Jewish upper class tended to live in the western arrondissements. Of the thirteen synagogues controlled by the Association Consistoriale des Israélites de Paris (Consistorial Association of the Israelites of Paris [ACIP]), seven were in bourgeois *quartiers*.[15] The immigrants' choice of location was governed by social and economic factors. Those who had arrived in the late 1920s settled in the fourth arrondissement, their point of arrival in Paris. This was soon referred to as the Jewish district. Generally immigrants congregated according to occupation and economic status. The majority of immigrant workers lived in Belleville, in the twentieth arrondissement. Artisans, small traders, or *travailleurs à façon* (home workers) usually lived in the third. The fur trade settled in the tenth, while the eleventh arrondissement, rue du Faubourg Saint-Antoine, attracted the furniture trade. Market traders lived in Clichy and Saint-Ouen. Regardless of the tendency to take up residence according to professional occupation, by 1939 the largest number of immigrants lived in the eleventh arrondissement. Still, despite high concentration of Jews in given areas, no one *quartier* could be said to constitute a ghetto.[16]

While this residential sprawl was not conducive to community cohesion, the degree of concentration of immigrants in particular districts was sufficient to concern the Consistory, which regarded it as politically dangerous and prone to xenophobia and antisemitism. The immigrants, on the other hand, believed that those French Jews from the Consistory were seeking to dissociate themselves from their poorer "cousins." It has to be borne in mind that although the growth of the Jewish population of France and Paris had been an historical process, the differences in degrees of acculturation arising from the length of residence in France did not make for a mutual understanding of each others' needs. In the period of political crisis that characterized the French political scene in the 1930s, with its accompanying outburst of antisemitism, the continuous arrival of fresh groups of Jewish immigrants were viewed as posing a threat to those already well established. All immigrants were not always welcome. Unlike those who had arrived before the onset of the Great Depression in the early 1930s, the more recent arrivals were anxiously aware of their own status as unwanted foreigners.[17]

Inevitably the Jewish refugees who arrived in France between 1933 and 1939 faced problems vastly different from those faced by the earlier immigrants. They were without work permits or residence permits and many were unable to obtain visas into other countries. By their very presence they highlighted existing apprehensions about the future of Jews. When the German armies began their offensive in May 1940, that immigrant community was to grow larger yet: the war in the Low Countries brought a wave of refugees, many of whom were Jewish. They arrived in thousands from Holland, Belgium, and Luxemburg. In northern France they joined the general exodus south until the June 1940 Armistice.

We cannot establish how many Jews living in Paris joined the exodus but we do know that in this instance they acted in the same way as the non-Jewish population.[18] The census ordered by Roger Langeron, then prefect of police, following the German occupation, revealed that the population of Paris, which stood at 2,829,746 in 1936, had dropped to 1,101,030 at the end of July 1940. If we discount the number of prisoners of war we are left with a 30 percent fall in population. However, during the weeks following the Armistice some Parisians returned to their homes and by early September 1940 the number of inhabitants in Paris had risen to 1,700,000.[19]

The first precise information on the number of Jews living in Paris became available following the special census of the Jewish population in the Occupied Zone ordered by the German authorities in September 1940. To the German criterion of who was a Jew were added the criteria introduced by Vichy's own Statut des Juifs which appeared on 3 October 1940, and which further increased the number of those who qualified.[20] To ascertain the total number of Jews in France at the outbreak of the hostilities it is necessary to examine, in conjunction with the German census, Vichy's own census taken in its zone in June 1941. The combined results show that 287,962 Jews had complied by registering, 149,734 in Paris and surrounding districts.[21]

The overall number of Jews living in France at the time was only of relative importance to the authorities. The number of Jews revealed by the censuses represents a valuable source which conclusively establishes the number of Jews who lived in France before the war and more importantly provides their national origins.

To give the census figures the needed precision, a number of elements should be taken into account. First, we need to add the number of Jews who, as prisoners of war, were not recorded: estimates vary between 7,000 and 10,000.[22] Then we must include those who succeeded in leaving the country in June 1940, as well as those who left later but before the Vichy census. The Jewish organization that handled Jewish refugees and immigrants, the HICEM, was best placed to evaluate the number of Jews who had left France and according to their own source some 7,000 were known to have departed.[23] A number of other Jews had also left France via Spain or had taken refuge in Switzerland. Others probably left France by their own means but available evidence suggests that they numbered only in the hundreds and thus do not significantly affect the overall figures.

Finally there is the question of how many refused to fill in the census forms. Jewish sources claimed that the Jews overwhelmingly obeyed the law.[24] On the other hand, Xavier Vallat, Vichy's first head of the Commissariat Général aux Questions Juives (General Commission for Jewish Affairs [CGQJ]) told the German authorities that as many as 10 percent might not have registered. Because France was a secular state a Jew was indeed able to avoid declaring himself without fear that he would be found out through official sources. But there were two obstacles to overcome: the Jew could not be known as such by neighbors or associates and his surname could not suggest that he might be Jewish (it was better still if his surname was French-sounding).[25] Jewish women married to non-Jews could thus avoid detection. Nevertheless, few Jews refused to register. The October 1940 census, for instance, showed that 8 percent of the Jewish population were married to non-Jews, a figure consistent with communal estimates.[26] If we accept that Jews could safely avoid detection by having previously adopted a French-sounding name, and that the legal process was both expensive and drawn out, and that the number of those who did benefit from such names was not significant, then we can accept that the Jewish population did, generally, comply. Why then did Vallat claim that as many as 10 percent had failed to register? It can only suggest that both Vallat and the Germans were themselves surprised at the relatively small number of Jews living in France. Believing their own rhetoric that Jews not only were a major danger but also that they had invaded France in numbers that were unacceptable, Vallat and the Germans sought justification in the view that many must have hidden their Jewishness.

Furthermore, the 287,000 Jews who had been registered until June 1941 included 7,450 from Baden and the Saarland who had been expelled by the Germans and sent to the Vichy Zone on 22 October 1940.[27] Within the overall figure were also included some 45,000 Jewish refugees from Belgium and Holland who had decided to remain in France after the cessation of hostilities in June 1940.[28] Therefore, taking into consideration this vast movement of population, those who had succeeded in leaving Europe, those who had crossed into Spain and Switzerland, and those who had not been actually included in the census (prisoners of war), we can conclude that no more than 260,000 Jews lived in France at the eve of the war.

That figure is all the more significant when we note a statement issued by Vallat in April 1941, well before Vichy conducted its own Jewish census, that the Jews represented 2.4 percent of the French population, that is 900,000.[29] Vallat's need to advance such fanciful figures was due no doubt to his own vision of the "Jewish menace." It was also clearly designed to justify among the general population Vichy's own anti-Jewish policies and thereby silence critics.

The German and Vichy censuses revealed a new geographical distribution of the Jewish population. Previously the overwhelming majority of Jews were believed to be residing in Paris; now as a consequence of the exodus and of the German Occupation, many had chosen to abandon their homes in the capital rather than live under German rule. Among those were the French Jews who had followed the French government south, as well as Jews from Alsace-Lorraine who had refused to live under German law like their ancestors in 1871. Although the percentage of French Jews in the Vichy Zone was only 60 percent of their total number in France, it must also be noted that included in that total were the refugees from the Low Countries who remained in France after the Armistice. In fact, the percentage of French Jews in the Vichy Zone in relation to the number of Jews in France at the eve of the war stood closer to 75 percent of their prewar estimated numbers.[30]

The results of the October 1940 census of the Occupied Zone affords us the possibility of examining, in some detail, the composition of the Jewish population of Paris. It numbered, as we have seen earlier, 149,734 for Paris and surrounding suburbs. The most significant feature of that population was its national composition. There was an equal proportion of French to foreign Jews. And even more interesting was the proportion of French-born Jews to their overall number. Indeed, only 25 percent of the Jewish population was effectively of French ancestry. The overwhelming majority of the Jews in Paris were recent arrivals or, at least, no more than first-generation French (Tables 1 and 2). The second feature of the census was not only that foreign Jews had larger families but that three quarters of the immigrants' children had acquired French nationality, indicating thereby the desire to remain in France and have their children become French citizens. The pattern of birth differentiation between French-born and immigrants was also consistent with the general finding that birth rates tend to be higher in the lower socioeconomic groups of a community (Table 3).

Table 1. Number of French and Foreign Jews, Paris and Suburbs,[a] October 1940 Census

	Paris		Suburbs		Subtotal		Total
Categories	Males	Females	Males	Females	Males	Females	Males and Females
French	23,824	26,201	3,519	3,566	27,343	29,767	57,110
Protected and from Administered Territories	359	90	43	11	402	101	503
Foreigners	25,656	25,374	2,505	2,319	28,161	27,693	55,854
Subtotal	49,839	51,665	6,067	5,896	55,906	57,561	
Total	101,504		11,963				113,467

a Fifteen years of age and over.

Source: Department of Demography, Institute of Contemporary Jewry, Hebrew University of Jerusalem; French Collection, nonclassified (hereafter Department of Demography, Jerusalem).

Table 2. French Jews: Origin of Citizenship,[a] Paris and Suburbs, October 1940 Census

Categories	Males	Females	Total
By origin	13,718	14,784	28,502
By marriage	—	2,511	2,511
By naturalization	11,525	9,789	21,314
By declaration	1,074	1,090	2,164
By reintegration	253	857	1,110
No indication	773	736	1,509
Total	27,343	29,767	57,110

[a] Fifteen years of age and over.

Source: Department of Demography, Jerusalem, French Collection, nonclassified.

As for the countries of origin of the foreign Jews, the returns show that although they came from fifty-six different countries, 80 percent of them came from East European countries. The largest group came from Poland, 26,158, and this represented 50 percent of all the foreign Jews. Of the other 30 percent, the Russian group, was the largest with 7,298 members; they were followed numerically by the Rumanian and Turkish groups (Table 4).

The census also provides us with the geographical distribution of the French and foreign Jews. Their residential pattern, in October 1940, shows that the French Jews lived predominantly in the bourgeois *quartiers* where they outnumbered the foreign Jews by two to one. The foreign Jews lived predominantly in the working-class districts. Indeed, 18 percent of all immigrant Jews lived in the eighteenth arrondissement, while no similar concentration of French Jews is noted (Table 5). If any conclusions can be drawn from this limited information, it is that the French Jews were better integrated in French life and, unlike the foreign Jews, did not require the mutual support necessary to immigrants, particularly in the first phase of their acclimatization in a new country.[31]

Table 3. Number of Children, French and Foreign,[a] Paris and Suburbs, October 1940 Census

	Children of French Families	Children of Foreign Families		Total Children of Foreign Families	Total French and Foreign
		French Nationality	Foreign Nationals		
Paris	11,296	14,864	4,415	19,279	30,575
Suburbs	1,916	1,631	435	2,066	3,982
Total	13,212	16,495	4,850	21,345	34,557

[a] Under fifteen years of age.

Source: Department of Demography, Jerusalem, French Collection, nonclassified.

Table 4. Distribution of Immigrant Population According to Countries of Origin,[a] Paris and Suburbs, October 1940 Census

Poland	26,158
Russia	7,298
Rumania	4,382
Turkey	3,381
Hungary	1,926
Germany	1,703
Greece	1,642

[a] The figures only refer to males and females over fifteen years of age. Only seven nationalities have been selected as they represent over 85 percent of the immigrant population. The census returns show that immigrants came from fifty-six countries, including one from China; one from Haiti; one from Thailand; one from Ireland; and sixteen from Afghanistan.

Source: Department of Demography, Jerusalem, French Collection, nonclassified.

Table 5. Distribution of the Jewish Population of Paris,[a] October 1940 Census

Arrondissement	French			Foreign			Total French and Foreign
	Males	Females	Total	Males	Females	Total	
1st	225	226	451	175	127	302	753
2nd	520	443	963	685	609	1,294	2,257
3rd	1,506	1,639	3,145	2,197	2,172	4,369	7,514
4th	1,569	1,640	3,209	1,844	1,750	3,594	6,803
5th	566	626	1,192	483	452	935	2,127
6th	284	313	597	213	184	397	994
7th	324	337	661	141	129	270	931
8th	621	621	1,242	299	247	546	1,788
9th	1,750	1,680	3,430	1,704	1,386	3,090	6,520
10th	1,837	2,048	3,885	2,470	2,428	4,898	8,783
11th	3,101	3,658	6,759	4,369	4,962	9,331	16,090
12th	1,104	1,227	2,331	895	832	1,727	4,058
13th	676	738	1,414	502	547	1,049	2,463
14th	572	650	1,222	429	374	803	2,025
15th	747	774	1,521	672	686	1,358	2,879
16th	1,576	1,878	3,454	816	924	1,740	5,194
17th	1,790	1,965	3,755	772	733	1,505	5,260
18th	2,889	3,055	5,944	2,337	2,183	4,520	10,469
19th	945	1,081	2,026	1,509	1,508	3,017	5,043
20th	1,581	1,692	3,273	3,144	3,141	6,285	9,558
Total	24,183	26,291	50,474	25,656	25,374	51,030	101,504

[a] Fifteen years of age and over, and according to arrondissement, nationality, and sex.

Source: Department of Demography, Jerusalem, French Collection, nonclassified.

It was after October 1940, following the census, that the Jewish population, French and immigrants, began to fluctuate inordinately. If the reasons for holding such a census were not obvious to the Jewish population, there was sufficient common sense to realize that it had not been an idle exercise. In fact, it had been undertaken with the objective of using that information in order to map out a strategy for the introduction of anti-Jewish policies based on concrete information.

It was in May 1941 that the first measures were taken that directly affected the number of Jews living in Paris. On 14 May 1941, 3,710 immigrant men were interned in camps outside Paris, in the Loiret department.[32] From then on, for varying reasons, to which we shall return, Jews were continually arrested. In August 1941, this time in a localized police operation, the eleventh arroundissement was completely surrounded and 4,232 men were taken from their homes, identified by names and addresss available from the October 1940 census. This time, however, some French Jews were also arrested. Meanwhile, between August 1941 and December 1941, individuals as well as small groups of Jews, such as the fifty-two Jewish lawyers also arrested during August 1941, found their way to camps. December 1941 saw the next major operation undertaken against Jews. On that day the German Feldpolizei (German Military Police) arrested, throughout Paris, 750 prominent French Jews as well as 250-odd immigrant Jews to complete the 1,000 men set as a target.[33]

By the end of 1941, close to 8,000 were still interned in four different camps. The majority were immigrants, although some French Jews had also been taken. By then Jews had begun to be concerned at the shape of events and had begun to leave Paris. In order to retain a tight control over the number of Jews in Paris the authorities introduced measures restricting their movements. On 10 December 1941, the Paris prefect of police, Admiral François-Marie-Alphonse Bard, announced that any change of address by Jews had to be reported at local police stations and that no Jew was permitted to leave the Seine department without police permission.[34] By 12 February 1942, even tighter controls were introduced with the order that Jews were forbidden to be out of their homes between 8 P.M. and 6 A.M.[35]

To evaluate the shift in numbers resulting from the year's internment, and more particularly whether the Jewish population had actually been docile, a new population count was held during December 1941. The results showed that there were, in Paris, 83,346 Jews, fifteen years of age and over (Table 6).

Between October 1940 and December 1941, the number of Jews in Paris had fallen by more than 18,000. Some 8,000 had been interned and 10,000 remained unaccounted for. A comparison between the October census and the December population control shows that it was from among the French Jews that the largest number were missing. When we relate this fact to the numbers of immigrants and French Jews who had been arrested between May and December 1941, we see that it was those who were less likely to be arrested who had left Paris in greater numbers.

Table 6.   Decrease of the Jewish Population in Paris, December 1941[a]

	French			Foreign		
Arrondissement	October 1940	December 1941	Missing %	October 1940	December 1941	Missing %
1st	451	392	13	302	266	12
2nd	963	794	17	1,294	969	25
3rd	3,145	2,374	24	4,369	3,529	19
4th	3,209	2,623	18	3,594	3,086	14
5th	1,192	898	25	935	844	10
6th	597	461	23	397	339	15
7th	661	551	17	270	211	22
8th	1,242	854	31	546	407	25
9th	3,430	2,703	21	3,090	2,393	22
10th	3,885	3,066	21	4,898	3,960	19
11th	6,759	5,620	17	9,331	7,776	17
12th	2,331	1,927	17	1,727	1,435	17
13th	1,414	1,217	14	1,049	876	16
14th	1,222	1,023	19	803	661	18
15th	1,521	1,303	14	1,358	1,128	17
16th	3,454	2,627	31	1,740	1,352	33
17th	3,755	2,899	23	1,505	1,196	20
18th	5,944	4,854	18	4,520	3,904	14
19th	2,026	1,681	17	3,017	2,669	11
20th	3,273	2,867	13	6,285	5,681	16
Total	50,474	40,734	av.% 20	51,030	42,612	av.% 17

[a] Fifteen years of age and over, according to arrondissement and nationalities. The percentages of missing Jews in Paris have been calculated on the basis of those present during the October 1940 census.

Source: October 1940 census: Department of Demography, Jerusalem, French Collection, non-classified: December 1941 population count, in Roblin, *Les Juifs de Paris,* p. 183.

Population controls assumed ever greater importance as the anti-Jewish policies of the German occupiers emerged and took shape. This is evident in the eighth German ordinance, which appeared on 29 May 1942, ordering all Jews over the age of six to wear a "Yellow Star of David."[36] Basing their estimates on the December 1941 controls, the CGQJ and the Germans had calculated the precise number of Jews who should have collected their Yellow Stars: 100,455, a figure that included the Jews living in the surrounding districts as well.

The German ordinance was to come into effect by 7 June 1942. But by that date only 83,000 Jews had collected their stars.[37] The population differential between December 1941 and June 1942, although it was now based upon a larger area and included children, suggests that a further number had meanwhile decided to leave Paris. The report from Theodor Dannecker, the *Judenreferent* (Jewish expert) for the Reichssicherheitshauptamt (Central Security Office of the Reich [RSHA]) for France, had recognized that Jews were leaving Paris for the Vichy Zone in order not to have to wear the star.[38]

Dannecker was convinced that unless stricter police controls were established the plans being devised in Berlin for the Jews in France were in jeopardy.[39] But then it must also be remembered that the German insistence on precision, for example, the estimated numbers for how many should have collected their stars, was tempered with the confidence that ultimately all Jews, including those in the Vichy Zone, would fall under their control.

The application of the policies designed to ensure that no Jew would remain in France took effect from July 1942 onward. During that month, on order from Dannecker, 12,884 men, women, and children were arrested and soon deported from France to Auschwitz.[40] By then there were only 80,000 Jews left in Paris. From then on the French police carried out internments of specific nationalities. By the middle of 1943 there were only 60,000 Jews in Paris and the majority of them were French citizens.[41] Some 52,000 foreign Jews of various nationalities had been deported from France to Eastern Europe.[42] A number of Jews from certain countries were protected by their governments and owed them their survival. Upon request from some of these governments the German authorities allowed repatriation for some Jews. The largest groups were the Turks and Hungarians, but Jews from Italy, Spain, Portugal, Switzerland, and Denmark were also repatriated. Yet fewer than 3,000 in all were thus saved.[43] The whole question of consular protection for the Jews was at all times problematic. The chance element was characteristic of the procedure even when the respective consular authorities did decide to intervene. Once interned there were never any guarantees that release could be obtained regardless of the goodwill of the consular officers.

Although records were kept by the French police in charge of Jewish affairs of the number of Jews who should be present in Paris at all times, after July 1942 the reliability of these records became increasingly questionable. Too many people were leaving for the countryside or for the Vichy Zone for these records to remain accurate. In fact all Jewish population controls appear to have lost value. At best the French police could only work from estimates. Jewish births, for instance, were never recorded. Yet by law Jewish women could not be treated anywhere else but at the Rothschild Hospital. For those Jewish women living illegally the problem of birth presented insuperable obstacles and was fraught with the danger of internment and deportation.[44] As far as deaths of Jews were concerned, of those resulting from natural causes or from the consequences of internment in camps, we could only obtain data from 1 October 1941 to 7 June 1944; they numbered 1,420. This figure does not include those who died in the camps, or those who died before 1 October 1941, or those who died while living illegally.[45]

The last population control made by the Prefecture of Police was in January 1944; it showed 6,472 foreign Jews still in Paris.[46] They had been allowed to remain free because they were among those considered useful to the German economy. But by the end of January and early February 1944 the Germans issued orders for their arrest. From then on only French Jews were supposed to have been left. Yet, foreign Jews are known to have remained in their legal abodes until the Liberation of Paris totally undisturbed by police.

The records of the Prefecture of Police were never proven to have been tampered with by policemen who objected to the arrests; it would appear that the French police had lost its efficiency.

How many Jews were left when Paris was liberated in August 1944? Estimates vary considerably, from 20,000 to 50,000.[47] But one fact is certain: the overwhelming majority were French. Even when the Germans no longer acknowledged the Vichy demands that the French Jews be spared, the French police could no longer be counted upon to carry out the orders to arrest the French Jews. French Jews had never been selected for large-scale internment; they were more likely to be the victims of accidental arrests in the streets. The French Jews' status, tragically enough, threatened all the other Jews. The French police would always, upon demand from the Germans to proceed with arrests, select the foreign Jews rather than the French. The foreign Jews were more exposed than the French, but because they were not as well integrated in French society as the French Jews they were less well equipped to deal with the situation; their isolation and separateness made them particularly vulnerable. Although a small number of them did benefit from consular protection, as far as the Germans were concerned foreigners belonged to two categories. In the first were Jews from the Allied bloc or from neutral countries who usually were spared largely because the Germans had to consider the safety of their own nationals in those countries. Whenever deportations occurred for those in this category, it ended in the exchange camp of Bergen-Belsen (Germany) where they were not singled out as Jews. But this comparatively fortunate group was numerically small. Most immigrants were from the second category, from countries that had come under total German control, such as Poland, Czechoslovakia, Greece, and Yugoslavia, or from Axis countries, Rumania and Hungary, allies of Germany until the end of 1942. The Germans felt free to do precisely what they wanted with these immigrants. The destruction of Parisian Jewry was therefore, in the main, the destruction of immigrant Jewry from Eastern Europe: of the 76,000 Jews deported to the extermination camps, 16,000 were of French descent, 60,000 were either naturalized or immigrants. If we include all the other Jews who found themselves on French soil when the Armistice was declared we find that 10 percent of the French Jews had died, compared with 40 percent of immigrant or recently naturalized Jews.

2

The Politics of Expropriation

The anti-Jewish laws established in France in October 1940 marked the beginning of the application by the Germans and Vichy of an anti-Jewish policy that was still in the process of elaboration. Neither the German authorities in France nor the Vichy government had yet decided on a definite course of action. However, options were under consideration in Berlin. Central to the various solutions considered in Germany was that France would be *Judenrein*—free of Jews: the Jews would be expelled. It was thus inevitable that such schemes as the famous "Madagascar" reservation for Jews remained under consideration by the RSHA for so long.[1] The defeat of Poland, in 1939, resulted in the Lublin Project, which consisted in turning the region into a Jewish reservation.[2] This solution, much closer to home, also had its supporters in the RSHA. But no firm commitment to a particular solution had yet been made by Hitler. This was the situation when Germany defeated France in June 1940 and when the first serious anti-Jewish measures were taken against the Jews in France in October 1940. But the absence of a definite Jewish policy did not prevent the RSHA's representative in France from pursuing a policy designed to place the Jews under firm administrative control until a decision was reached.

The new government that emerged in France after the Armistice rapidly showed itself to be not only xenophobic but antisemitic as well. It also proceeded, on its own accord, to take anti-Jewish measures, though at first of a definite xenophobic character rather than strictly anti-Jewish. Although Vichy soon proceeded to legislate against the Jews, unlike the Germans, it did not entertain any specific project designed to resolve what it saw as the "Jewish Problem." The *Militärbefehlshaber in Frankreich* (Military Command in France [MBF]) announcement, in September 1940, of a Jewish census in the Occupied Zone, did not therefore cause undue apprehension at Vichy. The commonly shared assumptions about the Jews certainly contributed to Vichy's acquiescence. It marked the beginning of the application of the administrative phase of the German solution to the Jewish problem and Vichy's cooooperation with it. The second German ordinance, announced four weeks later, which imposed a special census of Jewish commercial enterprises, properties, and economic activities and set down the principle of their expropriation, heralded the radical policies.

It was with the challenge to the continued material existence of the Jews that German policy in France laid the foundations for its anti-Jewish course. Such a decision immediately brought the Vichy government into action. It was not that Vichy was fundamentally opposed to the imposition of some measure of economic controls, but in the context of the German occupation of half of France the German decision raised basic questions of state interests. For Germany the dispossession of the Jews was the logical application of state ideology and the prize of victory. For Vichy, it was the extension of a particular vision of the Jewish menace, but the threat of German takeover of Jewish properties remained a constant source of concern.

Vichy's own views on the Jewish Question, which had appeared as an official statement on the eve of the publication of the first Statut des Juifs, on 17 October 1940, read in part:

> The government in its task of national reconstruction has, from the very first day, studied the problem of the Jews and of certain foreigners, who, having abused our hospitality, have contributed to a significant degree to the defeat. Although there are some notable exceptions, in the Administration and everywhere else, the influence of the Jews has been undeniably corruptive and finally decaying. The government as a whole intends quite sincerely not to engage in reprisals. It respects the individual Jew as well as his possessions. It will forbid him however to hold certain administrative responsibilities, authority in the national economy and education. Past experience has shown to all impartial minds that the Jews represent an individualistic tendency which leads to anarchy. Our disaster imposes upon us the task of rebuilding French energies, the characteristics of which have been defined by a long tradition.[3]

Germany's own views on the Jewish Question were well known. The Jews were the inferior race, the enemy that threatened the Aryan's vital space. The question, however, from the Jews' point of view, was not whether the Germans would apply racial laws, but to what degree they would seek to apply in Occupied France the legislation and treatment that the National Socialist regime had introduced in Germany. Most Jews in France believed that the answer to that question resided in Vichy and that Vichy would never allow Germany to introduce such laws or, at least, it would be capable of controlling German excesses. Vichy's first official statement appeared to confirm that view. The French-born Jews sought solace in the reference to foreigners in that statement, while the more vulnerable foreign Jews sought comfort in the assurance that they would not be physically harmed or materially disadvantaged.

Yet there was little to rejoice about. Two days after the statement Vichy promulgated a law that gave prefects the power to intern foreign Jews.[4] Even more threatening was the second German ordinance, which appeared on 18 October 1940, ordering all Jewish firms to be registered with the French police. This was the first step in the expropriation of the Jews.

Until the economic census, little had been known about the Jews' economic position, although the antisemitic Right on the French political scene had always claimed that Jewish-owned banks dominated the French economy. The specter of Jewish financial power had been a traditional theme of that Right. Undoubtedly the dominant position of certain Jewish-owned commercial establishments such as the Galleries Lafayette or the role played by Bloch in the aeronautical industry and Citroën in the automobile industry had made easy headlines in the specialized antisemitic press.

But the economic census of 18 October 1940 had not been conceived or designed to confirm or deny the veracity of these antisemitic stock-in-trade allegations. Its aim was to establish the precise extent and whereabouts of all Jewish economic activities and assets with the explicit purpose of taking them over. The process by which this was to be achieved necessitated, to a certain extent, that public opinion be manipulated. Ordered by the German authorities, executed by Vichy, the census immediately presented problems for the French government. In order not to permit the Germans to take advantage of the situation, Vichy had to act swiftly, and in order to manipulate public opinion, it had to grant some concessions to some Jews who could not be equated with the foreigners. Such parsimonious concessions granted by Vichy were based on different though sometimes related criteria. Those French Jews who could claim outstanding military records or whom Vichy recognized as "exceptionally important" to the state could still engage in certain professions, and the same measure of "exceptional importance" applied also, although to a much smaller degree, to immigrants.[5] But the overall majority of Jews in Paris found themselves powerless before the economic sanctions. Between October 1940 and November 1941, a series of decrees appeared which resulted in the almost total exclusion of foreign Jews from the liberal professions. All Jewish enterprises, no matter what their owners' backgrounds, were placed in the hands of administrators who were to dispose of them. Within that thirteen-month period the German authorities and Vichy saw that the Jews were deprived of control over their own properties, banned from trade, and significantly impeded in their occupations.

While the legislation applied to all Jews, the French Jews were particularly affected because they had most to lose. Many of them were dismissed from the public service, their access to the liberal professions was severely curtailed, and their stronger economic basis became the target of German and French interests. The immigrants, while also affected in the conduct of their businesses, were not so immediately threatened. Their very weakness was for the time being a protection. The relatively small size of their establishments, commercial or industrial, meant that they did not attract the attention of those anxious to acquire Jewish property at bargain prices, nor did the appointed administrators, whose remunerations were calculated on a percentage of the proceeds of the sales, direct their attention to them initially. Admittedly, many foreign Jews working for Jewish employers lost their jobs, but this could be remedied more easily than their employers' loss of their businesses. In the final analysis, the pauperization resulting from the expropriation affected the

middle class most. Both the comparatively rich upper classes and the poorer
working population were better able to adapt to the resulting situation. The
former had means of cushioning the effect of the legislation, the latter a skill
on which to depend.

On 13 April 1941, about one third of the way through this period of intensive economic legislation against the Jews, the CGQJ released to the press
some preliminary results of the economic census of 18 October 1940. If the
intention was to justify the economic measures Vichy had taken against the
Jews, the results must have been disappointing. It certainly did not support
the contentions of the antisemitic press that the Jews had controlled French
finances.[6] The statement emphasized two aspects of Jewish economic activities: that a significant number of them were engaged in trades related to the
clothing industry, but that they were overwhelmingly small traders; and that
the number of Jews in the medical profession was very high, Jews constituting
about 12 percent of all medical practitioners. Neither of these two findings
seemed particularly germane to the general antisemitic argument. The press
report further revealed that the Jewish population's economic activities were
distributed in the following proportions: 25 percent in manufacturing, 30 percent in commerce, 4 percent in the liberal professions, and 3 percent in activities related to personal care, all of these being employers or self-employed,
and the remaining 38 percent were employees.

Vallat's press release did not distinguish between French and foreign Jews
(Table 7). Only through a fuller examination of that census do their economic differences become clear. It confirms the view that the Jewish upper
classes were to be found among the French Jews. They predominated in a

Table 7. Comparative Distribution of Occupations of the French and Foreign
Jewish Population, Paris and Suburbs (Expressed in Percentages). Economic
Census, October 1940[a]

Nationality	French	Poles	Russians	Rumanians	Turks	Hungarians	Germans
Total of Each Group	57,109	26,158	7,298	4,382	3,381	1,926	1,703
Industry	19.0	39.4	29.9	25.9	13.2	36.5	7.3
Commerce	36.6	18.4	25.8	20.7	33.8	17.1	16.9
Personal Care	3.0	3.1	3.6	3.2	2.5	5.0	—
Liberal Professions	4.9	1.1	4.3	5.2	1.4	4.4	4.2
Nonworking	35.0	37.0	35.9	35.2	48.4	36.5	69.2
	98.5%	99%	99.5%	90.2%	99.3%	99.5%	97.6%

a The six groups of foreign nationals we have selected accounted for 80 percent of the immigrant population and as such can be accepted as representative of immigrant economic activities. The percentages express the relative distribution of occupations within each nationality.
The discrepancies in the percentage totals are due to our selection of the five major groups of
occupation of the census returns from the eight groups used in the classification.

Source: Department of Demography, Jerusalem, French Collection, economic census, October
1940, FR021.

range of enterprises that required substantial capital. In the banking industry 31 French Jews held directorship compared with 4 immigrants, on the stock exchange the numbers were 13 to 3, in the wholesale clothing trade they were 447 to 286, and in the fur trade 631 to 357.

The differences between French and foreign Jews were also reflected in occupations of lower economic status. French Jews easily outnumbered immigrants in the census figures for white-collar workers, where accountants numbered 410 French to 111 foreigners, commercial travelers 1,962 to 661, and shop assistants 3,343 to 945. It was in less capital-intensive and more labor-intensive occupations that the foreign Jews were more numerous. In the food trade, for instance, we find 59 French to 106 foreigners, in handbag manufacturing 293 to 765, among hawkers 551 to 1,433, among second-hand dealers 659 to 937.[7]

The economic census showed that 33,984 people were engaged in commerce, of whom 20,918 were French and 12,766 foreigners. In commerce, therefore, the French represented 61.7 percent of the total, while in manufacturing industries the foreigners constituted the dominant group with 62 percent of the total number engaged (Tables 8 and 9). It was in the clothing industry that the foreign Jews appeared to concentrate most; they constituted 70 percent of those Jews connected with it (3,858 French and 9,114 foreigners). But then these figures do not indicate the respective share of the business; for all we know the French Jews, despite their superficial numerical inferiority in the field of industry, may well have dominated it by the financial control of that industry. These figures, however, like all statistics, are significant insofar as they give us some broad indication of general patterns in trade and occupation. And in this respect they provide us with information not previously available.

Table 8. Occupational Distribution of the French and Foreign Jews in Paris and Suburbs. Economic Census, October 1940[a]

Category	*French Jews:* 57,109 Numbers in Each Category	No. Employed in Each Category (%)	*Foreign Jews:* 55,854 Numbers in Each Category	No. Employed in Each Category (%)
Industry	10,887	19.0	17,948	32.0
Commerce	20,918	36.6	12,766	22.8
Personal Care	1,752	3.0	1,812	3.2
Liberal Professions	2,836	4.9	1,453	2.6
Nonworking	19,999	35.0	21,733	38.9

a The census recorded a total of 113,467 Jews of working age who were classified into eight groups. The discrepancies in our totals are due to our retention of only five of the most significant groups of activity, and our omission of the Jews from the Protected Territories and those who became French by reintegration.

Source: Department of Demography, Jerusalem, French Collection, October 1940 census. FR021.

Table 9. General Occupational Distribution of the Jewish Population of Paris and Suburbs.[a] Economic Census, October 1940

Category	No. of French and Foreign Jews in Each Category	% of French	% of Foreigners
Industry	28,918	38.0	62.0
Commerce	33,894	61.7	37.7
Personal Care	3,605	49.7	50.2
Liberal Professions	4,317	66.3	33.6
Nonworking	41,868	48.0	52.0

[a] The discrepancies between the number of Jews of working age, 113,467, in this table are due to our selection of the five major classifications in the census and the deletion of Jews from Protected Territories and those who became French by reintegration.

Source: Department of Demography, Jerusalem, French Collection, October 1940 economic census, FR021.

At the other end of the spectrum of occupations, Jews directly involved in unskilled labor were proportionally very few and appear to be equally divided between French and immigrants (515 French to 568 immigrants). This remarkably low incidence of unskilled laborers was due to the fact that the majority of the prewar Jewish immigrants had arrived in France equipped with a skill.

In the public service, where French nationality had always been a precondition for recruitment, the naturalized Jews had been dismissed in conformity with Vichy policy announced in the Statut des Juifs of 3 October 1940. But French Jews remained; some were never dismissed. They were present in every branch of the administration, from the municipal police to the fire brigade. By the end of 1941, despite the laws barring Jews from a whole range of administrative positions, 602 were still employed in various departments, including one as a department head at the Seine Prefecture.[8]

The problems in the liberal professions were, however, vastly different to those in the administration. There, the possibility of pursuing their profession was governed by a limiting factor, a "numerus clausus." There was indeed a disproportionately large percentage of Jews in certain liberal professions. Whereas the Jewish population numbered 0.7 percent of the French population, they numbered 12.5 percent of the medical profession in Paris. Inevitably this high proportion of Jews had helped to fuel antisemitic commentaries. According to Vallat, the problem faced by France was the concentration of Jews in a number of economic fields, a concentration which, in his view, clashed with national economic interests. It would appear, according to his count, that the Jews in Paris made up 57 percent of all bankers, 57 percent of all those engaged in the fur trade, 61 percent of shirtmakers, 71 percent of music publishers, 45 percent of diamond dealers, and 43 percent of hatmakers.[9]

The argument with Vallat's report does not reside in whether these figures are or are not accurate. The problem is that they were published in order to promote the concept of the "Jewish menace" and so conveniently avoided presenting the distinctive contribution made by Jews to French manufacturing industries. If there were indeed large numbers of Jews in some of these industries, such as the diamond or fur trade or shirtmaking, it was because of the skills they had brought as immigrants when they arrived in France. The other aspect of the question that Vallat omitted concerns the conditions under which immigrant workers lived and worked in Paris, more often than not for non-Jewish employers. While they had been invited to come to work in France, administrative harassment never ceased. It affected particularly those who had come in the late 1930s. The economic depression had led the French government to curtail work permits and it affected a considerable number of those foreign Jews. The infamous fourth floor of the Prefecture of Police in Paris, where every immigrant Jew had to call for renewal of the work permit, was known as the *vallée des pleurs* (valley of tears). And then there were the frequent police raids in working-class districts where Jews lived and the inevitable explusions of those who no longer had a valid work permit and could not show that they had sufficient resources on which to live.[10] Vallat's attention to the successful and long-established members of Parisian Jewry and their presentation as objects of envy provided a far from complete picture of the economic basis of the Jewish population of Paris.

The economic census of the Jews of Occupied France ordered by the Germans in October 1940 has allowed us to briefly outline the dominant characteristics of the economic activities of the French and foreign Jews. But it should be viewed in the context of the permanent conflict of interest between Vichy France and the occupying authorities over how best to deal with the Jews' assets. When Vichy was informed of the German law, it immediately moved into action to avoid leaving the matter in the hands of the Germans. The Vichy representative in Occupied France, Général Benoît Léon de Fornel de La Laurencie, instructed the prefects in Occupied France to oversee the selection of these administrators-to-be and to ensure that these men be French.[11] Vichy had no intention of leaving the Germans open access to Jewish properties by allowing them to select the appointment of the administrators whose task it was to dispose of the Jewish establishments.

On 12 November 1940, the MBF published the general guidelines for the administrators who were soon to begin operating.[12] It was the German view that to achieve the elimination of the Jews from the economy three methods would be approved: the Jews would be permitted to sell their own businesses; in the event that they did not do so, the administrator would be empowered to force the sale; and, the administrator would have the power to dispose of stock and equipment if there was meanwhile no economic interest in keeping these businesses in operation (interest being defined as benefit to the state).

On 12 December 1940, the MBF informed the prefects of the Occupied Zone that they were authorized to nominate administrators to all Jewish-owned shops.[13] Three days later, on 15 December, de La Laurencie sent a note to the prefects in which he reminded them that the Germans' instructions were to be executed; however, he added, the prefects were to ensure that the Jewish shops, which would be sold by the administrators, would remain *entre les mains françaises*.[14]

If it was immaterial to the Jews whether their businesses were sold as a consequence of a German or Vichy decision, for Vichy the problem of what was to become of Jewish-owned commercial undertakings was a serious matter. Indeed Vichy's Ministry of Finances was very much concerned at the likelihood of the Germans' seeking to gain particular Jewish firms.[15] A special law was passed at Vichy which ordered ministerial approval for the selection of administrators to Jewish banks or insurance companies.[16]

The establishment of a junior ministerial post for Jewish affairs was certainly influenced by the problem of the "aryanization" of Jewish businesses. The whole Jewish Question was considered serious enough for Admiral François Darlan, then head of the Cabinet, to place Vallat under his direct supervision.[17] The establishment of the CGQJ indicated that Vichy was treating the Jewish Question with all the seriousness with which the Germans appeared to endow the question; furthermore Vichy was committing itself to a constant control of the question. With the centralization of the responsibility for Jewish affairs into the hands of a single authority, a more aggressive line was pursued. Within less than a month two new measures were introduced by Vichy: a law ordered the blocking of Jewish bank accounts and added a number of amendments to the first Statut des Juifs.[18] The German authorities, however, pursued their own policy, which was to constantly reduce the field of activities available to Jews. On 26 April 1941, the third German ordinance appeared, issuing a list of business activities forbidden to Jews.[19] The two measures, Vichy's order that Jewish bank accounts were to be blocked and the third ordinance, were further reinforced by initiatives from the private sector of the banking industry. On 23 May 1941, the Union Syndicale des Banques informed its members that a new German ordinance which would adversely affect the Jews' right to withdraw funds and shares would soon appear. It requested all the associated member banks to immediately apply the order, even though the ordinance had not yet been issued.[20]

Although by May 1941 many administrators had already been appointed to Jewish firms, the German authorities wanted the process speeded up. The fourth German ordinance of 28 May 1941, sought to bring the whole program close to completion. It banned all Jewish firms with gross sales above 15,000 francs per month from taking part in any financial transactions without prior referral to the Service de Control des Administrateurs Provisoires (Control Organism of the Provisional Administrators [SCAP]).[21] Thus, it was hoped, the most significant portion of Jewish firms would finally be firmly controlled. All that remained of the Jewish assets to be disposed were the artisan workshops and the insignificant businesses.

Two months after the establishment of the CGQJ the second Statut des Juifs appeared, essentially designed to correct anomalies stemming from the earlier *statut*. Among these was the problem of the status of converted Jews and children of mixed marriages. And, of course, each and every new addition of newly found Jews meant added Jewish assets to be aryanized. This second *statut* not only extended the earlier definition of a Jew, but also introduced a list of more occupations no longer open to Jews. However, to placate critics Vichy allowed new classes of Jews to benefit from some dispensations. To the earlier categories were added the descendants of former servicemen who had died for France on the battlefields and families who had lived in France for more than five generations.[22]

The SCAP was Vichy's administrative instrument to eliminate the Jews from the national economy. M. De Faramond, the general director, addressing himself to the administrators on 9 June 1941, once more reminded them that it was imperative that no Jew remained in any business that could bring them into contact with the non-Jewish public.[23] The activities of the CGQJ and SCAP made sure that this particular aspect of aryanization was fully carried out. A week later, the Paris Prefecture of Police ordered that hawkers, traders in public places, commercial travelers, *marchands de quatre saisons* (street vendors), and lottery ticket sellers stop all activities forthwith and return their traders' permits to the Prefecture.[24]

The first phase of the program of expropriation had been directed at commercial and industrial enterprises. The second phase was to be aimed at properties and shareholdings. Until June 1941 Jews were still permitted to own a single property, and its contents, as long as it was for personal use. On 22 July 1941, a law established the legal basis for the expropriation of the rest of Jewish properties.[25] Even the Jews' homes could now be confiscated and sold. The very basis of private property, as far as Jews were concerned, had become nonexistent. The law gave the administrators the power to control all properties owned by Jews and the discretionary power to decide whether such ownership constituted a possible basis for Jewish influence in the national economy. It authorized the administrators to take over existing leases as well as any valuable articles of furniture. The Jews were at the total mercy of the arbitrary decision of the administrators. Furthermore, unlike earlier legislation this law allowed no dispensations. But Vichy, desirous to appear magnanimous, and to avoid any adverse reaction by the French public, included a clause which stated that "l'administrateur doit gérer en bon père de famille" (the administrator must manage as if the head of the family). The essentially expropriatory nature of this law was further camouflaged by a statement that the Jews would be allowed to retain articles for daily use.

The aryanization program was applied more radically in the Occupied Zone than in the Vichy Zone. Vichy's commitment to the program, however much it was due to German pressure, remained constant. At all times Vichy sought to show the Germans that it was determined to pursue the program to its conclusion. There were, of course, a number of reasons, not least the need to protect what it viewed as French property. But Vichy also needed to justify its actions to French public opinion. The severity of the legislation had to be tempered with a grain of fair play. The law of 22 July 1941 provided precisely the amount of benevolence that would pacify likely critics. It provided that 10 percent of the value of the Jewish properties sold would be set aside, part of which would be available for the relief of the Jewish poor. The balance of the proceeds of the sale would be placed in a special account in the vendor's name and held by the French administration. The other part of the retained 10 percent would cover the cost of the program of aryanization. The law was intended to show the public that provisions were made by the government to help the poor and that the whole program would not cost the taxpayers. In this way two opposing types of criticism could be met.

Problems did arise in the application of the aryanization program, however. Particularly troublesome was the question of Jewish companies that had their main offices in the Vichy Zone and needed to transfer funds there from the Occupied Zone. In such cases, since they immediately involved the German authorities' control over the banking system, there was a conflict of interest between the German and Vichy authorities. Each sought to retain its share of the booty. On 25 August 1941, the CGQJ enunciated a compromise policy, which confirmed in principle the absolute control of the bank accounts but nevertheless permitted the transfer of funds to Vichy. Such a compromise was not likely to be satisfactory to the Germans, whom Vichy was anxious not to provoke. Two factors affected the issue: the accelerated dispossession taking place in Occupied France, in which Vichy always feared German interference; and the need to keep the Jews in the Vichy Zone firmly under the CGQJ's control. Vichy feared that if less stern measures were applied in their zone it would attract Jews from the Occupied Zone. And this Vichy did not want. Government policy was clear on that issue: no more refugees would be accepted into the zone, and efforts would be made to have the largest possible number repatriated. Vichy had neither the work to occupy nor the food to feed any additional people. The issue of bank accounts for firms operating from the Vichy Zone was finally resolved at the expense of the Jewish firms. On 13 October 1941, all Jewish bank accounts, irrespective in which zone they were, were frozen.[26] The principles of blocked accounts and strict limits upon the amounts that could be withdrawn were uniformly imposed for the whole of France.

The material dispossession of the Jewish population went hand in hand with a ban on a whole range of occupations. The first targets were positions in the public service. In line with the policy formulated on 17 October 1940, which had declared the need to remove all Jews from positions of responsibility in the public service, the Secretariat of Education instructed all its departments to dismiss them, unless such individuals could show active wartime service. Educational institutions were given two months to put the decision into effect.[27]

The professions were the next to suffer. In their case, criteria for the exercise of the liberal professions had already been set out for the medical profession in the law of 16 August 1940, which decreed that only those born of French parents could practice medicine. This applied to the whole range of medical practices, including dentistry, pharmacy, and midwifery. The legal profession fell under a similar status on 10 September 1940. These general principles were further developed with the first Statut des Juifs, which advanced the principle of the "numerus clausus." The legal profession was the first to be affected when a July 1941 law announced that the number of Jews could not exceed 2 percent of the total number of lawyers in each locality.[28] These 2 percent were to be determined on the basis of special dispensations awarded to outstanding individuals for either military services, for more than five generations of residence in France, or for exceptional merit.

The same principles applied throughout the professions. But the severity of their application and the speed with which Jews were eliminated from the various professions depended on the individual professional associations, for the criterion of dispensation allowed room for interpretation. The general principle of a 2 percent "numerus clausus" was not always strictly applied. In the medical profession, for instance, the number of candidates entitled to dispensations outnumbered the maximum 2 percent. In such cases, although the final decision rested with the CGQJ, some professional associations such as the Ordre des Médecins (Medical Board) defied CGQJ orders when it permitted 203 Jews to practice when there should have only been 108.[29]

Although Vichy promulgated its own anti-Jewish laws during this period, these laws carried no weight in Occupied France unless confirmed by the MBF. What resulted was a see-saw action. Vichy laws were examined by the German military administration and accepted only if the Germans thought they were likely to further the anti-Jewish objective. For example, the fifth German ordinance of 28 September 1941 confirmed the provisions of the Vichy law of 22 July 1941. The result of this interaction between Vichy and the Germans was that at times measures were harsher in the Vichy Zone, but never for long. In the final analysis, Vichy legislation acted as a pacesetter. Vichy's desire to maintain administrative cohesion and to ensure the prevalence of French law resulted in laws being framed in such a way so as not to be rejected by the MBF.

The accumulation of the proceeds of the sales of Jewish establishments held in trust by Vichy, and the blocked bank accounts, were never to revert to their legitimate owners. If it appeared, for a brief time, that these funds could assist the Jewish poor, the illusion did not last long. The illusion had been fostered by the provision of the law of 22 July 1941, stating that part of the proceeds of the sales would be available for such a purpose. It was enhanced by the establishment of the Union Générale des Israélites de France (General Union of the Israelites of France [UGIF]) in November 1941. Its charter stated that UGIF funding would be constituted in part by these proceeds. Instead these funds became pawns in a broad German maneuver designed to involve Vichy even further in its anti-Jewish policy.

On 14 December 1941, a special German ordinance imposed a fine of a *milliard* francs (a billion francs) on the Jews in Occupied France, as reprisal against "terrorist" attacks on the German army. Given the immediate application of the order, it was clear that the fine could only be met from the proceeds of the sales of Jewish properties as well as from the frozen Jewish bank accounts. While Vichy was debating how to handle the problem, the MBF, on 22 December 1941, ordered the Association Professionelle des Banques

(Banks' Professional Association) to present a full report detailing the credit balances of all Jewish bank accounts. The report was also to include the names and addresses of the depositors as well as the value of all shares held by Jews. The MBF's desire to push the process of aryanization to its ultimate limit is evidenced in this same note, as it ordered the French banks to deny Jews access to safety deposit boxes as well as to report the existence of such boxes forthwith to their *Devisenschutzkommando* (foreign exchange unit).[30]

The fine was finally paid by 15 April 1942. Vichy had ordered the banks to advance the necessary funds, using the Jewish assets, the proceeds of the expropriation, and the frozen bank accounts as collateral. The Caisse des Domaines paid 856 million francs from the special accounts holding the proceeds of the forced sales; a further 393 million francs were taken from private bank accounts, and in its haste to meet the German dateline for the payment of the fine Vichy had ordered the sale of shares owned by Jews, a move resulting in the unnecessary disposal of 250 million francs' worth of shares.[31]

The final acts of expropriation were announced on 15 September 1943. Two ordinances stated that all properties that had formerly belonged to Polish and German Jews and Jews from Bohemia and Moravia would be declared the property of the Third Reich.[32]

What were the consequences of the anti-Jewish legislation? As far as the Jews employed in the public service were concerned, a report presented to the MBF indicates that by 27 January 1942, 1,947 public servants had been dismissed, and by 2 March 1942, a total of 3,346 had been dismissed, the largest number from the Ministry of Education.[33] By June 1942 some 215 Jews remained in various ministries (the largest number, it would seem, in the Ministry of the Interior).[34] This situation prompted German protests, but Vichy, which considered that certain Jews were needed, refused to act.[35] By March 1943, the situation was still unchanged. Joseph Antignac, head of the CGQJ, wrote to SS-Obersturmfürer Heinz Röthke, the *Judenreferent,* to express the view of the CGQJ: "I am convinced that the total deportation [of the Jews] would simplify all these questions, notably the dismissal of the Jews from the Public Service, even from the Ministry of the Interior."[36]

A similar situation had arisen in the liberal professions. The second Statut des Juifs of 2 June 1941, and the further amendments of 17 November 1941, had maintained the principle of dispensations. Inevitably, conflicts arose over the numbers still allowed to practice. In the medical profession, as we have seen, the Council of the Medical Board did not endorse the CGQJ principles, yet there were pressures exerted upon it from within the profession. The Association Amicale des Anciens Combattants Médecins des Corps Combattants, 1914–18 (Friendly Association of Former Fighting Doctors of Fighting Units), continually campaigned to have the Jewish doctors expelled from the profession. It claimed that young doctors were having difficulties establishing a practice on account of the number of foreigners and sons of foreigners who were blocking their opportunities. As far as they were concerned the law was not being well policed.[37] In fact, by July 1942, some 250 Jewish doctors had already been deregistered.[38] The attitude of the German authorities and the

CGQJ notwithstanding, the Council of the Medical Board, whose task it was to enforce the laws, readmitted some Jewish doctors without the knowledge or approval of either.[39]

This same council also controlled pharmacists and midwives. It continually argued with the CGQJ in favor of allowing the largest possible number to be permitted to practice. These two branches of the profession had been legislated against in December 1941 and were also faced with the "numerus clausus." Pharmacists who owned outlets, however, were never allowed to benefit from dispensations. The appointed administrators treated them in the same manner as any other Jewish commercial undertaking. Those permitted to work could only do so if they never came into contact with the non-Jewish public. As far as midwives were concerned, the question remained academic. By March 1943 there were only thirteen left in Paris.[40] Dentistry was the last of the professions to be aryanized. The difficulty in the dentists case was that their practice verged on commercial activities. The CGQJ sought to appoint administrators but the Council of the Medical Board refused to view the profession as a commercial venture. In April 1943, forty-six Jewish dentists, in accordance with the "numerus clausus," had been allowed to continue to practice.[41]

The practice of law had been the first of the professions to be singled out for aryanization because that profession had traditionally been led by right-wing elements. As Vallat was a lawyer, it was no accident that the Jewish lawyers were the first to be affected. The legally acceptable exemptions from disbarment were kept as low as possible at all times. Vallat, in a letter to the MBF, stated that in January 1942 there were 250 Jewish lawyers (48 of whom were war veterans) still practicing.[42] By April 1943 there were only 92 left.[43] However, even these figures were inflated because they included members of other paralegal professions, notaries, valuers, and others, whose practices fell under the laws governing commercial activities. To allow them to carry on in accordance with the law, SCAP had to appeal to the MBF for approval of its decision not to appoint administrators.[44]

Artists, writers, and composers were affected by the two Statuts des Juifs of 1940 and 1941, which decreed that no Jew could be employed in any institutions or theaters that received government subsidies. The elimination from public performance was total. The works of published Jewish authors sold in bookshops were seized by the Police aux Questions Juives (Police for Jewish Affairs [PQJ]) and later, after its reorganization, by the Section d'Enquête et de Control (Office of Control and Inquiry [SEC]).[45] No publisher could enter into contracts with Jews or issue any works by Jews. Jewish painters were not allowed to exhibit or sell their paintings. A whole class of artists was reduced to poverty.[46]

Every section of the Jewish population was affected by the aryanization program, even the Jewish labor force. As soon as a branch of industry was named in a law as no longer open to Jews, the Jewish employee was immediately threatened with unemployment. Appointment of an administrator to a Jewish firm resulted in the dismissal of its Jewish workers. Dr. Blanke, of the economic division of the German military administration, addressed himself to that situation. In a letter to the Ministry of Industrial Production at Vichy, dated 7 February 1941, he noted that the Jewish employees of Jewish firms controlled by administrators were sacked while non-Jewish companies in the same industry could continue to employ Jews. Blanke suggested that this anomaly could easily be remedied by banning all Jews from employment in the same occupational group, a radical measure indeed.[47]

Artisans were particularly affected by the aryanization process, since they had limited resources and were totally dependent upon their own productivity. The appointment of an administrator often had dramatic consequences. Not only were their tools of trade and small stocks immediately impounded but, even worse, their homes (which were also their workshops) were offered for sale. The German view was that because of their independence and potential mobility these skilled workers represented a permanent economic threat and should be eliminated.[48] Nevertheless the German ordinance of 26 April 1941 had overlooked them. Stenger, the MBF's representative on SCAP, pressed for adoption of the German point of view. He was willing to compromise if Jewish artisans were placed under binding contracts to non-Jewish employers, received raw material only from them, sold finished products only to them, and were each permitted to employ only one person, also a Jew. If these conditions were not met, wrote Stenger, then their workshops should be sold or taken away.[49] Darlan, however, rejected this proposal on the grounds that a danger would be created by an "increase in Jewish unemployment and on this subject the current situation is already troublesome."[50]

Meanwhile, awaiting a decision about their fate, most of these artisans as foreigners found themselves out of work. They were unable to obtain raw materials for their small workshops and had to close; even those who still held stocks were not permitted to trade. In order to operate, these artisans had to apply to the Prefecture for permission to work at home as *travailleurs à façon*. But the Paris Prefecture had never looked with favor on that class of self-employed workers. The lack of sympathy on the part of the French authorities and the artisans' own fear of presenting themselves at the Prefecture aggravated their already difficult material situation. The German authorities nevertheless did want some artisans to remain, if only because certain trades were becoming useful in war production. Glovemakers, knitters, and furriers were required to outfit German troops on the Eastern Front, and Parisian firms needed workers with these skills. The German military administration agreed, in January 1943, to permit Jewish artisans to carry on their work on a limited basis.[51]

The consequences of economic aryanization still remain to be examined. The October 1940 census of commercial and industrial firms had shown that there were 11,000 Jewish enterprises in Paris, of which 7,737 were privately owned and 3,455 were incorporated companies.[52] Pierre-Eugène Fournier, then general director of SCAP, stated that within a week of the decision to appoint administrators, 4,500 Jewish firms had been taken over. This haste stemmed from the need to complete the appointments by the date demanded by the German military administration, 26 December 1940.[53]

The initial set of figures is markedly lower than those given in April 1941. By then, we learn from Fournier, 20,000 enterprises had been registered; the SCAP had presented the German military administration with a list of 3,000 nominations of administrators and 700 had been accepted and were already functioning. At an interministerial meeting in May 1941, Yves Bouthillier, the minister of national economy, had announced that following the order of the military administration to SCAP to place administrators in firms dealing directly with the public, on penalty of closure, SCAP had appointed administrators to 10,500 firms within three weeks.[54] At the end of 1941, 17,000 Jewish firms were still registered: 2,195 commercial enterprises, 12,230 shops, and 2,500 artisans.[55] The difficulty in establishing precise figures for the number of Jewish establishments, a problem that constantly annoyed the German military administration no less than the French authorities, was due to the complexity of establishing once and for all who was a Jew. This problem led Vichy, for instance, to constantly introduce new clauses into the Statut des Juifs.[56] Furthermore, some Jews from certain countries were considered protected nationals. This meant there were individuals registered as Jews whose property could not be aryanized.

The aryanization of real estate, which had been ordered by the law of 17 November 1941, began before the year was over. The number of properties affected was estimated at between 3,000 to 3,500.[57] Jewish properties could be disposed of in three ways: by full aryanization, that is, direct sale or auction; by "de facto aryanization," disposal by the former Jewish proprietor to a non-Jew (this method only existed in the early phase and had been approved by the German administration); and by liquidation, that is, a separate disposal of stock, equipment, and assets.

To evaluate the monetary value of these transactions and the numbers in each category, we must turn to statistics that include real estate transactions but not other kinds of dispossession. For, besides enterprises as such, there were also partnerships with non-Jews, commercial agreements, patents, shareholdings, art works, and the contents of apartments, which in their rightful owners' absence were crated and sent to Germany.

A CGQJ report on the number of enterprises it had controlled until April 1944 shows that for the Occupied Zone there had been 29,831 enterprises and 12,396 buildings rgistered as Jewish-owned, all of which had been placed with administrators.[58] This same report informs us that 7,972 enterprises had been aryanized, 1,708 buildings sold, and 7,340 enterprises and buildings "liquidated." A total of 17,020 commercial and privately owned properties had been disposed of. Within this total there had been 1,930 artisans; we can well accept that from the 7,340 that had been "liquidated," there must have been a very high percentage of artisans' so-called enterprises. This CGQJ report, viewed in conjunction with the CGQJ's June 1944 statistical report, shows how these properties were aryanized: 50 percent had been sold straight out; 25 percent were liquidated, that is, sold in parts to various buyers; and 5 percent were de facto aryanized, that is, carried out in the early phase of the program when Jews were still permitted to dispose of their own properties without resorting to an appointed administrator. The high number of liquidations, 7,340 from a total number of 17,020, could only indicate that either these businesses were of no financial value whatsoever, or, as in the limited number of those with annual sales exceeding 200,000 francs, they must have been the object of a dismemberment by interested parties.[59]

After September 1942 the CGQJ began to give the German authorities monthly returns of proceeds of sales of aryanized properties.[60] Yet these figures were always questioned by the Germans. Despite repeated demands the Germans were never able to obtain accurate figures from Vichy.[61] It must have been clear to Vichy, especially after the December 1941 *milliard*-franc fine was imposed on the Jews, that the Germans might be tempted to try that tactic once more.

What was the total amount of Jewish expropriation? According to the last Administration des Domaines balance sheet of July 1944, after the payment of the billion francs, the proceeds of the sales were 899,201,477 francs for Paris and 86,550,406 francs for the other departments of Occupied France.[62] To this sum must be added the monies deducted from private accounts in December 1941 and January 1942 when the Germans had imposed the *milliard* fine. Then there were the forced sales of Jewish shares owned privately and confiscated apartment contents shipped to Germany.[63] And there were the works of art seized by the Einsatzgruppe Rosenberg (the Rosenberg Action Group).[64] The Jewish community of France claimed after the war that the final cost of aryanization had amounted to 8 billion francs.[65] It is beyond us to judge whether such a claim is above or below the actual financial losses suffered by the Jews of France. But a number of points can be made. We do know that war profiteers took advantage of the possibilities offered during the war. Jewish properties were sold at give-away prices despite Vichy's attempt to endow these sales with a semblance of respectability. The 40 percent of the Jewish properties that were liquidated might not have represented to the profiteers worthy opportunities, but to the Jewish artisans they represented a lifetime of patient accumulation of tools of trade. Though of no market value, their worth was inestimable to the artisans. Furthermore, replacement costs, loss of earnings, and delays in regaining possession from those who acquired such properties must be quantified. It therefore seems that the claim advanced by the Jewish community was legitimate. In the archives of the Ministry of Finance, the files concerning the whole sordid episode would certainly establish a more precise figure, but until 1994 all access to them is denied.

The Jews of Paris could not have anticipated that the special census of October 1940 would be the first in a series of discriminatory acts and regulations that would soon deprive them of their livelihood. It took a full year for the significance of Franco-German collaboration against the Jews to be fully understood. In overall terms, no distinction ultimately could be made between the German and Vichy positions on the issue of aryanization and the elimination of Jews from the professions. There were sufficient differences in emphasis, however, to generate among certain Jews illusions as to Vichy's real intentions. The French Jews, particularly those who could claim their families had lived in France for a number of generations or had gained distinctions in wars, believed that Vichy would protect them from complete destitution.

Vichy had made its position clear to the Germans: war veterans and a limited number of Jews would be given special consideration. This had been stated when the issue had first been raised by Dr. Blanke of the German military administration. Vallat's reply to Blanke's question indicates the number of Jews to whom Vallat wanted to extend protection. Of the Jews in Paris, on the basis of the population control of December 1941, 8,000 could benefit from the available dispensations. Vallat further stated that no more than 2,000 of these were likely to remain in business, which from France's point of view "would not constitute an economic danger." In order that the French position be clearly understood Vallat emphasized that the "numerus clausus" constituted a safe limit.[66]

Thus a whole class of French Jews had some ground for hope. That hope resided in the essential difference between German racialism, which was total and absolute, and Vichy's xenophobic antisemitism. Vichy held that Jews could be accepted only in homeopathic quantities, that is, 2 percent.[67] Germany had a radical position which nothing short of a Final Solution would satisfy.

Three laws sealed the economic fate of the Jews, both French and immigrant: the law of 2 June 1941, the decree of 28 July 1941, and the law of 17 November 1941. From 1942 onward, 98 percent of the Jewish population was deprived of all basic economic rights. Only those within the privileged 2 percent who benefited from Vichy's protection could still hold out hope. From then on the combined German and French laws set out to rob them of their properties. It was only because the Germans, for reasons of their own, had tolerated Vichy's demand that hope could be sustained. This hope, though misplaced, remained strong among French Jews, who believed the Vichy legislation was particularly directed at foreign Jews. This illusion was eventually shattered as their economic bases became as exposed as the immigrant Jews'.

3

Life under the Occupation

It was physical survival that was at stake for the Jews of Paris during the Occupation, yet few Jews realized this soon enough. Until July 1942, faced with harsh measures that affected their economic and social existence, they viewed their survival in terms of overcoming material deprivations and social isolation. Even the deportations to Eastern Europe, which began in March 1942 and which seem now such poignant indications of what was to come, did little to alter their evaluation of events. Today we can see why. The decision that France be cleared of Jews was not made in Berlin until June 1942.[1] It is therefore understandable that the Jews did not relate the measures taken prior to that date to the unbelievable policy that was to threaten their very survival. Perhaps it was the massive increase in the scale of deportations, in July 1942, that radically altered their outlook. Still ignorant of the significance of deportations, they intuitively perceived a sinister threat.

Interpretations abounded. French Jews, deported from Compiègne in March 1942, boarded the trains singing the "Marseillaise." Arrested as hostages, they saw themselves above all as prisoners of war being sent to camps not unlike POW camps.[2] Even the foreign Jews, deported from the camps of Beaune-La-Rolande and Pithiviers, preferred to believe the German propaganda that they were being sent to labor camps.[3] Reasons for accepting these interpretations appeared well founded. Had not the collaborationist Paris press clamored for Jews to be put to work?[4] The true meaning of deportations was not apparent. The nature of the camps they were being sent to was unknown. They went in total ignorance. It was a German state secret: so well kept in fact that historians have had to accept that aspects of the genesis of the Final Solution are still obscure.[5] It is small wonder that the significance of the German moves was not clear to most of those affected by them.

There was a second factor affecting the Jews' interpretation of German policy, namely, its divisiveness, its concentration on particular groups. Essentially the Germans were dependent on Vichy's assistance for the execution of their policy, and Vichy insisted that foreigners rather than French Jews be deported.[6] It seemed then that only certain Jews were to be the target of the German policies and this caused, or rather accentuated, divisions in the Jewish community. Worse still, Jews failed to recognize that the German policy would, in the end, affect all of them. This confusion was compounded by Germany's foreign policy considerations which made some Jews immune. Furthermore, there were Jews who received protection because their skills were necessary to the German war effort. All these objective factors help to explain why Jews readily regarded deportation as a police measure rather than recognizing it as a major action in a war of extermination.

Illusory hopes of survival were thus sustained by plausible explanations. Jews in various categories of survivors and condemned understood deportation differently. The less likely personal deportation seemed, the less fearsome the interpretation.

The situation changed dramatically in July 1942: the deportation of women and children, the aged and the dying, canceled all the earlier interpretations. Deportation was no longer viewed as a police measure. It was suddenly seen as a dreadful trial, a leap into the unknown. The total ignorance of what awaited those deported to Eastern Europe gave the notion of survival a significance hitherto unthinkable, for those threatened as well as for those who felt safe.

An avalanche of anti-Jewish—and antiforeigner—laws, decrees, and circulars had been issued by Vichy and the German authorities.[7] They had come in such rapid succession, and in so many cases were unknown to the Jews, that their real significance was not understood until it was too late. In the end, taken collectively, the laws turned the Jews into a hunted people. But these laws in themselves only set the stage. It was in how the administration applied them, in how these laws were experienced by the Jews in daily life, that they acquired their real significance.

On the eve of the German Occupation, even though Paris had been declared an open city,[8] the collective fear that had engulfed Holland, Belgium, and northern France also gripped Paris. Jews joined the ensuing exodus. All Jews had particular reasons for fleeing; the violent racism that prevailed in Germany could leave them in no doubt. But not all left, some remained unable or afraid to join the exodus.

The government of Paul Reynaud had decided to leave Paris. The Central Consistory of French Judaism, at an extraordinary session on 5 June 1940, decided to follow the government.[9] It closed its synagogues as well as the various institutions it controlled. The Alliance Israélite Universelle and the Comité de Bienfaisance also closed. The departure of these institutions affected in turn the immigrant organizations. The Fédération des Sociétés Juives de France closed its offices. The continuous exodus of Jews brought an overnight cessation of all activities by Jewish political parties. Even the illegal organization of the Jewish Communists, which could have been expected to react differently, ceased to exist. Communist leaders and membership reacted no differently to the general panic. The general press, acting on government orders, stopped all publications; Jewish editors did likewise.[10]

By mid-June 1940 the Jewish districts were as deserted as the rest of Paris. But Paris was not entirely denuded of its population. As Robert Geissmann, whose family was later to play an active role in the Vichy-imposed representation, recalls, "Despite the menacing news, many had chosen to wait at home rather than seek uncertain security in the provinces."[11] Jean Jacques Bernard, a well-known writer, claimed that those French Jews who did remain in Paris did so out of loyalty to their country.[12] Most foreign Jews stayed simply because they did not have the resources for the uncertain journey. Others, because of indecision about where to go, had been overtaken by the advancing German armies.[13] Whether they stayed in Paris or fled, the fear was genuine and seemed well founded.

The German invader, however, dissipated this initial fear with a most unexpected "correctness" of behavior; the relief that the population felt as a result was all the greater. The word soon spread that the German soldiers did not pillage or maltreat the population. Parisians, Jews included, began to return to the capital.[14]

After the Armistice of June 1940 a significant number of Parisians returned to their homes. Yet, already, there were signs that should have alerted and deterred the Jews. The Armistice had divided France into two zones. Access to Occupied France was firmly policed by the German authorities. By September 1940, signs appeared at the crossing points to the effect that Jews were not admitted into occupied France.[15] Despite the notices and the orders, Parisian Jews were still seeking to return to their homes. The German military authorities in Paris readily granted travel permits without asking racial questions.[16]

The early months of the German Occupation were a time of reorientation and resettlement for the Jewish population. The Jews, like the rest of the French population, were seeking to come to terms with a totally new situation. Notwithstanding the presence of German troops, the French administration continued to ensure public order and maintain public services. The orderliness that prevailed in Paris in the early months of the Occupation encouraged people to resume their former activities. Jewish workingmen, anxious to return to work, sought out former employers. Artisans, *travailleurs à façon,* and shopkeepers were eager to resume lives that had come to a halt in June 1940.

Some immigrants had a command of the German language. They used this to advantage when dealing with the soldiers who seemed not at all concerned that they were Jews. One could see Jewish youths, unable to find work, selling postcards to the soldiers as though this army of occupation was but a new wave of tourists.[17] Fears of the German policy toward Jews receded. In their place came material frustrations. Trade was brisk, and as stocks dwindled in the fur and clothing industries, traders worried about the shortage of materials. How were they to renew the stock of manufactured goods? Although these uncertainties were causing concern, the traders urged friends who were still in the Vichy Zone to return to Paris. Despite the census taken of Jews and their businesses in October 1940, some Jews were still returning to Paris as late as November 1940.[18]

In day-to-day living the Jewish population faced the same difficulties as their non-Jewish counterparts. Long queues in the food shops had become a feature of everyday life for all Parisians. Shortages created a struggle for basic family necessities common to Jews and non-Jews. The growing unease among the Jewish population at the first anti-Jewish measures and the level of anti-Jewish propaganda on the radio and in the press was reflected in particularly high attendance at services in the synagogues. During the Jewish New Year holidays of October 1940, the synagogues of the Consistory as well as those of the more orthodox immigrant Jews had never been so well patronized. Jews were not afraid to behave in ways that clearly distinguished them from Gentiles in the Parisian population.[19] Indeed, during the early months of the Occupation, daily life for the Jews in Paris had regained a normalcy reminiscent of the days before the exodus. The return of relatives and friends, together with the absence of overt anti-Jewish measures, cloaked the city in an aura of normalcy.

October 1940 was important for the Jews of Paris—it was during that month that the earlier antisemitic propaganda began to acquire legislative muscles. The uncertainties regarding Germany's well-known anti-Jewish positions found expression in two ordinances. Vichy's own legislative contribution added in no small manner to popular concern. Indeed, Vichy's legislative action against the Jews dated back to the law of 22 July 1940, which announced the establishment of a governmental commission that would reexamine all naturalizations granted since 10 August 1927.[20] At the time the announcement had passed unnoticed among the Jews. The Jews, like the French population, were still too traumatized by the military defeat and the exodus to evaluate the significance of the law. Despite the suspended threat of denaturalization for some, the German censuses of Jewish population and property and Vichy's own *Statut des Juifs,* which affected all the Jews, produced no more than a superficial, temporary, commotion.[21]

The return of many Jews to Paris enabled the dormant Jewish institutions and organizations to renew their work. The return of communal activists, and donors, provided the basis upon which community life could resume. It was in the cafes of the Jewish districts, particularly where Jewish businessmen met, that communal life found its former energies. Indeed, the place of the cafes in prewar Jewish political and social life has never been granted due recognition. It was there that interest groups gathered, news and views were exchanged, and support for causes was marshaled. It was in these cafes, as regular meeting places, that the reborn Jewish organizations found the support they needed for their activities.[22] There was little disagreement then among Jews about the need to establish relief organizations; it was accepted by all that there were many in need of assistance. The wives of prisoners of war, the families of unemployed, the refugees, and the families of soldiers not yet demobilized all needed immediate help.[23] Fortunately an official framework existed and this was soon reinforced by the efforts of various immigrant and radical groups. As the German army marched into Paris on 14 June 1940, remaining immigrant communal workers met and formed a coordinating committee. Its aims were to reopen canteens formerly operated by the participating organizations and to revivify the then-closed institutions. Within weeks of the German Occupation the canteens were once again feeding those in need. The activities of these groups were not restricted to relief work. By July 1940, the Jewish Communists began publishing their illegal news-sheet *Unzer Vort*—Our Opinion.[24]

The early period of the Occupation had witnessed the Jews of Paris gradually returning and resuming their former occupations. Everyone lived in the shadow of anti-Jewish legislation but the Jewish population was surprised: they had been anticipating material and political persecution. The Eastern European population, accustomed to state-promoted persecution, looked to their organizations for guidance and help; the French Jews, not endowed with the myriad organizations that characterized communal immigrant Jewry, found their defense in the hands of those who had traditionally represented French Judaism: the Consistory. The ACIP had also reopened its offices in August 1940. Albert Manuel, the general-secretary of the Central Consistory, returned to Paris at the end of July, and his presence attracted many worshippers back to the main synagogue on the rue de la Victoire. Chief-Rabbi Julien Weill's own return in August led to the reopening of the Consistory's synagogues.[25]

By October 1940, the immigrant Jews were already organized. Former political organizations had, individually or collectively, reopened welfare centers and were helping a sizable segment of the population. Food, medical care, clothing, and financial help were distributed to anyone in need. At first, because the resources were limited, only the most needy were helped. But, as the community adjusted itself to the new conditions, further financial resources were found. The French Jews, through the institutions of the Paris Consistory, meanwhile reopened some centers of assistance, though on a reduced scale.[26]

Before the Occupation, it was refugees, escaping persecution, who needed material help. Now a part of the immigrant population was also affected. As a consequence, the broad network of communal institutions, ranging from orphanages to schools and homes for the aged, strove to meet the growing needs. Families and organizations busied themselves with the problems of daily existence in conditions of material hardship, which would soon become secondary preoccupations as the fight for survival came to eclipse daily concerns. The repressive anti-Jewish legislation had not yet made its mark on people and institutions. In spite of the gradual return to normal of Jewish communal life in Paris, it would be wrong to assume that the community resumed its former level of activity. While the immigrants had already laid the foundations for future activities, the French Jews of the Consistory had only made hesitant moves to revitalize their institutions. In short, at this stage, the impact of the Occupation was limited and the responses of the various groups in the Jewish community were unorganized, tentative, and parochial. They reflected self-interest more than collective fear or anticipation of hard times.

The first measure to affect the Jewish population became effective during

October. All Jews, French and foreign alike, were ordered to register with the police. Everyone obeyed the German ordinance: the French-born, in spite of their resentment at being placed in the same category as the more recently arrived foreigners, because they believed that the law should be upheld; the naturalized French and the foreign Jews, less certain of the protection the legal system offered them, because they feared the consequences of disobedience. This particular German ordinance carried three significant paragraphs. First, it was officially announced that Jews would no longer be permitted to reenter the German-occupied part of France. Second, all Jewish-owned establishments would have to display a poster, in French and in German, stating that their owners were Jewish. Third, the leaders of the Jewish communities were, on demand of the French authorities, to give all information and documentation needed to carry out the census of the Jews. The Jewish population of Paris saw the order singling out Jewish stores as the most disturbing of the three clauses. It was the first manifestation of the German intention to segregate the Jews. And although the German order for registering every Jew was menacing, the order that Jewish leaders were to cooperate in the fulfillment of the census was even more sinister.

At the time the Jewish population and organization did not react. Jewish shops affixed the bilingual sign in their windows. In an attempt to demonstrate their place in the nation, some displayed along with that sign their family's war record. But the French police forbade that practice.[27] Shopkeepers in Jewish districts did not feel particularly vulnerable because they had the support and sympathy of the local population. For example, on the day following the announcement French Fascist groups attacked some Jewish shops in the third arrondissement. When they returned the next day for a second attack, they were met by Jews prepared to defend their rights physically.[28] It was rather different for Jewish shops sparsely spread along the *boulevards;* they were prone to victimization. The same Fascist organizations sent their gangs to smash storefronts and to create havoc in the shops, but unlike those in the third arrondissement the Jewish shopkeepers were defenseless.[29] It was also during October that the press and the radio actively engaged in anti-Jewish propaganda. Certain non-Jewish business houses joined in the chorus. Les Frères Lissac was a large chain of opticians; it ordered its branches to display prominent signs that read "Les Frères Lissac ne sont pas les Frères Isaac" (The Lissac Brothers are not the Isaac Brothers). A chain of cafes trading as "Dupont" displayed signs that prohibited "Jews and dogs" from entering.[30]

The first arrests of Jews occurred in November 1940. The victims were a group of left-wing Zionists, members of "Hashomer Hatzair." The Gestapo had found a prewar list of donors during an investigation of Jewish organizations and these individuals had become the first victims. Their sudden arrest and incarceration in army barracks outside Paris brought temporary panic among the immigrant population. Most Parisian Jews soon viewed their arrest as a repressive measure of a political character. Zionist circles in Paris tried vainly to convince the immigrant Jews that these arrests had a much broader significance but to no avail.[31] The limited nature of the arrest and the fact that it was an isolated incident reduced the affair to insignificance.

In late 1940 and early 1941, Jewish relief organizations, under pressure from Theodor Dannecker, agreed to form a Coordination Committee. The Jewish population was faced with serious problems. There were substantial numbers of unemployed, many families of prisoners of war needed help, intellectuals were particularly affected by the difficulties in obtaining employment, some artisans were unable to work due to the shortage of raw materials. There was an urgent need for the community to centralize its efforts. The Jewish organizations' need to pool their resources in order to meet communal hardship occurred simultaneously with Theodor Dannecker's demand that a central Jewish organization be voluntarily formed to represent and assume responsibility for the Jewish population. The Coordination Committee, formed at the instigation of the Gestapo, fell under the control of the Jewish department of the RSHA, Department IV B4* Yet the Gestapo's involvement in communal affairs was not immediately seen as something to be feared.

The Jewish population was still trying to understand the significance of that change when the French police interned 3,710 foreign Jews on 14 May 1941. The number of men arrested marked the first qualitative change in the life of the Jews in Paris. Overnight the problem of relief increased immeasurably. Those interned as well as their families required assistance. The community responded quickly. Shopkeepers whose businesses had not yet been placed in the hands of government-appointed administrators donated money and goods. Subscription lists were circulated in workshops and businessmen in the cafes organized their own collections.[32]

An increasing number of Jewish families were in need of a different kind of help: the small traders and craftsmen whose premises had been placed in the hands of government-appointed administrators. Increasingly, the Jewish organizations were called upon to provide legal assistance to these traders in the inevitable conflicts with the administrators. The sudden and total dispossession faced by these families arose not only from the iniquitous aryanization laws but also from the ruthless manner in which the majority of these administrators set out to enforce the laws. Whether the conflicts between the dispossessed and the administrators always had a basis in law or not was not necessarily significant, but the Jewish organizations did find themselves called upon to provide legal advice. Between the two extremes of the destitute and previously independent businessmen newly deprived of their businesses, was the working population. That group constituted over a third of the population, and the workers were anxious to retain their employment.

Providing material subsistence for 65,000 Jewish families was, of course, beyond the combined resources of the Jewish organizations, particularly when there was an overt plan to reduce them to utter poverty in order to prepare for their elimination from France. The issue of employment was suddenly

* The Coordination Committee and Dannecker will be discussed in the following chapter.

brought to the fore in July 1941 when Dannecker demanded that the Coordination Committee of the Jewish relief organizations supply manpower for a German agricultural firm operating in northern France.

The Coordination Committee, because it was under orders from Dannecker, and because it also saw the demand as a way to alleviate unemployment, organized a recruitment drive. Promises of security and benefits were made to attract volunteers. Yet the results of the campaign were negligible. Unemployed Jews neither trusted the promises nor wished to be employed by a German company in an unfamiliar place. Neither the inducements nor the warnings of the Coordination Committee that the Jewish population as a whole would be exposed to reprisals if enough men did not volunteer succeeded in generating the required numbers.

The Coordination Committee was neither heeded nor trusted. The problem remained; a large number of Jews were destitute and the Jewish organizations, trusted or not, were the only bodies Jews could call upon for assistance. These organizations could only continue to function and provide if they could muster the necessary resources. The Coordination Committee made many public appeals for funds, warning that unless donations were voluntary the Germans would impose special taxes upon the Jewish population.

To show that German commands were to be taken seriously Dannecker ordered the French police to proceed with mass arrests and internments. In the early hours of the morning of 20 August 1941, the French police surrounded the eleventh arrondissement. At every Metro exit they checked identity papers. Commuters were allowed in but no Jew was allowed out. That day the police conducted door-to-door searches and 4,232 Jews, French and immigrants, were arrested.[33]

The Jewish population was stunned. Panic reigned among the French and the foreign Jews. In the following days few Jews ventured into the streets of the eleventh arrondissement.[34] The 4,232 internees were the first to suffer. They had been taken to Drancy, just outside Paris, where neither the German nor the French authorities had made any preparations for such a large number of men. There was an immediate problem of providing food and clothing. Medical facilities did not exist and many men had been taken regardless of their condition. When families and organizations offered supplies for the internees, the French police guarding the camp refused them. Drancy rapidly became a place to be feared. To the families of men previously interned in Pithiviers and Beaune-La-Rolande could now be added the families of men in Drancy. Eight percent of the Jewish adult population of Paris was now under guard in camps; one family in eight was affected.

A German military commission inspected Drancy in October 1941, and, appalled at the conditions in the camp, ordered the release of more than 900 of the sick and dying.[35] The French prefectoral authorities included among those to be released war veterans, fathers of large families and, significantly enough, among those who belonged to these categories, an overwhelming number of French Jews. This particular development gave credibility to the French Jews' belief that internment measures were primarily directed at the immigrants. Some of the released immigrants who had served in the French army concluded that their release was due to that fact. Fathers of large families also reasoned that some sense of justice still prevailed. Although the immigrants were obviously the most exposed, the releases led Jewish public opinion to the view that the authorities were gradually re-examining the policy of arbitrary internments.[36]

As a result of the Drancy internments and reports of the unbearable conditions there, those captive in Pithiviers and Beaune-La-Rolande no longer attempted to escape. Indeed, after three months of internment these men had succeeded, with the help of Jewish organizations, in improving their conditions. Food parcels and mail were allowed in. Some who had escaped before August 1941 returned of their own volition to Beaune-La-Rolande and Pithiviers to face punishment rather than chance a second arrest which could result in their internment in Drancy.[37]

The growing number of internees, 8,000 in three months, stepped up the tension already present, particularly among the immigrants. The plight of the internees and their families called for all the resources that the community's organizations could muster. The ruthless progress of aryanization and its consequences compounded the material difficulties. Immigrant organizations and the Coordination Committee were hard-pressed to meet the various needs, but they did open youth clubs, medical centers, and more canteens.

Threats to survival came from every side. Pauperization or internment were certainly the most obvious and direct results of anti-Jewish measures. Antisemitic propaganda, although not directly affecting particular groups of Jews, was equally insidious. The general aim of that propaganda, carried by the press, radio, and billboards, was to incite the Gentile population against the Jewish population.[38] Such propaganda used every opportunity to bolster popular support for the anti-Jewish measures, despite the danger that these harsh measures might prompt a backlash of sympathy from the general population. On 3 October 1941, seven synagogues in Paris were bombed. The Jews, French and immigrant, were suddenly reminded that anti-Jewish propaganda could easily become violent. The Paris Consistory, although aware that these bombings could not have occurred without the complicity of the German authorities, decided nevertheless to protest to the French police and demand that the guilty parties be brought to justice.[39] The Rabbinate appealed to the Catholic and Protestant churchees for support in this effort.[40] The German department of propaganda examined the effect of the bombings on French public opinion and was forced to conclude that opposition arose when action was taken against any places of worship. The official Jewish protests certainly did not lead to the prosecution of the guilty parties, but unknown to the Jewish Consistory, General Otto Von Stülpnagel, the military governor, was strongly opposed to such actions. Such deeds could only disturb public order and as governor this was his main concern. He ordered the punishment of the Gestapo officer who had engineered the bombings; this same officer was recalled to Germany.[41]

It is not our intention to examine the important question of the MBF and Gestapo relationship in France nor to examine the respective responsibility of the MBF or Gestapo Jewish section in the drafting and application of anti-Jewish measures. There was a degree of compliance on the part of the MBF to Gestapo policy until the end of 1941. It certainly becomes apparent when, following attacks upon German army personnel, Stülpnagel decided to execute 100 hostages, of whom 53 were Jewish, in an effort to stop anti-German hostile acts. Together with the decision to impose such reprisals, the MBF also decided to arrest 750 prominent French Jewish citizens who, together with 250 immigrant Jews from Drancy, would be deported to labor camps in Germany. Although the special arrest of French Jews should have indicated to the Jewish population that the formal differentiation between French and immigrant Jews was only temporary, the Jewish community, as a whole, chose to view these arrests as part of the German authorities' attempts to eradicate resistance and not as evidence that the Jews were an expendable commodity, irrespective of their nationalities.

The year 1941 came to a close with executions and further internments. Between December 1940 and December 1941, some 8,000 men were still interned, and the economic and social conditions of the Jewish population had deteriorated severely. Jacques Biélinky, a well-known Jewish journalist with access to French and immigrant leaders, noted then that "the Jewish masses, who have never dealt on the stock-exchange, are in atrocious misery. . . ."[42] The destitute who were too proud to ask for community assistance were left with only one option: to work in the factories supplying the needs of the German war effort.

In December 1941 the Jewish population was informed that Vichy had formed a national Jewish representation: the UGIF. Among the various reasons given by Vichy for the establishment of this representation was the increased poverty resulting from the previous measures. At any rate this was advanced as one of the reasons by those Jews who chose to lead this Vichy creation. Indeed the problem was serious. The suffering Jewish population could only call on the network of immigrant organizations, operating semilegally or illegally, or upon this newly and legally formed UGIF.

Anti-Jewish legislation reached its peak during 1942. Almost every function of daily life was curtailed and governed by restrictive laws. Jews could not change places of residence without informing the local police stations; they could not leave the Seine department without travel permits; they had to be home between 8 P.M. and 6 A.M.; radios had been confiscated; bicycles were also confiscated and could only be used with special permits; telephones were disconnected and even the Jewish medical practitioners had to apply for special permits, which were often denied; and no Jew was permitted to enter a non-Jewish store except between the hours of 3 P.M. and 4 P.M., when food stores, for instance, were already sold out. Entry into any public establishment, even public gardens, was forbidden. In the Parisian Metro Jews were only allowed to use the last carriage. In order to enforce these restrictions thoroughly (apart from other motives) the Germans ordered every Jew over six years of age to wear the Yellow Star of David; and even these stars had to be paid for in cash and with textile coupons at the local police stations.[43]

Of all the measures taken against the Jews, the Star had the most profound psychological impact. It had to be firmly sewn on the left side of the outer garment so as to be clearly visible at all times. Even in the workplace the Jews had to wear the Star at all times. The removal of the outer garment was not permitted unless there was another Star on the garment immediately underneath. The Star marked the Jews as distinctly separate and exposed them to the physical abuses of French Fascist thugs and to continual police harassment. It was a simple matter to charge a Jew with intent to conceal the Star, a crime that would result in immediate internment. There were, of course, even before the Star had been introduced, other forms of identifying the Jews. Jews' identity cards had to be stamped "Jew" and this practice was not abandoned after the introduction of the Star.

Until July 1942 only men had been interned and immigrants had been the main victims. The official reason given for internment was that the Jews had to be put to work. No lasting panic had resulted, no doubt because the French police had conducted the arrests seemingly according to decisions by French authorities. But after July 1942 the situation altered radically. From then on, women, children, the old, and the sick were indiscriminately interned. Again they were all foreigners.

On 16 July 1942, more than 12,000 men, women, and children were arrested by the French police.[44] All the immigrant communal networks collapsed. Total panic resulted. This, the largest arrest of Jews, had been conducted over three days and had a profound effect. In the immigrant districts, few Yellow Stars could be seen in the streets. The sight of police escorting whole families, sometimes old people and children, or, more often, women and children carrying meager bundles of clothes brought fear to French Jews and despair to other immigrants.[45]

It was only after the arrests had ceased that the remaining Jews realized the scale of the police operation. The stories of mothers who chose to throw themselves with their children from apartment windows rather than face arrest, caused the most anguish.[46] Then there were the hundreds of children who had been left behind by their parents. And, finally, there were the men who, expecting to be the targets as in the previous mass arrests, had hidden with neighbors or friends and returned the following day to find that their homes had been sealed off by the police and their families vanished.[47]

During the weeks after these events two questions dominated the lives of the remaining immigrants: what would the authorities do with those arrested and what was to be done next? By the end of the first week after 16 July, two convoys had left Drancy for Eastern Europe. No one doubted anymore what the fate of the others would be. The remaining question was what to do now. The immigrant Jews began leaving Paris. Until then, it was mainly the French Jews who left. Now the situation had reversed. The only remaining safe area was the Vichy Zone. The immigrants began seeking smugglers who would take them out of Paris and across the line into the Vichy Zone. Although internment was still a possibility there, the fact remained that Vichy France had not deported anyone. Furthermore, if one was equipped with adequate financial means it was possible to avoid internment.[48] It is not surprising, therefore, that many chose this escape to partial freedom rather than remain in Paris.

The precise number of Jews who left Paris in the aftermath of the July events is impossible to establish, although evidence indicates a significant shift of population. Reports from various UGIF offices in the Vichy Zone, particularly those bordering the demarcation line, stress the large numbers arriving during August 1942. They asked for assistance and advice. In the Limoges area 1,000 persons, including many unaccompanied children, arrived in the four weeks following 16 July. The Toulouse office also reported an unusual number of new arrivals. Even Marseille reported that 400 people had presented themselves in the UGIF offices.[49]

For those who remained in Paris after July 1942, it was a matter of beginning life anew. Why had they chosen to remain? Some feared the largely unknown problems they would face once they had abandoned their homes. Generally, however, it would appear from surviving immigrant Jews that the decisive factor was finances. Those with the wherewithal left Paris; survival through escape was the privilege of those who could afford it. Others remained because employment afforded them protection from internment. Gradually the remaining Jewish shops reopened, schools prepared for the forthcoming academic year, and synagogues resumed services. The UGIF and the immigrant organizations tackled the massive task of providing for children whose parents had been interned, people wanted by the police, and the old, sick, and poor.

Ironically, one of the consequences of the arrests was that certain sections of the Jewish population gained a measure of confidence that never existed before. The French Jews had their hopes reinforced; they had been protected from internment. The staff of the UGIF and their families, whether they were French or not, were immune from arrest. The particular nationalities which had earlier gained exemption from wearing the Yellow Star realized that they were also immune from arrest. And the largest group, those working for German industry, were equally privileged; regardless of their nationalities, they were immediately released in case of arrest.

Each protected group owed its immunity to specific reasons, not, as the Jewish population assumed then, to a policy that only sought to reduce the number of Jews in France. In the case of the French Jews, it was because the Germans needed the French administration to carry out the arrests as well as Vichy's demand that the French Jews not be harmed. In the case of certain national minorities such as Turks, Hungarians, or Rumanians, immunity depended on the German Foreign Affairs Ministry in Berlin with which the Jewish section of the RSHA had first to clear whom it could or could not arrest. Dannecker, and after July 1942, his successor Heinz Röthke, never overrode foreign office orders. The Berlin Foreign Affairs Ministry retained the final decision about all the foreign Jews in France; whether they were from Germany's allies, neutral countries, or from countries at war with Germany.[50] The skilled workers employed in industry owed their protection to their role in the war economy. As for the UGIF personnel, their protection was entirely related to the usefulness of the organization to the application of the deportation program. As mentioned previously, in June 1942 the decision had been made that Jews from France were to be deported to Eastern Europe.

Once the remaining Jews in Paris realized that protection from arrest and deportation could be obtained, either through employment in the special factories or as a UGIF member, a scramble for positions ensued. Large sums of money were offered to factory managers or to UGIF leaders to be listed as employees and so obtain the necessary documentation.[51] Those who did not succeed in obtaining protected employment were at the mercy of the deportation program. The survival of the immigrant Jews depended on chance or resourcefulness within the confines of a clandestine existence. There were no further mass arrests equal to those of July 1942. Although successive police arrests were carried out on one nationality after another, they never resulted in more than 3,000 arrests in one incident. But they continued throughout 1942. It was the unpredictability that intensified the tensions in daily life for the Jewish population. The race for protection had been a race of the immigrants, while the French Jews could still carry on an existence as permitted by the restrictive laws and remain temporarily unaffected by the tragedy confronting the immigrants.

Regardless of the various types of protection available to the immigrant Jews, they still remained the most vulnerable for the remainder of 1942. They were particularly vulnerable primarily because the Vichy government wanted to see them leave France and return to their country of origin. If they were not to sit and await their fate they had but two choices: either to assume a non-Jewish existence with forged identity papers or to find non-Jews who were willing to hide them. In reality, neither option was accessible to the majority. Most had recently arrived in Paris, they had only a smattering of the French language, and their contact with the non-Jewish population was too limited to open many doors. Furthermore, non-Jews feared punishment if they were found to be sheltering Jews. This fear probably deterred even those charitable enough to have considered such a venture. Inevitably the majority of immigrant Jews looked to their own groups and organizations for the help they needed if they were to survive.

In the first place the defenseless immigrants sought identity papers that would pass the continual and all-too-frequent police inspections. A whole industry evolved after July 1942 to meet this need. Production of such documents expanded from limited beginnings to massive proportions, extending from mass-produced documents to highly sophisticated and control-proof counterfeits.[52] Having obtained false identity papers, it was then necessary to find somewhere to live. This was complex and difficult. The concierge had to be neither inquisitive nor observant. Then there were neighbors who might be alerted by such factors as physical appearance or language difficulties and denounce the offender to the police. But even when these problems were overcome by good fortune and constant moving, financial difficulties remained. To subsist for an indefinite period without work required sufficient personal funds or a regular source of financial aid. Many were able to survive through the help given by various organizations, but for most it was a struggle against starvation. Despite the seemingly impossible odds, many managed to overcome the obstacles. They abandoned familiar districts, separated from their families, refrained from meeting old friends, and led a lonely existence.[53] When Paris was liberated in August 1944, some 10,000 to 15,000 immigrant Jews emerged from hiding.[54]

The end of 1942 marked the end of an era for the Jews in Paris. The only group that emerged relatively unscathed were the French Jews. Those French Jews who had been interned and deported so far were regarded as victims of German antiresistance policy rather than fated victims of the anti-Jewish policy affecting the immigrants.

News reached Paris, at the end of 1942, that effective protection for the Jews was available in areas formerly in the Vichy Zone. The German occupation of the Vichy territory in November 1942 had resulted in an expanded Italian Zone of Occupation. The news told of Italian refusal to hand over immigrant Jews to the French police. Yet, despite the temptation, few Jews from Paris took the journey; the risks involved in passing the numerous identity controls were too great.[55] The remaining Jews in Paris were geographically too isolated to look elsewhere for salvation.

By 1943 it became evident to the French Jews that Vichy's former protection was no longer respected by the Germans; the supply of foreign Jews was drying up. The Germans adhered to their deportation schedule and the convoys required a minimum number of people; these facts overrode all previous considerations. French Jews began to fill Drancy and their numbers in the deportation convoys increased rapidly. After a halt of two months, the deportations were resumed in February 1943. The first convoy consisting of French Jews only left on 13 February 1943.[56] From then on, despite Vichy's policy, the French Jews were as vulnerable as the immigrants.

Each successive police raid upon selected groups brought to those affected their accompanying tide of dramas. But for the remaining Jews there were, besides the permanent fear of being the next victims, the constant uncertainties of the morrow. Material conditions worsened immeasurably during 1943. Economic aryanization had run its full course and family incomes were totally dependent upon remaining funds still left in the single bank account accessible. It was almost impossible to find employment outside factories producing for the Wehrmacht. The number resorting to communal help was growing. The security formerly enjoyed by those in possession of an *Ausweis* (protective pass) was no longer taken for granted. The factories that previously ensured protection had been raided by the Gestapo, as were UGIF of-

fices. All former protective devices had lost their credibility.* The reasons for
this change are easily discerned. Following the German defeat at Stalingrad,
and the consequent changes in German war plan, the skills of Jewish artisans
in certain areas such as the fur trade were no longer vital. The winter campaign was over, fur garments were no longer required. Even the usefulness of
the UGIF to the Gestapo appeared to be outweighed by the more immediate
need to fill deportation quotas. Although French Jews were still favored when
arrests of UGIF personnel occurred, they could no longer assume that they
were protected because they were French. The only Jews fortunate enough to
retain some hope of survival were those who could still be repatriated to their
own countries. Few in number, they were the only ones left with any expecta-
tion of survival.[57]

Deportation inspired fear, a fear born of total ignorance of the conditions
of the Eastern European camps. Early in 1943 letters began arriving from the
camps to which some of the Jews from Paris had been deported. These were
the first communications received since the departure of the first convoy in
March 1942. They provided some comfort for families fortunate enough to
receive a letter but for the many who did not the letters aggravated fears
about their relatives' whereabouts.[58] Furthermore, there were some disturbing
features about the letters. That they were all alike was easily accepted: there
were standard forms and most likely all internees had to conform. But none of
the letters were from elderly people who had been deported, nor was any
news received from known sick people or from children. This lack of information clouded whatever rejoicing occurred.

To understand the impact of these letters, they have to be seen in relation
not only to the daily existence of the Jews left in Paris, but also in relation to
the paucity of information about conditions in Eastern Europe. Admittedly,
many immigrant Jews had a clearer understanding than the French Jews of
the situation in the east. Mail had reached Paris from Poland soon after the
Armistice and it told of hunger and death. Although no details had come
through, the Polish Jews in Paris knew from the mail that Polish conditions
were exceedingly grave. Until early in 1942, food parcels and money orders
were still accepted for Poland by French postal services.[59] But no news had
reached the Jewish population of Paris before the end of 1942 about labor
and extermination camps. The UGIF leaders knew that a camp existed at
Auschwitz and that the Jews from France were directed to it. Even later,
when the UGIF leaders were first informed of mass extermination in Eastern
Europe, without knowing the real function of Auschwitz, they did not share
this limited information with the Jewish population.

The fears generated by deportation were not irrational. Until July 1942
only men of working age and in reasonable physical condition were deported.
They had been told that they were going to labor camps and they had accepted the information at face value. Although these men were anxious about
how hard that labor would prove to be and how their families would manage

* It was during March 1943 that holders of *Ausweise* and immigrant employees of
the UGIF were arrested and deported; the question will be discussed in Chapter 7.

without them, even these worries did not seem to affect some of the men who volunteered to join the first convoy of March 1942.[60] Even the deportation of women, which commenced after 16 July 1942, did not result in a general dread. The deportation of babies and children too young to know their names was more sinister, but even then some argued that those deportations were aimed at reuniting families. It was only when the old, the physically impotent, and the dying were also deported that the early apprehension turned into fear.[61]

This fear was first experienced by immigrants; only after February 1943 did their fear find an echo among the French Jews. Fear became a mass experience for all the Jews and the lack of information only intensified it. Georges Wellers, director of the Centre de Documentation Juive Contemporaine, who spent two years at Drancy before deportation to Auschwitz, has written:

> Until the end [the eve of deportation] almost everything about the fate of the deportees was unknown. Everyone knew of Radio London's broadcasts about the gas chambers and other means of extermination were known, but no one could believe them.[62]

In this period, without doubt, Jewish people in Paris were unable to acknowledge that their fears were based not only upon the unknown, represented by the east, but also upon the impact, even if unconscious, of the information that was available. They were unwilling to believe and unable to comprehend that any state could adopt a policy of deliberate extermination. Yet reports of what was occurring in the east were available from sources other than British broadcasts. The Central Consistory in Lyon was informed of Jewish mass extermination, most likely through Swiss sources. In a letter to Pétain, as early as August 1942, the Consistory stated it openly.[63] But the Central Consistory in Lyon and the UGIF in Paris made the deliberate choice not to disseminate the information. In November 1942 the Jewish Communist underground press published the information, based upon a report from a Pole who had returned to Paris from Poland.[64] Although fragmented, the evidence existed and was known to the UGIF. That body chose a policy designed to placate public fears and to ensure that the Jewish population did not resort to extreme responses; the UGIF leaders deliberately chose a policy of silence. Understandably, the German authorities adhered to the use of euphemisms—when referring to the extermination camps they called them labor camps. This practice was consistent with their need to conceal the truth for fear of complicating their task of deportation. The German instructions were observed in this matter, because it was an order and because of UGIF's own reasons. Most likely the UGIF took the view that nothing could be done to stop the deportation; therefore there was no point in making the victims' last moments before deportation even more unbearable.[65] Even when octogenarians were being deported the UGIF answered inquiries with the suggestion that they were, in all probability, being sent to Theresienstadt, a model camp for the elderly which had been reported in the Parisian press.[66]

The letters that arrived in Paris in January 1943 from Birkenau (Silesia), and later from other camps, were part of a German operation to deceive and pacify public opinion. The letters also added to the credibility of the UGIF's reply to inquiries from the population. Despite the fact that letters arrived from various camps until November 1943 and certainly succeeded in confusing the public, they failed to quell the basic fear: the letters were too few in number; they were all alike; and not one family ever received more than one single communication.[67]

Because the number of available immigrants no longer filled the convoys, the arrest and deportation of French Jews had become routine during 1943. Yet there remained significant numbers of immigrants in Paris, some still living in the apartments they had always occupied. This was not due to sabotage on the part of the French police but rather to bureaucratic fallibility. The famous Tulard index card system was intended to ensure that every Jew was entered on a card, but apparently its original thoroughness had degenerated.[68] Most probably the constant German calls for lists of names in various categories was the real cause of its malfunction. Whatever the reason, the numerous demands for the arrest of Jews of various nationalities, who theoretically should have been dealt with already, persisted well into 1944.[69] Until March 1943 the only immigrant Jews still living legally in Paris were those protected by either UGIF employment or an *Ausweis*. There were some 3,000 families in this category. There were also Jews from Rumania, Hungary, Turkey, Italy, Spain, Portugal, Switzerland, Britain, the United States, and the Scandinavian countries. The Rumanian and Hungarian Jewish nationals only began to receive consular protection when Germany started to lose the war, particularly after the defeat of Stalingrad. By June 1943 most of the Jews from these various nationalities had been repatriated. A marginal group of Jews without consular protection, UGIF membership, or *Ausweis* who had remained unaffected by police measures now became the most exposed. The chronological lists of nationalities to be arrested, recorded at the Jewish section of the Prefecture of Police from May 1941 to the Liberation of Paris in August 1944, shows most clearly the vagaries of the selection of various national groups and also the loss of control over who was still free and who was yet to be arrested.[70]

The Jews who lived illegally were thrown onto their own resources. They were at once the neediest and the most difficult to help. A large group, impossible to quantify with any degree of certainty, they existed on a day-to-day basis, uncertain of tomorrow. The ever-increasing tension in 1943 due to heightened Resistance activities had dotted Paris with large concentrations of repressive police forces. Inevitably the already precarious existence of the illegal Jewish residents came under greater threat. As identity controls became more frequent, they were compelled to limit their movements to an absolute minimum.[71] The Allied landing in Normandy in June 1944 brought them the first spark of hope. It was the first real signal for all the remaining Jews that Liberation was in sight. The struggle for survival became even more critical then, because there was no abandonment of the deportation program from Paris. In the short time between the Normandy landing and Liberation, the

Germans carried out two more massive deportations from Drancy, numbering 2,200 people on 30 June and 31 July 1944.[72]

How the Jews lived through the four years of Occupation in Paris is best understood when viewed in the light of their chances of physical survival. In the first place, the order of priority in the deportation program determined the levels of hope and fear. The French Jews, the last major group subject to deportation, did not perceive survival as the urgent issue until 1943. For those immigrants who had been able to obtain a reprieve through the *Ausweis,* the fear of deportation was tempered by hope, but at all times proportional to the degree of protection the *Ausweis* appeared to offer. A range of responses existed, therefore, according to one's exposure to danger. A second factor was the material situation, best reflected in the constant number of persons who depended upon communal assistance. Despite the ever-diminishing number of Jews in Paris, the proportion of indigent Jewish families never seemed to moderate. Indeed, from 1942 onward, a constant 20 percent of the overall Jewish population depended entirely upon the UGIF's soup kitchens and other UGIF facilities for all their needs.*

Added to the constant threat of internment and the struggle to secure daily necessities were psychological factors. Existence for the Jewish population had become an unending nightmare. Accidental arrest was always a possibility. Once arrested, even those with documents became victims of chance. Those Jews still free had to adjust to a particularly circumscribed daily existence. A barrage of laws had excluded them from normal social interaction. The Yellow Star guaranteed their segregation and exclusion. The uncertainties and the isolation profoundly affected morale. Even Jews with legal identities who locked themselves up in their apartments by day were forced to find alternate accommodation at night because they feared sudden police raids.[73]

From July 1942 onward, each family, sooner or later, had to face difficult decisions. Those with children had to decide whether to keep them or place them in safety elsewhere. Countless parents at first entrusted their children to the care of Christian families, then, believing that they had overreacted, took them back and found themselves shortly thereafter arrested with their children. Numerous families rejected entirely the notion of separation, choosing to face the future together. We will never know how many parents trusted their children to smugglers, to have them transported to Switzerland, and later learned that they had been arrested by the border guards. Nor will we know how many children left with Christian families remained unclaimed after the war because their families did not survive the camps in Eastern Europe. No figures are available for children converted to Christianity by their guardians in the absence of immediate families or relatives. We cannot know the number of Christians who, by giving Jews food and shelter, enabled them to survive. Although there are no figures available we do know that some Jews could not find anyone to answer their pleas for help and finally had no alter-

* The evidence for the number of Jews depending upon communal assistance will be presented in Chapter 7.

native but to surrender to the police. Finally, we will never know the numbers who were victims of betrayal based on greed.[74]

The Jews of Paris, in June 1940, had no idea what life would be like under the German Occupation. Before the war the French press had widely reported the physical abuses to which the German Jews had been subjected, but there was no way these Jews could have made the connection between what was taking place in Germany and the likelihood of similar occurrences in France. Nor could these Jews ever imagine that the French government would be a party to such a possibility. No effort of imagination, however pessimistic, could conceive of it happening in France.

Those who stayed in Paris as the German armies marched in or those who chose to return to their homes during the early months of the Armistice were no less aware of what the Nazis had done to the Jews in Germany. Yet they had opted to remain under German rule. None of them could believe that the Germans would dare to apply the same methods in France. When Liberation came, 40 percent of immigrant Jewry had been exterminated. The question of survival is, however, an issue that needs to be viewed in wider terms than the countless individual tragedies of the overwhelming majority of Jewish families in France. For although it remained primarily an individual question, much could have been done by organizations to support and protect that population. The following chapters examine the role of the Jewish organizations and their effectiveness in tackling the complex problems that flowed from the application of the anti-Jewish policy.

II
THE FATE
OF COMMUNAL
ORGANIZATIONS

4

The Coordination Committee of Jewish Relief Organizations: September 1940 to November 1941

Both the needs of the Jewish population of Paris and those of the German authorities called for some kind of unified organization that would represent the Jews. The first such body was not established on Jewish initiative but at the instigation of the Gestapo. This was the Coordination Committee, and it bore the marks of its origin throughout its existence. By the end of 1940, French and immigrant organizations had agreed to cooperate. But none of the participating organizations had ever envisaged that this cooperative movement would extend its role from providing relief to representing the entire Jewish population, or that the various Jewish institutions would need to unite in order to formulate appropriate responses to Gestapo pressures already manifest.

Regardless of the intentions of the participants, this short-lived cooperation became the basis upon which the Gestapo built its campaign to compel the Jews to voluntarily form a unified representation that would accept Gestapo control.

If, as it seems likely, there was nothing the Jews could have done to deflect the Gestapo from its objective, nevertheless much could have been done to counter the threatening consequences of a central organization, led by well-known and respectable Jewish figures, but operating as an instrument for the execution of Gestapo orders. The necessary preconditions for the formation of an alternative response did not exist. The French Jews refused to view the situation in the same terms as the foreign Jews; they had a firm desire to distance themselves from the immigrants. The immigrants were consistently more apprehensive about Gestapo controls and the French Jews were less fearful of negotiations with the German or Vichy authorities. As a consequence, and under constant Gestapo pressure, the French Jews not only assumed leadership of the forced association but also ensured that they themselves retained control. Such a step inevitably precluded the emergence of a cohesive opposition to German policies and blocked the development of an alternative united response.

It was in the decade before the Second World War, when the issue of immigrants and Jewish refugees became a French national issue, that the old established Jewish community's leaders adopted political positions that ran counter to the interests of Jewish immigrants and refugees.[1] Rising xenophobia and, more specifically, anti-Jewish propaganda during this decade demanded appropriate communal structures to combat these manifestations, but the differences between the French and the immigrants' organizations made a meeting point impossible. At the heart of these differences were conflicting perceptions of identity, of cultural, political, and national dimensions. The immigrants insisted on retaining their former customs although the process of acculturation was slowly making inroads on patterns of behavior, particularly among their children. Their cohesiveness was expressed through a vast network of organizations.[2] The French Jews, on the other hand, already had undergone cultural integration. The overwhelming majority no longer had any ties with communal Jewish life. A number of them, however, had chosen to retain past religious practices and had grouped themselves around the ACIP.

As a strictly religious organization, the ACIP limited its activities to matters connected with faith and charity. It operated a network of religious schools, attended to the appointment of rabbis to congregations, and through its Comité de Bienfaisance dispensed charity to the poor, the sick, and also to immigrants. Although it was the most influential, the ACIP was not the sole organization through which French Jews expressed affiliation to Judaism. Their other major organization was the Alliance Israélite Universelle. A lay organization, the AIU was independent from but much influenced by the Consistory. In Paris, where its headquarters were located, AIU organized cultural activities. But its main activities consisted in maintaining a network of schools in the French colonies of North Africa and the Middle East, where classes were taught in Jewish faith and French language and culture. The other important channel through which French Jews expressed their interests in Jewish issues was the journal *L'Univers Israélite*. But at all stages, the ACIP effectively functioned as the political liaison with the French government.

Although the ACIP never numbered more than a few thousand members, successive French governments always regarded it as representing the Jewish community. Accordingly, during the 1930s, when the German refugees began arriving in France, the government of the day had appealed to the ACIP to organize their relief.[3]

Headed by the Rothschild family, the ACIP represented the Jewish upper bourgeoisie and had extensive connections with the Establishment. What distinguished the French from the foreign Jews even more than their differences in economic and social class was their total identification with France. As a historical entity they held in special regard the country that had given them equal rights. Gratitude for this equality, together with the sacrifices made by successive generations on the battlefields, had made them fervent patriots.

The political crisis of the 1930s revealed perhaps most clearly the political attitudes of the leaders of the ACIP. The former republicanism of the previous leaders of the ACIP had given way to a form of patriotism that easily accommodated the French Right. Rabbi Jacob Kaplan, later France's chief-rabbi, then welcomed colonel François de La Roque and his Croix de Feu into the ACIP's main synagogue. Some of the ACIP leaders' support for the Right manifested itself in other forms as well: the Rothschild Bank, among other Jewish banks, also financed anti-Communist movements.[4]

The Jewish immigrant organizations, faced with ever more virulent xenophobic campaigns on the part of movements of that Right and the ACIP sympathies for such movements, saw themselves threatened and isolated. It was clear to the immigrant organizations that French Judaism was a politically conservative body which, in the context of the antisemitic character of the right-wing xenophobic campaigns, was more concerned about its own position within the French polity than with the fate of the immigrants or of the Jews of the rest of Europe.

Although in practice the ACIP's relief organizations never refused requests for help by immigrants or refugees, the assistance dispensed was so often accompanied by advocacy of assimilation into the French community or further migration, for example to America, that the immigrants easily believed that their readiness to listen to such advice was a condition of help.[5]

The rise of Nazism in Germany and the pervasive growth of antisemitism in East European countries brought about various attempts by the immigrants to draw French Judaism into public protest campaigns. But they all proved unsuccessful. The ACIP rejected the view that public campaigns would be of any assistance in stemming the tide of antisemitic policies.[6] By 1939, the immigrant organizations, isolated and despondent, withdrew into themselves. The year after the Germans occupied Paris, the consequences of disunity became apparent. The French and immigrant organizations were unable to reach a consensus on what needed to be done when the issue of representation was forced upon them.

The gravest problem faced by the Jewish organizations during the early part of the Occupation (that is, at least until October 1940) was the difficulty of interpreting the available information about German and Vichy intentions.

Professor Robert Debré had already been warned in July 1940 by Jean Chiappe, a former prefect of police for Paris, that the Germans would institute an anti-Jewish policy. Isaïe Schwartz, chief-rabbi of France, had been warned in July 1940 that grave measures would be taken against the Jews. In August 1940, the Central Consistory, which had followed the French government in its tribulation, had also been advised that there were rumors of an imposed representation.[7] The failure to acknowledge these warnings stemmed from a number of causes. The lack of authoritative information about the overall direction of the Vichy and German anti-Jewish policies was but one of the major reasons. Perhaps more important was the inability to integrate that partial knowledge into a general political evaluation. But an evaluation based on what criteria? French and immigrant organizations, each according to their own concerns, advanced their own analyses. As far as the immigrant organizations were concerned, Vichy's early legislation was, under the cover of xenophobism, unmistakably antisemitic. In the view of the French Jews, that is, those who could claim generations of residence in France, the issue of xenophobism was totally outside their concern. Unfortunately, on 27 August 1940, Vichy published a law revoking the provisions of the Loi Marchandeau of 21 April 1939, which had banned all publications that attacked people on religious or racial grounds. The consequences of Vichy's annulment of this law immediately opened the floodgates of antisemitic writings. French Judaism should have seen Vichy's notification of an intended policy, but the Consistory failed to respond to it.[8]

The immigrant organizations, defenseless, waited passively for further developments. The Consistory's representatives looked to former associates in the French administration and to the Vichy government for reassurances. In Paris the situation was totally new. Until the German authorities announced their own policies neither the immigrants nor the Consistory could take a position.

The problem in Paris resided with the German military administration. Until it began to act against the Jews, their organizations were unable to make an informed estimate of the scope of the German designs. The situation was, however, far more threatening than the early inactivity of the German administration seemed to indicate. In fact, all their major administrative departments had either specialists on the "Jewish Problem" on their staff or leaders who considered that the Jews constituted a question worthy of their personal interest. The main German state organism that initiated the application of anti-Jewish measures was the RSHA. That organization coordinated all actions, planned the overall strategy, and ensured its enforcement. A special department, IV B4, was in charge of planning and controlling the Jewish policies, and every occupied country was assigned a representative. Theodor Dannecker, a close associate of Adolph Eichmann who headed the department in Berlin, had been appointed to France. Originating from Vienna, like so many other members of Department IV B4, he had been appointed as *Judenreferent*. While in Berlin, Dannecker had been associated with the Madagascar Plan. His transfer to field work in France was made in order to ensure that an expert would control all activities. Department IV B4 belonged to the SD (*Sicherheitsdienst*—Security Services of the Gestapo), the controlling organ of the *Gestapo* (*Geheimstaatspolizei*—Secret State Police). Since Jews were considered one of the main enemies of the Reich, it was logical that the security forces be entrusted with their elimination.[9]

But the SD was not the sole administrative unit that concerned itself with the Jews. Each administration had its "Jewish desk." At the MBF were two chiefs of staff, military and civilian. The military section (*Verwaltungsstab*) was headed by Dr. Werner Best. A former SD officer and a member of the RSHA's general staff since 1939, he had been appointed to head the civilian administration in France in July 1940. As a former member of the SD, he was well acquainted with Nazi policy on the Jewish Question. The economic department was led by Dr. Elmar Michel. His second-in-command, Dr. Blanke, was his principal adviser on Jewish problems and had a particular interest in the planning of economic expropriation.[10]

The appointment of Otto Abetz, in August 1940, as the Third Reich's ambassador to France, with the position of political adviser to the army and the police, introduced additional "expertise" on the Jewish Question. Nominally, Karl-Theodor Zeitschel was the embassy's Jewish expert; attached to the political department, he had the task of ensuring effective liaison with the SD in France. His immediate superior in the department, Dr. Ernest Achenbach, who, according to some sources was Abetz's "eminence grise," also devoted particular attention to Jewish problems.[11]

A very wide network of "experts" and interested parties, collectively and individually, helped make decisions on the fate of the Jews in Occupied as well as non-Occupied France. Yet unlike Eastern Europe, the presence of numerous Jewish experts among the various branches of the German administration did not result in the immediate application of an anti-Jewish policy. Whereas in Eastern Europe the Jewish department of the RSHA was free to apply its policy, in France the MBF held full and final authority over all matters. Dannecker was unable to proceed without prior approval from the military administration.[12] Because of the lightning German victory in June 1940, the RSHA in France had only a small representation, headed by Dr. Helmut Knochen, whose principal task was to ensure the security of the German army. From the available evidence it appears that the RSHA appointed Dannecker as *Judenreferent* for France in August 1940.

Under Dannecker's direction the Gestapo began its activities in France with an investigation into the Jewish organizations and some of the remaining prominent members of the community. Dannecker based his activities on his department's experience gained in Germany, Austria, and, more recently, in Poland. Soon after his arrival in Paris he contacted Chief-Rabbi Julien Weill to inform him that he expected the ACIP to acknowledge itself as the representative of all the Jews in Paris and accept responsibility for their social and charitable needs.[13] This was the first indication of the German intention that the Jews would be officially represented by a single body responsible for their needs; the German policy had been unofficially stated and those authorities in charge of that policy's execution had revealed themselves.

Dannecker spelled out that policy clearly. There was to be a *Gleichschaltung*—ideological unification—of the Jews of Paris with those of the rest of Europe. The Jews would have to conform to a common policy. As there would be *Ausschaltung*—exclusion—Jews would no longer be permitted to have any contacts with any organizations other than the German ones—they would have to form a self-sufficient representative organization.[14]

Dannecker's choice of the chief-rabbi of Paris as the one to begin the implementation of Nazi policy was not just due to the fact that at the time Weill appeared to be the only representative leader available. In Germany, Austria, and all the occupied European countries, rabbis and their supporting organizations had been used by the Gestapo in the establishment of the Jewish councils.[15] They were viewed in these countries not only as the Jewish spiritual leaders but as their true representatives. In fact, the Gestapo were not the only ones to see them in that light; even France under the Third Republic had regarded them as such. But the situation in France was vastly different from that in Central or Eastern Europe. An overwhelming majority of Jews, those who had been living in France for countless generations as well as the more recently arrived, had long since refused to regard rabbis and consistories as their representatives. French Jews who sought to maintain Judaism had developed their own institutions, without ever seeking to involve the more recently arrived immigrants, while the immigrants themselves had formed their own specific organizations.

The differently organized communities in Paris were to be one of the main causes of Dannecker's early difficulties in establishing a Jewish representative organization. Despite Dannecker's clear directives, he was unable to force the ACIP to act as he desired. The by now traditional weapon of terror, used so effectively in Poland, was not applied. Dannecker decided to try other means but, hampered by the military administration, found himself unable to enforce his will. The overall German authority in France, the MBF, was more concerned during September 1940 with the preparations of the campaign against England. The Gestapo agencies in France consequently were occupied with military security. Furthermore, Dannecker's own efforts were frustrated by the paucity of resources available in his own department. Nor had he yet been able to secure the relevant support from the other Jewish "experts" in the German administration. Even Abetz, in spite of having brought with him special instructions from the Führer himself regarding the Jewish Question, had not yet begun to assert his own authority with the German military administration.[16]

Dannecker, having to account to Eichmann, refused to wait for more propitious circumstances. He therefore pursued the only course of action available: to sustain pressure upon the ACIP by ordering it to report regularly. The subsequent meeting with Dannecker involved three representatives of the Consistory: Chief-Rabbi Weill, Rabbi Marcel Sachs, and Alphonse Weill. By then, September 1940, the ACIP had formulated a strategy.

The 1905 Law of Church and State Separation provided the ACIP with the legal basis to reject Dannecker's demand. According to that law no representatives of religious institutions were permitted to assume responsibilities in secular organizations. Dannecker sought to overcome the legal objection by nominating Sachs and Weill as representatives of the Jewish population, with Sachs as its leader. Dannecker's first attempt at forcing the ACIP to recognize itself as representing the Jews of Paris failed when Sachs himself rejected the order by citing the same legal proscription.[17]

September 1940 proved to be a critical month in the negotiations, even though they were inconclusive. Dannecker, who had installed himself at the Prefecture of Police, began to organize a special Jewish department there. The instructions brought back from Berlin by Abetz complemented Dannecker's own objectives. Jews would not be allowed to return to the Occupied Zone; the French authorities would be asked to establish a special register of the Jews; Jewish shops would be clearly marked by a distinctive sign; and Jewish firms whose proprietors were absent would be handed over to appointed administrators.[18]

Despite Abetz's support, Dannecker was not able to proceed with his plan. He was unable to force the Jews to voluntarily join in a central Jewish organization. In a major report on the question, Dannecker chose to interpret the difficulties he encountered as the result of the command structure in France. The army, he argued, was not the least interested in the Jewish Question. As far as the army was concerned it was a political issue, the responsibility of the embassy and the SD.[19] This was a rather surprising interpretation, given that the army had not been so disinterested in Eastern Europe, where *Judenräte* (Jewish Councils) were established without concern for local laws or administration. It is more likely that Dannecker's difficulties in securing support stemmed from different notions of how best to proceed. The army's administration, headed by Dr. Best, believed that different methods were needed in France. In the first place, anti-Jewish measures would need to be seen by the population as coming from Vichy rather than as being imposed by the army of occupation.[20] Because the army was not prepared to legislate over that issue in the occupied territories, Dannecker hoped that if he succeeded in compelling the Jews to form their own representation, and make the initiation of special measures appear to be the result of the Jews' own demands, then the army administration would not fear a popular backlash.

September 1940 was also a critical month because the ACIP, fearing that Dannecker might be able to force it to carry out his orders, sought French administrative advice. Jean François was the director of the department dealing with foreigners at the Paris Prefecture. The ACIP decision to call upon François had resulted from an earlier order from Dannecker that required the ACIP to maintain regular contact with the French police, as, allegedly, it was preparing a law which would overcome the legal difficulties.[21]

Unwilling to break off relations with Dannecker in the event that a law would be issued, the ACIP leaders wanted to find out from François whether this was the case. François reassured them that the French police were not empowered to issue such a law but that the German military administration could do so. François therefore advised the ACIP not to take any initiatives, to adhere strictly to the law, and to wait for the legislation. The ACIP, reassured that the French police would not issue such a law, returned to Dannecker and informed him that existing French law forbade them to participate in any secular organizations.[22]

On 27 September 1940, while these negotiations were proceeding, the first German anti-Jewish ordinance appeared. It announced a census and included a clause that read, "The leaders of the Jewish community will have to supply, on demand from the French authorities, all necessary documentation for the application of the ordinance."[23] The inclusion of such a clause, totally irrelevant to the conduct of the census, could have originated only from a source unfamiliar with the situation in France—where since 1905 no Jewish organization had had any connection with censuses. It was meant to remind the ACIP that sooner or later a comprehensive representative and organizational role would be administratively assigned to it. With hindsight this period appears as a critical one. Admittedly, a month of negotiations had passed and Dannecker had not been able to overcome the ACIP's objections. But the Consistory had made the crucial concession: they continued negotiations after their first refusal. By doing so they conceded that with the appropriate legislation they would accept secular repsonsibilities.

The leaders of the ACIP wanted to be seen, certainly by Vichy in the first place, as acting in accordance with French law and as advised by the French administration. But evidence suggests that alongside this strategy, they had already accepted the inevitability of some form of central organization formed by Dannecker. If this was to be the case, the ACIP could not continue to raise obstacles. For, sooner or later, Dannecker would appoint a communal leadership and the ACIP's leadership could not afford to leave a vacuum that could be filled by outsiders. By October 1940 the ACIP had made its decision; it informed Dannecker that an association "of various Jewish organizations in a single organism [was possible] if the legal barriers between religious and secular organizations could be removed."[24]

Dannecker, unable to overcome the ACIP's legal objections with the necessary legislation, decided to try to find other leading Jews outside the ACIP. Dannecker called on Dr. Reichman, former chairman of the Union of Polish Jews, and asked for a list of names of other community activists, even foreign Jews, whom he wanted to address on the important issue of a central Jewish organization. Reichman did supply the list of names demanded. Concerned, however, at the possible consequences of his actions, and in consultation with the Amelot Committee, Reichman extracted himself from any further contacts with Dannecker by claiming that none of the parties concerned were prepared to take up communal responsibilities.[25] Dannecker, left without any contacts other than the ACIP, then demanded that the ACIP call together a group of communal leaders in order that he might explain the aim of such an organization.

Dannecker had been powerless to enforce his wishes and could have done little had the ACIP decided to boycott all contact with him. The only power available to Dannecker rested with the MBF, and so far it had not been prepared to act as Dannecker had wanted. But powerlessness did not preclude resourcefulness.

Early in November 1940, Dannecker offered the ACIP permission to launch a financial appeal among the Jewish population to finance its welfare activities. To prove his good intentions he instructed the Prefecture of Police to hand over to the ACIP the list of 6,000 Jewish-owned stores so that every Jewish business house could be solicited. The text of this appeal, however, had to be first submitted to Dannecker and he made sure that the final version conveyed what he had in mind. The final version thus read that all donations would be considered as "an advance on a tax which would be shortly imposed on the Jews." It was no surprise that the appeal never yielded a significant amount. Over a period of five months only 335,000 francs were donated by the Jewish population.[26]

Dannecker had permitted the ACIP to undertake a major financial appeal with no preconditions save his final twist to the text of the appeal. As a consequence of Dannecker's initiative and, it must be borne in mind, of the existing and very real needs of the Jewish population, the ACIP had committed itself to the development of relief activities and to the revitalization of dormant institutions. There was, no doubt, an obvious need both for funds and institutions, but under such conditions the decision to accept Dannecker's offer proved self-defeating. No sooner had the appeal been launched, on 24 November 1940, than Dannecker informed the ACIP that the funds collected could only be used to finance the organization he had wanted from the start.[27]

It must have become clear by that time to the ACIP itself and to the immigrant organizations that Dannecker's assurances could not be relied upon, that he would use all available means in order to compel the Jews to accept his orders. The appeal for the collection, signed by Chief-Rabbi Julien Weill, Rabbi Marcel Sachs, and Alphonse Weill, could not at that point be withdrawn. The ACIP had to decide what it was to do next. If any lesson could be drawn from the experience, there was only a single road available: to stop all further cooperation, irrespective of the immediate cost. But the ACIP chose another course. It sought, while continuing negotiations, to draw the immigrant organizations into the process. The ACIP hoped thereby to deflect Dannecker's attention from itself.

The meeting of communal workers requested by Dannecker some weeks earlier, which was to include immigrants, took place on 2 December 1940.[28] Only one immigrant was present, a lawyer, Jacques Rabinowicz, who was to act as legal adviser during the discussions. All the other participants were either members of the ACIP or representatives of the Comité de Bienfaisance. None of the immigrants had wanted to establish any contacts with Dannecker or participate in any discussions.[29]

The meeting proved to be an exercise in authority on Dannecker's part. To prove to the assembly that he was in charge, he expelled Chief-Rabbi Weill from the room for daring to ask what the intentions of the authorities were.[30] Instead of presenting a case for a central Jewish organization, given the existing material need, Dannecker declared that he would not tolerate the existence of separate organizations and that it was German policy that they should amalgamate. Having hit hard with the stick, Dannecker dangled a carrot: if a coordination committee of relief organizations was formed it would be free to operate without any control by him.[31] In order to show his goodwill he named Rabbi Marcel Sachs as head of Parisian Jewry. Once more Sachs declined that dubious honor. Finally, the continuous pressure upon the ACIP, backed now with assurances that there would be no interference and that such a coordination committee would be based on French laws, induced Sachs to approach the Amelot Committee to form the Coordination Committee that Dannecker wanted.[32]

By December 1940 Dannecker had succeeded, through guile and deceit, and a significant change of policy on the part of the ACIP, in successfully concluding this first stage in the establishment of a central representation. The question remains why there had been such a change in ACIP policy. It would seem that on the Jewish side, among the French Jews no less than among the immigrants, some individuals believed that despite Nazi intentions there was a real need to achieve a coordination of relief organizations. A substantial number of families were in dire circumstances and this appears to be the decisive factor in the eventual decision to agree to Dannecker's order. That Dannecker's objectives did not correspond to the objectives of the organizations was certainly clear, by then, to all. It was a choice between two evils: acceding to Dannecker's demand with all the risks involved or sacrificing the welfare of the population. The pressures of the immediate needs prevailed over political judgment. Certainly the continued anti-Jewish legislation, particularly the economic measures taken by the Germans leading to the appointment of administrators to Jewish trade and industry, foreshadowed even further hardship and even greater dependence on relief.[33]

Contact between the ACIP and the Amelot Committee was established in September 1940 through Chief-Rabbi Weill and David Rapoport.[34] The immigrants, unlike the French Jews, had been actively engaged in relief work from the first day of the German Occupation.* As they had renewed their own activities, they also encouraged every known Jewish institution to do likewise. Amelot had approached the Oeuvre de Secours aux Enfants (Children's Relief Committee [OSE]) and through its representative further extended contacts with the ACIP.

When in September 1940 Amelot organized a special meeting to launch a drive for financial support, the chief-rabbi not only approved of the initiative but expressed the desire to be represented on the special committee. Amelot and the ACIP considered that their relations had become harmonious and based on mutual understanding.[35]

When Dannecker began to demand that the ACIP assume responsibility for a central representation, Amelot had been informed. But Amelot held back from proffering advice, leaving the ACIP free to handle the problem as it saw fit. When Dannecker asked Dr. Reichman to prepare a meeting of immigrant communal workers, Amelot advised him not to offer any assistance. Amelot took this position because it was opposed to entering a dialogue with Dannecker but also because it held that its participation in the negotiations would serve Dannecker's purpose and introduce another element in the process of negotiations begun by the ACIP.

Amelot then debated whether it should become involved in discussions about the creation of a central Jewish organization. It decided, by the barest majority, that it would participate at the appropriate time.[36] The majority decision was not decisive enough to be conclusive. In the interests of unity within the committee no action would be taken and the committee would limit itself to remaining in contact with the ACIP.

When the ACIP decided, in December 1940, that despite the risks involved it would seek to form a committee of relief organizations, Amelot decided in turn, after being informed of Dannecker's assurances that he would

---

* Their early activities will be discussed in Chapter 8.

not interfere in the organizations' activities, that it would participate in discussions with the ACIP. As the association was to be voluntary, Amelot remained confident that it could withdraw at will.

Amelot debated the issue again during January 1941, and decided to accept the principle of participating in a Coordination Committee of Jewish Relief Organizations. By then, however, the ACIP was under renewed pressure from Dannecker. Representatives from Dannecker's office called daily upon Rabbi Sachs for reports of activities. Sachs was even ordered to collect from the Prefecture of Police a copy of the October 1940 census of the Jewish population.[37] But none of these activities appeared to have been communicated to Amelot.

On 20 January 1941, the Comité de Bienfaisance, on behalf of the ACIP, officially invited Amelot to send delegates onto a Coordination Committee which was to be formed in order to help stimulate social welfare.[38] Three second-level organizations were to participate: the Comité de Bienfaisance, the OSE, and the Colonie Scolaire, (Holidays for children), an organization of Amelot. The Comité de Bienfaisance had reopened its various branches; the Amelot operated canteens, clinics, an orphanage, and a clothes distribution center, and OSE specialized in child welfare. Practical and procedural questions were easily resolved.

When the Coordination Committee of the Jewish Relief Organizations of Paris officially came into existence on 30 January 1941, the constituent members were in fact representatives from earlier organizations: two from the ACIP (the Comité de Bienfaisance and L'Asile de Nuit de Jour); one representative from OSE, which was supported by the French and immigrant organizations. Organizational procedures were rapidly approved.[39] It was to be led by a board of six members. Each organization was to be autonomous but activities were to be coordinated in order to avoid duplicating the distribution of relief. Budgetary problems were to be jointly resolved but each organization was to remain free to decide internal allocations of resources.[40] This agreement, which protected the independence of the French and the immigrants, created the conditions for harmonious relations. Plans were made for the centralization of activities, which generated much hope that the newly established Franco-immigrant relationships would prove productive.

The relative peace in which the newly formed committee could work was short-lived. The German anti-Jewish program, continually under examination by the German experts in Jewish affairs in France, was in the throes of a reexamination. Massive deportation was one of the solutions to the Jewish problem already being considered, although a destination had yet to be decided upon. Zeitschel, the specialist from the embassy, had already begun to suggest a number of preliminary steps in late 1940. The Jews would first be eliminated from the professions. A central administration was considered, which would control their persons and their properties; a centralized card index of the Jewish population at the Prefecture of Police was to be extended; special Jewish concentration camps were to be established, for the foreigners at first, on the basis of the Vichy law of 4 October 1940; there was to be a firm control of the compulsory central Jewish organization, which had just been established.[41]

In order to complete the groundwork for the day when a "final solution" would be adopted, one that would also be applicable to France, Dannecker wanted to go beyond the existing centralization of the Jewish organizations. By mid-March 1941, Dannecker informed Sachs that the funds which had been collected since November 1940, and which he had held back until the existing organizations had amalgamated, would not be available unless all the Coordination Committee members signed a personal statement that they would continue to participate in the work of the committee and carry out all orders given by its secretary.[42]

This demand provoked consternation in the ranks of the participating organizations. They had voluntarily joined, under the assumption that Dannecker would hold to his promise that he would not interfere. Neither the ACIP nor Amelot had envisaged such an eventuality. At issue was not only Dannecker's interference in the matter of finances but a principle: the assertion of Dannecker's authority. It signified a formal announcement that the newly formed committee would operate as ordered by Dannecker.

The strategy that had been followed until then, based on temporizing and a degree of confidence born of the protection that the French law seemed to have held, could no longer be sustained. The earlier view that Dannecker would need the support of a special law to force the Jewish organizations to carry out his orders had outlived its pertinence. A new and more threatening climate had developed, one that jeopardized the belief that French law would suffice to check any dangerous trends. Dannecker informed the ACIP that he had requested and obtained the establishment by Vichy of a government department for Jewish affairs, which would control all matters pertaining to Jews.[43] This was the most serious blow to the strategy of legalism. Dannecker's claim that the CGQJ would create the desired compulsory organization completed the rout. The problem became even more acute when Dannecker informed the ACIP that in order to facilitate this transformation, and because the ACIP had been so uncooperative, he had decided to bring to Paris two "technical advisers" who would assist the Coordination Committee.[44] This final development completed the bankruptcy of the existing political line. The attempts to unite in forming a legally acknowledged body that could assist the Jewish destitute had culminated in the forging of an instrument of Nazi anti-Jewish policy.

The news of these developments—the creation of a CGQJ and the importation and imposition upon the committee of two specialists—further complicated the difficult decision about how to handle Dannecker's demand for personal pledges. Within the Coordination Committee the appointment of two of Dannecker's men was viewed as the more dangerous development. The ACIP still believed that the CGQJ, as a French administrative body, would ensure that respect for the law would prevail, and that it would not leave ACIP at the mercy of Dannecker's demands. Amelot held that the CGQJ was a secondary threat to the Jewish population and that the real danger came from German sources. This evaluation was not wholly correct; indeed, it had been the Vichy legislation so far that had given the Germans the necessary legal basis as well as the administrative manpower to carry out its own policy.

Dannecker's two technical advisers, Israel Israelowicz and Wilhelm Biberstein, former members of the Vienna *Judenrat,* arrived in Paris on 18 March 1941. No evidence has as yet come to light to explain their former activities in Vienna, or how they came to be selected for the task, or whether they were Gestapo agents.[45] They were said to be from Vilna in Lithuania. Israelowicz was vaguely Zionist and a practicing Jew; even less is known about Biberstein. Because they were brought to Paris and placed on the Coordination Committee by Dannecker, they were naturally considered Gestapo agents. Their special position as Dannecker's representatives, conveying his orders and regularly reporting to him, was seen as a threat to the members of the Coordination Committee. Israelowicz's statement that they had been brought to Paris to help the Jews organize their leaderless community appeared to confirm fears that these two men had been brought in to take over the Coordination Committee.[46]

On 27 March 1941, Israelowicz and Biberstein met the full committee for the first time. It was then that the first full debate took place over Dannecker's demand for the personal pledges. Amelot, for its part, had already decided that its representatives would not sign such a blank check, which committed individuals and organizations.[47] The arrival of Dannecker's two men now complicated the issue. As Amelot was represented by the delegates from the Colonie Scolaire, who in the end would have to assume the personal responsibility for carrying out the committee's decision, Amelot decided to give these delegates the right to make their own decision. The delegates from Colonie Scolaire informed Sachs that they would not sign the pledge.

Dannecker's demand was unequivocal, and the ACIP itself also needed to find a solution to protect institutions and leadership. A compromise formulation was prepared for submission to Dannecker. The committee had decided to elect Sachs as chairman and undertook to carry out all instructions given to him as leader of the committee.[48] The Coordination Committee members believed that if Dannecker would accept such a declaration they would have released themselves from a commitment to any other leader. Clearly, the committee assumed that Rabbi Sachs would never submit to unacceptable orders.

When Dannecker did accept the compromise the committee members believed that they had won a victory. In fact, it was another significant defeat. They had taken another step in the acceptance of Nazi control over their organization. They had been manipulated into accepting the *Führerprinzip*—the Nazi leadership principle. No sooner had they signed the amended pledge than Dannecker requested that the president of each organization sign a similar promise. Albert Weill, who had agreed to lead the Comité de Bienfaisance, was the first to be ordered to sign a declaration that he would fulfill all orders given or transmitted by or on behalf of the Occupation authorities. The general mood in the Coordination Committee grew somber as they realized that Dannecker was totally misinterpreting the compromise pledge. The activities of the committee reached a standstill.[49]

Although the committee had stopped meeting, Dannecker was now in a controlling position through his two "advisers." Dannecker, who had previously demanded of Sachs that he prepare the Coordination Committee's articles of association, something which had not yet been done, now ordered Israelowicz to have them completed by 1 April 1941. Israelowicz, now acting as head of the Coordination Committee, promptly submitted the organization's constitution to the Prefecture of Police in order that it be duly registered and recognized by the French authorities.[50]

One aspect of the Coordination Committee's work went on: the publication of a newspaper. In February 1941 Dannecker had ordered Sachs to take the necessary steps to publish a newspaper and had asked for proposals regarding content, format, and distribution.[51] Most likely Dannecker had in mind similar newspapers in other Jewish communities, particularly Vienna, his hometown, where such newspapers were used to publicize the activities of the *Judenrat* and as a general channel for the dissemination of orders affecting the Jewish population. The arrival of the two Viennese advisers also resulted in a prompt execution of this previous order. By 26 March the title of the paper had already been decided upon. The *Informations Juives de Paris* was to

> address itself not only to practicing Jews . . . but to all those defined as Jews by the law . . . given that they are bound by such a tie which will necessarily impose duties and obligations which will need to be indicated.[52]

The ACIP was not enthusiastic about this latest project, however, and did not wish to be associated with it. It certainly did not approve of any projects in which French and foreign Jews would be made to appear as one and the same in a legal capacity. The proposed constitution of the Coordination Committee was already implicitly reducing the French Jews to the same legal status as the foreign Jews. The notion of a newspaper was also objectionable to French Judaism, for it equated Judaism with secular Jewishness, which had always been rejected by French Judaism. Sachs, on behalf of the ACIP, protested to Dannecker pointing out that the ACIP would be in breach of the French law if it became associated with such a publication.[53]

The main groundwork, however, was completed by Israelowicz and by the beginning of April 1941 all was set to prepare the first issue of the paper and distribute it to the 65,000 families that had registered in the census.[54] The only practical question was the appointment of an editor. The fact that the Coordination Committee no longer met provided Israelowicz with the opportunity of assuming the position. Without consulting Sachs or anyone else he began preparing the first issue.[55]

The issue appeared on 19 April 1941. It provoked a furor among the committee members and brought consternation to the Jewish population. Israelowicz, left to his own devices, had presented the issues as he understood them. He had been brought to Paris to ensure that a central organization was formed. In Vienna the process of amalgamation of the Jewish organizations had long since been completed and the Jewish population itself had accepted that there could only be one Jewish organization to represent it. Israelowicz proceeded to state his views on the relationship between the population and the Coordination Committee:

> It will no longer be possible for the Coordination Committee to dispense advice or to give financial aid unless you become members of the Jewish community of Paris. You are hereby invited to join the Coordination Committee. . . .[56]

This appeal was followed by a list of the addresses of the organizations comprising the Coordination Committee, where enrollments could be made.

The following day, 20 April 1941, the Coordination Committee met. All the representatives of the various organizations sharply criticized Israelowicz for having published such an editorial without consulting the committee. Israelowicz was attacked for using threatening injunctions to force the Jewish population to enroll. Israelowicz, in his defense, warned the committee that its earlier lack of resolve and failure to pursue an active policy placed the future of the whole population in jeopardy.[57]

The argument had not rested on the need to ask the Jewish population to become members of the Coordination Committee but on Israelowicz's assumption of power and his introduction of a style of authority foreign to the committee. But in fact the committee was now paying the price for abdicating its authority and leaving Israelowicz to his own devices. The committee objected to the use of threats, which since they were accompanied by the names of the member organizations appeared to originate from those organizations. The issue was complicated by the fact that the editorial immediately intensified existing anxieties within the Coordination Committee about the organization itself. The ACIP members viewed their representation on the committee as purely voluntary, and, consistent with their legalistic approach, refused to accept any other criteria. The ACIP sought to bring Vichy into the discussion. They presented an argument based on French law to the effect that a union can receive donations only from its constituent organizations and not from the general public. Although the argument was designed to draw the CGQJ into the argument, it never had any consequences. The committee remained at Dannecker's mercy. On the practical level, however, the Jewish population was left with the impression that only members of the Coordination Committee could benefit from its support, and, further, that the ACIP supported such a policy. Naturally the ACIP strongly resented this state of affairs. Nevertheless, despite the ACIP's reluctance, it was inexorably drawn into a position in which it could overnight become an instrument of compulsion. Furthermore, by trying to avoid association with the establishment of an official central Jewish organization, the ACIP had avoided the real issue, that of fighting the very proposition.

The immigrant representatives also refused to be identified with the editorial of the *Informations Juives*. Indeed, since Dannecker's demand that the organization pledge to carry out orders from the leader of the Coordination Committee the Amelot Committee was divided on the issue. Amelot, unlike the ACIP, was constituted of representatives from various immigrant organizations who had joined to assist the Jewish population in its needs. Three political organizations, the Bund (Jewish Socialist Union), the Left Poale-Zion, the Right Poale-Zion, a communal organization, the Fédération des Sociétés Juives de France (Federation of Jewish Societies of France [FSJF]), and a number of communal activists constituted Amelot. When the issue of signing an organizational pledge had arisen, Amelot had been undecided. Even though Amelot representatives on the Coordination Committee, in the end, had not signed the pledge, representatives of the Bund and the Left Poale-Zion meanwhile had resigned from Amelot to protest the failure of Amelot to adopt an unequivocal opposition to the principle.[58] The impact of the first issue of the *Informations Juives* gave the remaining committee members the responsibility of taking a public stand on the issue. They were compelled either to support Israelowicz's announcement publicly (and be a party to his and the Germans' threats) or to disassociate themselves from the Coordination Committee.

The Coordination Committee irretrievably was led to assume the character sought by Dannecker. Less than two weeks before the *Informations Juives* appeared, on 7 April 1941, Dannecker ordered the Paris Prefecture of Police to supply the local branches of the Comité de Bienfaisance with lists of Jews living in their areas; these local committees were ordered to display prominently in their offices the names of the heads of each family.[59]

Although an insignificant measure in itself, this indicated the close contact Dannecker was expecting between the Coordination Committee and the population. On 27 April 1941, the Coordination Committee, despite its failure to be constituted according to French civil law, was duly recognized by the Prefecture of Police. Furthermore, all other organizations desirous of joining the Coordination Committee had to apply to the police, naming their leaders and presenting their membership lists.[60]

The gradual transformation of the Coordination Committee into a police-controlled organization did not meet effective opposition from its leaders. But popular opposition began to manifest itself. Few people enrolled at first. The majority were French and of the immigrant Jews who did join, few paid any dues. The intensity of popular opposition, both verbal and in print, was such that Dannecker felt he must stem it. Believing that it originated from the Colonie Scolaire, Dannecker warned David Rapoport that if this campaign did not stop he would be arrested. He also required Rapoport to sign a pledge that he personally would refrain from further attacks on the Coordination Committee.[61] But the hostility did not abate, for besides the opposition of Amelot, which Rapoport might have been able to control, there was organized opposition from the Jewish Communists. For some time they had pursued an opposing political line that defined the Coordination Committee as a Gestapo instrument. The leaflets that Dannecker thought came from Rapoport had come from the Communists' presses. Furthermore, the Bund and the

Left Poale-Zion also provided strong opposition. Still connected through their institutions with Amelot, they had been pursuing an independent political line since their resignation from the Amelot Committee.[62]

Amelot's decision to resign from the Coordination Committee was not immediately acted upon, however. It was delayed after Rapoport's plea that an attempt be made to organize a collective resignation from the whole committee. But the ACIP, mindful of Israelowicz's oft-repeated warnings that reprisals would be taken against the population if the Coordination Committee did not function, refused to resign. On 12 May 1941, Yehuda Jakoubowicz, Amelot's secretary, informed the Coordination Committee that Amelot's representatives had resigned on personal grounds and that therefore Amelot would no longer be represented.[63] A flimsy excuse had been used in order to resign without provoking reprisals from Dannecker.

Neither the temporary failure to obtain the necessary legal powers to establish a central Jewish organization nor the lack of cooperation on the part of the Jewish organizations prevented Dannecker from seeking alternatives in order to achieve his goal. It was during April 1941, when Alphonse Weill had assumed temporary presidency of the Coordination Committee because of Sachs's absence, that Dannecker believed he had found a solution to his problem.[64] The difficulties he had encountered so far resided in the dominant place occupied by the ACIP on the Coordination Committee, and the ACIP's legalistic opposition could only be overcome if new elements were brought into the committee. Dannecker therefore ordered Weill to submit proposals for a committee that would effectively correspond to the actual national composition of the Jewish population, so that that there would be equal representation of French and foreign Jews.[65]

The ACIP realized immediately the danger in allowing immigrants to share the leadership. They had taken note of Dannecker's comment that "Each time he addressed himself to the French, they invoked French legislation, while they [the immigrants], ignoring French law, could quite easily establish the desired organization as had been done in their countries of origin."[66] The attitude taken at that point by the ACIP is the key to the policy they had followed until then. They were prepared to remain at their posts out of fear of the irresponsibility they attributed to the foreign Jews; they were also hoping that the French government, though the CGQJ, would take over the whole Jewish issue from the occupying Germans. The French Jews believed that the immigrants, given full rein, would destroy that possibility. Dannecker's demand was therefore viewed as an immediate and direct threat. Weill, unable to convince Amelot to remain and extend its participation on the Coordination Committee, viewed with concern Israelowicz's activities among the foreign Jews.[67] Indeed, as soon as he had arrived in Paris, Israelowicz sought to make contacts with them, particularly former community activists. Not many responsible immigrant communal workers were willing to have any dealings with him. Those he did contact, on hearing of his assurance of police protection (at a time when such a question did not seem to be relevant), immediately broke off contact. In some cases, upon hearing such a proposition, individuals began to make preparations to flee Paris; the implied need for police protection did not augur well.[68]

Alphonse Weill, pressed by Dannecker, and unable to find suitable candidates, called upon Elie Krouker, a former president of the FSJF, the Anciens Combattants Juifs Etrangers dans l'Armée Française, and numerous other organizations including the Comité de Bienfaisance. He was asked to join and to use his connections to find other suitable individuals.[69] Krouker eventually accepted the offer. Two events, apparently only loosely related, added to the sense of crisis. On 14 May 1941, 3,710 immigrant Jews were interned. Although the measure had been under consideration by Dannecker for some time, he had used this particular moment to order the French police to use the powers granted by Vichy in October 1940 to intern the foreign Jews. The Coordination Committee viewed the arrests in the context of its own problems, as a warning of measures to come.[70]

Shortly after, in June, Dannecker, dissatisfied at the rate of progress in carrying out his instructions, ordered the arrest of Alphonse Weill and informed the committee that his release was conditional upon the establishment of the representative committee he had been demanding since April.[71] This was the second time Dannecker had used internment of some members of the Coordination Committee in order to impress them. During April, following Dannecker's order to the Comité de Bienfaisance to utilize the October 1940 census returns, Louis Frank, its seventy-eight-year-old secretary, had written to him requesting an explanation. Dannecker's reply was to have Frank interned at the Santé prison for a brief period, on the grounds that he had not shown enough respect in his letter.[72]

The arrest of the immigrants and of Weill precipitated the changes sought by Dannecker. The ACIP became concerned about the future leadership of the Coordination Committee. The possibility occurred to the leaders of the ACIP that Dannecker would appoint outsiders and such a likelihood was too dangerous to contemplate. The ACIP moved into action—Chief-Rabbi Weill convinced his nephew André Baur to join the committee. Krouker and Baur began preparations for a special conference to resolve the situation.[73]

On 13 June 1941, Krouker asked Amelot to attend a meeting due to take place three days later, and warned that failure to be represented would incur serious consequences.[74] At a preparatory meeting, Amelot's secretary, Jakoubowicz, informed Krouker and Israelowicz that his committee had decided not to be represented.[75] Krouker, who had assumed the secretaryship of the Coordination Committee, and Baur decided to proceed. Elie Danon, of Rumanian origin, was brought into the committee by Krouker. Together with Albert Weill, these men constituted an executive body representing the demanded proportion of French and immigrant Jews. All that remained was to complete the membership of the whole committee on the same basis.

The special conference took place as announced on 16 June 1941. Present were Dr. Eugène Minkowski, of foreign extraction, representing the OSE; Elie Beilin, a French Jew, on behalf of the Philanthropic Association of the Night and Day Shelter; Fernand Musnik, of Lithuanian background but a veteran of the 1939–40 war; Alex Klein, a Hungarian; Jacques Rabinowicz, of Polish origin; Rabbi Marcel Sachs, French; and Georges Edinger, French.[76]

André Baur, president of the Union Libérale Israélite, a former president of Keren Kayemet (a Zionist land reclamation organization), and a member of a banking family, assumed the leadership. As the chief-rabbi's nephew and because of his personal qualities he became the uncontested leader.

The meeting's discussions demonstrated that the new leadership had accepted that concessions could no longer be avoided. Baur was the first to concede that "it is no longer possible to continue fighting [with Israelowicz and Dannecker] and that it had become necessary to 'make the first step on the road to concession.' " Krouker, as secretary, appears to have made an openly collaborationist speech which was condemned by all the others.[77] A new committee that conformed with Dannecker's demand was formed.

As the new secretary, Krouker not only alienated the Coordination Committee by his political position but also offended the Amelot Committee by his authoritarian methods. He demanded that Amelot give precise reports of its activities when the previous Coordination Committee had accepted its resignation. Amelot, not prepared to be placed under anyone's control, rejected his demand. After alienating both the French and the foreign Jews, Krouker found himself bereft of support within the organization and was left with no other alternative but to resign.[78]

During the interim period, when Baur and Krouker had been sharing the leadership, they had set into motion a new style of activities. Having agreed that it now was necessary to show Dannecker that the new committee would work in earnest, the new committee undertook several organizational steps. An overall evaluation of all member institutions was made. A control commission was established to report on the situation within each institution and evaluate their personnel.[79]

During this period a new crisis developed in the committee which, following Krouker's resignation, led Baur and his associates to assume full leadership. The crisis arose from the *Informations Juives* of 4 July 1941, prepared under Krouker's secretaryship and edited by Israelowicz. In a leading article, Krouker advanced two propositions that were anathema to the ACIP and over which Amelot had previously resigned. The article unequivocally stated that "the Coordination Committee was committed to the establishment of a unique Jewish organization which would incorporate all the existing organizations." This proposition particularly angered Amelot. The ACIP had previously accepted Amelot's desire for independence when they first decided to join forces, a position that suited the ACIP. It was over that issue that Amelot had resigned from the Coordination Committee in May 1941. Amelot, although aware of Israelowicz's role in the publication of the paper, nevertheless feared that in their absence from the committee the ACIP might have radically altered its own course and decided to assume full control.[80] Amelot therefore viewed the public statement as a declaration of intentions, which was to be read as a warning. The ACIP, for its part, viewed the statement as a move by Krouker, on behalf of immigrants, a move designed to compel ACIP to grant the immigrants equal footing on the Coordination Committee. In the article's reference to themselves as *Juifs* rather than *Israélites,* the traditional term preferred by the French Jews, the ACIP perceived a threat to their status as French citizens. Although by then the ACIP had already conceded that its former opposition to a central organization could no longer be sustained, its reaction to the article was designed to conceal from Dannecker its change of policy. The second proposition included in the article was that the Jews of France should follow the example of those from Vienna and emigrate. Krouker's advocacy of such a position suggested that it was Coordination Committee policy. While the foreign Jews found no grounds for objection in this, the French Jews received the proposition with anger. It challenged their attachment to France. The Coordination Committee emerged from this latest crisis transformed: the ACIP was determined to remain in control of the committee and Amelot, suspicious of ACIP's intentions, was more determined in its opposition to the Coordination Committee.

Early in July 1941, Marcel Stora, the new secretary, and Baur constituted the tandem that was to lead the Coordination Committee until it became the UGIF in November 1941. They had retained the former personnel, people such as Elie Danon, who as head of the canteen services had previously called upon the Communist canteen, rue Saintonge, and with promises of financial aid and German protection had attempted to bribe the director into joining the Coordination Committee.[81] The Communists, unlike the Bund and the Left Poale-Zion, were totally opposed to the Coordination Committee. Unlike the Bund and the Poale-Zion, they were not prepared to allow the slightest compromise.*

July 1941 represented a turning point in the life of the Coordination Committee. Under André Baur's leadership a new decision-making body emerged. This new-style Coordination Committee was formed at the critical moment when a vacuum had been created by a failure in leadership, resulting from Dannecker's actions. There had been a serious risk that because of Israelowicz an alternative leadership could have been formed, one that would have been totally subservient to Dannecker. In that crisis Baur proved capable of forming a united committee able to sustain and carry through a coherent line of defense. However, this new leadership, which included immigrants as well as French Jews, resulted once more in the dominance of the ACIP, and in the application of strategies that set out to defend the interests of French Jewry rather than all Jews. An important factor in the composition of the restructured Coordination Committee was the nature of the immigrant representation. Bauer had not made any efforts to win over the representative immigrant forces. Amelot chose to sever its connection with the new leadership not only because it opposed, as a matter of principle, any negotiations with Dannecker, but above all because it believed that the ACIP had taken a course of compromise. The few immigrants who did participate

---

* The Communist positions will be examined in Chapter 8.

in this new leadership agreed to do so because they accepted the ACIP's political line. They were represented by men like Danon, typical of one type of
immigrant who, having lived in France for dozens of years, had forgotten
the more recent immigrants' experience of antisemitism so common in Eastern and Central Europe.

Episodic challenges, grounded in mutual distrust, were a constant re-
minder of the relationship between the French and the immigrants, but during
the Occupation they never became serious enough to turn into open antago-
nism. If anything, according to ACIP sources, despite occasional incidents,
"relations . . . were generally correct and even at times friendly." As far
as the foreign Jews were concerned, they appreciated the noninterference
and the protection that the ACIP occasionally extended.[82] The French
Jews were appeased when immigrant organizations refrained from any initiatives with Dannecker and did not interfere with the general negotiations. As
long as they did not attempt to assert their rights to a share of the leadership
relations would remain satisfactory.

The new leadership under Baur soon confronted the gravest issues since
the formation of the Coordination Committee. On 18 August 1941, the committee found itself faced with Dannecker's demand for an immediate supply
of 6,000 men and 1,000 women for agricultural work in the Ardennes. All
the foreigners on the committee were to list their full names, addresses, and
identity card numbers, accompanied by a statement of the number of people
they could each supply. Dannecker further informed the committee that if
it complied with the order there would be no new internments and the liberation of some of those previously interned could be expected.[83]

Never before had the Coordination Committee been asked to engage in
such activities, never before had Dannecker made such demands. Until the
establishment of the committee the issue of unemployment among the Jews
had troubled only the relief organizations. The immigrant organizations in
Paris had tried to meet the situation as resources permitted. The aryanization
program had aggravated unemployment and presented unsuperable difficulties as a growing number of trades and professions were closed to Jews by
the Germans and Vichy. Even in the Vichy Zone, where the hardships arising
from aryanization were much slower to appear, the Central Consistory acknowledged the problem and addressed itself to Vallat. On 21 April 1941,
the Central Consistory forwarded a resolution asking, among other things,
that "given the shortages of agricultural manpower, foreign Jews actually
unemployed or interned in camps [in the Vichy Zone] be utilized to the best
of their abilities for the national economy." Vallat replied that he was "willing to see foreign Jews actually unemployed used to overcome the deficiency
in agricultural manpower in France."[84] The problem was that when the leaders of the Central Consistory appealed to Vallat to reduce unemployment
among the Jews, they did not offer French Jews but immigrants, attempting
to show that they did not consider themselves in the same class, as well as
reaffirming their devotion to the interests of France. Just as in the Vichy
Zone where the representatives of French Judaism sought to distance them-

selves from the foreign Jews, in Paris, the ACIP viewed the problem of unemployment as a specifically immigrant question.

The demand that the Coordination Committee supply workers was first raised by Dannecker during the period when Krouker was secretary of the organization. Posters were placed in Jewish relief institutions, advertising agricultural employment. Danon, as canteen supervisor, saw that they were prominently displayed. Indeed, he threatened the manager of the Communist canteen that he would call on the German authorities to force compliance, if necessary.[85]

Dannecker had not indicated that he wanted only immigrants, therefore the Coordination Committee thought the decision might affect French Jews as well. In order to placate the Germans, the Coordination Committee approached the CGQJ and asked it to request the Ministry of Labor to find employment for Jews on the land. The ministry, desiring to avoid involvement in Jewish problems in Occupied France, evaded the question by making a specious demand for figures of the likely numbers willing to accept such employment. The Coordination Committee was unable to advance any figures. It resorted to advertising in the *Informations Juives* for volunteers. The volunteers were promised "Good food, particular care for their families who would remain behind, and a quiet life."[86]

It was through the efforts of the Coordination Committee to find volunteers that its interpretation of the labor problem as essentially a problem for foreign Jews became explicit. Georges Bloch, who was handling the question on behalf of the committee, submitted a report that clearly stated it in those terms. His views were based upon discussions held with various representatives from the Service des Cartes d'Identités for immigrants at the Prefecture of Police, where Bloch had discovered that the foreign Jews had to reapply every three months for a work permit. He had been informed that because many foreign Jews were unemployed, many ended up being sent to labor camps. The possibility of using the Service des Cartes d'Identités as a venue for the recruitment seemed to Bloch most appropriate.[87] His plan needed, however, the cooperation of the Secretariat of Labor, which had so far proved uncooperative, and that of the Prefecture of Police, which was quite ready to reissue a special identity card allowing the bearer to work on the land.

Whether Dannecker would have ever considered demanding manpower from the committee if a German agricultural company—Ostland—had not requested it is not clear. In May 1941, Israelowicz had reported to Dannecker that a certain Tuvel had promised that he could deliver 20,000 workers for agricultural purposes. This offer had been made to Israelowicz during his attempts to find support within the immigrant population. Furthermore, the offer had come during the period when the May internments of 3,710 men had generated public fears; these fears had been further magnified by Israelowicz's own stories of Gestapo ruthlessness which he had experienced in Vienna before his arrival in Paris.[88]

The emergency meeting of 18 August 1941, to which, besides the executive of the Coordination Committee, Tuvel, Jakoubowicz from Amelot, and representatives from the camp of Pithiviers were invited, took place because Dannecker had informed the committee that he was no longer willing to wait. The situation had reached a critical point. All previous efforts had been unproductive. The Coordination Committee had neither the legal means nor the desire to compel anyone to volunteer. It found itself a hostage in the situation. Unable to handle the question, unwilling to proceed forcefully, all it could offer Dannecker was a resolution agreeing with the principle of placing unemployed Jews on the land and undertaking to campaign for volunteers. Israelowicz tried to convince the meeting that it could use the available population index in order to select those of working age, and order them individually to present themselves, but this suggestion was rejected.[89]

Without awaiting Dannecker's reply, the committee prepared a special appeal to the Jewish population. The first draft, headed "Jews and Agriculture," read as follows: "We have done our duty, it is up to you to do yours. If you want to save the existence of the Jews of France . . . you must come in mass, for it is with you that our salvation lies." Because of concern for the impact of such formulation, the appeal finally read "Through the kindness of the authorities, we are able to offer employment to 6,000 Jewish men and 1,000 Jewish women. We are hoping that in the interests of the community many will answer the call."[90] Dannecker, displeased at the failure of the Coordination Committee, ordered reprisals. On 20 August 1941, the eleventh arrondissement was surrounded by the French police and 4,232 Jews, French and immigrant men, were interned at Drancy.[91]

The number of families affected in Paris, only three months after the May 1941 internments, exacerbated the already difficult financial problems of the community. The committee decided to launch a public appeal that emphasized the issues confronting the population.[92] As in Chief-Rabbi Weill's first appeal, it stressed the need for Jews to give voluntarily, in preference to a Vichy- or German-imposed special tax.

To the Coordination Committee and French Judaism the issue of Jewish taxation was of special concern. It was viewed as an integral part of the overall anti-Jewish legislation that had turned the French Jews into a foreign minority. French Jews considered the whole matter a question of principle. In order to avoid a further loss of status it was vital that the Jewish community find resources to finance its own relief activities. The failure to generate internal communal resources was bound up with the fear that the Germans themselves might introduce taxation measures to cover these needs. The danger was that in such a case Vichy might emulate the Germans in its effort to ensure the predominance of French law. Furthermore, Vallat had already passed a law establishing the Fonds de Solidarité (Solidarity Fund) in order to meet the social cost of aryanization. At this stage the Coordination Committee was not yet prepared to apply to the CGQJ for access to such funds. It was vital, from all points of view, that the Jewish population make an extra effort and donate the funds necessary to meet communal needs.

The second issue, only alluded to in the committee's appeal, was that it had effectively become the only Jewish organization accredited with the authorities, the only one officially allowed to distribute help. The reaction of the Jewish population, especially the immigrant population, did not indicate that the committee had found much support; if anything the chasm between the committee and the population appeared to be significant.

The appeal for financial donations was caused by a real financial crisis in the organization. The committee's report of activities for August and September 1941 stressed the growing material difficulties, particularly among the working population, which necessitated large sums of money. Revenues, the report pointed out, were totally insufficient. Georges Edinger, who controlled the financial operations, had been a strong advocate of higher membership dues, in preference to gifts in order to meet those needs.[93] Notes, which Edinger prepared for the Coordination Committee, reveal that the income derived from the existing sources, membership dues, gifts, and subscriptions to *Information Juives* would yield 110,000 francs for September 1941.[94] Such amounts were totally insufficient to meet even a fraction of the overall needs. During the same period, the Amelot Committee, whose monthly expenditure for August 1941 had amounted to 240,000 francs, found even that sum far from sufficient.[95]

The Coordination Committee's assessment of its resources and corresponding levels of spending and activities were not, however, determined solely by a real lack of funds. It was a question of policy.* Under Baur's leadership, since July, the Coordination Committee had decided to proceed cautiously while maintaining a minimum of relief activities. The view was that it was not in the interests of the Jewish community for the Coordination Committee to assume an important role. But prodded by Dannecker and by mounting demands from the population, the committee had to begin serious relief activities. Meanwhile, the lack of activities generated an adverse popular reaction.

Popular opposition, particularly among the immigrants, was widespread. The arrival of Israelowicz and Biberstein had provided a focus for the opposition. The Coordination Committee's leaders were commonly referred to as the "Broner Yiden"—the brown Jews—from the Nazi "Brownshirts."[96] The internments of May 1941 produced a further backlash against the committee. Immigrant public opinion linked the presence of the two Viennese on the committee with the arrests. The first public manifestation of this opposition occurred on 20 July 1941, when deputations of Jewish women began presenting themselves in the committee's offices demanding the release of their husbands, as if it were up to the committee. The demonstrations continued daily until 31 July. The number of women and their militancy was such that Israelowicz called Dannecker for protection, who advised him to seek help from the French police to reestablish order.[97]

The demonstrations, at times involving 500 women, were taken seriously by Baur and the committee, who appealed to Dannecker and the CGQJ for

---

* The issue of the financial resources of the Coordination Committee and the UGIF will be discussed in Chapter 7.

the release of particularly deserving cases.[98] A few war veterans or particularly sick people were released, which had the effect of strengthening the view of the popular opposition that the committee could have done more in the past to help the internees.

The appeal for funds conducted by the committee through *Informations Juives* occasioned a further expression of public opposition, this time from French Jews as well. After the August 1941 internments hundreds of letters were addressed to the committee attacking it for daring to call upon the population for money. Again it was accused of having been party to the internments. Furthermore, it was now being attacked for protecting the rich against the poor.[99] Unwilling to carry out Dannecker's orders, unable to protect the population from internments, unable to explain its actions to them, the Coordination Committee appeared to the immigrants and to some French Jews not as their protector, but as the cause and instrument of their plight.

Dannecker, while constantly on the heels of the committee, pursued his original objective of forcing the establishment of a compulsory central Jewish organization. All the other maneuvers were peripheral, merely designed to facilitate the achievement of that objective. No sooner had Baur and his team established themselves, in July 1941, than Dannecker informed the committee that no Jewish institution would be permitted to operate outside the committee. On 1 August 1941, the ACIP was informed that it would have to join if it wanted to continue to exist. On 8 August 1941, Chief-Rabbi Weill accepted the order on behalf of the ACIP.[100] Following this, Dannecker took a further step in his dealings with the religious institutions: he issued an order that forbade all associations of a religious character to function unless they also joined the committee. But in their case they also had to accept the authority of the ACIP on all religious, moral, and national questions.[101] By the end of September 1941, seven immigrant religious associations had joined the ACIP, and through it the committee.[102] Every month new institutions, besides religious institutions desiring to remain in existence, joined the Coordination Committee. By the end of 1941, some twelve separate institutions had enrolled, the majority of them formerly controlled by the ACIP.[103] Underlying the ACIP's decision was not only a concern for these organizations' existence but a concern for their assets which could be regarded by the CGQJ as akin to any other type of Jewish asset and so aryanized. The Coordination Committee's protection was sought even though it meant strengthening Dannecker's own creation.

As long as the Coordination Committee was legally a voluntary association, organizations had a choice. They could join or refuse. The same applied to individuals. Enrollment as supporting members had begun in April 1941. At first, despite the use of threats, enrollments were very low; neither the French nor the immigrants hastened to join. The Coordination Committee, keen to develop popular support, used the columns of its paper to entice the population to join. When the appeals proved unsatisfactory, it was decided to apply sound commercial techniques by hiring some professional recruiting agents. The advertisements placed in *Informations Juives* indicate the committee's attitude about its role in the Jewish community: "Wanted, representatives to collect subscriptions for the newspaper and for membership dues, high percentages offered and job security."[104]

Despite these efforts and inducements, few took up the offer, and few people joined the Coordination Committee. Under Baur's leadership, however, some support was gained. At the end of 1941, 6,057 had joined, even though 1,961 were nondues-payers.[105] An examination of the membership rolls shows that the French Jews constituted most of the dues-paying majority and the immigrants free members. From a Jewish population of 65,000 families in Paris, 10 percent had chosen to join. The motivation for joining varied, but doubtless the influence of the ACIP was significant. After all, the Coordination Committee, led by well-known Jewish personalities, did represent a guarantee that lent the organization respectability. The support of the ACIP was certainly the decisive factor in inducing French Jews into joining. As for the immigrants, their motives are harder to establish. Some, swayed by the early threats of the *Informations Juives,* would have joined for fear of losing whatever assistance might be obtained from the committee. In view of the large number of immigrant poor who needed communal help, it was not surprising that many of them did not want to rely wholly on the Amelot Committee. But the majority of the population did not join the Coordination Committee because they thought it was controlled by the Germans.

Even though Dannecker had insisted that foreign Jews be equally represented on the committee and a number had been coopted, in terms of responsibilities and function its leadership was overwhelmingly French. Its executive of seven included only one foreigner, Alex Klein, and one naturalized citizen, Elie Danon.[106] By October 1941 the situation was still unchanged, except that another French Jew had been taken into the executive. As for the general staff, where it no longer mattered, the nationality of employees was inconsequential. In August 1941, the Coordination Committee employed 67 persons of whom 31 were French and 37 foreigners; by October 1941 the number of people employed had risen to 140, and the personnel department was no longer concerned about maintaining the ratio of French and immigrant members that Dannecker had earlier ordered.[107]

The reason for the increase in employees was due to the extension of the committee's range of activities, as well as the inclusion of personnel accrued from affiliated institutions. But as the August 1941 mass internment had shown, arrests could affect the proper functioning of any institution. The question of how to maintain stability in the management of institutions and ensure permanence of personnel was most likely raised with Dannecker by Israelowicz. Israelowicz knew that in Vienna the Gestapo did grant immunity to certain groups, particularly the leaders and employees of such organizations as the Coordination Committee. It appears from the evidence that such a practice had already been approved by Dannecker in August 1941.[108] But such protection had not yet been made available to the general personnel of the committee. On the same day that the committee requested this special protection from the French police for Danon, the committee had rejected a similar request from one of its employees.[109] The protection available to the committee leaders, though not publicly acknowledged, was an open secret that only served to alienate the Coordination Committee from its personnel and the population.

The issue of the special protection for the leaders of the organization should be seen in the context of the need by the Jewish population for similar protection. The Coordination Committee was judged by the population on the basis of its activities. Indeed, by the end of 1941 it was sufficiently well organized to have agencies in all arrondissements of Paris with large Jewish population. The relative peace that prevailed after the August arrests had restored some confidence. In the quarters where immigrant Jews predominated, immigrant Coordination Committee personnel staffed the various offices and their participation helped maintain an aura of peace. The presence of the Amelot Committee, officially a member of the Coordination Committee but unofficially totally independent from it, contributed equally by its presence as a relief organization in sustaining the temporary popular belief that despite present material hardship all difficulties would be overcome.

It was while the Jewish organizations were coming to terms with the population's problems that Dannecker finally gained support from the German military administration for his plan for imposed representation. Indeed, by September 1941, the negotiations between Vallat and the military administration were already well advanced.[110] Still, the high-level negotiations did not keep Dannecker from trying again to force the Coordination Committee to supply manpower for the Ostland company in the Ardennes. Once more his order was accompanied by the demand that the executive accept responsibility for the fulfillment of the order, and with threats of reprisals for failure to comply.[111] Baur succeeded in avoiding reprisals with the usual evasive declarations. Again Dannecker relented, but then the Coordination Committee was already involved in negotiations with Vallat over Vichy's intentions to form an imposed representation, which could well have accounted for Dannecker's refusal to execute his threats. On 29 November 1941, a Vichy law established the Union Générale des Israélites de France.

It had taken Dannecker from September 1940 to September 1941 to force through his plan of imposed representation, and the delay had hardly been due to the Jews' resistance alone. The German military administration and the embassy, despite strong support in their ranks for a Nazi solution to the Jewish Question in France, had opted for the "soft" plan. This plan required that Vichy enact the necessary legislation. Vichy obliged because in its own political perspectives the Jews were expendable. Equally important, it was Vichy policy to ensure the predominance of French law over the whole of France.[112]

But what of the Jews themselves? We have seen how, partly out of fear for the consequences of their own actions and partly out of their own communal needs, the French Jews had been drawn into a dialogue with Dannecker. The strategy devised by the ACIP, of recourse to French law, proved useless. Leaders of the ACIP had realized it early in 1941, but had continued to negotiate with Dannecker because they believed that ultimately Vichy would intervene in their favor because they were French. In the process the French Jews of the ACIP overlooked the consequences of their actions upon the whole of the Jewish population.

The French Jews wanted to defend their sectional interests, and by so doing provided Dannecker with the first step toward imposed representation led by well-known Jewish personalities, who by their presence conferred an aura of respectability. Yet the actions of the ACIP must be judged in conjunction with the internal needs of the Jewish population itself. Between September 1940 and January 1941, while Dannecker was exerting pressure, many Jews faced serious material hardships. This factor had great bearing not only on the ACIP but also on the immigrant organizations, from the Amelot Committee to the Communists: it encouraged them to seek communal agreement to confront these problems. The establishment of the Coordination Committee following the early cooperation between the ACIP and Amelot was a reflection of this common concern. By seizing upon this development just as he was negotiating with the ACIP to turn itself into the representative of the Jews of Paris, Dannecker fused these two separate elements. From then on any legal relief activities could only assist the Germans in controlling Jewish communal activities. By the use of threats and announcements that legislation would soon force the Jews to establish their own representation, Dannecker succeeded in compelling the ACIP to voluntarily organize and lead the first form of representation. It is to the representation imposed by Vichy under German pressure that we must turn to examine the French Jews' responses when they were granted an opportunity to reconsider their participation in an organization conceived as a bureaucratic device to imprison the Jewish population.

5

The Establishment of the
Union Générale des Israélites de France:
September 1941 to January 1942

The news that Vichy was to introduce an imposed representation brought in its wake a debate among Franco-Jewish organizations of a kind that had not occurred since the Dreyfus Affair.[1] The news had followed a shattering catalogue of laws, which was gradually but inexorably turning the French Jews into foreigners in the country of their birth. They had viewed successive anti-Jewish laws with mounting apprehension. But occasional reassurances, given privately to some Jewish leaders, that there would be reviews in order to protect the French Jews, had contained some of their fears. The new threat, however, was of a fundamental nature: it irrevocably cast them out of French society. It was no surprise, therefore, that the official notification by Vichy of the forthcoming legislation on an imposed representation, which they were expected to lead, evoked such strong responses.

The debate among the leaders of French Judaism centered around the elaboration of a policy that would ensure the survival of the Franco-Jewish community. Only two courses of action were available: a strategy that would lead to open conflict with Vichy or a policy of compromise. The debate was divisive. Those opposed to compromise were not willing to pursue their opposition to the law to its logical conclusion, open conflict with Vichy. They assumed a sterile opposition through private protestations. Those in favor of compromise, believed cooperation with Vichy was the only course available that took into account the need to keep the existing Jewish organizations operative and, above all, to ensure that "responsible" Jewish leaders remained at the helm.

Central to the conflict was that the law was being prepared by the Vichy government. Indeed, in retrospect, had the legislation been German it might not have evoked the same division within French Judaism. The problems facing French Judaism would have remained the same and might well have been resolved in the same manner, but the opposition to the question of direct Jewish participation might have taken on different forms. In any event, because the projected law had been communicated by Vallat to the Central Consistory it influenced the proceedings of the debate.

In September 1941, Jacques Helbronner, as president of the Central Consistory of French Judaism, received from Vallat the draft of a law on imposed Jewish representation. The draft law was based, in its main lines, on directives from the German military administration which Best had earlier communicated to Vallat.[2] Even if it was not clear to the French Jews, Vallat himself had not been very enthusiastic about the project.[3]

The German decision to proceed with the establishment of an imposed central Jewish organization through Vichy did not mean that it was willing to leave the matter in Vichy's hands. In fact, Best's communication to Vallat clearly defined the terms of the legislation the Germans wanted to see introduced by Vichy. Best's guidelines were clear, first, all Jews in Occupied France would be members, and so would their religious institutions; second, the organization would be responsible for Jewish welfare and representation to the authorities; third, it would be permitted to collect dues from members to fulfil its obligations; fourth, it would be controlled by the CGQJ; and finally, all Jewish organizations would be dissolved and their assets would become the property of the new organization. Best's communication also included an ultimatum:

> In the event that a French law did not establish such an organization, I am envisaging issuing an ordinance to that effect and would charge the French authorities with its application as well as with the control of the organization.[4]

Vallat had been ordered to submit a report by 25 September 1941, on the progress achieved in the elaboration of the law. Yet Vallat was not ready to proceed as the Germans demanded; he tried to gain time by arguing that general relief work for the Jews did not in itself necessitate the establishment of a compulsory organization. But the deadline remained and Vichy needed to take action now if it wanted to avoid the German authorities' taking unilateral measures.[5]

None of the previous anti-Jewish legislation had evoked disagreement between Vichy and the Germans. A conflict of economic interests arose over the question of aryanization but no one disagreed about its necessity. Vichy viewed the Jewish Question as a political problem, and in the context of the overall Franco-German relationship it was treated as such. Fundamentally, though different methods may have been considered appropriate in dealing with the Jews, the German command and Vichy shared an underlying ideological position.

Although Vichy's views on the Jewish Question were close to the German position, Vichy's policy was ambivalent. On the one hand, Vichy accepted the premise that the Jews as a group were "nonassimilable" and could have no place in the new France. At the same time, however, Vichy recognized that some Jews had earned the title of Frenchmen by past sacrifices and contributions.

This basic difference became apparent during 1941 when restrictive legislation was applied. Whereas Vichy viewed the Jews either as foreigners or as deserving Frenchmen, the Germans refused to recognize such a distinction. This important disagreement was further complicated by Vichy's own administrative policy, which sought as a matter of principle to retain administrative control over the occupied parts of France. This policy had particular consequences for the Jews. Each new French law needed German assent in occupied territories, particularly in the case of the Jews. The need for German acceptance necessitated that Vichy conform broadly to German policy. Vichy would have taken into account in its own legislation the special position of the French Jews, but the Germans were not prepared to accept such a modification.

Vichy's anti-Jewish legislation reflected both its fundamental positions on the question and its need to satisfy existing constraints. The early legislation passed under Pierre Laval, during 1940, had been both xenophobic and antisemitic. It was only from 1941 onward, under Darlan, that Vichy had begun to introduce finer distinctions between those it considered 100 percent French and the others. Once that principle had been established all further legislation followed this rule. But until the establishment of the CGQJ in March 1941, all legislation reflected Vichy's own ideological views rather than German pressure.[6]

Under Darlan, from February 1941 to March 1942, the Jewish Question began to present problems for Vichy. The gradual development of a parallel German Jewish policy in Occupied France led to increased demands by the Germans concerning Vichy's own policy. Gradually Vichy found itself not only having to accommodate German demands but also, because of the Vichy policy of ensuring predominance of its own legislation, having to anticipate German objections and German legislation. If at first the treatment of the Jewish Question had proved merely a useful opportunity to demonstrate its willingness to cooperate in developing a new Europe, Vichy now found itself more and more involved in the application of the German Jewish policy.

The problems faced by Vichy in the application of its own anti-Jewish policy were bound up with broad policy considerations, German demands and the need to satisfy them, as well as its own anti-Jewish ideology which did not meet the German racist requirements. By August 1941, when Vichy faced a new German demand, it had already become so familiar with the German technique of extracting the desired legislation that its reaction was predictable—as the Germans were well aware.

Vichy decided to meet the German ultimatum with a counterproposal to legislate for the whole of France in order to maintain national administrative unity. The Germans approved. Even though Dannecker was still not satisfied with the limited powers of the proposed organization, particularly for its anticipated future tasks, he had to recognize that Vichy had taken a step in the right direction. The Jews in the Vichy Zone perceived this latest measure as the gravest threat so far. It was the final and all-embracing codification of all previous discriminatory measures. The French Jews saw it as the first step in some comprehensive plan to place all the Jews in a real ghetto.

The reactions of organizations governed by French Judaism in Vichy France were even more violent than among the immigrant organizations. These strong reactions stemmed from the French Jews' objection to being reduced to the same level as the foreign Jews. On that score they were unanimous. Previously, they had acted as if there was a political problem only because of the excessive number of foreign Jews—a problem that justified the special legislation. This is why in April 1941 the Central Consistory suggested to Vallat that the immigrant Jews could be placed either in work camps or labor brigades.[7] René Mayer, a leading member of the Central Consistory, wrote to Vallat during the negotiations over the imposed representation with suggestions that foreign Jews be encouraged to emigrate.[8]

The French Jews were all the more shocked because they had assumed all past measures to have been dictated by the Germans; furthermore they had not questioned until then their own future in the new France, which would emerge if Germany were victorious. Darlan's views on the Jewish question were well known:

> The stateless Jews who, for the past fifteen years have invaded our country do not interest me. But the others, the good old French Jews, are entitled to all the protection that we can give them: I even have some of them in my family.[9]

Jacques Helbronner, president of the Central Consistory, regularly brought back comforting messages from Pétain. Even Vallat had reassured Helbronner that the Statut des Juifs would be modified in order to save 95 percent of the French Jews.[10]

The reality of Vichy's anti-Jewish policy did not square with these assurances. French Jews had not even been given dispensation from the special census of all Jews.[11] The proposed legislation did not admit conflicting evaluations. The problem for the French Jews was to decide a course of action. Some held that the survival of French Judaism was the central task; others took a much broader view and believed that all Jewish institutions were at stake. Should they oppose Vichy or cooperate? Those who favored opposition saw participation in the imposed representation as a symbol of tacit approval and believed those in favor of cooperating were capitulating. But what would happen to the Jewish institutions and organizations if a boycott was agreed upon?

The Central Consistory's leaders were outspoken opponents of the principle of a central representation. The projected incorporation of all existing organizations, including those of the foreign Jews, into a single body controlled by the state but under the possible leadership of men who could well be outsiders was viewed as the most fundamental threat to the Consistory's position as the representative of French Judaism. The Central Consistory's network of charitable institutions would be swallowed up, signifying the end of what had been an integral part of its activities. By secularizing its social work, as the projected law would, the Central Consistory would be reduced to a purposeless body.

The rabbinical corps fully supported this reaction. The existence of the imposed representation would create a rift between the spiritual and social character of French Judaism.[12] It, like the Central Consistory, feared that the relief work formerly centered around the religious communities would be taken over by an organization that was a "body alien to the synagogues."[13] Chief-Rabbi Maurice Liber, addressing a general assembly of the Association des Rabbins Français, argued that with the establishment of the imposed representation a situation must inevitably result in which alongside or in opposition to religious Judaism there would also arise a secular and enforced Judaism. As far as the Association des Rabbins Français was concerned, no concession could be made that would not only jeopardize religious Judaism but would concede that Judaism had a national connotation.

What had occurred in Paris was too recent and too meaningful as an example of what could happen elsewhere to be dismissed by the Central Consistory or the Association des Rabbins Français. With the formation of the Coordination Committee, the Paris Consistory had become isolated from the Jewish population and was no longer recognized by the authorities as the representative of the French Jews. It had been reduced to holding religious services. Although the leadership of the Coordination Committee was in the hands of Consistory members or its supporters, the influence and significance of the Consistory had been destroyed.

> By wanting to save the Consistory from playing the role of *Reichsvertretung*—national representation—the outcome of that tactic in fact resulted in the establishment of a real *Reichsvertretung* side by side with the Consistory and, whether this outcome was wanted or not in opposition to the interests of the ACIP.[14]

Neither the Central Consistory nor the rabbinical corps wished to suffer the same fate, the same collapse of power, as the Paris Consistory.

There was another component in the Central Consistory's opposition to the law. It refused to be placed on the same footing as recently naturalized or immigrant Jews. This was clearly articulated in each and every letter of protest it sent to the government.[15] The old enmity of the Central Consistory to the foreign Jews found, during the many debates over the law, numerous opportunities to express itself.[16]

The Central Consistory, as a body representing the local consistories, did not require unanimity to function. In fact, there were many instances in the past when some of its members were highly critical of its political positions. The most outstanding occurred in the 1930s over the issue of the ACIP's relationship with the French Right.[17] In the context of the debate over Vichy's proposed law, some members of the Central Consistory, although opposed to the law, did not accept the nationalist argument. Professor William Oualid, well known in the prewar period for his sympathies for the Central European Jews, disputed the nationalist position.[18] During the debates, while sharing the general concern about the future of French Judaism and the independence of Jewish organizations, he refused to view the survival of the leading role of the

Central Consistory as separate from the survival of all the Jews. Some other Jews of long-established families in France shared his attitude. Jules Isaac, who had devoted much of his life to furthering Judeo-Christian understanding in France, was equally concerned with the problem of Jewish identity and French Judaism. Other French Jews went even further, defining themselves first as Jews and only second as French.[19]

Another Franco-Jewish organization took an active part in the opposition to the law: the Commission Central d'Oeuvres Juives d'Assistance—Central Commission of Jewish Relief Associations (CCOJA). This committee, created and led by French Jews after the exodus of June 1940, included some immigrant organizations.[20] Its opposition to the law therefore was not based upon the same criteria used by the Central Consistory. It rejected above all the Central Consistory's claim to represent French Judaism. Addressing itself to the Consistory during one of its plenary sessions, the CCOJA felt it necessary to stress that although the Consistory believed it spoke on behalf of 180,000 Jews there were in fact over 300,000 Jews in France.[21]

Despite these important differences in the reasons that groups and individuals opposed the law, agreement was total about its pernicious character. Consequently, as long as the debates were only dealing with the general problem, no one thought it very harmful to enunciate facile oppositional formulations. Divisions began to emerge when Vallat, wishing to conclude the draft of the law, also began to seek Jewish participants who would ensure the proper operation of the projected organization. Vital questions began to challenge the early unity. What would be the fate of the organizations once integrated into the new organization? How would the controls be exercised? What would be the overall nature of this central organization?

The French Jews were not the only ones to find themselves divided. The immigrants also reacted to the projected law in diverse, conflicting ways. Essentially two positions emerged. Marc Jarblum, the leader of the FSJF, during the negotiations with Vallat was opposed to the principle of Jews' participation in such an organization. He consistently sought to extend the process of discussion by advancing demands that Vallat could not meet. He hoped, Jarblum said, "that in following this strategy Vallat's aim would become clearer for all to see and that perhaps it would be possible to achieve a collective refusal at the very last minute."[22]

Jarblum achieved limited success with this strategy. Unlike the members of the Central Consistory, he had no illusions about the motives behind Vichy's anti-Jewish legislation. In his assessment, the projected legislation was the clearest evidence that little distinction would be made between French and foreign Jews. The billion-franc fine imposed by the Occupation authorities to be paid by the Jews of the Occupied Zone and the collection of that fine by the UGIF should have convinced those called to participate in the UGIF to reject the offer.[23] In Jarblum's view this last measure, with all the earlier legislation and police actions, made the overall policy of the German authorities, but above all of Vichy, irrefutably clear. He believed that no Jew ought to collaborate with a body aimed at extending further controls over the Jewish population.

The other view that found support among some immigrant leaders was based on more pragmatic considerations. It called for participation in the UGIF so that some control or at least some measure of knowledge would be obtained through presence on the board of the new organization. This view was espoused by Israel Jefroykin, honorary president of the FSJF. Jarblum presented Jefroykin's position in the following terms:

> We national Jews have always wanted Jewish autonomy. . . . We consider ourselves to be a national group. That which we should have done but did not wish to do voluntarily is now being imposed upon us by force. Therein lies our guilt. But why should we not accept it? True this is not the autonomy that we had preached. This is indeed a political action directed against us. But upon us alone depends whether this new institution will be properly utilized. And, if we are hindered in our activities we shall be able to leave at any moment.[24]

The immigrant organizations other than the FSJF also took positions. The Jewish Communists were convinced that no collaboration with Vichy was acceptable. They felt Vichy's antisemitic activities were sufficient to categorically condemn participation in any organization that existed under its control or even with its blessing. The projected imposed representation would only mislead the Jewish population into believing that Vichy's claim of wanting to help the Jews help themselves was genuine. Furthermore, if Jews were to participate in the imposed representation it would lull the population into believing that the prime function of that body was to assist the poor. All decisions should be aimed at helping the population recognize the true function of this organization.[25]

The Bund, the Jewish Social-Democratic party, also opposed participation. For the same reasons as the Communists, the Bund appealed to all Jews to refuse to participate in it. The Bund believed the new body would become the "concentration camp of the Jewish organizations which would be compelled to join it."[26] Some individual Bundists were even more outspoken in their opposition. Attacking those who had opted to work in it, one illegal Bundist publication characterized these Jews and their attitude to the question thus:

> They want to organize the Jewish shame. To the argument that we must enter into it because the needs among the Jewish masses are great we reply: it makes no difference if we are shot singly or collectively. Let the torturers do their own work.[27]

The positions adopted by organizations and individuals were not so clearly expressed when Vallat first notified the Central Consistory and Raymond Raoul Lambert, the general-secretary of the Comité d'Assistance aux Réfugiés (CAR). The negotiations with Vallat lasted from September 1941 to January 1942. When they were finally over a UGIF had been formed with the participation of Jewish representatives and the Central Consistory had lost its former position as the representative of French Judaism.

The first official notification to the Jews that a compulsory representation was being prepared was received by the Central Consistory in September 1941. It was, despite feigned surprise, no surprise to the Consistory's leaders. There had been ample warnings. Only the timing and the degree of inclusiveness, that is, whether French and foreign Jews would be forced into a single organization, could have remained uncertain. Some French Jews had hoped that it would not affect them, but the immigrants never doubted that a *Judenrat* would be imposed. Except under Léon Blum, during the Popular Front government of 1936, the immigrants never had access to government circles. The Vichy legislation had made its xenophobic policy abundantly clear to the immigrants. The French Jews did have very influential friends at Vichy, for example, the close acquaintance of some leading Jewish personalities with Pétain and Vallat. Furthermore, the responses of the French Jews were limited by their inability to consider any opposition to the government other than the traditional forms of negotiation. The leaders of the French Jews also had not realized that the system of justice under Vichy would no longer provide them with the protection of the law. They failed to perceive that under the conditions that prevailed the government would continue to pursue its anti-Jewish policy, gradually placing them outside French law and finally depriving them of what they had assumed were their traditional rights.

The notification that a law would soon impose representation had stated that it would apply to the whole of France, and would be led by French Jews. There were a number of ways the law could be applied: with the cooperation of the present leaders of the Jewish organizations, with the collaboration of Jews outside these organizations, or through the appointments of state administrative personnel. The negotiations over the modalities of the law began with the Central Consistory.

Vallat had sent a draft of the proposed articles of association to Helbronner in September 1941.[28] Helbronner, as president of the Central Consistory and a member of the Conseil d'Etat, the highest legal state advisory body, was certainly the most influential Jewish personality in France at the time. From Vallat's point of view, it was essential to obtain the approval and support of such an important member of the Jewish community. Helbronner's assent would have resolved many technical difficulties, ensuring the support of the most important organizations and certainly accelerating establishment of the organization.[29] But the problem faced by Vallat was time: he had been warned by the Germans that unless Vichy immediately promulgated the desired law the Germans would proceed unilaterally.[30]

The draft presented to Helbronner for consideration was much more comprehensive than what the Germans themselves first suggested. Whereas Best emphasized the problem of relief as a justification for the establishment of the imposed body, Vallat, with traditional French bureaucratic thoroughness, aimed at an all-inclusive law. The draft grouped all the Jewish organizations into a single representative body and made that body responsible for welfare and economic reorganization. As a French-instituted body it was to be led by a board of sixteen French Jews with the assistance of representatives from the Ministries of Finance and National Economy. It was to be financed by legacies and gifts, by the assests of the dissolved organizations, by a special tax on the Jews, and by subsidies from the CGQJ, which in turn would come from the "Solidarity Fund." The religious institutions were to be compelled to join in a separate union.[31] There is no doubt that Vallat's scheme was designed to prove to the Germans that France was equally capable and determined to deal with the Jewish Question. But perhaps as important was that its very comprehensiveness would elicit German approval, thereby helping to see that French and not German law prevailed in Occupied France.

Vallat needed to form the new organization as rapidly as possible—Helbronner's approval was essential. Vallat decided to offer him the presidency, but Helbronner was too experienced as a lawyer and too conscious of his responsibility to be tempted with such a puerile bribe. Then Vallat passed on the assurance he had received from the Germans that the leaders of the organization would not be held personally responsible in the event that they chose to refuse to carry out an order.[32]

The Central Consistory viewed Vallat's draft as a basis for negotiation with the full knowledge that it had been a Vichy decision to proceed with the legislation. Helbronner's strategy was twofold: to call on every source of support at Vichy in order to obtain assistance in the negotiations and to seek out areas in Vallat's draft likely to be modified in favor of French Judaism. Helbronner's counterproposals aimed at protecting the Central Consistory by ensuring its total independence from the projected union. The Central Consistory sought government recognition of its leading position in representing the moral and spiritual interests of the French *Israélites*. It also wanted to avoid being pressed into a union of religious institutions which would make it only equal to the immigrants' own religious institutions.

Helbronner demanded that the Jews' religious freedoms be respected in accordance with the 1905 and 1907 French laws of church and state separation. As confirmation of the Central Consistory's representative authority, Helbronner also insisted that the administrative board of the new union be nominated by the Central Consistory in conjunction with the CCOJA. Furthermore, Helbronner set out to formulate clearly the aims and objectives as well as the areas of responsibility of the organization, to remove from Vallat's draft the ambiguities inherent in the concept of representation.

As a concession to Vallat, Helbronner offered that the new body should be responsible for education in addition to the proposed areas of relief, welfare, and economic reorganization. Helbronner was also prepared to accept that the financial resources should be augmented through the application of special laws for exceptional funding, and that the CGQJ should be empowered to select from those nominated by the Jewish organizations the president, two vice-presidents, a treasurer, and a general-secretary. Helbronner had also made provision for the appointment of two controllers from the Finance Ministry with powers to cancel the board's decisions, with such powers equally vested in the CGQJ.[33] At this early stage of the negotiations, it was clear that the Central Consistory's leadership had engaged in a course of concessions in order to ensure its position as the authorized representative of French Judaism.

Vallat's search for the suitable influential personalities to form the representation was not limited to Helbronner and the Central Consistory. Vallat was well aware that alongside the Central Consistory there were a range of organizations headed by responsible leaders who, although connected in a myriad of ways to the Central Consistory, were somewhat independent of it. And then there were the immigrant organizations, which accounted for half the Jewish population. He decided to contact Raymond Raoul Lambert, general-secretary of the CAR.

R. R. Lambert came from an old established French family, and always had been associated with French Judaism. Between 1935 and 1939 he devoted much time to editing the Univers Israélite. During that period he played an important role in a number of Jewish welfare institutions, particularly the CAR. But most of his public career had been spent in the corridors of power of various governments, particularly those of Georges Clémenceau and Edouard Herriot. He was as well acquainted with the senior levels of French public admiration as with Jewish communal affairs.[34] Lambert, with the consent of Albert Lévy, CAR's president, met with Vallat on 27 September 1941. According to Lambert the decision to meet Vallat had been made with the specific understanding that Lambert would not act as the representative of CAR, and with the understanding that replies to all questions raised by Vallat involving the CAR directly would first have to be cleared with the CAR Committee.[35]

Vallat thus set into motion a process of negotiations that ensured him contact with both the Central Consistory, whose influence within the community of French Jews extended far beyond its own members, and Lambert, whose knowledge of the Jewish personalities and institutions outside the immediate control of the Central Consistory could allow Vallat room to maneuver. The contact with Lambert was important if Vallat was to achieve a rapid outcome to the projected organization, for he was well aware that the negotiations with Helbronner and the Central Consistory would be a drawnout process.

When Vallat met with R. R. Lambert for the first time on 27 September 1941, he took a conciliatory line to create the atmosphere for a continued dialogue. He expressed regret at the conditions in the Vichy camps, particularly Gurs and Rivesaltes, and even promised to raise the question with the appropriate ministry.[36] The second problem was that of the Jews in the Occupied Zone. Vallat informed Lambert that the Germans were contemplating taking even more severe measures against the Jews. Without going into details about those measures, Vallat opened up the point of the meeting: the issue of a "unified community" for the two zones. Vallat's decision to link the situation in the Occupied Zone with this issue was obviously designed to imply that a "unified community" under Vichy's auspices would be of assistance to the Jews under German rule. To prove his goodwill Vallat advanced the question of the funds held by the AIU. They amounted to some 13 to 18 million francs and Vallat suggested that it would be possible to arrange their transfer to Vichy to prevent a likely German confiscation. According to Lambert, Vallat sought to convey that it was only because of the Germans that Vichy had adopted anti-Jewish measures. At the conclusion of the meeting, however, Vallat "ironically" rejected the protests made by "Rabbis and State Councillors." Vallat, the politician and the antisemite, thus made light of the manner in which French Judaism and Helbronner had sought to bring to the attention of their contacts at Vichy their bitterness and sorrow at being treated like foreigners.[37]

By the end of September 1941 the issue of an imposed representation could no longer be confined to the closed ranks of the Central Consistory's leadership. The question was of such fundamental importance that a general meeting of all the members of the Central Consistory was called for 19 October 1941. This was to be the first general assembly since the Armistice; 100 delegates were summoned from every part of the Vichy Zone. Two documents were submitted for discussion: Helbronner's amended draft, which had been given to Vallat, and a general analysis of the project.[38]

Although the ostensible items for discussion were Vallat's draft constitution and Helbronner's counterproposals, what dominated the debate was the real question of what needed to be done if Vichy decided to proceed with the law regardless of the Central Consistory's objections. A decision had to be reached on recommendations to be made to members of the Consistory if they were solicited by Vallat to join the board of the organization. The problem was whether cooperation was to be rejected on principle or whether there was room for compromise and at what cost. The meeting considered the appropriateness of the two options. The first was an uncompromising refusal, based on the honor and dignity of French Judaism, to participate in the workings of a law that negated the contributions made by the countless generations of French Jews. Such a position, however, demanded that the Consistory be prepared to sacrifice its public image with Vichy, that of a law-abiding and responsible body, and incur the risk of losing the network of institutions it had established over generations. The second option was to compromise, and was conditional upon the outcome of negotiations. In this case, even though concessions were inevitable, the Consistory would remain at Vichy, would still be able to appeal for the redress of grievances, and above all would have neither lost control of its organizations nor forfeited its leading role. The general assembly was too well acquainted with the consequences in Paris of earlier anti-Jewish laws not to fear total defeat. The assembly dreaded the possibility that in the event of a refusal by the Consistory and its members to participate in the projected organization, Vallat would have to decide to operate these institutions without their former leaders.

The assembly debated the issues and formulated its positions around the two alternatives. Three principles were adopted. In the first place there was a general protest against the proposed legislation which extended the previous discriminatory laws to institutions, whether those of the French citizens of Jewish faith or (given French law) those of the foreign Jews. Second, all efforts were to be directed at maintaining the distinctions between religious questions and social solidarity. Finally, the assembly declared its opposition to the establishment of an organization which, once granted its own juridical and fiscal status, would become implicitly or explicitly a quasi-political organization.

On the basis of these principles, the assembly formulated its strategy. It would demand, first, that the 1905 law of church and state separation remain applicable to Judaism. Next, a protest would be made against the further attempt to limit the Jews' civic rights by imposing a specific political representation. In the area of philanthropic activities, however, the assembly would accept the principle of government control, but only under certain conditions.

It was in the conditions under which the Central Consistory was prepared to accept government controls that the essence of the strategy was mapped out. Under no conditions should the rights of French Jews to government assistance be prejudiced by the various relief activities being dispensed by the coordinated efforts of existing Jewish welfare organizations. Moreover, under no circumstances should the private efforts of these organizations be augmented by the proceeds of the forced sale of Jewish-owned properties. Further, the budgetary resources of the organization the government wanted to establish should only originate from voluntary donations or legacies; compulsory dues should be considered by the government only in the case of the most serious shortage of funds. Finally, regardless of these considerations, the law regarding the imposed representation should be enforced only after a study in depth, in which representatives of the existing institutions should take part. The secretariat of the Consistory drew up a note outlining these recommendations, which together with Helbronner's counterdraft constitution, was to be given to Vallat.[39]

When the Consistory had completed its deliberations and taken up its positions for the forthcoming negotiations, the CCOJA began its own evaluation. It concluded its meeting with a resolution attacking the law as well as the Consistory's positions. Although Helbronner's draft had, in anticipation of criticism, allocated the CCOJA a leading role in the selection of the board of management, the CCOJA was far from satisfied. The CCOJA challenged the Consistory in its claim to represent the Jews of France, and even French Judaism. The CCOJA took the view that the Consistory had refused to recognize that a large number of Jews who were not French needed help. The Consistory had presumed to negotiate with Vallat on behalf of Jews it did not represent. The CCOJA claimed that if any one group was required to present positions on behalf of the majority of the Jews, the CCOJA was certainly far more representative than the Central Consistory.[40]

The challenge to the Consistory's position of authority, coming from such a source, could not be left unanswered. The Consistory was well aware of its strengths and its weaknesses. Indeed, although it did have entrées at Vichy it could never assert that it held any authority over all the Jewish relief institutions. Unwilling to relinquish its authority, yet recognizing the problem arising from the CCOJA's challenge, it called for a combined discussion of the issues to avoid becoming isolated.

On 26 October 1941, a meeting of both leaderships took place. The Consistory's line of argument was clear. It justified its claim by presenting to the CCOJA its counterdraft constitution and made much of its connections with Pétain. In support of this line of argument the Consistory presented a letter it had received from André Lavagne promising valuable support.[41] The difficulty encountered by the Consistory was not easily overcome, however, for in their early negotiations with Vallat, the Consistory had neither informed the CCOJA nor attempted to seek its views.

Both the Consistory and the CCOJA were well aware of the necessity to find grounds for agreement during such a critical period. It was on the need to continue relief activities that unity was achieved. The final resolution adopted at the meeting shows the Consistory's concessions on the general strategy regarding the proposed constitution. Similarly, the CCOJA made concessions in order not to be accused of dividing Jewish opposition. Neither party could afford to reject the other's particular contribution.[42]

The agreed course of action was to leave to the Consistory the responsibility for carrying on negotiations with Vallat and for continuing to develop political support with Pétain. In line with this, the CCOJA was to prepare a document presenting the various aspects of their relief work, with the objective of convincing the authorities that subordinating these organizations to one central body, as proposed by Vallat, would impede rather than assist the aims and objectives of the law. It was for the Consistory to ensure that the CCOJA's case be presented to the relevant Vichy authorities.

While the Jewish organizations were formulating a defensive strategy, trying to develop support at Vichy and testing the limits of compromise, Vallat was busy finalizing his legislation and ensuring that the German authorities would not find it wanting. By 7 November 1941, Vallat was sufficiently advanced in his work to give Lambert the names of those he was considering as possible leaders of the organization.[43]

It was during this crucial meeting with Lambert that Vallat finally stated the limits of his concessions. Vallat's terms demonstrated the erroneous assumptions that guided the Franco-Jewish strategy; namely, that further negotiations were still possible and that an acceptable compromise was still within reach. The basis for the Consistory's assumptions had been a letter Helbronner had received from Lavagne, a member of Pétain's personal staff. Lavagne's claim that the proposed law had met objections from some ministries and that it would most likely go before the Conseil d'Etat had given rise to the Consistory's confidence. But Vallat had been able to overcome all ministerial opposition by using the threat of German unilateral legislation. In the process, however, Vallat had had to make a number of concessions to Helbronner to overcome opposition to the law.

Three concessions were actually made. First, the religious institutions would not have to enter into a union. For the Central Consistory this was a significant victory, not only because it retained its independence but, more important, it could continue to view itself as the legitimate representative of French Judaism. Whether this particular concession was due to Vallat's refusal to enter into a debate with the churches in France on the issue of church/state relationship is not clear; what is clear is that Vallat had avoided being drawn into such a complex issue. The second concession made by Vallat was on the funding of the proposed organization. Vallat conceded that while the organization's overall funding would be based on gifts and donations the imposition of a special tax on the Jewish population would not take place without prior discussion with the Finance Ministry. Finally, as a gesture to the Jewish organizations in the Vichy Zone, Vallat agreed that, due to the different conditions prevailing in the two zones, a slightly different mode of operation would be allowed, though the same constitutional principles would remain valid. Vallat was effectively telling his interlocutors that the Jews would be treated less harshly in the Vichy Zone than in Paris.

For all intents and purposes, Vallat had successfully overcome all objections. He had obtained the necessary support from his government and the Consistory's opposition had been silenced. Vallat could now turn to the practical problem of forming a suitable leadership. He advanced to Lambert the names of some of the individuals he envisaged as the leaders of the Vichy organization: René Mayer, Albert Lévy, Oualid, David Olmer, and Lambert himself as general secretary. He asked Lambert to inform these people and to report their replies by 21 November 1941. As far as Vallat was concerned the issue of the articles of association was settled and awaited final German approval. He felt confident enough of that approval to give Lambert its main lines for transmission to the prospective candidates.[44]

Upon receiving Lambert's reports, the Central Consistory felt that the concessions had been substantial, and continued to hold that further concessions were within reach if all Jewish parties held fast to their positions. It viewed the acknowledged independence of the religious institutions as a breakthrough. The removal of the special tax was received as a victory, as it implied that the Jews would be allowed to fund themselves; there was hope that the institutions' blocked funds in the Occupied Zone might become available. And the Consistory interpreted the recognition that the Jews in the Vichy Zone would be treated differently than those in the Occupied Zone as meaning that existing organizations would be maintained and not dissolved into the body to be formed. The fact that Vallat had not referred to education was seen as another important gain. From their original fear that an organization would be imposed upon them which would contain all the attributes of a national minority—judicial, fiscal, religious, and educational—the members of the Consistory now believed that the outcome was an organization oriented chiefly to relief activities. The problem was to see that this limited role was clearly defined and stated.

The resolution of the problem depended on maintaining the momentum of negotiation, and the Consistory interpreted Vallat's own actions as acknowledging this. However, the Consistory was only one of two centers of negotiations. Lambert remained. The Consistory's objective was now clear: Lambert had to go so that Vallat would be compelled to deal directly with the representative organizations. Yet Vallat was never in a position to grant significant concessions, unless Vichy was prepared to alter its fundamental political line. Vallat had always insisted that he was obeying "superior orders"; German sources indicate the extent of their control.[45] All this suggests that on this particular issue, Vallat had no power to make significant changes for the benefit of the Jews.[46]

The Consistory had transmitted its counterproject as well as the CCOJA's memorandum to Pétain and various ministries.[47] On the eve of the promulgation of the law, 24 November 1941, Helbronner received a letter from Lavagne which appeared to offer new hope:

> I have shown the Maréchal your letter as well as the memorandum concerning the Jewish relief and welfare institutions. I had earlier written to the CGQJ that it should send the draft law to the Conseil d'Etat but regrettably the CGQJ has refused. Lagrange has also asked the CGQJ to submit it to the Conseil d'Etat but has met with a similar refusal. I shall insist anew, and I have suggested to the Minister of the Interior, who had not been consulted, and has since been, that he also proposes that the law be submitted to the Conseil d'Etat.[48]

It was no surprise that the Consistory, faced with such expression of support, held out hopes for a negotiated settlement and continued to believe that the issue was not yet closed.

The nature of this letter, no less than the earlier one from Pétain's office, reveals the extent of the contacts with Vichy available to the Consistory leaders. Indeed, there was a close association between Helbronner and Maréchal Pétain dating back to the First World War, when Helbronner headed the military department of the Minister of War Paul Painlevé and was alleged to have supported Pétain's nomination to lead the French armies in 1917. Their acquaintance was sufficiently close for Helbronner to have stated, according to one source, that until July 1941 they had met once a week. This state of affairs was so well known in the Jewish community that Helbronner was referred to as the "Juif du Maréchal." Helbronner's former position on the Conseil d'Etat explained his contacts with a range of personalities extending from Pétain's own staff to Cardinal Gerlier with whom he had studied law in his youth.[49] But then such contacts were typical of the social integration of the leadership of the Consistory. René Mayer had been Laval's Chief of Cabinet in the 1925 ministry; and even Laval's personal secretary until December 1940, Stora, was a Jew.[50] These factors were, no doubt, a major influence upon the course of the whole debate, and more particularly upon the positions taken by the leaders of the Consistory during negotiations. It was no surprise that the CCOJA castigated the Consistory, accusing its leaders of lacking fighting spirit because it neither could nor wished to oppose Vichy.

Vallat's promise to Lambert that he would be shown the final text of the law before publication, so that he could pass it on to the individuals Vallat was considering, also led the Consistory to assume that there was still a margin of time available. They were wrong again. Vallat had other priorities, for he urgently needed to have the law published, and only then would he seek willing participants.

On 29 November 1941, the text of the law announcing the establishment of the Union Générale des Israélites de France went to press. The next day, Lambert was told he would get his copy to show to those Vallat had decided to solicit: Albert Lévy, president of CAR; David Olmer and William Oualid from ORT; René Mayer from HICEM; Maurice Pléven from AIU; Dr. Joseph Weill from OSE; Gaston Kahn, from CAR; Marc Jarblum from the FSJF; and Lambert himself from CAR. Vallat would not publish the names of these individuals until they had consulted with their respective organizations and agreed to participate.[51] Vallat had now advanced a full list of prospective candidates who effectively represented the major Jewish organizations and were well known enough to guarantee that the UGIF would be led by responsible leaders.

As the first phase of the establishment of the UGIF was finalized and its legal basis completed, it was obvious that despite the attempts at negotiations the Jewish organizations had achieved very little. The second phase in the struggle for independence began as soon as the law had been made public, on 2 December 1941. It ended on 8 January 1942, when the names of eighteen French Jews who had agreed to lead the UGIF appeared in the *Journal Officiel*.

The five-week period, until Vallat finally decided upon whom to call to lead the UGIF, was characterized by indecision on the part of French Judaism despite some semblance of resistance. However, unlike the first period, the immigrants now, through Jarblum, were to play a far more significant role. Their influence was expressed in an open opposition, directed at attempting to persuade those selected by Vallat to refuse. Although Jarblum failed to convince all of Vallat's nominees, he was able to turn a number of individuals against cooperating with Vallat.

The articles of association of the UGIF were very close to what Vallat had told Lambert they were going to be.[52] They retained the loosely worded formulation of representing the Jews to the authorities *notamment* (especially) in questions of assistance, welfare, and economic restructuring. Such a formulation left the assignment of unspecified responsibilities wide open. Helbronner had been unable to alter it. This ambiguity had been planned to satisfy the Germans, for had the articles of associations limited the role of the UGIF to relief the Germans would certainly have rejected them. On the other hand, had the articles of association clearly stated the possible extension of responsibilities to include political questions it might have given rise to a stronger Jewish opposition to participation. Vallat had struck the *juste milieu,* confusing the Jews and giving the Germans what they wanted. Article 2 of the law followed the same path: all Jews were compelled to be affiliated with the UGIF and all the Jewish organizations and their assets were to be absorbed by the new organization; only the religious associations were to remain untouched. The Consistory had won but as a consequence was isolated and neutralized. The law had resulted in the French and foreign Jews being placed on the same legal footing.

In the funding of the UGIF the French Jews were more severely dealt with than the immigrants. The law had defined the UGIF's funding as originating from gifts and legacies; membership dues, to be set by the incoming board; the assets of the incorporated organizations; and funds from the Solidarity Fund which would be controlled by the CGQJ. But of all the existing organizations that were to form the UGIF those belonging to French Judaism were the wealthiest. The French Jews were made to support the poorer immigrants. Although the financial provisions of the law had not introduced special taxation clauses, the use of the Solidarity Fund had been enshrined in the articles of association. The UGIF was to be administered by a board of eighteen members, divided into two boards, one for each zone, with two government representatives under the direct CGQJ control. All board members had to be French—no doubt to make sure the organization would remain under French control and to soothe the fears of the French Jews that the organization would be dominated by the immigrants.[53]

On 1 December 1941, some of the nominees met to consider whether to accept. Present were Olmer, Oualid, Lévy, Kahn, Jarblum, and Lambert. They decided to send Vallat their acceptance, conditional upon certain reservations which they wanted approved by the CCOJA.[54] Indeed, none of these men were prepared to act in a personal capacity. The CCOJA, which represented in the Vichy Zone the overwhelming majority of Jewish relief organizations, needed to be consulted. It was for the CCOJA to determine under which conditions these men should accept the responsibility offered or whether they should refuse.

The nominees themselves could not reach agreement. Opinions were divided on whether to accept and whether there was any point in reiterating once more previous objections. On 3 December 1941, they met again, this time without Jarblum. His absence makes it clear that he was the most resolute opponent of participation. Those in favor of participating thought that his presence could have influenced a majority decision. Upon Lambert's suggestion it was agreed that Lambert be authorized to meet Vallat and submit a statement. It was agreed to participate in UGIF only if Vallat met certain conditions: that the term *notamment* used in the law be understood as referring only to welfare activities; that under no circumstances would the incoming board ever ask for the imposition of special taxation measures; that under no circumstances were they prepared to use any funds originating from the Solidarity Fund; and that they would want a representative of the Rabbinate on the board.

The qualified decision to participate did not resolve the problem of the incoming leadership, which Vallat was anxious to settle as rapidly as possible. Only two alternatives appeared likely; either a solution based on acknowledged conflict, that is, the nominees be summoned to lead the UGIF without prior agreement, or a peaceful solution. Given that the law could no longer be altered, Lambert proposed that Vallat be asked to give verbal assurance to a deputation that their acceptance was technical and would not imply acceptance of the legislation. Furthermore, all instructions received from Vallat would be based on mutual agreement, between them and Vallat. Lambert argued that the following principles would help resolve the impasse: that the UGIF's responsibilities in the Vichy Zone would extend only to philanthropy and social work; that the board would not have to act in matters of taxation but would receive instructions from Vallat; that sufficient time be allowed to establish that voluntary donations would suffice to support activities; and that under no circumstances would money originating from the Solidarity Fund be directly handed to the UGIF except in the form of subsidies.[55] Such a line of argument on Lambert's part demonstrated that he personally had decided to participate, irrespective of Vallat's willingness to accede to any assurances. Lambert was intent on finding a formula that would overcome the objections and the fears of the other men.

The following day, 4 December 1941, there was a plenary meeting of the CCOJA to examine the conclusions reached by the meeting of Vallat's nominees. Two issues dominated the debates. No one argued any longer that there should be a general refusal to cooperate with Vallat. The issues raised no longer affected the outcome of Jewish participation; now they focused on Lambert's role as intermediary and how to balance organizational representation on the UGIF's board. The assembly believed that Vallat's nomination of certain people and not others followed from Lambert's privileged position in the negotiations. It was inevitable that Lambert would become the focus of general criticism. Vallat's refusal to deal with accredited representatives was interpreted by the CCOJA assembly as a result of Lambert's manipulation, because he had numerous meetings with Vallat at which no other Jewish representatives were present. The predominance of the CAR representatives on Vallat's list was seen by the assembly as clear evidence of Lambert's desire to gain control of the board.[56] The assembly directed the nominees to make one last attempt to renegotiate with Vallat on some of the issues. They were instructed not to accept nomination unless Vallat gave formal guarantees on the fundamental questions: the nature of the UGIF's representation, its leaders' personal responsibilities, the taxation issue, and the use of the Solidarity Fund.[57]

Lambert, despite explicit orders from the assembly, met Vallat again on 5 December. Without the assent of anyone, Lambert took it upon himself to present to Vallat the views he had proposed at the previous meeting of the nominees, on the eve of the CCOJA's own assembly. During this last meeting, on 5 December, Vallat had handed him a complete list of the names of those he wanted to lead the UGIF in the Vichy Zone. Lambert was told by Vallat that it had become imperative that a UGIF leadership be immediately constituted. Of those nominated by Vallat—Oualid, Olmer, Lévy, Weill, Joseph

Millner, Jarblum, Mayer, Maurice Leven—Lambert already knew that some would refuse. Mayer had already told Lambert that his reservations were such that he was unlikely to accept appointment.

When Lambert indicated to Vallat that some of those on the list were unlikely to accept, Vallat informed Lambert that he reserved the right to make the final decision on the choice of individuals. Lambert, anxious to protect himself from further criticism by the CCOJA for having acted without prior clearance, demanded that Vallat agree to meet other Jewish representatives besides himself, possibly the president of one of those organizations that would be affected, a financial expert, and a representative of the naturalized Jews. Vallat, wanting to continue to use Lambert, indicated that he would meet Oualid, Weill, and Millner. In order to ward off the expected criticism, Lambert received from Vallat a verbal but official statement in which four points were elucidated: (1) on no account was it envisaged that the existing organizations would suspend their activities while they were being integrated in the UGIF; (2) the Solidarity Fund would not be administered by the UGIF and the CGQJ alone would be responsible for its allocation; (3) gifts and legacies would be part of the UGIF's funding; and (4) until the establishment of a scale of compulsory dues, voluntary dues would be acceptable.[58]

Lambert could thus return from a meeting with Vallat to face the CCOJA equipped for the first time with a statement from Vallat clarifying some of the issues of concern, as well as with the names of other Jewish representatives Vallat was prepared to meet. In fact, however, despite his own original claim to have remained passive during the negotiations, acting only in a technical capacity, Lambert had taken initiatives that confirmed the various organizations' suspicions. Indeed, by continuing to meet Vallat he seemed to indicate that he was prepared to cooperate in the imposed representation regardless of Vallat's terms.

The latest developments, Vallat's clarifications, and the opportunity of a wider meeting than just with Lambert compelled the Consistory and the CCOJA to hold a combined session. The Consistory's position had altered since the law appeared on 2 December. Having retained its independence as a religious organization, it now confronted the practical problem of seeing that its position as the representative of French Judaism would not be affected by a strong UGIF. It was therefore necessary for the Consistory to continue to participate in the general debate in order to exercise whatever influence possible so that the UGIF would be led by individuals willing to recognize its leading position. The Consistory, despite its protestations of opposition, came over to the view that given certain conditions collaboration with Vallat was acceptable. The CCOJA, representing all the Jewish organizations, was immediately affected and needed the Consistory's support in order to justify its actions, as it appeared likely that some of its members would accept nomination.

The meeting of both leaderships took place on 7 December 1941. The adopted resolution reflected their concern to show those who accepted Vallat's nomination where their responsibilities rested. The resolution was more like a plea than a clear and unequivocal statement of opposition:

> In the present circumstances and faced with the terms of the law of 29 November 1941, it is impossible for the committee members of the organizations to accept the functions of board members as stated in the articles 1 and 4 of the law [article 1 stated its representative character as well as its ambiguous aims and objectives; article 4 stated that the CGQJ was to nominate the board members, which made it impossible for the organizations to regard the proposed board as a representative body]. It therefore asks those invited by the General-Commissioner for Jewish Affairs to take these considerations into account.[59]

At the same meeting Oualid was instructed to prepare a note for Vallat stating the general position.

While the Consistory and the CCOJA were formulating their position in preparation for the meeting with Vallat, the Association des Rabbins Français was also in session seeking to forge its own policy. Although controlled and dominated by the Consistory, the relationship between the two bodies had not been fully harmonious since the June 1940 exodus. The general breakdown in communications and the dispersal of the Jewish population had resulted at first in the rabbis acting autonomously. Their day-to-day contacts with the Jewish refugees, particularly those in the Vichy concentration camps, had made them more responsive to the people's plight. The establishment of the CCOJA by the chief-rabbi and the active participation of the rabbinical corps in the various relief organizations had resulted in a greater affirmation of independence from the reconstituted Consistory. This was the reason Lambert, at the meeting of 3 December 1941, when attacked by the CCOJA for his single-handed negotiations with Vallat, attempted to gain support from the rabbinical corps by suggesting that one of their number be nominated to the board of UGIF.

The assembly of the Association des Rabbins Français of 7 December passed two resolutions referring to the debate over the UGIF. The resolution concerning the Solidarity Fund effectively placed a religious ban upon its use. The other resolution dealt with the issue of rabbinical representation on the board of the UGIF. But the authority of the Central Consistory over the rabbis' association was too strong for any expression of independence, and the assembly produced an ambiguous resolution which finally left the decision to the Consistory.[60]

Oualid's note, presented to Vallat at the 12 December 1941 meeting, was another significant landmark in the negotiations.[61] It was the swan song of French Judaism. Before the final capitulation the French Jews restated their fundamental objections, to make their capitulation appear honorable. Reaffirming its opposition to the law, French Judaism sought for the last time confirmation of a legal distinction between French and foreign Jews. It demanded that a special place be given to the Franco-Jewish organizations to acknowledge their leading role. Oualid's note, expressing the views of French Judaism, pleaded that the presidency of the UGIF be given to a president of a Franco-Jewish organization. Significantly, Oualid's note sought to have Lambert removed from the scene as one of the conditions of acceptance by demanding that the future general-secretary be nominated by the incoming board and be made a member of the board. This final attempt to extract some modifications of the UGIF did not blind Vallat to the underlying tenor of the note: it was not a collective rejection but an expression of acceptance on the part of those he had nominated, provided that he gave some assurances.

Sensing that the issue was about to be resolved, Vallat gave Oualid a formal assurance, given that the law could not be altered now, that he would never ask the board of the UGIF in the Vichy Zone to carry out any other functions than attending to the needs of the organizations they represented. Vallat finally promised Oualid and the other two representatives that in the event that the UGIF was requested to carry out orders they did not approve, the board members would be free to resign.[62]

From all appearances, Vallat and the leaders of French Jewry had entered into a "gentlemen's agreement." All that remained was for the delegates to obtain a letter from Vallat stating his assurances to take back to their organizations. But Vallat refused to write the letter. Instead he offered to accept from all those he had invited to join the board a statement of reservations on their part in their reply to the official invitation.[63]

The issue appeared resolved. Now each prospective board member was to decide his personal attitude and state the conditions under which he was prepared to accept his nomination. Vallat knew by then who would and who would not accept. Lambert, Millner, and Lévy had accepted, so had Robert Gamzon, the general commissioner of the Eclaireurs Israélites de France, who had been introduced to Vallat by Général Emile Lafont.[64] Those in favor of participating on the board on Vallat's terms had taken Lambert's view that with a little *sage diplomatie* and without prejudicial haste it would be possible to ensure that the UGIF retained its technical independence and each organization within it would retain its administrative autonomy.[65]

On 15 December 1941, the Consistory and the CCOJA met again to evaluate the result of the meeting with Vallat. They faced the problem of the drafting of a letter of acceptance. There was a general agreement to accept nomination, and the statement of reservations did not present any difficulties: the board members would engage only in relief work and refuse to act in a representative capacity; in no case would the board use the proceeds of the Solidarity Fund; membership dues would not be imposed as long as voluntary contributions sufficed; the general-secretary was not to be a board member; and the board members would not accept remuneration.[66]

Between 15 and 18 December 1941, eight persons had received Vallat's offer to sit on the board.[67] Vallat's invitation had not made any reference to the "gentlemen's agreement," however. Vallat's omission necessitated a redrafting of the letters of acceptance which had been approved by all.

On 22 December 1941, another meeting considered the new draft replies. Jarblum read out his own version, which was filled with so many reservations that it was tantamount to a refusal; Mayer refused the invitation on personal grounds but suggested someone else on his behalf; Olmer refused on the grounds of the principles of the law; Oualid rejected the offer unless Vallat gave the desired guarantees. Lévy, Gamzon, Millner, and Lambert were prepared to accept nomination, but, in solidarity with the other candidates offered to abide by a majority decision. It was unanimously decided that Vallat should be informed that his offer was conditionally rejected.[68]

It was then that the news of the German imposition of the billion-franc fine on the Jews of Occupied France became known. Those opposed to participation seized upon the most threatening aspect of the fine: the UGIF's responsibility for the collection of the fine. Indeed, the news resulted in an immediate hardening of positions among all the candidates: those opposed saw it as a confirmation of their fears; those in favor concluded that they could no longer postpone taking up their responsibilities. The fine created corresponding problems for the UGIF, and since the UGIF was a Vichy responsibility, it was up to Vichy to see that the UGIF carried out the order. It therefore became imperative, from Vallat's position, to have a UGIF board assume responsibility immediately.

On 30 December 1941, Lambert and Millner met Vallat to resolve the differences. Vallat, no longer able to wait, threatened: "I shall find eight margoulins [petty speculators] who shall accept." Pressed by the situation, Vallat finally sent word to the candidates confirming the gentlemen's agreement of 12 December.[69]

Vallat's confirmation of assurances, which were never officially recorded, failed to alter the position of those in opposition. They demanded that he confirm in writing the terms of the agreement, only then would they reconsider.[70] Furthermore, the imposition of the fine raised totally new questions.

The UGIF had been formed as a single organization, even though because of the German Occupation it was to operate as two distinctive branches. But how was the imposition of a fine upon one branch to affect the other? It raised anew the whole problem of responsibilities, individual and collective. Could the Vichy UGIF branch be compelled by the Vichy government to shoulder other impositions also? Candidates opposed to an unconditional acceptance of Vallat's offer raised these questions, while those in favor of accepting Vallat's terms believed certain objective factors as well as fundamental differences between Occupied France and Vichy had to be accepted. In the first place Vichy had not imposed the fine, nor had Vallat ever suggested that the UGIF in Vichy France would be made a party to German orders. But above all it was now urgent to act responsibly by ensuring that the Jewish organizations remained operative under their existing controls.[71]

By 5 January 1942, Vallat had decided not to persist with those who had expressed reservations, which he neither could nor wanted to placate. On 9 January, the *Journal Officiel* and the Parisian press published the names of the individuals who were to lead the UGIF in both zones. Vallat had found other individuals willing to accept his terms and thus completed the Southern Zone's board.[72]

In Paris, unlike in the Vichy Zone, no wide debate took place over the imposed representation. The experience of the establishment of the Coordination Committee had resulted in adoption by the leadership of a pragmatic approach to the questions that had troubled the southern leaders.

The Coordination Committee's activities continued but under a different name. Its domination by the same people with the same objectives meant that Vallat did not encounter any difficulties. Vallat had nominated the former leaders of the Coordination Committee to lead the UGIF. But if the fundamental issues of participation in an imposed body were not as broadly debated in Paris as in the Vichy Zone, the Parisian leadership did not remain passive either. Stora, an executive member of the Coordination Committee, stated:

> We held back our approval to participate to the UGIF until the very last moment. During the early part of the negotiations, we even presented a counterproposal in the form of an enlarged Coordination Committee in order that there be no counterpart in the other zone. But the MBF created it [UGIF] with the imposition of the billion franc fine and the government was compelled to legislate rapidly. Our names were in the press even before we ourselves were informed.[73]

The Paris Consistory, like its counterpart in the Vichy Zone, had conducted the negotiations with the CGQJ, with Edinger, Roger Olchanski, and Baur acting on its behalf.[74] Without doubt, the Paris leadership did hold back its agreement to participate in the new body until the very last minute. But at no stage were the problems viewed in the same manner in Paris as in the Vichy Zone. There had been no conflict of opinion among the leadership, nor had there been any conflict of personalities. In the first place, the fact that these leaders were in Occupied France, living under German rule, colored every aspect of their behavior on the question. Unlike those living under Vichy, the Parisian Jews could still believe that all antisemitic measures emanated from the Germans. And, to be placed under the direct control of Vichy seemed, if anything, a possible source of protection, for it introduced another element into the conflicts with the German authorities, and one that could prove a moderating force. They did not set much store by that possibility, however.

The evidence shows that the Parisian leadership had little confidence in Vichy's willingness to help. Except for matters affecting the French Jews, Vichy had so far refused even to discuss the question of mitigating some of the harsher laws. The decision in Paris not to make any difficulties for Vallat stemmed from the latest German measure taken against the Jewish population: the fine and the announcement that some Jews would be shot as hostages in reprisal for attacks on German army personnel. Baur, among others, was convinced that if the fine was not met, arrests and massive deportations to Eastern Europe would occur.[75] This fear thus precipitated the Parisian leadership's decision to take part in the UGIF.

The Paris negotiations with Vallat only involved leaders close to the Paris Consistory. Vallat, like the Germans, sought at first to deal with his peer group, those Jewish representatives who had standing in the community. Unlike in the Vichy Zone, the debate had been restricted to a narrow group of men and it had not been due solely to the absence of similar representative organizations such as the CCOJA. The Amelot Committee, which represented an equivalent representative opinion, was never consulted nor even informed of the developments of the negotiations with Vallat. The negotiators of the Coordination Committee had assumed responsibility on behalf of all the Jews, including the immigrants, not only because of Vallat's choice of Jewish negotiators, but because they believed that as French Jews they were better qualified.

Though the Amelot leadership had not been asked for its views, it made its own position known to the Coordination Commiteee leaders in Paris. Without ambiguity it declared that in the event that the Consistory decided to cooperate it would find in the FSJF "pas un homme, pas un sou," and, furthermore, immigrant public opinion would judge their behavior to be every bit as reprehensible as that of the two "pioneers."[76] Yet the French leadership in Paris, unlike in the Vichy Zone, needed to pacify immigrant organizations, however. The recent experience of the Coordination Committee could not be ignored.

As soon as a UGIF board for Paris was formed, it met representatives of the Amelot Committee. Baur informed them that the board would not interfere in their activities and that they could be assured of their independence. In the Vichy Zone, throughout the period of negotiations between Vallat and representatives of the Central Consistory the French Jews had never sought immigrants' opinion, nor did they solicit it later. The immigrant organizations, on their part, had refrained from advancing their own opinions.

After the SD had brought in the two Austrian Jews to control the Coordination Committee, Vallat had not met any difficulties in finding suitable people to head the UGIF in Paris. And because of the different political situation in the capital, the contact between the CGQJ and the Jewish leadership were much closer there than in the Vichy Zone. When Vallat decided that he needed to proceed with the law instituting the UGIF, he approached the Paris leadership and the Central Consistory leadership in Lyon simultaneously. He then also showed Baur the first draft of the articles of the law.[77]

The first meeting of the Paris UGIF board marked the beginning of a new phase in the relationship between the Jews of Paris and Vichy. Yet there were still echoes of the more hopeful past. At this meeting, on 11 January 1942, a letter of protest was sent to the CGQJ and to Pétain rejecting the moral exclusion of the French Jews from the nation. In what must appear in retrospect a desperate effort to maintain the position of the French Jews in respect of the law, the letter stated:

We accept—with goodwill and to the extent that we shall not have to relinquish our twin dignity of Frenchmen and as members of the Jewish faith—to act as intermediary between you and our companions in faith, compatriots or foreign. We take the liberty, however, as Frenchmen whose families had long since testified to it, to state that we shall never accept the principle that Frenchmen of the Jewish faith shall not belong to the nation.
  . . . Furthermore, however, we would like to bring to your attention that although you have nominated us, we have not received a mandate from our companions in faith, French or foreign, to represent them.[78]

Mandate or not, the board of the UGIF, by then, felt that it had no option but to accept the role thrust upon it.

Looking back on the whole process by which the UGIF was formed, it is clear that uncertainties grounded in fears dominated the debates. The purposely ambiguous character of the law establishing the UGIF only partly explains the conflicting attitudes that resulted. There was also a belief among some French Jews, just as among much of the French population, that Pétain would succeed in bringing peace and getting the Germans out of France. It was unthinkable to anyone, French Jews included, that Pétain would be associated with collaboration with Nazism. The Central Consistory, in spite of its close links with the French administration and with Pétain's Cabinet in particular, did not accurately assess the relation of forces operating within the Cabinet and Pétain's own position. Consequently there was a failure to understand Vichy's relationship to Nazi racism. Yet some evidence existed. Vichy's policy had consistently paralleled Germany's own racial legislation, and in the early days of the Occupation had been even harsher; Germany's own prewar anti-Jewish legislation had been too well known in France for the leaders of the Consistory not to have noticed the similarities.

Consideration of these important questions was complicated by concern about two other problems: what would be the fate of the Jewish institutions, and how could the material needs of the Jewish population be met. Again uncertainties and fears prevailed. These secondary problems began to assume a central position as the debates and negotiations developed. In the process of elaborating a viable strategy, these considerations, which should have been subordinated to the general problem of defining a policy designed for and adapted to the deteriorating situation, instead came to overshadow it. The approaches of those who favored participation for the sake of the institutions, and of those who opposed participation on nationalist grounds, proved unresponsive to that central need. A general strategy based on negotiations—which failed to take into account what had occurred until then and which concluded that negotiations were a viable course of action—was to be tested in practice by the UGIF.

Unfortunately, cutting across the debates and negotiations were many inner conflicts among leaders and organizations. Once imposed representation became inevitable, each organization sought a share of power. Thus at the crucial moment the Jewish leadership, far from facing the situation with a clear understanding of the stakes, found itself divided. The French Jews sought protection at the expense of the immigrants, personal ambition overrode the interests of the population, and rivalries and mistrust between organizations blocked the development of a unified response.

No one had considered the consequences of participating in such an organization or its effect on the overall need to prepare the Jewish community to cope with its uncertain future. There was no attempt to examine ways and means of supporting communal structures to oppose the new body and squarely place survival as the central task. In this respect assent to the establishment of the UGIF was a costly compromise.

For the Jews of France the situation early in 1942, though deteriorating, had not yet become unbearable. Internments had become common practice in both zones. A large impoverished population required communal assistance. The shooting of hostages (many of them Jews) by the Germans was becoming more frequent. The specter of deportation, however, had not yet begun to manifest itself. It was with this next stage in the Final Solution to the Jewish problem that organized responses began to assume communitywide dimensions.

Jacques Adler, far left, with his unit, December 1944.

Adler, front row, with the same unit, February 1945.

Jacques Adler, front row, second from the right.

Adler, back row, second from the left, with surviving members of his underground unit, August 1944.

III
THE FRANCO-JEWISH
RESPONSE

6

The UGIF and Its Functions:
January 1942 to December 1942

Regardless of Vichy's intentions in establishing the UGIF and the Jewish participants' motives for taking part, the UGIF was and remained a German creation, conceived as an essential agent in the administration of the Final Solution to the Jewish Question. In every European country the Germans had imposed a *Judenrat* as part of their Jewish policy. Dannecker was determined to follow this same procedure in France.[1]

The unique conditions in France were to make the imposed council there, the UGIF, singularly different from similar bodies already established in other conquered countries. What distinguished the UGIF was not the caliber of the people who assumed its leadership, but rather the nexus of political factors that influenced its intended role, and which in the final analysis saved the UGIF and its leaders from the fate similar "councils" suffered throughout Europe.

The political relationships between the Nazi department in charge of Jewish affairs, the German military administration, and Vichy were complex enough in themselves to be beyond the capacity of many a Jewish leader to correctly evaluate. But Vichy's own misleading attitude certainly helped spread confusion in the ranks of French Judaism. Vichy's predominantly xenophobic anti-Jewish policy lulled those leaders who assumed the responsibility of directing the UGIF into believing that the anti-foreigner component in Vichy's policy would suffice to protect the French Jews from the worst excesses of that policy. During the two and a half years of the existence of the official Jewish representation, organized Jewry pursued two parallel but distinctive lines of response: the French Jews through the UGIF and the immigrants through their own organizations. The following two chapters will examine the development, through the work of the UGIF, of the French Jews' response.

The sense of communal responsibility motivating those leaders who had agreed to head the UGIF in Paris was put to the test during the events of December 1941. A number of repressive measures were taken by the German authorities which, although directed at curbing the activities of the French

Resistance, primarily affected the Jews. Some 1,000 Jews, including 750 notables, were arrested. One hundred people were executed, 53 of whom were Jews.[2] The UGIF leaders had been made individually and collectively responsible for the payment of the billion-franc fine and had been warned that in the event of their failure to pay there would be public hangings of Jews. It had indeed required moral and physical courage to agree, under such conditions, to head the UGIF.[3]

It was under the shadow of these measures and threats that the UGIF leadership for Occupied France began its work. A board had been nominated by Vallat: some were former members of the Coordination Committee, others were new to it. From the nine members constituting the UGIF board, the effective leadership rested with André Baur, Marcel Stora, and Georges Edinger who had previously led the Coordination Committee. From the other six, only Albert Weill and Fernand Musnik were former members of the Coordination Committee, while Lucienne Scheid-Haas had acted as a legal adviser.

The remaining members, Juliette Stern, Dr. Benjamin Weill-Hallé, and Dr. Alfred Morali, had only recently agreed to participate. Baur, an intellectual, was from a banking family; Stora, experienced in administrative matters, had already proven himself by participating in the organization of the World Jewish Congress inaugural meeting of 1936; and Edinger, as a former company director, made a first-rate treasurer.

The newly constituted board's first step was to direct the transition of responsibility from the Coordination Committee to the UGIF. A new organization had to be created which would be subject, unlike the Coordination Committee, to French administrative control. This supervision was to be exercised under the overall management of the CGQJ by representatives of the Ministry of Finances which would control all its financial transactions. The UGIF board was also to create a centralized administration to meet the needs of the Jewish population.

The law creating the UGIF stated that all Jews would automatically become members and that all institutions and organizations and their assets would be transferred to it.[4] Its board set out to form the new organization within the terms of the law, and according to its own vision of what its function was to be. It chose to build on the premise that primarily it existed to protect and assist the French. Assistance to the foreign Jews was provided only because the law had so ordered. That approach proved to be politically unrealistic as well as particularly indifferent to the fate of the foreigners.

It became Edinger's responsibility to establish local UGIF branches throughout Occupied France wherever there were sizable communities. Local Consistories were approached in order to find suitable individuals to form committees. It was Edinger's view that these committees would need to have the support of the French Jews. Indeed it was not sufficient for him that they be led by French citizens, as the law required; he believed, above all, that the UGIF should "be solely led by French Jews."[5] Writing to a representative of the Rouen Consistory, Edinger expressed his views:

It appears to us that you are meeting in Rouen the same difficulties that we had earlier encountered in Paris. It appears however that it will be possible for you to gather a number of people of goodwill who will find support in the French elements of the population, and begin to react against the hostility of the foreign Jews who will constitute, it is quite certain, the majority of those who will appeal to you for assistance.[6]

From the very inception of the UGIF, its leaders assumed that the inevitable anti-Jewish measures would be directed mainly against the foreigners; more important, they feared that the foreign Jews were a political danger to the French Jews in that they might influence some French Jews against the UGIF and thereby erode the support they needed to be effective leaders.

These broad problems were partially eclipsed during the first few weeks of the UGIF's existence by the complexities of the issue of the fine. The German order was explicit: the fine was to be met in four installments, the first 250 million francs to be paid on 15 January 1942. No sooner had the UGIF been informed of the amount and the date than a German ordinance appeared which stated that the fine was to be raised from Jewish properties in the Occupied Zone.[7] For the UGIF leaders the gravity of the fine overshadowed all other considerations. The problem was that the UGIF, barely formed, had neither legal powers to compel the population to make contributions nor means of assessing how much each family could pay. It had access to neither frozen Jewish bank accounts nor the proceeds of sales of Jewish business which had already taken place.

The German ordinance, officially published on 17 December 1941, specified that the French authorities were responsible for ensuring that the UGIF assigned to each Jew his due share. Vichy thus became linked to the execution of the fine. Dr. Michel, chief of the economic administrative staff of the MBF, writing to the Ministry of Finances, indicated the various sources of funds available for the fine:

> Jewish possessions in the Occupied Zone may be used even if the Jews themselves are outside the Zone. Properties in the hands of the provisional administrators can also be used, but permission must first be obtained from the German authorities and Jewish assets presently in the Caisse des Dépots et Consignations are also available.[8]

Michel further informed Vichy that the following three installments were to be met on 10 February, 10 March, and 31 March 1942.[9]

The Paris UGIF leadership was powerless, at the mercy of both the Germans and Vichy. Vichy, however, also had a problem, essentially the same one it faced when the issue of appointing public administrators to Jewish properties arose in 1940: either to be a party to the spoliation or to leave the field wide open to indiscriminate German actions. Vichy decided to act. Two courses of action were available, to involve the Bank of France or to grant the UGIF permission to seek a loan through the commercial banking system. By 8 January Vichy had decided to allow the UGIF to go to the private market.[10] By 13 January the Comité d'Organisation Professionnelle des Banques advised Baur that, following a special Vichy law permitting the UGIF to borrow 250 million francs,[11] it had decided to organize a consortium of banks to float the loan; twenty-nine banks headed by the Banque Française d'Acceptation were prepared to participate.[12] Vichy had also taken a further step to ensure that the first installment be made, as demanded by the Germans, by 15 January: it ordered a massive sale of shares owned by Jews.[13] The UGIF leaders had no choice but to accept the arrangements made on their behalf. They had to take the loan, on any terms, and they could not refuse to allow Vichy to dispose of the privately owned shares. Collaterals for the loan were frozen bank accounts, properties under the control of appointed administrators, shares still held by banks, and proceeds of the forced sales of Jewish businesses made to date which were deposited at the Caisse des Dépôts et Consignations.

Although the UGIF was relieved by Vichy's intervention, there was still much to be feared. The amount outstanding, 750 million francs, still had to be raised, and as the UGIF was not privy to the amounts held in the various banks and at the Caisse it had cause to fear. Baur decided therefore to solicit assurances from the CGQJ that in the event of insufficient funds in the Caisse there would not be a further indiscriminate sale of assets. Vichy, unwilling to close down those Jewish enterprises still operating, assured Baur that the situation would not arise.[14]

When the second installment of 250 million francs came due on 10 February 1942, the UGIF was in the same situation as at the eve of the first payment: it was again at the mercy of Vichy policy. Baur had to write to Dannecker informing him that the UGIF had appealed to the CGQJ to obtain a new loan.[15] Once more the UGIF faced the question of further bank accounts indiscriminately drawn upon and more hasty sales of Jewish properties and enterprises. Vallat, however, informed Baur that the money would definitely be made available because Vichy was not in favor of the Germans helping themselves to Jewish properties.[16] The remaining 500 million francs were settled by the Bank of France which recovered its advances from the funds held at the Caisse and from individual bank accounts.[17]

The UGIF was concerned not only that the fine should be paid promptly, but also that an "equitable" distribution of the amount among the whole Jewish population should be achieved. However, neither the Germans nor the French were concerned with that aspect of the question. They made arbitrary deductions from some accounts. In principle, accounts holding between 10,-000 and 200,000 francs were reduced by 50 percent while accounts with balances exceeding 250,000 francs were reduced by 80 percent. In practice, in the haste to assemble the funds, there were indiscriminate withdrawals affecting some, leaving others untouched.[18] It remained beyond the UGIF leaders' power to judiciously apportion the fine. It was not until the fine was settled that the UGIF's leadership could effectively turn to internal problems and feel free of the fear of mass reprisals.[19] The uncertainty over how the fine would be met was typical of the problems confronted by the UGIF in all financial questions. It highlighted the impossibility of framing a long-term financial strategy while permanently exposed to both German measures and Vichy's ineffective and equally costly protection.

The law creating UGIF stated that its resources would originate from four sources: gifts, membership dues, the assets of integrated organizations, and the Solidarity Fund. The UGIF in Paris had officially taken over from the Coordination Committee on 15 January, and quite apart from the problem of the German fine, had faced an immediate financial crisis. No funds were at its disposal nor was it able to call immediately upon any of its possible financial sources. Since the only funds available were from the Solidarity Fund, Baur began to plead with Vallat for the necessary credits.[20] Vallat then recognized that given the practical impossibility of an immediate application of imposed dues upon the Jewish population the principle of advances from the Solidarity Fund would be CGQJ policy.[21]

The early financial policy of the UGIF was formulated on 29 January 1942, at a meeting of its financial commission, when it decided that "it was not in the interests of the UGIF to have at its disposal more funds than is necessary to meet monthly needs." The financial commission could have recommended that meanwhile the UGIF should use the cash reserves of some of the organizations that were now part of the UGIF but the commission chose to recommend that the cash reserves "be used with the greatest circumspection and only for the purposes specified by the original donors of these funds."[22] The implications of such a policy were clear: the assets of the Franco-Jewish organizations would only be used to help the French Jews; the immigrants would be assisted solely from whatever other funds were available.

Vallat's approval of the principle that the UGIF's main income would come from the Solidarity Fund did not mean that he would take immediate steps to place some of these funds at the disposal of the UGIF, however. During its first month of operation the UGIF was able to assist financially 618 families, but with no further funds at its disposal it was only able to provide for 248 families during February.[23] Such a critical situation led the UGIF to appeal to Dannecker in order to put pressure upon Vallat:

> Following Vallat's demand we have submitted a provisional budget, but Vallat has not so far informed us whether the budget has been approved or whether he will give us the necessary funds.[24]

The UGIF's financial problems were not due solely to Vallat's refusal to grant it the necessary credits, nor even to the inevitable problems arising from its recent establishment. The UGIF's financial crisis was complicated by the fact that Vallat was no longer acceptable to Dannecker. Vallat had outlived his usefulness: he had established the compulsory organization. Now another commissioner for Jewish affairs, far more aggressive in the application of anti-Jewish measures, was required.[25] The difficulties Vallat faced in Occupied France found their echoes in the Vichy Cabinet. His conflict with Dannecker was detrimental to Franco-German relationships; Vallat, as far as the Cabinet was concerned, had to be replaced.[26] Vallat's problems with Dannecker and with Vichy had resulted in the UGIF being the scapegoat: the Vichy Ministry of Finances meanwhile had held up the appointment of an auditor-accountant to supervise the UGIF's financial affairs. The news, early in March, that Vichy had appointed Maurice Couturier as auditor-accountant was received with relief by the UGIF.[27] It was not that the appointment of a public servant would resolve the problem, but at least he was not a political appointee. Indeed, there was cause for concern, for much of the flexibility in the uses of budgetary allocations would depend upon this financial controller. Couturier soon showed the UGIF leaders that he would not create any difficulties. In his first report on the UGIF's activities he strongly advised an urgent allocation of funds as the organization had been able to operate only by gifts and advances from the board members themselves.[28]

The temporary financial crisis did not keep the UGIF leadership from taking organizational steps. The old structures of the Coordination Committee, which had operated on a voluntary basis, and only in Paris, were no longer adequate. The law stated that the UGIF would not only absorb all the former organizations and institutions but that all Jews, as defined by the law, would automatically become members. A new organizational framework had to be created which would fulfill the conditions set by the law. Inevitably, the organizational structures inherited from the Coordination Committee formed the basis upon which the UGIF began recasting the organization.

The Coordination Committee, since its formation in January 1941, had grown, regardless of the intentions of its leaders, from a network of relief organizations into a complex structure. Its controlling bodies, the SD in particular, and the CGQJ to a lesser extent then, had seen to that. Dannecker's incessant demands for reports of activities, and especially his introduction into the leadership of Israelowicz and Biberstein, had resulted in greater control over the activities of the committee, and especially in formalizing that control by the establishment of a special department within the Coordination Committee responsible for permanent contact with the German authorities. Similarly, the frequent contacts with the Prefecture of Police arising from the unofficial but representational character of the committee over numerous problems affecting the Jewish population brought about the establishment of yet another department in the organization. Dannecker's order that the Coordination Committee be open to dues-paying members led to the establishment of a membership department. The appeal from Jewish internees for assistance in a camp near Poitiers led to the formation of a committee of assistance for internees.[29] The May 1941 internment of immigrants by the French authorities resulted in the establishment of a legal office to assist those for whom a case could be made for release. By June 1941, an official liaison with the Secours National was formed.[30] By then the general structures of the Coordination Committee were established: an executive body that was accredited with the authorities; an SD liaison, a CGQJ liaison; a Prefecture of Police liaison; accreditation with the Secours National; a membership department; a camp commission; a medical committee; a social welfare commission; a legal department; a bulletin committee; and a youth commission.

Dannecker was still not satisfied. By August 1941 the ACIP was told that it was to be represented on the Coordination Committee and furthermore that "no religious association would be permitted to function unless they recognized the authority of the ACIP in all religious questions." By the end of August twelve organizations were already affiliated with the Coordination Committee.[31] The arrests of August 1941, during which some of the Coordination Committee members found themselves in Drancy, led Dannecker to grant some of its leading personnel special protective passes.[32] On the eve of the transformation of the Coordination Committee into the UGIF, it already employed 140 people.[33] By November 1941 the general structures of a self-managing Jewish representation were set.

In the view of the Parisian leadership, the Vichy law that made the UGIF effective for the whole of France was only a change of label. It legalized the current situation by giving to the existing leadership the status resulting from Vichy recognition.[34] There was no need to introduce any major changes, but the executive set out to place the former voluntary organization on a firm administrative basis. Perceiving themselves as directing an autonomous, government-approved institution, the UGIF leaders set out to remodel the various commissions on the lines of the French public service. The executive introduced a code governing recruitment, promotions, salaries, and work discipline. It offered to its staff all the current benefits attached to the public service: paid holidays, social security, and family allowances.[35] This code, composed of fifteen paragraphs, expressed a confidence in the future quite unwarranted in view of the problems encountered so far by the Jewish population.

The UGIF leaders based the reforms of the former organizational structures on the principle of directorate responsibility. Groups were created and within each related departments were assembled: Group I included all general services; Group II, administration and finances; Group III, social services; Group IV, vocational training and youth activities; Group V, clinics and children's homes; Group VI, canteens and food supplies. This last group was for a time divided into two groups; Group VII was specifically responsible for supplies.

Group I, under Stora's responsibility, was the most important one. It included besides the general secretariat, personnel, the population card index, the legal department, dispatch of food supplies to the camp inmates, the *Bulletin de l'UGIF,* liaison with the Germans and the Prefecture of Police, the control commission, the administrative committee, and the administration of the UGIF's provincial committees. Group II was under Edinger's control. It dealt with finances, properties, and the financial aspect of supplies, as well as direct control over certain UGIF country offices: Seine-et-Oise, Lunéville, Nancy, Bordeaux, and Rouen. Group III, under Juliette Stern, attended to all departments dealing with social work, including employment centers, youth social welfare, children's homes in the provinces, isolated children, and those placed with foster parents. Group IV, led by Musnik, controlled all other activities dealing with youth, as well as OSE, ORT (Organisation pour la Reconstruction et le Travail) and the Jewish agricultural workers in the Ardennes. Group V, led by Weill-Hallé and Morali, attended to socio-medical services as well as five children's homes. Group VI was under Weill, who supervised all the canteens and the commission that controlled the stocks of food and equipment.

This presentation of the complex bureaucratic organization does not give a clear understanding of the functioning of the UGIF, however. A closer examination of this structure reveals that by the second half of 1942 there were forty-eight different departments.[36] Evidently, as an organization the UGIF was required by law to meet the needs of the Jewish population; but on the contrary, the archives of the UGIF indicate that despite the impressive number of departments, there was much that was illogical in the organization. The leadership's desire to maintain firm control led to confusion in the functioning of the organization. Each department was subject to a tripartite supervision: finances, supplies, and personnel. No independence of operation within departments was tolerated. Control commissions were constantly operating. Although there was, in the early period at any rate, a deliberate attempt at balancing controls with decentralization to minimize police interference, it is by the end product that the UGIF is to be evaluated, and not by its leaders' intentions or claims. If the French Jews who called upon the UGIF for help were given sympathetic consideration, the foreign Jews who called for assistance never found the kind of response they needed. Each demand for help was processed not according to its urgency but according to public service practices. The UGIF's social services, led by the same people who before the war directed the ACIP's philanthropic institutions, had found in the UGIF's administrative policy a familiar mode of operation.

Although by the end of January 1942 the issue of the payment of the billion-franc fine appeared about to be resolved and organizational structures were in the process of being established, the real task the UGIF leaders had set themselves when they agreed to be nominated by Vallat, to assist the poor, had yet to be tackled. The central problem was political: to win support from the Jewish population in order to meet the threat from without. To achieve that objective the UGIF leaders had to solve the material problems now faced increasingly by the French Jews, but they also had to win the trust of the immigrant organization: Amelot. The previous attempt by the French Jews to achieve an understanding with Amelot was short-lived. Amelot had refused to accept what the ACIP believed could not be avoided: Gestapo control. But the deterioration of the situation and the compulsory establishment of a central representation necessitated a reappraisal of earlier Franco-immigrant relations. On 28 January 1942, UGIF and Amelot representatives met.[37]

The UGIF leaders had called the meeting to resolve former differences and to establish a modus vivendi. Although Amelot was not prepared to give the UGIF its blessing, and certainly not its support, it was prepared to set aside its differences so that the UGIF could immediately work on relief activities. To show goodwill Amelot refrained from attacking the UGIF and the UGIF leaders promised Amelot that they would not impose controls or interfere with its activities. Central to the compromise for the UGIF was the desire to neutralize immigrant opposition and thereby gain a position of authority within the Jewish population. Amelot, on its part, was well aware that the UGIF could have forced it to become integrated into its organization. Amelot was therefore protecting its independence.

Two previous police measures contributed to the rapprochement. The UGIF had been informed by the Prefecture of Police that the French Red Cross would no longer be permitted to handle food parcels for the Drancy inmates. And, second, the Secours National supplies, which previously sustained Amelot's canteens, would be wholly allocated to the UGIF for internal distribution.[38] Neither the UGIF nor Amelot could afford to remain estranged. Amelot needed the supplies for its canteens and the UGIF was not yet ready to supply the Drancy inmates on its own, nor was it able to dispense with Amelot's canteens.

The overall strategy pursued by the UGIF during these early weeks had been to play for time and to seek support from any available source. From Vichy it had sought an immediate solution for payment of the fine; in its dealings with the Jewish population it had wooed the French by presenting itself as their organization and the immigrants by assuring them of continued friendly support. The test of that strategy in respect to the Jewish population itself resided in the UGIF's ability to justify its actions by positive results. It was in the area of relief that both the foreign and French Jews could be won over.

The camp population was the largest single group of people needing constant assistance. In January 1942 there were four major camps holding Jews: Pithiviers, Beaune-La-Rolande, Drancy, and Compiègne. Compiègne, where the French Jews last arrested were interned, had a distinct political status: it was directly under German control, unlike the others which were under French administration.[39] There were interned Communists, Resistance members, and after June 1941, Soviet citizens. The Jews were in a special compound. Conditions in the camp were particularly bad for the Jews whose rations were below subsistence level and the number of food parcels permitted was strictly limited. In the particularly harsh winter of 1941 the physical conditions of the men deteriorated further.

Drancy was a special camp. Originally a complex of municipal high-rise apartments built for low-income families, it was not yet completed when war broke out in September 1939. In June 1940 an unexpected use was found for it as a temporary camp for French and Allied prisoners of war until their transfers to *Stalags* (POW camps) in Germany.[40] "Drancy-la juive," as it was later called, was assigned a definite function in August 1941: it became the center for the deportation of Jews from the whole of France.[41]

However bad conditions were at Compiègne, Drancy was worse. Conditions were so grave that in October 1941 a German military commission, upon inspection, decided to order the release of 900 men.[42] The supplies sent by the Coordination Committee and Amelot were totally inadequate to meet the most minimal needs of the inmates. When, on Dannecker's orders, the French police stopped the French Red Cross from delivering these supplies, the UGIF became directly responsible for relief. This decision although innocuous in itself, marked the beginning of the UGIF's involvement with Drancy. As a consequence, the French camp commander, Lamant, informed the UGIF that it would have to attend to food supplies, that public welfare personnel would no longer be allowed into Drancy, and that the UGIF would need to supply nursing staff as well as medical supplies.[43]

The deportations of Jews from France began in March 1942 and the Germans applied the same techniques used in the rest of Europe, enlisting Jewish participation in the execution of the orders.[44] The organization of deportations required a central Jewish organization which was forced to make all the necessary preparations besides the actual transportation. In Eastern Europe, the *Judenräte* were made to deliver the required numbers for each transport. In France, however, the UGIF was never actually made to do so. The reasons are readily apparent. In the first place, the ghetto system, an important part of the deportation process, had not been introduced in France by the military authorities despite Gestapo attempts.[45] The resulting dispersion of the Jewish population made the internment a necessary transitional stage. This dispersion had also created problems for the police in the execution of the orders of internment. The limited Gestapo manpower in France, some 2,500 men, made the French police a major link in the whole process.[46] The UGIF was not yet ready to play the role Dannecker would have assigned to it when deportations from France began in March 1942. Its legal basis had barely been completed and it had just begun to be drawn into the concentration camp vortex.

Dannecker chose the issue of supplies for those about to be deported as the next stage in the UGIF's transformation. At the beginning of March, Dannecker ordered the UGIF to conduct home collections of shoes and blankets for 1,000 men.[47] The UGIF immediately perceived the special significance of the order. Yet, it was faced with a political and moral dilemma: it neither wished to collaborate in a police measure nor did it want these men to be deported without basic survival equipment.

While the UGIF leadership was not prepared to confront Dannecker with an outright refusal, it nevertheless decided to seek ways and means to avoid carrying out the order. To pacify Dannecker the UGIF launched a special appeal in its bulletin.[48] But meanwhile, Baur appealed to Colonel Chomel de Jarnieu, Vallat's director of Cabinet, for assistance on the ground that Dannecker's order was incompatible with the UGIF's charter. Jarnieu advised Baur not to comply as Dannecker did not possess the relevant authority to issue such an order.[49] The issue of supplies became the object of a CGQJ-Dannecker conflict. Jarnieu's advice to Baur had come at the time when Vallat himself was no longer allowed in the Occupied Zone and it is in that context that the CGQJ's defiance can be understood. Vallat was fighting for his political survival no less than objecting to a minor police officer such as Dannecker ordering a French-controlled body such as the UGIF without prior approval. The CGQJ's show of independence was immediately countered by Dannecker: Lionel Cabany, Vallat's chef de Cabinet for the Occupied Zone, was arrested by the Gestapo for failing to assist the UGIF in obtaining the goods.[50]

On 26 March 1942, Dannecker once more ordered the UGIF to comply with his order. Although Jarnieu was no longer allowed in Paris by the German authorities, Baur called once more upon the CGQJ for help to avoid carrying out the order:

> It appeared clear to us that this demand was incompatible with the social objectives of the UGIF, as defined by the law. . . . The discussions held with Jarnieu have confirmed our point of view. . . . We have been told . . . that the regulations governing requisitions, which have been established between the services of the MBF and the French authorities, do not permit us to give satisfaction to such a demand without written confirmation on the part of the relevant authorities. . . . A new demand has been made since Jarnieu's departure. . . . Do let me know, in all urgency what I am to do with this new demand.[51]

By 31 March the CGQJ officially informed the UGIF that Dannecker's order was to be complied with, and furthermore, that the UGIF would need to hold a constant reserve of material in readiness for any future demand.[52] The UGIF had not wanted to be involved in the deportation process or any activities connected with it, but its official status had forced it to cooperate with the Nazi measure. It had sought support from the CGQJ, and Vichy, and it had not been forthcoming.

Between the end of March and July 1942, Dannecker made repeated demands upon the UGIF for goods to equip the convoys of Jews leaving for Auschwitz. By 20 April, the UGIF informed Dannecker that it held a stock of equipment for 1,000 men.[53] By mid-May the UGIF was once more pressed to increase the size of its reserves. The UGIF's Supply Commission pleaded with the CGQJ for the allocation of the necessary credits as well as the purchasing orders for the rationed goods from the respective ministries. The UGIF was then trying to establish reserves sufficient for two months.[54] The CGQJ, under the newly appointed commissioner, Louis Darquier de Pellepoix, was not providing the necessary support. On 21 May, Marcel Lévy, head of the Supply Commission, reported back to the UGIF that the CGQJ had been in possession of a new demand from Dannecker since 6 May and had not even bothered to inform the UGIF. Dannecker, however, soon saw to that, and the CGQJ granted the UGIF the necessary credits.[55]

The UGIF's inability to build up the required stocks resulted in threats of reprisals. Dannecker decided to apply the well-tested Nazi principle—the *Führerprinzip*—whereby leaders are to set an example and be personally responsible for the fulfillment of orders. Each board member, each head of services, was ordered to deliver personally a complete set of the goods demanded. Baur was ordered to acknowledge, in writing having received such an order. Dannecker personally ensured that the CGQJ gave the UGIF the necessary purchasing orders to equip 1,500 people.[56] The UGIF, in the face of such firmness, complied. But the difficulties in obtaining the required goods, with or without orders, proved insurmountable.[57] By 15 June 1942, the UGIF had still not been able to locate firms holding such stocks. Four transports left Drancy, on 5, 22, 25, and 28 June, with 3,937 persons, only partially equipped.

Throughout that period from March onward, the UGIF found itself under constant pressure from Dannecker. Lengthy correspondence with the CGQJ and various French ministries show the extent to which the UGIF tried to fulfill Dannecker's orders. The political and moral dilemma involved in either agreeing to or refusing to comply with the orders could not be resolved. The UGIF had been drawn into the process of deportation and that process was beyond its control—5,000 people had been deported, more or less equipped, and paid for by the Jewish population. Fears for the safety of their own persons had combined with their sense of communal responsibility to make the UGIF an unwilling instrument, but an instrument nevertheless of German anti-Jewish policy.

After July 1942 the UGIF was required to supply goods on an industrial scale. These goods, ostensibly for Jewish deportees, eventually stocked Nazi relief stores. After July 1942 the deportations escalated. Between then and November 1942, 36,802 persons had left Drancy for Auschwitz.[58] The UGIF had to equip each man, woman, and child on these convoys from funds derived from the proceeds of the expropriation as well as from gifts collected from that population. Of these 36,802 people, over 24,000 were selected immediately upon arrival in Auschwitz for the gas chambers.[59] The clothing and equipment that accompanied each convoy were stored upon arrival in compounds commonly known among the camp population as "Canada." But these goods did not remain there, they were used by the German war relief organization to help German families in need.[60] From the beginning of July 1942, when mass deportation was placed on the agenda, the problems faced by the UGIF in meeting Dannecker's demands for supplies made the preceding three months' difficulties seem minute in comparison.

The political and police preparations for the deportations had begun in Paris during the second half of June, after Dannecker's return from a conference in Berlin. Eichmann had called a meeting of SD representatives from Western Europe to establish a timetable for implementing the Final Solution. A target of 100,000 people to be deported had been set for France, and Dannecker was responsible for its fulfillment.[61] Following Dannecker's return to Paris, a round of negotiations at the highest levels took place to prepare for execution of the measure.

The Germans, mindful of Vichy's desire to protect the French Jews, and to reduce the number of foreigners on French soil, advanced the proposition that foreign Jews from both zones should constitute the bulk of the numbers required and be supplemented by 40 percent of the Jews who had been naturalized since 1918. A compromise was reached with Laval giving approval to the principle and support for its execution, as long as naturalized Jews were not included.[62] The issue was resolved with the Germans conceding that they would not arrest naturalized Jews if Vichy supplied foreign Jews from its own territory. The French Jews had been saved but at the price of Vichy's cooperation in the application of the Final Solution in France: it was to provide manpower and the necessary administrative resources for the execution of the program. The original target of 100,000 was to have been of both sexes aged between sixteen and forty-five, and was to include only 10 percent unfit for work. Laval, desirous of making up the numbers solely from among the foreign Jews, had insisted that children be included with the spurious argument that families should not be separated.[63] Thus began the calvary of 4,000 children. This demand from Laval caught the German representatives in Paris by surprise and it took fourteen days for a reply to arrive from Eichmann: Berlin agreed to have them included in the transports for the sake of "keeping the families together."[64]

The preparations for this new round of internments and deportations first became known to the UGIF on 1 July 1942. It was then clear to the UGIF leadership that there was a direct relationship between the demands for stocks of supplies and deportations. On that day, the UGIF received a note from the CGQJ with a new demand:

> Such an eventuality [the need for supplies] is likely to repeat itself at very brief notice. . . . A great urgency must therefore be given by the UGIF to the immediate constitution of a stock of equipment which would meet the needs of about 7,000 people. . . . Given the difficulties in obtaining such equipment you are to take immediate steps in order to constitute such a stock from voluntary contributions by Jewish families.[65]

What was different about this demand was the magnitude of the order: equipment for 7,000 people. The very size of the demand, coming from the CGQJ and not from Dannecker, indicated that unusual measures were about to be taken: major, massive internments and deportations. The UGIF leadership, although it had already conceded that it had to comply with such orders, decided to seek clarification of the significance of this unusually large order. On 6 July, Baur replied to the CGQJ:

> We do not a priori refuse to ask, once more, that our co-religionists donate such articles. It seems to us, however, particularly dangerous to inform the Jewish population that it may expect a new and vast measure of deportation. It is not our function to spread panic by making known, even partially, the content of your letter, which we consider confidential. It is not possible however to appeal for donations without letting the population know the purpose of these articles. . . . This is a grave responsibility

which we cannot assume without asking for written approval from both you and the German authorities to disseminate such information. Furthermore home collections are forbidden by law and only the Secours National is empowered to do so.[66]

It had taken the UGIF board a full week to prepare its answer to the CGQJ's letter and within it are found all the contradictions faced by its leaders: the conflict between its functions as seen by Vichy and the Germans and its desire to assist the population; the moral dilemma in the execution of orders. If the UGIF took its time to elucidate the significance of the order, the CGQJ itself did not appear to be in any hurry to reply to the UGIF's letter. Another whole week passed before the answer came. It instructed the UGIF not to reveal any part of its original letter and, more particularly, not to mention the figure of 7,000 which "had only been advanced in order to fix the magnitude of the effort required. . . ."[67] The CGQJ had let the cat out of the bag and was trying to backtrack to allay the fears it had generated. It was during that period, between 1 July, when the UGIF received from the CGQJ the order to prepare massive stocks of equipment, and 16 July 1942, when the mass internments began, that the role and function of the UGIF must surely have become explicit to its leaders.

Remaining UGIF sources do not reveal whether during that period any meeting occurred between UGIF representatives and Dannecker or the CGQJ. Most likely Dannecker and the French police representatives were too busy putting the final touches to the technical preparations: availability of transport, establishment of lists of persons to be arrested according to nationality and places of residence, and the mobilization of the necessary police forces to carry out the projected mass arrests. But if no records are available of any official contacts between the UGIF and the authorities, two developments occurred which certainly revealed the imminence and grave character of what was soon to take place. On 6 July, the German authorities began issuing UGIF personnel with *cartes de légitimation*—official passes—certifying that the holder was a UGIF employee.[68] Each special pass granted the holder and his immediate family immunity from arrest and internment. The issue of such a document was novel. Until then these papers had only been the prerogative of UGIF leaders. Their sudden distribution to all employees, paid or voluntary, must surely have indicated to the UGIF leadership that the organization had acquired special importance.

The other development that must also have alerted the UGIF leadership was a demand by the CGQJ, on 8 July, to indicate the number of children that could be accommodated by the UGIF.[69] Baur informed the CGQJ that the UGIF held sufficient space for 300 beds and that a further 700 beds could become available if French and German authorities released Jewish-owned properties they presently occupied.[70] This demand for information, coming as it did in the wake of the earlier demand for large stocks of equipment and the issue of protective documents, certainly should have confirmed the scope of the planned operations. But even if doubts remained as to the magnitude of the measures, further evidence was at hand to fully confirm the worst fears. On 2 July, the Jewish camp leaders of Drancy had been told to make room for 3,000 new inmates: 2,000 men and 1,000 women. Furthermore, Beaune-La-Rolande and Pithiviers had been emptied of their Jewish inmates at the end of June when they had ben deported to Auschwitz.[71] By 9 July, therefore, the UGIF was in possession of sufficient evidence that large-scale internment and deportations were imminent.

What was done by the UGIF's leaders during these two critical weeks? No evidence has remained in the accessible archives about how the UGIF leadership viewed the mounting threat of massive internments or whether they devised a counter-strategy. We do know, from immigrant sources, that Baur and Stora met Amelot representatives on 13 July 1942, but no records remain of the discussions.[72] Jakoubowicz, the sole survivor of the then Amelot leadership, only recorded in his memoirs that Baur had offered to issue *cartes de légitimation* to Amelot's personnel.

Although no one knew officially when the arrests would take place, the Jewish population had already been alerted by numerous sources other than the UGIF.* The UGIF had not launched a comprehensive campaign of warning. It had not used its own wide network of institutions to disseminate the information. Until evidence to the contrary emerges we must assume that the UGIF leaders were aware that these measures would affect only the immigrants and were fearful of reprisals upon themselves and the French Jews if a leakage of information could be attributed to them. They were, however, men of conscience and thus decided, in extremis, at least to inform the Amelot leaders. Given that according to the original timetable the arrests were to begin on 13 July, it had indeed been a last-minute case of bad conscience.[73] As it happened the police operation had been delayed until 16 July in order to avoid massive arrests coinciding with the National Day, 14 July. The UGIF's last-minute move proved more valuable than intended, two days' grace had been won.

The UGIF leaders were not, however, callous. They did what they believed was the next best thing: they organized teams of social workers and medical services. The social workers were assigned to manufacture hundreds of name tags to be used for the children about to be arrested in the event of separation from their families. Doctors were kept ready to enter the precincts of the Vélodrome d'Hiver where those with families would be kept until directed to camps.[74]

At dawn on 16 July 1942, thousands of foreign Jews were arrested regardless of their physical condition. Claude Lévy and Paul Tillard have described the preparations and execution of the most massive police operation ever undertaken in Paris against any group of civilians.[75] They have drawn on numerous reports from eyewitnesses and underground organizations describing the barbarous conditions under which the orders of arrest were executed by the French police. Some 12,884 Jews were arrested. Those with families, more than 8,000, were directed to the Vélodrome d'Hiver. Baur,

---

* This question will be discussed in Chapter 8.

during a visit, was revolted at the conditions under which these poor people were held. For five days they were locked up without water or food, save some biscuits from Quakers, in a totally enclosed precinct where the temperature never fell below 100 degrees Farenheit and there were no adequate toilet facilities.[76] Then the men were sent to Drancy and the women and children transferred to Beaune-La-Rolande and Pithiviers.

The fate of the children was sealed on 20 July 1942, when Eichmann informed Dannecker that they would also be deported.[77] The earlier deportation orders which had not included children meant that mothers were separated from them and sent on to Drancy to fill the convoys. According to one source, "tragic and revolting scenes have taken place when mothers were separated . . . the gendarmes used bludgeons to force the separations and did not spare the children."[78] With each departing convoy the number of children left on their own in the camps grew. Their number reached 4,000 by mid-August, when their own deportation came. The first convoy for Auschwitz to include children under the age of twelve left Drancy on 14 August 1942; from a total of 991, more than 100 were under the age of sixteen. The following four convoys were to include some 500 children each.[79]

The massive arrests and deportations created immediate problems for the UGIF's relief departments. Considering itself to be a first aid organization, it set out to dispense that aid. The helpless children became the focus of a major campaign of rescue. Some, either French-born or naturalized, were likely to be released if application was made. Then there were the children left behind by their parents as they were arrested; these children needed immediate help. The first issue of the *Bulletin d'Information de l'UGIF* that appeared after 16 July contained an appeal asking for the names and the whereabouts of such children. But the plight of those who had been arrested with their families was the most serious of all. In the case of those who were French, parents' consent was necessary in order for the UGIF to apply to the authorities for their release. The parents had to agree to allow the UGIF to become the child's guardian, but many refused to separate themselves from their children. And then the UGIF faced the problem of housing them: it only had accommodation for 400.[80] The solution was to farm them out to foster parents or foster homes. Between July and November 1942, 1,080 children had been placed by the UGIF.[81]

The UGIF became the guardian, with SD consent, of some of the children who were released from Drancy. These children were referred to as *enfants bloqués*—controlled children—that is, they were only temporarily free and their names were recorded in special police registers. The UGIF housed them with orphans and other children whose parents though still free had left them in the UGIF's care. At the time there seemed to be sound psychological reasons for this procedure: after the trauma they had undergone a stable environment would help them readjust. At the end of 1942 the UGIF operated seven such homes which housed 386 children, free and controlled.[82]

The problem faced by the UGIF of how best to care for children, under the prevailing conditions, was bound up with political considerations. In the first place, it was UGIF policy that at no stage should the UGIF be found engaged in any practices that would jeopardize the authorities' confidence. The implications of this policy for the children in UGIF's homes were serious; lodged in residences whose addresses were known to the police the children were permanently exposed to the consequences of arbitrary arrest. The other assumption shared by the UGIF leaders was that the Jewish children should be given a Jewish environment and education. The consequence of this policy was that Jewish children were not usually placed with Christian families or in Christian institutions for fear that they would be exposed to the danger of conversion. Either as members of the Paris Consistory or because of personal conviction, the UGIF leaders in Paris were unanimous in the view that Judaism needed to be sustained. Wartime conditions had reinforced such views. Some of the UGIF leaders were connected with Zionist projects. Baur, although president of the Union Libérale Israélite, was the former president of Keren Kayemet which financed the purchase of land in Palestine for Jewish settlers; Dr. Weill-Hallé was the former president of Kerem Hayesod, a fund (for agricultural development in Palestine) to financially assist Jewish settlers in Palestine; Juliette Stern was the secretary of WIZO—Women's International Zionist Organization; Fernand Musnik had been a member of the Federation of French Zionist Youth Organizations.[83] Although Zionist ideas and French Judaism were at variance on most issues they concurred on a youth policy: the future of Judaism had to be secured. Such a policy expressed itself in every aspect of youth activities. In the Jewish trade schools, for instance, Jewish youths were directed to occupations equipping them to take their place in the Jewish national home to be in Palestine.[84] Such a policy was also supported by the Consistory although it was opposed to the very principle of Zionism. But French Judaism also supported Vichy's policy of a "return to the soil." The leaders of ORT felt that support for such a policy would

> allow Jews to fulfill their legal obligations to work and lead to a structural reform of the Jews' traditional professional occupation and [contribute] to the economy of the country [France]. The Jews affected by this plan must understand that it is their personal interest and must accept their responsibilities to the country which feeds them.[85]

The UGIF's policy toward youth was characterized by the need to find solutions consistent with its own philosophy in the face of the ongoing anti-Jewish legislation. It was during 1942 that general access to tertiary education was blocked to all those who could not benefit from parental derogation, but primary, secondary, and technical education was open to all Jewish youth. But whereas before the war there existed a Jewish educational system, the German occupation had restricted it to trade schools. The Coordination Committee and later the UGIF gave ORT, which specialized in technical education, the necessary support. The ORT schools had reopened their doors in October 1940 and continued to function. In July 1942 its student population numbered 374, but by October 1942, at the eve of the new academic year, only 285 of the former students reenrolled. Of a new contingent of 300 students, only 52 presented themselves at the beginning of class.[86] The fall in attendance was due to continuous arrests and the flight of families from Paris rather from the lack of support. The UGIF was, however, determined to sustain any youth establishment that would offer opportunities for an avowedly Jewish education. Throughout the war ORT schools received the necessary funding. The same principle of giving support to Jewish education led the UGIF to maintain a number of other youth centers. Besides four trade schools, by the end of 1943 the UGIF managed six children's homes, an orphanage, a girls' boarding school, a day center, and three youth clubs.

The management of the children's homes presented constant problems to the UGIF. Some had to be moved because of their proximity to bombing targets. Others became overpopulated and were moved to more spacious premises. The constant reorganizations that characterized their existence, as well as the background of the children residing in the homes, inevitably brought disruption. Some of the children had spent time at Drancy after having witnessed their families' deportation. Others had been separated from their families who had been arrested while attempting to cross into the Vichy Zone. Over and above these difficulties the UGIF also had to overcome problems arising from the constant fluctuations in the number of children in the homes. Families who had entrusted their children to the UGIF would reclaim them, while other children who were allowed out would fall victim to arrests in the streets or simply fail to return.

One group of children presented special problems: those children entrusted to the UGIF by families who had been deported and had themselves spent time in camp. Their release from camp had been due to the UGIF's having assumed direct responsibility. These children were under a permanent regimen. None were allowed out of the homes unless escorted. The escorts themselves had to enter their names and identity card number in a special register and assume direct responsibility for the children's return.[87] These children, although no longer in camp and subject to the ever-present danger of being placed on a deportation list, nevertheless lived under the constant threat of being taken back to Drancy. They were one step away from freedom but yet not free.

The events of July 1942 had not only brought about a totally new appreciation of the situation within the Jewish population but had also resulted in a newly found support in the Christian churches. The indiscriminate arrests in Paris of the sick and the old, of women and children in particular, had generated a movement of sympathy extending from the parish priest to the higher clergy. Catholic and Protestant clergymen alike condemned the mass arrests. This new development held out much hope for the persecuted immigrant Jews. Cardinal Emmanuel Suhard of Paris appealed to Pétain and Laval about the treatment of the Jews. In the Vichy Zone, Marc Boegner, on behalf of the Protestant Church, was even more outspoken in his criticism of the role of the French administration.[88]

This new development offered unprecedented possibilities to protect the children. In the Vichy Zone the Central Consistory had reached an under-standing with the Amitié Chrétienne—Christian Friendship—on the issue of their protection. Amitié Chrétienne, a recently formed committee of Christian laity and clergymen, was already well known to Jewish organizations. Two factors had influenced French Judaism to enter into a dialogue with the Amitié Chrétienne: the establishment of the UGIF meant the Central Consistory was no longer allowed to conduct charity work, and an increasing number of children needed immediate help. The Amitié Chrétienne appeared to be the most suitable channel for the use of Consistory resources. The problem that needed to be resolved, from the Central Consistory's point of view, was the issue of proselytizing. The two organizations entered into a secret formal agreement with guarantees given on both sides, thus opening new possibilities for the protection of a large number of threatened children.[89]

Robert Debré, a leading French pediatrician who was actively involved in the protection of children, and who was closely connected with the Amitié Chrétienne and the Jewish organizations, felt that "the official leaders of the Jewish organizations were at times timorous, fearing for themselves and of ul-terior conversions to which the children entrusted to Christian institutions may be attracted."[90] This central concern was one of the major factors that hampered a large-scale campaign for the defense of the young. The UGIF leadership in Paris never actively sought to take advantage of such a line of rescue. It chose to maintain those children who were not directly entrusted to it by the Germans at addresses known to the authorities. But then, until the end of 1942, the UGIF leadership although under constant pressure had not yet accepted that the internment and deportation measures would also extend to the French Jews.

The UGIF leadership's view of its place in the defense of the Jewish pop-ulation, which proved to be its Achilles' heel, was never more clear than in its relation to the question of deportation and the immigrant Jews. When depor-tations began in June 1942 the UGIF leaders had believed that it was a ques-tion of population resettlement. Already by November 1941 news items had appeared in the Vichy press to the effect that the Germans had established "experimental villages" for Jews in Poland.[91] Such news items, when viewed in the context of the economic difficulties faced by Vichy and the general pol-icy toward the foreign work force, views also shared by the Central Consis-tory, led to the acceptance of the idea that foreigners, and Jews in particular, should return to their country of origin.

When in December 1941 the German authorities announced that "1,000 Judeo-Bolsheviks" would be deported for hard labor, the UGIF leaders had not seen the measure as related to this same question. The UGIF certainly did not believe that French and immigrant Jews would be treated as a single group. The departure, in March 1942, of the first group of Jews had drawn attention to Auschwitz as a "work camp," and not to resettlement villages.[92] The UGIF attempted to obtain information on conditions in Auschwitz but without success.[93] The world of concentration camps was closed to all out-siders and neither the International Red Cross nor the International League of Red Cross Societies could gain access to it.[94] The UGIF therefore took the view that there existed in Eastern Europe camps for Jews similar to camps for prisoners of war, where inmates were made to work, and also general areas of resettlement for Jews. This was the UGIF's view as to the fate of those deported up to June 1942.

Difficult though it may be to understand, given hindsight, even the subsequent mass deportations that began on 17 July 1942, and that included women, unfit people, and later very young children separated from their families, do not seem to have evoked in the UGIF leadership serious concern about the real meaning of "labor camps" or "experimental villages." The UGIF leadership did not appear to be sufficiently moved by a crisis of conscience to reconsider its basic aims, which because they had so narrowly defined them, in the end resulted in compliance with demands from the authorities. Though moved by the hardship faced by their foreign coreligionists, the UGIF leaders from Paris could write to Pétain to thank him for the protection afforded to the French Jews, making no mention of the heart-breaking sights of the thousands of Jewish children being searched by French police in the most brutal fashion before boarding the cattle trains that took them to Auschwitz.[95]

Although during the first six months of the UGIF's existence increasingly repressive anti-Jewish policies were set into motion, the UGIF's broad policy, which could have been expected to be influenced by these developments, remained constant. Its leadership concentrated efforts upon relief activities, consistently keeping a low political profile and decidedly avoiding any steps that could be construed as opposing current anti-Jewish policies.

The UGIF had begun the year of 1942 with 618 social cases on its files, and with each passing month the number of families it assisted grew. By the end of June 1942 it was helping 8,235 families. The July 1942 arrests immediately reduced their numbers. By the end of July the number of recipients had fallen to 5,506. The internments as well as the flight of many to the Vichy Zone drastically affected the numbers during the coming months; during August they fell to 5,293 but by the end of 1942 they had once more climbed to 6,961.[96] Their number never again reached the pre-July 1942 figures.

By the end of 1942, almost 42,000 Jews had been deported.[97] A limited number of French Jews had also fallen victim, either as the hostages arrested during December 1941, or for having disobeyed anti-Jewish proscriptions. The main thrust of the UGIF relief work was directed at helping the immigrants. The arrests of such a large number of people resulted in a growth of UGIF administrative activities. The continuous internments, together with the special protection that allowed some Jews the possibility of release from Drancy, led to numerous calls upon the UGIF for intervention with the German authorities.

Department 14, which was responsible for representation to the Germans, became the most important office in the organization. Headed by Israelowicz, it prepared all submissions to the SD. As a liaison bureau, besides regularly reporting on the UGIF it also transmitted SD orders. The activities of this department extended to all matters of interpretation or appeal of anti-Jewish laws and their application. It submitted demands for liberalization of laws regarding the use of telephones, bicycles, travel permits outside Paris, and the easing of restricted shopping hours in particular cases. Its functions were so wide and all-inclusive that no major decision could be taken by the UGIF without first submitting it through Department 14 to the SD. It was the instrument that permitted the SD to control the UGIF's activities.

The problems faced by the UGIF leaders were to ensure that this controlling organism was kept at bay, that administrative cooperation, that is, the execution of orders, did not become collaboration, a distinction that was not always easy to maintain. Therein rested the UGIF's major dilemma. It was not always clear where collaboration stopped or began. Seemingly innocuous orders could easily become traps from which the UGIF could not extricate itself. Nevertheless, until the end of 1942, this passive cooperation, the more or less partial fulfillment of orders transmitted by Israelowicz, had led to few prolonged dilemmas. The UGIF's attempt to refuse to equip the convoys of deportees was easily overcome by the SD. In any event the UGIF leaders never judged this issue in terms other than as a moral question, and never saw that a decision to fulfill the order could prove injurious to the Jewish population.

In spite of the risks involved in working so closely with the German authorities, the activities of Department 14 were important insofar as they gained improvements in conditions or achieved liberation from internment for some: the department contributed to improving the UGIF's public image. And it was in securing releases from internment that Department 14 proved most successful. Between June and December 1942, 4,487 persons applied to the department for help in submitting applications for release from internment; of these, 817 applications were granted. That figure included 192 children, 76 persons over the age of seventy and 19 women due to give birth.[98] This result was positive in human terms, but it must be seen in perspective with the actual conditions too. The SD could afford to let some go, believing that sooner or later they would fall back into the net. Moreover, they were an insignificant number compared to the 41,951 who had been deported.[99] Many of those released were later rearrested and subsequently deported.[100]

Nevertheless Department 14 was important to the UGIF, for it helped sustain hope that release was possible. Alas, it was a false and dangerous hope, since in fact the total deportation of the Jews was German policy. By holding out false hopes, the UGIF was in the invidious position of contributing to the war of nerves to which the Jews of Paris were subjected. Even hope became demoralizing when it was shown to be ill-founded.

Of the two UGIF boards it was the Paris board which, during the second half of 1942, carried the heaviest burden and responsibility, and with infinitely less resources. Not only did Paris have to cater to more impoverished masses, it also had to bear the full cost of deportations. Arrested Jews from the Vichy Zone had begun arriving at Drancy in August and the UGIF in Paris had to meet the cost of maintaining them in the camp as well as their material preparation for deportation. The UGIF-South had both greater resources of its own and access to funds not available to Paris. It was therefore inevitable that sooner or later Paris would demand that the UGIF-South help defray the financial burden created by the arrival of Jews from their zone.

The Vichy law of 28 August 1942 brought to a head the whole issue of financing the UGIF and revealed the differences between the northern and southern leaderships.[101] The law that established the UGIF had set out the financial sources available to the UGIF, but until August 1942 the CGQJ had not given the problem the necessary attention. The reasons are clear. The crisis caused by the German refusal to deal with Vallat, soon followed by the appointment of Darquier de Pellepoix, resulted in a temporary lapse of attention to the question on the part of the CGQJ. No sooner were these internal problems resolved than the CGQJ became involved with the preparations of the July 1942 mass deportations. But then, although Vallat himself is not re-puted to have been a minister with any particular administrative skills, Darquier de Pellepoix was only known for the street brawler that he was, and for his rabid antisemitism. The UGIF's capacity to operate even within the terms of the law was only of limited interest to either of them. The UGIF leadership itself never pressed the question either, although its relief activities were consistently impaired by the lack of funds. The UGIF leaders feared any and all solutions that would originate from either the Germans or Vichy.

By August 1942, Darquier de Pellepoix was ready to address himself to the question of finances. The UGIF's monthly requirements had, more or less, stabilized, and it had become possible to establish the magnitude of the sums that would be needed to meet communal needs. The law of 28 August ordered the UGIF to raise the sum of 6 million francs per month from the resources of the Jewish families for the whole of France. If this amount could not be raised by voluntary contributions, the UGIF was to recommend an appropriate taxation measure.

This latest law, imposed on the UGIF as a whole, required, if it was to be satisfactorily resolved, a combined meeting between the two UGIF boards. The Paris leadership acted accordingly. The urgency of such a meeting was further emphasized by the CGQJ order that the first 6 million francs be paid into a special account by the end of September 1942.[102] Couturier, the financial controller, informed the UGIF's financial commission that it was CGQJ policy that the UGIF of the Occupied Zone should raise its own share of 3 million francs by gifts or imposed dues.

The UGIF's Paris leadership formulated its position at a special meeting and concluded:

> We cannot oppose the demand but it is necessary that we do all that is possible in order to avoid exposing our co-religionists of the Vichy Zone to the extreme measures which have not yet affected them such as the freezing of their funds.[103]

The Paris board saw serious difficulties in the execution of the law and Baur set out to present them to Couturier. One of the difficulties, Baur pointed out, was to define what the law meant by "resources" upon which the 6 million francs were to be raised. To Couturier's reply that it was the product of capital, Baur argued that if the Jews were to be assessed upon this basis the law was unworkable as no Jew in the Occupied Zone could be said to still have an income. The UGIF, however, was compelled to advance propositions in its reply to the CGQJ as a basis for negotiations. It therefore offered a scheme which while meeting the CGQJ's demand would also benefit some individual Jews:

(1) a flat tax of 120 francs for each adult over the age of eighteen in the Occupied Zone; (2) a 5 percent surcharge with each banking transaction; (3) access to be granted to those bank accounts which have been totally frozen when current accounts are no longer in credit; (4) in the event of these measures failing to generate sufficient funds that the UGIF in the Occupied Zone be permitted to seek a short-term loan.

In conclusion to these proposals, designed as a basis for discussion, Baur appealed for permission to convene a combined board meeting, north and south, in order to collectively arrive at a solution that could be effectively applied nationally.[104]

On 23 September 1942, the CGQJ informed Baur that it rejected his proposals and castigated him for failing to resolve the question. In order to force the UGIF to assume responsibility for formulating an acceptable scheme the CGQJ decided to take a punitive measure. The CGQJ informed Baur that it had decided to introduce cuts in the relief credits for the remaining four months and to transfer the available funds to general reserves for equipment purchases.[105] Clearly, such a move did not constitute a solution to the financial problem nor could it be interpreted as a basis for negotiations.

Such an attitude on the part of the CGQJ left the onus on the UGIF to resolve the practical application of the August law. Unable to draw the CGQJ into negotiations and unwilling to assume the responsibility for committing the whole of the UGIF to a specific course of action, the UGIF leadership in Paris had no other recourse but to persist with its demand for facilities to hold a combined meeting. Once more, in October 1942, Paris applied to the CGQJ for permission. This time, however, the CGQJ informed Baur that the SD had granted approval on the condition that the meeting be held in the Occupied Zone.[106] In order to facilitate the meeting, the SD was prepared to grant the southern delegates immunity from all current legislation affecting the Jews in the Occupied Zone. But the southern leadership had already informed Baur that it would not attend such a meeting in the Occupied Zone.[107] The SD even suggested that they meet at a border town, but the UGIF-South remained adamant.[108] The occupation of the Vichy Zone by the Wehrmacht in November 1942, following the landing of the Allied armies in North Africa, had altered the situation. Yet, although the Germans were now in the Vichy Zone, the UGIF-South still refused to alter its decision.

During this same period a new crisis began to loom for the UGIF. It was during November 1942 that the UGIF's foreign employees emerged as a problem for the organization, when Baur had been ordered by Röthke to dismiss a number of them.[109] It certainly must have been clear to the UGIF leadership in Paris that these employees would, at best, lose their special protected status, and, at worst, their freedom. A situation was developing, although at this stage it only affected the immigrants, which in fact threatened the protected nature of the organization as a whole.

The UGIF's first year of operation in Paris was drawing to a close, and it was ending on no happier a note than when it began. The UGIF faced financial problems that could only be resolved by further aggravating the Jewish population's material conditions. The order to dismiss foreign employees did not augur well, for in the long run it threatened the French employees as well. The first year of operation had been a succession of crises, each more serious than the last. The UGIF leadership had negotiated, made some compromises, given in on some issues in the belief that it was helping the Jewish population, if not directly at least by protecting it from even worse measures. But none of those dilatory tactics gained more than what the Germans were prepared to grant. Viewed from the immediacy of the need to overcome each crisis as it occurred, the UGIF leaders did what they believed was best. But in terms of a long-term strategy their judgment was flawed, not because they held any illusions about the Nazis, but because through their participation in the imposed representation, a Nazi creation became workable. It was from 1943 onward that the internal contradictions besetting the UGIF emerged.

7

The UGIF in Conflict:
January 1943 to August 1944

The year 1942 had seen the mass deportation of the foreign Jews in Paris. The deportations from France continued during the following two years, but they were no longer characterized by such a hecatomb. Never again were Jews deported in such large numbers in such a brief span of time from France. Yet January 1943 until the Liberation in August 1944 proved, in retrospect, far more difficult years for the remaining Jewish population of Paris. Mass arrests were no longer conducted in Paris on the same scale of July 1942, but this was not the result of any change of policy on the part of the Germans nor did it indicate a refusal by Vichy to collaborate in arrests. Pressure on Parisian Jewry was less devastating because the German authorities concerned with the application of the Final Solution in France were redirecting their efforts to the Jewish population in the former Vichy Zone, which the Wehrmacht had occupied in November 1942. Certainly arrests, internments, and deportations still continued in Paris, but the Jews of Paris had by then shed any illusion of security. Large numbers of the foreign Jews began to flee the capital. The French Jews, no longer confident of Vichy's protection, also took measures to secure themselves, and the holders of various protective devices learned the limited value of such protection. Of all French cities, Paris, until Liberation, continued to hold the largest number of Jews despite the thousands who had escaped and sought safety elsewhere or had hidden themselves.

The UGIF, representing that population's sole official source of support and assistance, occupied a central place in the Jews' struggle for survival. The UGIF continued to deal with the Gestapo and the CGQJ. It continued to believe in the importance of what it was doing; it refused to face the increasingly serious question of whether it was, by its relief activities, merely keeping the Jewish population alive and its whereabouts recorded until the SD decided its fate.

The last deportation of 1942, convoy number 45, took place on 11 November. It was the smallest ever recorded, only 745 people. Deportable Jews were becoming increasingly difficult to find in Paris and this figure of 745 had been reached only because the Gestapo had resorted to selecting deportees from the old people's homes run by the UGIF. It was a pathetic convoy: there were 74 children under the age of fourteen, and 129 men and women over fifty. Only 2 men survived and returned to France after the war; 599 were immediately gassed upon arrival in Auschwitz. After November the deportations ceased for a while, due to the protests of the French churches, though the requirements of the German army's winter offensive on the Russian front may well have contributed.[1]

The difficulties encountered by the SD in assembling the necessary numbers to fill the convoys had a direct effect upon the UGIF itself. The SD began to consider a new policy in respect to the personnel the UGIF was permitted to employ, which would lead to the dismissal of immigrants and thereby make available a new contingent of deportable Jews. A minor question from the SD's point of view, it brought the UGIF leadership in Paris to the brink of collective resignation.

On 30 September 1942, Lambert, the UGIF's general-secretary, informed all regional offices in the Southern Zone that the foreign employees would have to be dismissed. Although no records of this order exist in the UGIF's archives, it was surely the object of negotiations between the UGIF leadership and the SD, for Baur and Röthke had agreed in November to dismiss fourteen immigrant Jews.[2] But the UGIF board in Paris, it would seem, was satisfied with the outcome of the discussions with Röthke as no reference to its implications was recorded in the board minutes at the time.

The Paris UGIF board's lack of interest in the question has its antecedents in part in the law that established the UGIF. Article 4 stated that it would be led by French Jews. Vallat himself, when considering candidates for the board, even felt it necessary to reject naturalized Jews: UGIF leaders had to be of French ancestry. Furthermore, the view that the UGIF was primarily conceived as representing French Jews was held by such individuals as Edinger; such a view was widely shared by the Paris Consistory members, for these views corresponded to a particular brand of xenophobia that prevailed in its ranks. Chief-Rabbi Paul Hagenauer, who subsequently died in deportation,[3] expressed this to Baur on the issue of the Yiddish supplement to the *Bulletin d'Information de l'UGIF:*

> I must say that the Judeo-German insert . . . displeases me even more than my faithfuls. I cannot but think that all our miseries come from bodies, newspapers and journals which our foreign co-religionists have introduced in France since the Armistice [1918]. It is an error which we must not perpetuate.[4]

Similar attitudes existed within the UGIF administration itself and continued to manifest themselves despite the tragedy that had befallen the immigrants. These views found their worst expression in March 1943 when, following anonymous complaints about a Jewish firm of undertakers, a UGIF control commission concluded its examination by stating,

It is regrettable that this firm has been allowed to function; it would be of interest to all *Israélites* to see to the closure of this kind of establishment whose owners do not even speak French.[5]

The existence of such a body of opinion in the UGIF in Paris, however, was never permitted by Baur to become UGIF policy or to influence policies.[6] Still, the foreign employees were second-class citizens in the organization: the law ensured that they could not sit on the board and were merely tolerated.

The presence of immigrants on the various committees dated back to the days of the Coordination Committee. Dannecker, anxious to have a Jewish body whose authority no Jew would dispute, had insisted that there be an equal representation. But even then, despite orders to the contrary, a Franco-Jewish majority had dominated the organization. By the time the UGIF was formed, in January 1942, foreign employees were 30 percent of the total of the staff.[7] The earlier marked French prominence, particularly at management level, had not been due so much to directives from Vichy as to internments of foreigners, but it also arose from immigrants fleeing Paris and their general opposition to the organization. Albert Lévy, the UGIF national president, received from the CGQJ on 22 October 1942, the definite order that the UGIF be wholly French.[8] The UGIF leaders in the Vichy Zone were not really surprised. Indeed, given that Vichy had always sought to distinguish between French and foreign Jews, such an order appeared consistent with Vichy policy. Although it was a CGQJ initiative, no sooner had the process been set into motion than the SD moved into a controlling position. Röthke, seeing no need to give special protection to more people than necessary, supported the order.

The issue of dismissal became the object of prolonged negotiations. In the early phase the UGIF tried to stall. It argued that the presence then of 282 foreign Jews, only 34 percent of the total number of employees, was fewer than the 50 percent previously ordered by Dannecker.[9] To further strengthen the UGIF's case Baur claimed that their sudden dismissal would create major organizational problems in management. In fact the UGIF's reluctance to proceed with the CGQJ's order was a moral gesture, for despite the animosity between the French and the immigrants within the organization the Paris UGIF leadership was well aware that the dismissal of these employees would result in their immediate internment and deportation. And, perhaps equally important, it challenged the protective nature of the UGIF membership. If the foreign Jews were threatened today the French Jews' safety was in jeopardy. It was with these hesitations that the UGIF leadership entered into conflict with the CGQJ, and by proxy with the SD.

The question reached a critical stage on 28 January 1943, when the UGIF received a note from the CGQJ ordering the dismissal of the foreign Jews by 31 March. By way of concession, however, the CGQJ note added, it would allow the UGIF to retain foreigners as 1 percent of the total number of the UGIF's employees. The CGQJ note requested that the names of those retained be forwarded by 15 February.[10] The UGIF leadership could no longer avoid taking a definite position: it had to decide whether to defend or surrender its foreign employees. On 2 February 1943, the board decided

> . . . to make common cause with the personnel, to make all the necessary efforts in order to obtain from the CGQJ a reconsideration of the question, and if necessary to resign if satisfaction is not obtained. This unanimous decision is to be transmitted to the CGQJ and the foreign personnel is to be informed.[11]

The decision of the UGIF leadership to identify with the foreigners was a radical stand. It was the first expression of solidarity. The question remained, however, how far the UGIF was prepared to go in their defense. It was at this stage of the negotiations that Baur finally received a travel permit to attend a UGIF board meeting in the Southern Zone. On 9 February, on the eve of Baur's departure, the board decided to ask the CGQJ and Röthke for a postponement of the deadline until Baur's return. Röthke's approval arrived as Baur left Paris.[12]

On 10 February Baur left and the issue remained unresolved. Twenty-four hours later, mass arrests occurred, particularly noteworthy for the number of elderly people taken from the Rothschild Old People's Home and children taken from the orphanages. The day before Baur's departure for the south, convoys to Eastern Europe had resumed: on 9 and 11 February two convoys took 1,998 people to Auschwitz. These even included UGIF personnel from the Southern Zone who had been transferred to Drancy.[13] The renewal of deportations, which had ceased since November, made the situation tense. The respite gained when Röthke postponed the dismissals until Baur's return was shattered on 22 February when Röthke demanded immediate execution of the CGQJ's demand for the list of the foreign Jews who would be retained. This latest demand was particularly serious as Röthke demanded the list on that very same day and warned that failure to fulfill the order would incur severe measures against the board.[14] But once more the board was granted a twenty-four-hour extension. The board met in extraordinary sessions over two days. The first session of 22 February failed to achieve unanimity.

The CGQJ had allowed the UGIF to retain 9 foreign employees but some board members refused to abandon the rest of their staff. However, a majority was prepared to give in to the CGQJ's demand. Unable to decide which employees to sacrifice, the board decided that the 9 names were to be drawn by lots. In a final show of resistance, to pacify those board members opposed to any compromises, and to maintain unity, the board recommended to Edinger and Stora, who, in Baur's absence were to deal with Röthke, to attempt to renegotiate the issue. They were instructed to do their utmost not to hand in the list of 9 names, which would have condemned the others. Simultaneously, they were to seek terms of agreement in order not to precipitate a confrontation with the CGQJ and the SD, the consequences of which would be incalculable. On that same day the two men met with Joseph Antignac, representing the CGQJ, and, once more the CGQJ agreed to delay the execution of the order until Baur's return. At Edinger's and Stora's protests at the impossibility of selecting 9 names from the 282 foreign employees, Antignac told them they were free to reject the offer of 1 percent. They returned to their board, however, with the assurance that the foreigners would remain protected until 31 March 1943, and that Antignac would appeal to Röthke against their immediate arrest after their dismissal.[15]

Three days later Baur was back in Paris. Under his leadership the board reverted to its original position: it would resign rather than dismiss the foreigners. The board sent a note to the CGQJ rejecting the offer of 1 percent.[16] At the following meeting, on 2 March, the board decided that "if it proves impossible to reach an agreement the Board will demand to be relieved of its duties," and gave Baur full powers to negotiate.[17] The following day, Baur, Stora, and Armand Katz met with Röthke and the CGQJ. This time Röthke agreed to allow the UGIF to retain a number of foreigners not exceeding 15 percent of the total number of employees.[18] The board immediately went to work seeking to replace those about to be dismissed with some of their relatives who were French. The next day, 4 March, Baur wrote to Lambert: "You know our Board's attitude. Unfortunately the threat of measures against the rest of our personnel and against the French Jews has compelled us to reconsider our attitude."[19] All good intentions notwithstanding, in the face of having to bear the consequences of reprisals against the Jews collectively as well as against itself, the board had given in to pressures and threats. It had sacrificed the foreign employees to save the French employees, the foreign Jews to protect the French Jews. The director of ORT, Abraham Alperine, tried in vain to have the UGIF reconsider.[20] The problems faced by the board in deciding which employees would be dismissed had profoundly demoralized the personnel. In an effort to uphold morale the leadership circulated an internal memorandum:

> It is with profound sorrow that we learn of the forthcoming separation and we pay homage to the members of the Board for having tried, by all available means, that the "Union" not be destroyed.[21]

On 15 March foreigners who had not gone into hiding were arrested, together with 720 foreign Jews who had been working in factories producing goods for the Wehrmacht and had so far benefited from the *Ausweis*.[22] The UGIF had succeeded in retaining 50 foreign employees, including some working at the Rothschild Hospital and for the ACIP, but the other 232, together with their families, were immediately exposed to the Gestapo's arrest orders.[23]

The crisis that had threatened the UGIF revealed the extent of its vulnerability; it was powerless to protect even its own employees. It could only hope to survive by making concessions, and in the end by obeying German orders. It could not reconcile its self-imposed limitation to relief duties with an ever-worsening situation in which it was always at the mercy of the overriding policy needs of the authorities that had established the UGIF. The only justification available to the UGIF, and it was used from its very inception, was that by standing in the breach, between the authorities and the population, and through negotiations, it believed itself able to mitigate anti-Jewish measures. In the case of the foreign employees, it did win some vital weeks which permitted some of those under sentence to hide. Also, for a number of them it retained the protection that had come from being UGIF employees. Such small gains were of little comfort to the more determined leaders such as Baur.

One of the major problems faced by the UGIF, in Paris and in the Southern Zone, was the duality of leadership. This had arisen from the occupation of half the country by the Germans and from the fact that Vichy had established the organization. This division led to the development of two separate administrations, though Vichy continued to seek overall control in line with the general governmental policy of administrative unity of the two zones. But contacts between both zones were constantly at the mercy of the German military administration. During the crisis resulting from Laval's dismissal in December 1940, German authorities had closed the borders; even French ministers found their travel permits revoked. In February 1942, when Vallat was no longer acceptable to the Germans, he was unable to gain access to the Occupied Zone. The UGIF was in a similar situation. A nationwide organization, it had been established with two boards of governors, one for each zone, but with the presidency and the office of general-secretary in the Vichy Zone. These two boards had never met in common session. The need for consultation in order to elaborate common policies, no less than to arrange internal needs such as finances, made interzone contacts a most important objective.

In September 1942, the UGIF-Paris asked permission from the CGQJ to hold a combined meeting. The necessity for consultation had been prompted by the August law establishing the principle of a compulsory membership fee to the UGIF for the Jewish population. There were other far more important reasons for UGIF-Paris to seek a combined meeting, and to these we shall return. The two boards had developed their own styles of work, styles that corresponded not only to the particular political conditions in each zone but also to the communal structures that had merged into each half of the new body.

In the Vichy Zone, as a result of the negotiations with Vallat and the concessions he had made to speed up the formation of the UGIF, the overall organization had become a federated body. Vallat had permitted each major organization to carry on as before, with its own leadership, but acknowledging its place as part of the UGIF. In Paris, on account of the exodus from the city in June 1940, of the major organizations only two communal ones had re-emerged: the ACIP and a committee of immigrants. Dannecker's relentless pressure upon the ACIP to assume responsibility for the Jewish population as a whole had resulted in a centralized leadership dominated by the ACIP. Last but not least, because Vichy had created the UGIF it had been Vallat who had nominated its president and general-secretary, and Vallat had selected them from among the Southern Board. Paris, although operating independently, was therefore organizationally dependent upon the UGIF-South. The UGIF in Paris found this situation unsatisfactory; nevertheless it was constantly mindful of the need to maintain a presence in Vichy in order to sustain a possible line of defense. On the other hand, however, the UGIF-Paris, with its daily exposure to German demands, had developed lines of communication with the SD which, as the anti-Jewish measures grew in intensity, were becoming important to the UGIF-South as well. The UGIF-Paris believed that the question of protecting the organization, of ensuring its continued and unhampered activities, could, under the present conditions, only be obtained in Paris.

The UGIF in Paris, furthermore, never had a high opinion of the southern leadership. From the UGIF's inception, Paris had viewed its general-secretary, Lambert, and its president, Lévy, as inadequate to the task and too ready to give in to Vallat's pressure.[24] The goal for the Paris leaders was to take over the leadership through the removal of these two men. The Parisians' position was further reinforced by the knowledge that they had the support of the Central Consistory. Ever since the days of the negotiations with Vallat, the Consistory had opposed Lambert and Lévy and considered them traitors of Jewish interests and more particularly of its own role as representative of French Judaism. It was therefore no surprise that Paris sought a combined meeting to settle the matter or that the southern leadership was reluctant to take part in such a meeting.

At first, the UGIF-Paris demand for a combined meeting was not supported by the SD. But upon repeated insistence from Paris the SD gradually began to bend. They offered approval if the meeting was held in the Occupied Zone, offering the southern delegates immunity from the anti-Jewish laws.[25] But the UGIF-South remained firmly opposed to setting foot in Occupied France. The German Occupation of the Vichy Zone, on 11 November 1942, altered the situation. On 26 January 1943, the Paris leaders finally received travel permits from the SD for the south.[26] The permits had arrived just as the negotiations over the issue of the foreign employees had reached a critical stage, when a collective resignation of the board appeared imminent. At the height of the conflict, on 2 February, the Paris board found it necessary to discuss and officially record in its minutes a resolution calling for the centralization of the UGIF leadership with the head offices to be situated in Paris.[27] Furthermore, as if anticipating opposition from the south to its plan, the resolution included a proviso that such a centralization only be put into effect if appropriate liaison between both zones were approved by the authorities. Baur and Katz left Paris on 10 February to attend the first-ever combined meeting with such a plan in their bags. What Baur and Katz failed to mention to the southern leadership was that discussions had already been held by the Paris leadership to replace Lévy. A resolution had even been prepared for the CGQJ calling for Baur as the future UGIF president.[28]

Baur and Katz traveled first to Marseille. They left Paris as deportations were resuming and they arrived in Marseille in the aftermath of unprecedented arrests of not only immigrant Jews but of French Jews as well.[29] At the same time in Lyon the UGIF itself was the victim of police raids. The Paris representatives arrived just as the UGIF-South was facing a serious crisis. Baur and Katz initiated attempts to protect the UGIF organization, by demanding of the SD in the Vichy Zone that the same protective passes current in the Occupied Zone be issued to the UGIF-South.[30]

The meeting with the southern board took place at Nice on 15 February 1943.[31] Two questions dominated the debates: the reorganization of the UGIF and the Occupied Zone's financial problems. As expected, the question of Paris's bid for the leadership took precedence. Lévy's resignation from the leadership had provided the Parisians with the suitable opportunity. Baur set out to prove to the assembly the value of the Paris connection with the SD. To justify the Paris claim Baur informed the southern board of his demand for and the likelihood of success in obtaining protective passes. Through his report on Paris policy and the strategy adopted in negotiations with the SD and the CGQJ over the issue of the foreign employees, he sought to develop support for the view that Paris was effectively the most advantageous place for the national leadership, and that the UGIF in Paris was capable of handling the situation. Finally, to overcome remaining doubts Baur informed the southern leaders that the SD was prepared to grant five permanent travel permits for board members and another five for technicians. But although the UGIF-South decided to accept the permits, it still did not accept the Paris plan.[32] On the financial side of the Paris request, and following Baur's information that the Solidarity Fund was exhausted and that Paris needed 3 million francs a month to maintain itself, the southern board decided to grant Paris 5 million francs for February and March 1943, to be paid from gifts promised by individuals.[33]

Baur and Katz returned to Paris on 26 February. They had obtained a financial promise and, according to Baur's report, an understanding that the UGIF-South had accepted the Paris organizational proposals. On 3 March Baur submitted a report to the CGQJ. It recommended a centralization of the two boards into a single one located in Paris, but smaller in numbers, with twelve members instead of the previous eighteen. The body Baur proposed was to be made up of the existing Paris board and only three members from the southern board. Baur recommended that the southern leadership be situated either in Marseille or in Lyon with eight regional representatives based on the French administrative units. As far as the financial aspect of his report was concerned, Baur informed the CGQJ of the 5 million franc gift toward meeting the requirements of the August 1942 law requiring the UGIF in Paris to raise 3 million a month. He chose to emphasize, however, the possibility of financing the organization if the CGQJ allowed individuals to make donations from their frozen bank accounts.[34]

The debate between Paris and the south over the centralization plan continued at the southern board meeting attended by a Paris delegation. On 23 March 1943, at Grenoble, both sides presented their cases anew.[35] The UGIF-South had been shocked to hear that without its formal approval Baur had presented his recommendations for a reorganization plan to the CGQJ and the SD. Lambert recorded in his diary that the south resented being treated "as a minor in need of tutelage." Lambert's distrust of the north was so strong that he went on to record, "Baur . . . pretends that they [the Germans] are demanding regional unification,"[36] implying that Baur might have fabricated the argument to justify the Paris bid for control of the UGIF. There is no doubt that the south resented above all the Paris group's methods.

Lambert presented the southern position at this critical meeting. He rejected the implied charge of lack of competence which would warrant the dismissal of the southern board. To justify himself and his rejection of northern policy, Lambert rested his case upon two fundamental premises: the south had retained independence of the former organizations and it had never accepted monies from the Solidarity Fund.[37] Lambert went on to attack Baur for submitting a unification project to Röthke and the CGQJ without prior full agreement.

The main thrust of Lambert's argument was that unification would increase the representational character of the UGIF. This had been the organization's Achilles' heel and Lambert knew too well how telling this argument was with French Judaism. He therefore took refuge behind the claim that it was for the Central Consistory to decide whether centralization was acceptable: the UGIF, Lambert concluded, did not have the moral right to assume such a responsibility.[38]

The Paris delegates claimed in their defense that it had never been their intention to control the south and that under the new plan organizational autonomy would continue. Furthermore, despite the appearances of the plan, Paris had never acted autocratically: no board decision was ever made without the relevant commissions, representing the various organizations' interests, being first consulted. As for the implied strengthening of the UGIF's representational character, the Paris delegates argued that they considered themselves responsible for their own actions. Not only had they always acted in a purely individual capacity, but the reality of the situation rendered the whole question academic. Whether the UGIF had wanted the designation or not the authorities had always viewed it as representing the Jewish population. The real issue rested with the latest developments in the conditions faced by the Jewish population. There was no doubt that it was in Paris that the decisions affecting them were made and not in Vichy.

The evidence supporting the argument was irrefutable: the orders for internment were issued from Paris, the protective passes to the UGIF staff were issued in Paris, and the question of the foreign employees had to be dealt with in Paris and not in Vichy. Neither Lambert nor the southern board had been able to negotiate any of these issues and the very authority of the organization was affected when the president, Lévy, abandoned his post and went to Switzerland.[39] Even criticism of their use of the Solidarity Fund was rejected by the Paris representatives. Paris never had access to the funds available to the south, and as the billion-franc fine had shown, Jewish resources were totally at the mercy of the authorities and realism had to take precedence over moralism. The funds might as well be used to help the Jewish population. The two boards failed to resolve their differences. The availability of travel permits for the southern board to visit Paris, however, provided the south with an opportunity to ascertain how in fact UGIF-Paris functioned.[40] The northern delegates believed that such a visit would dispel mistrust.

On 4 May 1943, three delegates from the south, Maurice Brener, Jules Jefroykin, and Gamzon, arrived in Paris to examine its mode of operation.[41] Gamzon represented that wing of the southern board which opposed Lambert. He held the view that although the UGIF had a function to fulfill, alternate structures should be designed to help those most exposed. Brener and Jefroykin, although nominally UGIF technical advisers, were in fact the American Jewish Joint Distribution Committee (hereafter, the Joint representatives for France.[42] All three men firmly held that structures outside the UGIF were necessary for Jewish survival. It was therefore inevitable that such representatives would be critical of the UGIF-Paris whose very proposals were designed to strengthen the organization rather than diminish its role. They viewed themselves as representatives of a position motivated by ideals as opposed to the line pursued by Paris which sought administrative solutions to the problems. They reported back to the south in the following terms: "The Paris Board is divided into two clans: some are xenophobes, more or less antisemites and opposed to Zionism, and the others are more or less xenophiles, philo-semites and Zionists."[43] Given such an appreciation of the Paris board, they remained opposed to the unification plan.

On 16 June 1943, Baur and Stora returned to the south to push again for centralization.[44] The differences between the two boards had reached such a point that the southern board had passed a resolution stating that the northern delegates would not be permitted to participate in discussions of internal affairs. No northern delegates were invited to the following board meeting despite the obvious and urgent need for continued consultations.[45] Indeed, Lambert was mounting an offensive against Paris, claiming that already in December 1942, well before the first combined meeting, Paris was acting unilaterally by presenting to the authorities plans for a UGIF reorganization without the knowledge of the southern board.[46] A significant aspect of the whole question of centralization during that period was the support the CGQJ was giving to the UGIF-Paris. At a Paris board meeting, on 22 June 1943, Edinger reported on discussions held with CGQJ representatives. The issue was considered so delicate that it was not entered into the minutes: no one wanted to provide the UGIF-South with new arguments or invite interference from the SD.[47]

The opposition of the southern board to the Paris plan was not solely rooted in personality conflicts, nor in political differences between the parties. It stemmed in part from the southern group's view of its role due to the vastly different problems the Jewish population had had to contend with in the south. Until the German occupation of the Vichy Zone in November 1942, the UGIF-South had functioned in close relation with the French administration. The Vichy policy of maintaining a strict distinction between French and foreign Jews had helped sustain hope that the difficulties experienced might well prove temporary, at least for the French Jews. The southern UGIF's confidence was further strengthened by its financial independence, due largely to the support it received from the Joint and from the presence in its zone of Jews willing to make substantial contributions to the organization. These factors, when coupled with the high degree of independence of each constituent organization that came to compose the UGIF, explain the overall distrust at any change. Central to the south's reluctance to accept the Paris proposal was the fear of losing control of the one element which guaranteed its independence: the Joint's aid.

The American Jewish Joint Distribution Committee had been operating in France since 1932, when German Jewish refugees began arriving. Its guiding principle had always been to give financial assistance to organizations without assuming responsibility for its distribution. As a nonpolitical philanthropic organization it never funded political movements. The exodus of June 1940 had led to its withdrawal from Paris to the south. As Jewish organizations began to function after the Armistice the Joint resumed its funding.[48] The massive shift of the Jewish population resulting from the exodus had required unprecedented amounts of money. In the Vichy Zone alone, some 60,000 Jews benefited from its contributions. During the first semester of 1942 it had distributed 32 million francs, and, in the course of the Occupation, it gave some 480 million francs to a number of Jewish organizations.[49]

The distribution of the Joint's funds gave rise, however, to criticism. As a nonpolitical organization its charter did not allow it to finance political activities. The sole criterion guiding the trustees' distribution of funds was that they should be directed to helping the Jewish population. In May 1941, in Paris, the Jewish Communists had applied for funds for a canteen they operated for all Jews. Their application was rejected, and the Joint's trustees were attacked as anti-Communists.[50] Although the Communists' application presented political problems, the Joint's decision could not be justified on humanitarian grounds. After the establishment of the UGIF, the Joint was again attacked by Jewish organizations. For although the Joint had decided to continue funding individual organizations, the funding was made through the UGIF itself.[51] The justification for such a political decision was that since all the existing legal organizations had been incorporated into the UGIF, the Joint as a foreign organization was compelled to act within the law. The Joint's decision transformed the UGIF into the dominant relief organization in France and weakened those opposed to participation in the imposed representation.

During the second half of 1942, when mass deportations were taking place and mass rescues had become vital, the Joint's funds, controlled by the "official" Jewish organization, the UGIF, could not be used for that purpose. The Joint's general policy, formulated in New York, had not been adapted to the changing situation. Herbert Katzki, who controlled operations in France, was not prepared to assume responsibility for a change in policy.[52] Regardless of criticisms the Joint refused to reexamine its policy. The landing of the Allied armies in North Africa, followed by France's rupture of diplomatic relations with the United States and the occupation of the Vichy Zone by the Wehrmacht in November 1942, marked a decisive turning point in

Joint operations in France. Its official representatives left France for Lisbon and Jules Jefroykin and Maurice Brener were appointed as trustees and charged to continue activities.[53] Jefroykin began to reexamine the former funding policy. He organized a consultative committee which included, besides Brener, Léon Meiss from the Central Consistory and Joseph Fisher representing the Zionist organizations. Jefroykin presented the Joint's new policy at the first meeting of the consultative committee in Nice in February 1943, when Baur was attending the first-ever combined meeting with the southern leadership. Jefroykin had decided that the Joint's funds would be made available for illegal activities. Despite strong opposition, Jefroykin refused to reconsider. From then on illegal activities were assured of financial support.[54]

With no official representatives in France, the Joint's operations were reorganized. Until then, and certainly until the establishment by President Franklin D. Roosevelt of the War Refugees Board in 1944, U.S. currency regulations governed all transfers of funds abroad. It was U.S. policy not to allow financial transfers from the United States to German-occupied countries. Admittedly, the Joint had received special permission for limited transfers, but these amounts were totally inadequate in comparison to the sums required.[55] A method of self-financing based on local borrowings was established. Local lenders were approached and guaranteed repayment within three months of the cessation of hostilities at the ruling rate of exchange.[56] This method proved successful. In Paris, the UGIF and Amelot were thus able to secure funds outside official controls. The rupture of diplomatic relations between Vichy and the United States made Joint funding totally dependent upon such an illegal practice or upon illegal transfers from Switzerland.[57] This radical change helped Jefroykin and Brener overcome the objections of those who feared reprisals for illegal activities, and created possibilities for tailoring borrowing to needs rather than having needs without the necessary funds. Of the 480 million francs distributed throughout the Occupation, 260 million were spent during the last eighteen months of the Occupation. The Joint was thus able to present in its first postwar report of activities an impressive balance sheet. Of the 260 million, 70 million had been assigned to save children and 30 million for illegal activities.[58]

Yet despite an impressive record, despite Jefroykin's and Brener's forward-looking policies, there were still critics, but they came now from different quarters. The earlier critics had, by 1943, succeeded in organizing their own funding, for better or for worse. The majority were still helped by Jefroykin, the Communists through independent efforts. The new critics of 1943 came from the Central Consistory, Samuel Lattès, writing to Helbronner, was highly critical of the Joint's methods:

> I retain the distinct impression that the Joint could give at least a larger amount by accepting a lower rate of conversion. For otherwise, the deficiencies of that organization deserve to be qualified, given the terrible conditions affecting us, as criminal. . . .[59]

The point was, of course, that the Joint was borrowing from wealthy Jews who wanted to secure their money for after the war and who were seeking more remunerative offers. The problem was serious, as it interfered with larger public borrowing. Jefroykin's postwar assertion that there were always sufficient funds available was only true as long as it referred to the amounts necessary to meet the budget. In fact, the permanent financial difficulties encountered by all the organizations, including the UGIF, attest to the contrary.

The presence of the monied classes in the Vichy Zone made the financing of relief much easier for the UGIF-South. But in Paris, the absence of wealthy Jews, the increasing pauperization of the remaining middle classes, the strict financial controls exercised by the CGQJ and the German authorities, along with the stringent application of aryanization, continually imperiled the financial situation of the UGIF. Its main income came from the Solidarity Fund. The CGQJ, however, believed its own propaganda, that the Jews had money, that it was only a matter of applying sufficient pressure for the money to appear. Following the December 1941 fine, the UGIF had erred by suggesting that Vichy's appropriations to meet the fine had weighed unfairly upon some Jews and had bypassed others. That criticism found a receptive ear with Darquier de Pellepoix. The CGQJ regularly summoned the UGIF to work out an equitable basis to apportion the fine among the Jews of Occupied France. On 29 January 1943, the CGQJ once more returned to the question.[60] It ordered the UGIF to establish a nominal list of all the Jews in the Occupied Zone as a first step toward calculating the distribution of respective shares. The UGIF board did not, in truth, object, and in fact sought ways of rectifying a gross injustice. But the UGIF knew that it was beyond the organization to gather the necessary information to proceed with the task. Furthermore, the UGIF was reluctant to take any initiative in that direction, lest it bring in its wake further hardship upon the population.

The dominant question that faced the UGIF during that period was how to ensure a regular income. The problem remained that the organization was never granted access to Jewish properties, which were in the hands of administrators, held by the Caisse, or in bank accounts inaccessible to their owners. The financial strategy adopted by the UGIF was to gain access to the only two likely sources: the funds held at the Caisse and the frozen accounts. The UGIF applied to the Caisse first. A change of policy must have taken place for the UGIF was informed that in the event of the CGQJ's approval the Caisse would be willing to grant the UGIF access to the funds it held.

On 23 January 1943, Darquier de Pellepoix, faced with a bankrupt UGIF, conceded that in certain cases he would permit individuals to make gifts to the UGIF from their assets held by the Caisse.[61] Although the UGIF was finally granted what it had sought for so long, it found itself unable to generate sufficient gifts from this source; too many of the holders of large accounts had left Paris and too many could no longer be traced. Short of special legislation compelling the Jewish population to pay dues, the financial situation remained intractable. Only the Southern Zone could help Paris meet its budget and avoid the imposition of a per capita tax.

In April 1943 the UGIF-South promised Paris a monthly subsidy of 3 million francs. But the situation remained critical; the South itself failed to honor its promise. The situation was so desperate that the CGQJ, to force the south to meet its pledge, warned that it would impose a UGIF reorganization that would be particularly hard on the south.[62] The CGQJ's warning must have had some effect—the promised funds arrived during May.[63] But Paris needed 3 to 4 million a month.[64] The south's inability to guarantee regular payment as well as the continued insufficiencies of the Solidarity Fund could lead the CGQJ to make unpredictable decisions. Faced with such a situation Edinger proposed a number of alternatives. He suggested to the Paris board that the previously postponed sales of assets of institutions be resumed and that the Ministry of Finances be asked to collect a supplementary surcharge on the general taxes on revenues paid by Jews.[65] To negotiate with the CGQJ for permission to proceed with the sales of assets, Edinger went to Lyon on 26 May 1943, to consult with the Central Consistory and obtain its approval.[66]

The financial situation in Paris was so critical during April and May 1943 that the UGIF could only partly pay its salaries and general financial assistance to the population was temporarily discontinued. On 11 May 1943, the CGQJ imposed the UGIF's earlier recommendations of compulsory dues. In Occupied France each adult Jew was to pay 120 francs and in the Southern Zone 360 francs, with dispensations in both zones for those on welfare; there was to be a surcharge of 5 percent on each banking transaction, with exemptions for those holding civilian or military pensions. There were also, as in all laws affecting the Jews in particular, punitive clauses: the failure to meet this obligation would result in internment and all Jews were to carry proof that they had met their obligations.[67] The law was to become applicable on 1 September 1943.

Meanwhile, however, the problem of the UGIF's resources was far from being resolved. Even Auguste Duquesnel, CGQJ director responsible for the control of the UGIF, had come around to the view that the problem resided in organizational deficiencies and that the UGIF-South was not cooperating sufficiently. Only with Baur as president, Couturier was convinced, would the situation be resolved.[68] Back from the south, Edinger had brought the Central Consistory's approval for the sale of assets.[69]

The latest decree, together with the Central Consistory's approval, finally permitted the UGIF to look forward to a positive financial situation, though the CGQJ's permission was still necessary if the sale of certain assets was to proceed. But during July 1943 the CGQJ took the view that not all incorporated organizations' assets could be sold by the UGIF.[70] The CGQJ suddenly decided to adopt a legalistic position with respect to certain organizations; it maintained that some of these assets were gifts made by families and were the object of special endowments. In any event the CGQJ ruling affected such organizations as the AIU. The question may well be asked how this sudden concern by the CGQJ for legal niceties arose—until then there had been total disregard for such questions. In the case of the AIU it may well have originated from Darlan's earlier order to protect it, or perhaps from the CGQJ's concern to avoid endless litigations which would meanwhile place such organizations, and assets, in the hands of the courts. The Central Consistory and Baur opposed the CGQJ's latest ruling: as far as they were concerned these assets were French Judaism's property and it was the Central Consistory's right to dispose of them at will. Only a major loan could relieve the difficulty.

Two sources were available: the banking system or the Caisse, both requiring collateral to obtain the loans.[71] The UGIF wrestled with the moral problem of the use of properties without their owners' consent. The question was put to the UGIF-South's leadership. It agreed that since these assets were already impounded by the state and out of reach of their legitimate owners the UGIF was morally justified in attempting to borrow against them. The Paris UGIF decided to apply for a loan of 50 million francs from the Caisse which would be secured by the assets it held. It anticipated that the loan would be repaid in the same manner as when these assets were first used by Vichy to meet the December fine: the assets would be sold and the UGIF would become the debtor to the individuals affected.[72] Meanwhile, as the loan was being negotiated, the Paris board decided to proceed with the sale of shares it held to the value of 3 million francs and also apply to the Bank of France for a line of credit of 25 million francs which would again be guaranteed by the UGIF's assets.[73]

All these borrowings and financial manipulations did not, however, prevent the UGIF from attempting to regain for the Jewish population access to their own properties, especially the frozen bank accounts. The UGIF resorted again to the argument that its constitution allowed it to solicit gifts from the population and these gifts were an integral part of its financing. The UGIF demanded therefore that the CGQJ permit holders of such accounts to be allowed to make donations to the UGIF. The UGIF leadership was, of course, thinking about the possibility of using the Joint's guarantee to induce prospective donors.[74] But the CGQJ remained wary of permitting access to these accounts; it did not want to find itself in conflict with the German authorities who had ordered the original freeze.

By July 1943, the UGIF had, with CGQJ approval, borrowed 25 million francs from the Bank of France using as collateral shares held at the Caisse.[75] The UGIF was once more in a position to continue its relief work. But all these loans were only piecemeal solutions, barely sufficient to meet budgetary needs for a few months. The projected income from the compulsory dues might have contributed to the establishment of reserves but the UGIF faced constant difficulties in establishing complete lists of addresses of Jews. The French administration showed little interest in the UGIF's repeated requests for names and addresses. Furthermore, there was no assurance that by the time the dues were to be met the Jews would not have been arrested or that they would still be at their registered addresses. It was therefore an administrative impossibility to evaluate with any degree of certainty the projected income from the dues. The CGQJ was compelled to postpone until November 1943 the implementation of the law.[76]

There was still the Solidarity Fund but its holdings were not being replenished. Buyers of Jewish properties, sensing the likelihood of Germany's defeat, were becoming fewer. However the CGQJ examined the problem it could not avoid the frozen accounts as an immediate source of funds. During September the CGQJ forwarded to the UGIF a list of holders of large accounts so that the UGIF could apply to them for gifts.[77] Again the CGQJ had waited too long and the majority of these holders were long gone from Paris. The other immediate source of funds was the assets of organizations. In December 1943 the UGIF was compelled to sell another lot of them.[78] A floating fund of 5 million francs was constituted to form a reserve. To ensure liquidity the UGIF was forced to ask the CGQJ for an increase in its allocation from the Solidarity Fund. The CGQJ refused to consider the demand and the UGIF had to ask Röthke for the release of funds. By July 1944 the UGIF in Paris was financing the south from the sale of assets and its own reserves. Drancy alone was then costing the Paris Jews 4 million francs a month and most of the inmates now came from the south.[79]

The period between January and June 1943 had seen the UGIF devote its energies to problems of organization and finance. It found itself unable to advance in either direction: financial resources remained perilously limited and the organizational question was unresolved as UGIF-South refused to view the problem in the same light as Paris. It was within that context that the Paris leadership was confronted by an SD demand. On 7 June 1943, Röthke and SS Hauptsturmführer Aloïs Brunner met UGIF leaders and ordered them to take the necessary steps to ensure that the Jews become "productive." The UGIF was ordered to present a scheme, applicable for the whole of France. The UGIF was to open its own factories or seek industrialists willing to participate in projects. To make the proposition attractive, Röthke and Brunner assured the UGIF that those employed would be protected and that the UGIF would be granted the necessary capital.[80]

The UGIF immediately appointed a commission to study the question.[81] The proposal offered definite advantages: it would relieve the drain on resources for relief activities and also offer protection from deportation. By 29 June 1943, the commission had formulated questions for the UGIF to present to Röthke, then the commission would begin to examine in concrete terms agricultural, commercial, and industrial projects. It is clear that the UGIF, mindful of such previous demands, had decided to proceed cautiously by seeking to ascertain German intentions. The commission formulated key questions concerning the type of guarantees that would be offered to the workers, the nationality of those to be engaged, and, possibly more important, whether the work would be voluntary or compulsory.[82]

It was with Brunner's appearance in Paris that the UGIF began to confront new difficulties. Aloïs Brunner had arrived in Paris early in June 1943, at Eichmann's instructions, to speed up the deportations of Jews. Brunner brought his own task force, and was accountable only to Berlin, although Röthke remained the *Judenreferent* for France. Fresh from his successful deportation of all the Jews from Salonika, Brunner's orders were to introduce renewed vigor into the Final Solution in France.[83]

On 30 June 1943, Brunner presented Baur with an outline of the changes he was to introduce.[84] At Drancy SS were to replace the gendarmerie and the UGIF was to assume a greater participation in the internal organization of the camp. According to Brunner's plan the UGIF was to be responsible for all the camp's supplies. Individual food parcels would no longer be permitted, and the UGIF was to be responsible for an increased supply of clothing and equipment. Furthermore, the UGIF would assume full responsibility for all the necessary equipment of each deportee and each convoy. To ensure an equitable distribution of these goods UGIF staff would be allowed to witness the deportees boarding the departing convoys. The body searches previously occurring on the eve of departures would be altered to allow the deportees to take personal belongings and trade tools. Brunner further emphasized that to minimize the earlier indignities and brutalities of the body searches, and as far as consistent with deportation procedures, UGIF personnel would need to be present. Endeavoring to secure the UGIF's cooperation, Brunner took pains to present the proposed changes at Drancy; in a positive light he indicated that he wanted the infirmary rebuilt, that workshops would be established, and that a project was under consideration which would permit families to send monthly remittances to relatives in the camps in Eastern Europe.[85]

These minor alterations of camp regulations, seemingly designed to improve camp life and introduce an appearance of rationality, were prepared by Brunner to make his radical changes seem innocuous. In fact Brunner had transformed Drancy into a "KZ" (*Konzentrationslager*—concentration camp) functioning on Nazi lines and under direct control of the SS. The new regulations were designed to ensure, as in all KZ throughout Europe, the active participation of the internees themselves in camp administration.[86] From the UGIF's point of view the worst of the changes was not the change of status of the camp, but the UGIF's greater participation in the deportations.

Baur was also told by Brunner that the UGIF was expected to call upon the relatives of internees at Drancy to voluntarily present themselves at the camp so that the families would be deported from France as units. To make it more acceptable to the population Brunner suggested to Baur that the UGIF could allow these volunteers to take with them all their personal belongings, irrespective of weight.

It was also during this conference that Brunner demanded that Baur convene a meeting of the two UGIF boards where Brunner would present questions he wanted resolved. Indeed, Brunner was effectively taking in hand all the outstanding problems Röthke had not attended to so far. Included among these were the escape of Jews to Spain and Italy, the extension of the UGIF bulletin into a national paper, the comprehensive employment scheme the UGIF was already busy with, and 500 yellow armbands with the wording *Service d'ordre Juif* (Jewish marshals).

Never had the UGIF, nor for that matter the Coordination Committee before it, been faced with such a list of demands. The Paris board met in special session on 6 July to consider Brunner's orders, and unanimously decided to refuse to carry out or participate in any police measures.[87]

Meanwhile the SS had already taken over Drancy and left the French police to guard the perimeter of the camp. The UGIF was temporarily denied access. Within Drancy Brunner dismissed the former Jewish camp administration and selected a totally new staff, based upon new deportation criteria Brunner had imposed.[88]

All internees were grouped into six categories: Group A included Aryans, people wedded to non-Jews, and half-Jews; Group B included those not belonging to any categories; Group C1 was the camp administration; Group C2 included protected nationals; Group C3 included wives of prisoners of war; Group C4 included those awaiting the arrival of the remaining members of their families. The most privileged were in the categories A and C1. They were nondeportable on racial grounds or essential to the management of the camp. Group B, which accounted for the overwhelming majority of internees, were the French and foreign Jews who had very little chance of escaping deportation. The fate of those in the C2 category was dependent upon German foreign policy and were relatively safe. Those in Group C3, the wives of prisoners of war, only remained safe until May 1944 when they were sent to Bergen-Belsen. Group C4 could only hope for a postponement. They, after having been interviewed (and every single camp inmate was personally interviewed by Brunner), were found to have relatives still free. Given the policy of family regroupment, they were safe as long as their families were still at large or as long as Brunner adhered to this policy.

The introduction of these new criteria in the camp altered the situation overnight. All those previously thought safe found themselves candidates for deportation. Until then the Jewish camp administration had largely used its own discretion in the preparation of the lists of those to be included in the convoys. This previous administration generally selected foreigners rather than the French, and protected the French-born rather than the naturalized. Among former servicemen, those with decorations were less likely to be deported. Throughout the process of selection, however, the Jewish administration's policy was also influenced by personal judgment if not prejudice. Finally there remained the element of arbitrariness that hovered at all times over who was or was not included in the deportations. This element was the French police, who added or removed names from the lists without any seemingly justifiable reason. But generally the chance element in the whole process was secondary to the policy of the Jewish camp administration.[89] Brunner's changes radically altered the situation in Drancy. Gone was the confidence of the French, the former servicemen, or the decorated soldiers.

The administrative changes and the new internal organization were only two aspects of the changes. The new character of Drancy resided in the permanent presence within the compound of the SS and the establishment of a *bureau des missions* (assignment office).[90] To staff this office Brunner selected from among the camp inmates a group of individuals whose families were also interned. Their duties consisted in going out of Drancy and bringing back to the camp the relatives of those already in the camp. The perversity of the scheme rested in the selection of the members of that special group. In effect, they were blackmailed into carrying out the orders, otherwise they faced deportation. At first this *bureau des missions* only numbered a dozen men but during August 1943 its number doubled. These missionaries, as they were called by the camp population, would leave Drancy in the morning with the addresses of two or three families they had to bring back. If the victims refused to go willingly the missionaries were to call upon either the French police or the Drancy authorities to come for them. By the end of August 1943, however, Brunner abandoned the whole scheme, possibly because it did not prove productive or because the internees themselves no longer volunteered the addresses, or, equally likely, because Brunner had turned his attention to the Southern Zone where Jews were far more numerous than in Paris.[91]

Brunner's order for 500 yellow armbands for a Jewish police force was an integral part of the plan to make the interned Jews responsible for policing the camp. The removal of French police from within the precinct gave the Jewish police much wider responsibility than the previous Jewish camp management commission. The role of the new Jewish police was to guard the inmates, search them, and take responsibility for any escape.[92] This new police force was also made to guard UGIF institutions such as the Rothschild Hospital.[93] According to Georges Wellers, apart from a few corrupt individuals, this police force never exceeded orders and could not be faulted in its attitude and behavior toward fellow Jews.[94]

The UGIF's refusal to carry out the "regrouping of families" which it immediately recognized for what it was, had not been taken lightly. The board, expecting reprisals, decided on 13 July 1943, to ask the CGQJ to transmit to Laval a letter asking for a meeting.[95] Shortly after this refusal to cooperate, the escape of two men from Drancy precipitated a crisis which culminated in the decapitation of the Paris UGIF leadership. The escape, on 21 July 1943, of Baur's cousin Adolphe Ducas and another man, led to the immediate arrest of Baur by the SD as a hostage until their return. Brunner gave the UGIF eight days to have the men brought back to Drancy.[96]

On 30 July 1943, Brunner summoned Edinger and Stora for a report on what the UGIF had done so far to find the two escapees.[97] The Paris UGIF leadership had in fact set the whole organization to work to find the two men. Stora and Weill-Hallé had gone to the Southern Zone, Musnik was even reported to have gone into Switzerland.[98] The Paris board wrote to Lambert asking him to alert the southern UGIF.[99] The Central Consistory was asked to help trace the two men.[100] On 7 August Lambert replied to Paris that the two men had not been sighted but that he had alerted the French authorities and had asked the Jewish organizations in Switzerland to report their presence.[101]

The UGIF leaderships were leaving no stone unturned, but Brunner, dissatisfied with the UGIF's failure, ordered a raid on the offices of the Comité de Bienfaisance in Paris and forty-six of its staff were arrested.[102] The UGIF in Paris faced a serious crisis. Meanwhile Baur's family, his wife and four children, were arrested, and so was Israelowicz and his family. Katz, the UGIF's secretary in Paris, was interned at Drancy.[103]

The situation was deteriorating so rapidly that Baur, though at Drancy since 21 July, decided to address himself to the minister of justice asking for governmental assistance in demanding the extradition of the two men from Switzerland where they were believed to have gone.[104] Vichy, however, did not view the issue with the same urgency. A month later, on 4 September, Vichy wrote to the CGQJ rejecting all responsibility in the matter:

> Drancy being no longer under the control of the French authorities, the escape is not punishable by French law. Consequently, the French government cannot request Ducas' extradition.[105]

At a board meeting on 9 August 1943, Edinger and Stora, who had assumed the leadership of the organization, defended themselves against all charges of personal ambition, vehemently claiming that they had done all in their power to find the culprits. They asked the board to give them its full confidence until the situation was stabilized. On 4 September 1943, Brunner ordered Stora's and Musnik's arrest for the UGIF's failure to submit an employment plan as ordered.[106]

The arrest of most of the leaders of the UGIF in Paris did not mean its end, however, nor did it mean a change of policy on its part. A reconstituted leadership of Edinger and Juliette Stern took over the mantle. The issues of centralization and the financial problems continued to dominate the internal debates with the endless search for solutions or acceptable compromises. The new leadership's concern with the old question of centralization no longer found a responsive ear at the CGQJ. Duquesnel had given up the idea. As far as he was concerned it would result in the elimination of the southern leadership without a corresponding improvement in activities. Summing up his views, Duquesnel noted that the end result would be a growth of power in fewer hands with a corresponding growth in personal privileges and a loss of control by Vichy.[107]

The arrest of the Paris leadership was followed by Lambert's own arrest.[108] In the face of such a crisis, Edinger, the most senior leader, concluded that the situation could only be resolved by firm organizational measures: "The situation is grave on account of the deficiencies of the UGIF leadership." The CGQJ, uncertain about the UGIF's future, faced with misgivings about the appropriate solution, yet desirous of maintaining the UGIF if only to justify its own existence, decided there was no alternative but to dismiss the southern leadership and proceed with the centralization in Paris.[109] Edinger and the CGQJ, for different reasons, had opted for a continued

UGIF existence. But there were forces within the organization challenging this decision.

The southern board, following Lambert's arrest and the continual raids upon regional UGIF offices, had begun debating the question of the UGIF's future.[110] The first full plenary meeting of both boards following the arrests occurred on 25 October 1943. The southern delegates raised the question of a general dissolution but the Parisian policy of continued operation finally prevailed and was accepted by the assembly.[111]

The problem of the appointment of a president had remained unresolved since Lévy's departure early in the year. Darquier de Pellepoix, was not convinced that Edinger was the best person. He appealed to Röthke to release Baur from Drancy so that he might assume the presidency.[112] On 16 December 1943, the CGQJ, with Röthke's approval, appointed Edinger as president of the UGIF.[113] On 17 December 1943, Baur, Stora, Musnik, Katz, Israelowicz, and their families were deported.

The centralization of the UGIF administration in Paris with the corresponding improved contacts with the south did not improve the financial problems as Paris had earlier hoped. The policy of a self-sufficient Jewish community favored by the SD and the CGQJ could not be put into effect. The Solidarity Fund which was to help balance the budget was running down. The sales of Jewish properties were falling and the CGQJ refused to release funds from reserves, claiming that they were needed to meet the continued cost of administrating the aryanization program.[114] The Paris board continued to press the southern leadership for implementation of the agreed centralization, being more convinced than ever that salvation rested with a strong executive located in Paris which would be best able to represent the Jews and to run a strong relief program.

The Paris view that the continued existence of the UGIF was necessary was based on the number of Jews who depended on all the services it provided. It viewed itself as the only relief agency available to that population, and considered its function indispensable. What made reevaluation of its role and responsibilities impossible was the assumption that any action on its part might bring reprisals upon the Jews, those still free or those in the camps. The UGIF faced a situation, which if presented in these terms, was insoluble. By the end of 1943 the UGIF leaders were unwilling to consider alternatives to the problem of assisting the remaining Jews.

The most exposed Jews were in the camps and the UGIF faced constant difficulties in following the movements of the inmates. The SD constantly shifted some categories of inmates from one camp to another. No one was ever sure that some "safe" group of internees would not suddenly be taken back to Drancy by the SD to complete the numbers required for a convoy to Auschwitz. Jews married to non-Jews were interned at Drancy in July 1942 and remained there until November 1942. Then for reasons unknown to the UGIF, a number of them were directed by the SD to Beaune-La-Rolande and Pithiviers while others remained at Drancy.[115] In March 1943, some sick and elderly internees were released from Drancy by the SD and sent to the

Rothschild Hospital or Old People's Home.[116] This constant movement of internees from one camp to another, or in and out of institutions and camps, as well as the risk of deportation facing all internees, further confused the UGIF in its judgment. These factors also placed a great strain on UGIF services, thus intensifying the problems confronting the leadership.[117] Understandably, the UGIF leaders chose to deal with immediate needs rather than distance themselves from the problems, on the grounds that the deportation process would go on irrespective of the UGIF's actions. The UGIF continued to appeal to the remaining Jewish population to support its activities. Feeling that Parisian Jewry had given as much as it could give, it appealed to the UGIF-South for its share of help. Edinger, like his predecessor Baur, continually reiterated the need for great care in making appeals to the Jews, lest they be wrongly interpreted by the SD as notices of warning. Edinger, appealing to the Central Consistory for collections to be made at synagogues, asked for the utmost care: "It will be necessary to be extremely careful and maintain these appeals in general terms."[118] Throughout the remaining period, from September to August 1944, the UGIF leaders avoided making statements or tendentious comments that would give cause for reprisals. When deportations were a daily occurrence the UGIF persisted in referring to them as "departures" to the east.

The UGIF's commitment to those immediately threatened extended from those in the camps to those sheltered in its institutions. Despite occasional arrests carried out in these places, and despite the temporary relief felt by these people for being kept in institutions rather than at Drancy, the UGIF, fearing reprisals, maintained careful watch over them. Three women who had been transferred from Drancy to the Rothschild Hospital escaped in April 1943.[119] The UGIF immediately imposed a strict regimen. A week later the escape of a young girl from one of the children's homes resulted in the temporary internment at Drancy of the director of the institution.[120] The outcome was a near panic at the UGIF. There were serious grounds for concern: the UGIF was accountable for all those who, pending a decision about their future, had been released by the SD in its care. The UGIF had to submit monthly reports on their places of residence to the SD.[121] The UGIF housed all its charges together: those accountable as well as those who were not. All those who resided in the UGIF's institutions were grouped in a number of categories, each representing a degree of freedom. For instance, those of mixed marriages were permitted out between 8 A.M. and 8 P.M.[122] At the Old People's Home in the Rothschild Hospital some internees were also allowed out, but only by guaranteeing each other's return. The UGIF would request them to sign a pledge making each answerable for the escape of the other.[123]

Among the various institutions *cum* camps those housing children presented the UGIF with political problems. Because the children were the least able to protect themselves, their fate presented to those opposed to the UGIF the justification for an alternative course of action. By January 1943 the UGIF had seven such "homes" which housed 386 children either entrusted to the UGIF by families or relatives, or temporarily released from Drancy.[124] The arrests during February led the UGIF to open another two such centers.[125] The March 1943 special census for Jewish children in state and primary schools raised families' fears and more parents placed children with the UGIF. The additional pressures on the already limited UGIF accommodations were met by a new reorganization of the homes.[126] There were other problems. The youth centers and children's homes suffered from the constant changes in their population, and discipline was difficult to maintain.

The welfare of these children was of such general concern and became such a sensitive political issue that in January 1943 Baur himself was called in to deal with the problem.[127] The causes were not far to seek. The roots of the children's problems were in the conditions under which some of them had lived and in the events they had witnessed. The majority of the children in the UGIF homes were on parole, and they knew it. During February 1943 the police raided some of these homes and took some children back to Drancy for deportation. The police then raided the Rue des Rosiers technical boarding school and the Guy Patin Home, and all the older children knew that a recurrence was likely.[128] The UGIF leadership itself was conscious of the likelihood of a repetition of police raids, yet it could not refuse to accept the children and certainly not those the SD was willing to entrust to them. In March 1943 the UGIF housed 249 such children.[129]

Besides the children in institutions, the UGIF provided for an even larger number outside. Some had been placed either by relatives or by the UGIF with foster parents because of the shortage of accommodation. The CGQJ tolerated this situation until April 1943, when it suddenly ordered the UGIF to revise this item in its budget. Although the UGIF was then facing a financial crisis, the CGQJ's order was not designed to prune expenses and ensure that the UGIF remained within the budget. On the flimsy charge that the UGIF's rate of payment to foster parents was higher than the state's welfare department payments the CGQJ forbade the UGIF to place children with non-Jewish foster parents. The reason was well understood by the UGIF: it would be forced to take these children into its homes, thus facilitating police controls.[130] This particular CGQJ order became a further milestone in the history of the deterioration of the UGIF's reputation. The CGQJ ordered the UGIF to send out social workers, with appropriate police orders, to collect the children and bring them back, in some cases to the UGIF homes, in other cases directly to Drancy.[131] The deposition of one of those social workers at the postwar trial of Vallat showed how powerless and in the end how compliant the UGIF had become.[132] It was at this point that the basis of a clandestine Service Social was formed within the UGIF to counter the consequences of the CGQJ's ruling.

The UGIF's compliance was a direct function of its legal character and the policy so far adhered to by its leaders. Its first priority was to maintain the network of relief institutions and thus assist everyone in a position to benefit from them. The problem was that this number was ever-diminishing while the number of other Jews, those no longer permitted to live as law-abiding citizens, was constantly on the increase. The deportations which had stopped in August were renewed the following month. The space in Drancy created by the deportations was soon filled by new arrests. Between 18 and 25 October, systematic mass arrests of various nationalities, which had not occurred since July, resumed. The remaining Rumanian, Hungarian, Spanish, Portuguese, Danish, Swedish, Finnish, and Italian Jews who had not so far been repatriated were arrested.[133] But the number of deportations during 1943 never equaled 1942 levels. In 1942 there had been forty-five convoys, in 1943 there were only seventeen.[134] No change of policy on the part of Germany occurred to explain the reduction. It must have been caused by problems in obtaining the necessary trains and perhaps, more likely, by the increasing difficulty of arresting the requisite numbers. Once again a lull followed the October arrests; it lasted until February 1944. On 3 February, the French police raided the UGIF's children's homes, the Rothschild Hospital, and the Old People's Home.[135] The UGIF was powerless to protect the inmates in its institutions, so the illegal Service Social decided that the time had come to put its plan into action.

When the CGQJ ended the foster parents scheme, Gamzon had prepared the ground for the Service Social during his visit to Paris in May 1943 as a representative of UGIF-South. Plan B, as it was called, was now set into motion. The Zionist movement in the Southern Zone had conceived it. By reproducing all the UGIF departments in an illegal "ghost" structure, the aim was to assist all Jews who because they lived illegally could not call in person to collect financial help from the UGIF. Another purpose was to make regular payments and visits to the children placed with non-Jewish foster parents. Juliette Stern, from the UGIF board, nominally controlled the illegal activities.[136] In reality, the Service Social was led by Jacques Pulver and Albert Akerberg, who were supported by Dr. Fredy Menachem and privately by Toni Stern, a UGIF board member. The rank-and-file members of the organization were former Jewish scouts whose organization (the EIF) was disbanded by Vichy early in 1943 and who were sent by their leaders to Paris to carry out such activities. The funding of the organization originated from money illegally transferred from the Southern Zone as well as from irregular accounting practices at the UGIF itself.[137] The existence of such practices was known to the CGQJ and the SD but for some unaccountable reason they chose not to take steps to stop them.[138]

The existence of illegal activities within the UGIF, with the direct participation of some of its leaders, did not indicate that the UGIF itself was undergoing a change, however. All it indicated was the presence within the organization of individuals who no longer held the view that the UGIF's faithful respect of legality would necessarily ensure the survival of the remaining Jews. These people were challenging earlier UGIF assumptions and calling for a radical change of policy. Already during 1943 the OSE was operating totally outside the UGIF and its representative on the UGIF board had resigned.[139] In Paris, Dr. Minkowski, who headed OSE and was closely connected to the board, had also tried to persuade the UGIF leadership to adopt such a course. This pressure intensified early in 1944. This time it came from a newly formed body, the Comité d'Union et de Défense des Juifs (Committee for the Unity and the Defense of the Jews).* Headed by Alperine, this group tried to convince the UGIF leadership that its role had ended, and that it should disband.

The situation faced by the UGIF in Paris in 1944 was precarious. The "homes" had been raided in February and Brunner was constantly demanding information and reports about them.[140] The question of whether these homes should be maintained had to be resolved. Edinger, supported by most of his colleagues, refused to consider alternatives. As always, the fear of precipitating reprisals on the remaining Jews in Paris precluded any change of policy. Some witnesses have suggested that another consideration also influenced the UGIF's decision to remain operative: the fear of the leaders for their own safety.[141] However responsible and accurate such statements might be, it is nevertheless impossible to judge UGIF policy so simply. While personal anguish might have affected the decision-making process, these same leaders remained at their posts, accepting the accompanying risks. Nor must we forget that they knew from past experience that the SD would only tolerate their presence and thereby allow them to carry out their tasks as long as it suited the SD. Whatever the motives of individual leaders of the UGIF, the fact remains that there were indeed a large number of Jews still living in Paris, many still directly dependent upon the UGIF services. The situation was untenable: there was the obvious need for UGIF services and the equally obvious danger incurred by the population whenever it called upon the UGIF for assistance.

The new debate assumed the same proportions as the one that took place with the establishment of the UGIF in December 1941. But now there was one important difference. The immigrant organizations had come to occupy a central position. In the Southern Zone the immigrants' Comité Général de Défense des Juifs (General Jewish Defense Committee [CGD]) at a meeting of the Conseil Répresentatif des Israélites de France (Representative Council of the Jews of France [CRIF]) pressed for a change of policy.† The immigrant organizations in the Southern Zone had united to form a committee in July 1943 and the Central Consistory recognized the resulting CGD as representing the foreign Jews. The CRIF itself had been formed at the end of 1943 and for the first time in the history of the Jews in France brought together in one formal representative body both immigrants and French Jews. The Central Consistory's belated recognition that the fate of French Judaism was irretrievably linked with the foreign Jews had led to a fundamental reappraisal of the situation.

Léon Meiss, who, following Helbronner's arrest in October 1943, had as-

---

* The establishment of the Comité d'Union et de Défense des Juifs in Paris, and the Comité Général de Défense des Juifs in the South, will be discussed in Chapter 9.

† It subsequently altered its name to Conseil Representatif des Juifs de France, the term *Israélites* being considered too narrow. The establishment of the CRIF will be discussed in Chapter 10.

sumed the interim presidency of the Central Consistory, and who also presided over the CRIF, was one of a committee formed to examine the feasibility of an early closure of the UGIF. The debates over the issue, in which UGIF representatives also participated, proved inconclusive. The discussions reached a critical stage just as the Allied armies landed in Normandy in June 1944. The immigrant representatives demanded immediate closure of the UGIF. As far as they were concerned it was not only a moral and political question but above all a question of the survival of the remaining Jews. The UGIF's subservience to Vichy, the immigrants claimed, had made the Jews appear as collaborators, a political disaster that had divided the community. Moreover, the immigrants believed that continued operation of the UGIF represented now, more than ever, a threat to all those who resorted to its assistance. Raymond Geissmann, head of the UGIF-South, argued for the UGIF's continued existence. As a member of the Central Consistory, as well as a UGIF director, he was opposed to the very principle embodied by the UGIF. But Geissmann also believed that the UGIF had a function to perform which no other organization could have fulfilled and it was still needed. The problem, as he saw it, was that there were too many Jewish families currently dependent upon the UGIF's help for an immediate dissolution to be considered. Geissmann also opposed disbanding the UGIF on moral grounds: as far as he was concerned the pride of the French Jews was never tainted by their participation in the UGIF. Dissolving the UGIF would, Geissmann believed, place the remaining Jews at great risk. Geissmann refused therefore to assume the responsibility of declaring the closure of the UGIF-South without Paris approval.

The disruption of communications between the various UGIF leaders, and between Paris and the Southern Zone after the Allied landing in Normandy hampered the conduct of the debate. As it was, the UGIF itself was already disintegrating as an organization. In the south there remained only one senior leader, Geissmann. Throughout the rest of the former Vichy Zone, although the UGIF still distributed help, it no longer functioned from permanent offices. In Paris the UGIF leadership was collapsing. Toni Stern resigned in April 1944.[142] Weill-Hallé, already working with the Comité d'Union et de Défense, no longer considered himself a UGIF board member.[143] Edinger was highly concerned at the possibility of the former UGIF-South leaders openly supporting the closure of the UGIF and the remaining members of the board in Paris deserting him. He called a last-minute secret emergency meeting, attended by Geissmann, who had been summoned in a final bid to gather the necessary support for the policy to keep the UGIF operative. A resolution was passed, directed at the CRIF, reiterating one last time the opposition of the UGIF leadership to a premature closing down. There is no doubt that the board foresaw two possibly disastrous consequences: mass reprisals upon the remaining Jews and the chance that the forces who were ousting the UGIF would be incapable of planning and carrying out relief on the necessary scale until France was liberated.

The rapid advance of the Allied armies in July 1944 once more brought the question of the children's homes to fore. The Comité d'Union et de Défense was convinced that the SD was preparing a new and massive arrest of Jews in Paris and felt that it was imperative to warn the Jewish population. The fact that there were 350 children still in the UGIF homes became the first concern of the underground committee. It approached the UGIF leadership in Paris and offered to organize a mass escape of the children, but Edinger refused to accept the scheme. Edinger was not prepared to take steps that would contradict the decision to maintain the UGIF. Between 20 and 24 July 1944, the children's homes were raided by the Gestapo and 233 children were taken to Drancy; of these, the Germans deported more than 200 to Auschwitz on 31 July 1944.[144]

The arrests over the four days in July were the UGIF's worst indictment. Some children had been overlooked by the Gestapo, while others were so young that the Gestapo officers returned to Drancy without them. When Edinger was informed of this situation he immediately ordered the dispersal of the remaining children and ordered the homes' personnel to hide. But then, fearful of the consequences of this action, Edinger countermanded the order and brought everyone back, including the children. Two hours later the Gestapo returned, on Brunner's instructions, to collect them and take them to Drancy. The last of the children who could have been saved fell victim to a cruel policy.[145]

The UGIF had measured the survival of the children against the overall question of maintaining the existence of the organization and doing what it could to help the Jewish population. The early decision not to heed the warning of the Comité d'Union et de Défense and its offer to hide the children expressed the essence of the UGIF's grand strategy. To the very end it continued to view itself as a relief organization. Although it recognized that it had been created and allowed to continue to operate for reasons other than relief, its leaders had accepted the responsibility only because they believed in the imperatives of their task. They were determined never to allow themselves to participate in any action they considered injurious to the interest of the Jewish population.

The belated decision to hide the remaining children and order the staff away from a home that the Gestapo had overlooked was a moral reaction at variance with established policy. But as soon as Edinger recovered from his initial impulse he immediately canceled the order. Although the remaining UGIF leaders sensed that Liberation was at hand, they remained unwilling to take evasive actions. The UGIF refused to take any actions that might provoke Gestapo anger. The same fear of reprisals had characterized UGIF policy throughout its existence and was used as a justification not to act.

The final chapter of the UGIF was written during and soon after the Liberation. During the struggle for the Liberation of Paris, the units of the Jewish popular militia, the immigrants' armed units, occupied all the UGIF offices. The provisional government dissolved the UGIF. And, during the settlements of political accounts that took place following the Liberation, Georges Edinger was arrested by the Jewish militia, and briefly incarcerated at Drancy, which had been turned into a special camp for collaborators.[146]

The end of the UGIF did not mean the end of the UGIF as a political issue, however. Those opposed to the UGIF, particularly the CGD and Comité d'Union et de Défense, demanded that the CRIF publicly condemn both the institution and all those who had led it. Those believing that the UGIF had contributed, against impossible odds, in defending the Jewish population sought personal vindication. The purges that characterized French political life in the aftermath of the Liberation extended into the ranks of the Jewish community. On the demand of the CGD the CRIF appointed an honorary court to pronounce a historical verdict upon the UGIF.

The CGD, however, committed a cardinal error: it had accepted that the court should concentrate its investigation upon the case of the children arrested in July 1944, as an example of what it held was the least defensible UGIF action. Instead of demanding from the court a historical judgment based upon the performance of the UGIF over the whole period, the CGD accepted a procedure based upon a single if tragic event, which in itself could prove no more than cowardice or error of judgment on the part of Edinger. It took until October 1946 for the honorary court to present its findings. None of the UGIF leaders were found guilty of criminal actions. Even so, Meiss, as president of the CRIF, considered the terms of the judgment too harsh.[147] He took it upon himself to declare that the evidence was inconclusive and partly contradictory. Meiss therefore refused to accept the verdict, and demanded that the court reexamine the evidence. The court did as directed and returned a verdict that totally cleared the UGIF leaders. J. Lubetzki summed up the basis of the judgment thus: "Their courage and devotion to duty could never have succeeded. Let us however greet them with the respect [with which] one salutes the defeated fighter."[148]

But the immigrant organizations were far from satisfied with such a verdict. They demanded that the whole question be reexamined on much broader terms. The Association of Former Concentration Camp Inmates was not pleased with Meiss's summing up when he declared that "the commission had backed down before the impossible task of presenting a historical evaluation of the UGIF and could only limit itself to an examination of a specific instance of UGIF activity."[149] At the following meeting of the CRIF, the Association of Former Concentration Camp Inmates, supported this time by twelve other organizations, including Zionist groups, demanded a new trial. Meiss refused to reopen the case on the ground that it was beyond the CRIF's capacity to conduct such an inquiry.[150]

Unless the immigrant organizations were prepared to destroy the CRIF they were powerless: they did not have the numbers to overrule Meiss nor were they prepared to destroy the organization. French Judaism was not prepared to have the whole question publicly debated. The case was closed, the records of the depositions made before the honorary court have since been missing from the archives of the CRIF. Today it is no longer possible to examine fully even such a seemingly clear question of why the children were not saved. The disappearance of the evidence further limits any critical evaluation of the role of the UGIF leadership. Yet these difficulties should not preclude a discussion of some of the issues. Central to the examination of the place of the UGIF in the survival of the Jews in France was the role of the Central Consistory, without which none of the UGIF's successive leaderships would have dared to act. Unfortunately, the UGIF-Central Consistory relationship cannot be fully examined because the Consistory's archives remain closed to research.

Underlying that important question rests a serious political problem: the nature of the Vichy-French Judaism connection and its role in the development of an appropriate response to the deportation of the Jews. There is no doubt that the foreign Jews were the victims of this relationship. This is in no way to suggest that French Judaism was responsible for their mass deportation but simply that French Judaism failed to give them the necessary support at the appropriate time.

Finally, and perhaps more crucial, is the question of the importance of the UGIF-Consistory connection and the consequences of this relationship for the development of an alternative leadership that could have taken an active position against the UGIF. Though there was a viable alternative leadership, first among the immigrants and later among the French Jews, particularly in the Zionist movement, the continued existence of the UGIF blocked the development of a Jewish resistance that would effectively unite all the various groups into a single movement. The UGIF leadership, composed of French Jews, had continued to believe that the deportation measures were directed only at the foreigners and only because they had become difficult to find were French Jews substituted for them. This assumption and the UGIF's persistent adherence to it accounted for the disastrous strategy which assumed that French Judaism would survive. As a result, the main thrust of French Judaism's response was toward traditional philanthropic activities, admirable in themselves but totally unsuited to the situation. The path chosen by the successive UGIF leaders was the same path followed by French Judaism. Because the UGIF refused to view the problem of aid in any other terms but charity they foreclosed their own role as a unifying factor between French Judaism and the immigrant organizations. The UGIF remained a divisive force in the struggle for survival.

The history of the immigrant Jewish organizations traverses this same ground, but has a different effect. They acknowledged no duty to a distorted and annihilating perversion of the law, which the French Jews continued to respect. This was why, as shall be shown in the following two chapters, the immigrants proved to be the pacesetters in Jewish survival.

IV

THE JEWISH
IMMIGRANTS'
RESPONSE

8

From Self-Help to Resistance:
June 1940 to July 1942

It is to the immigrant organizations that we must look for the earliest, as well as the most appropriate, responses designed to assist and protect the Jewish population as a whole from the projected Final Solution in France. And it is in Paris that their organized responses first took shape. The reasons are clear: not only were the foreign Jews the first and most severely affected by the anti-Jewish measures, but above all and unlike the French Jews, the immigrants' past experiences had given them a better understanding of the problems arising from state antisemitism and more experience in dealing with them. Inevitably, they were more sensitive to Nazi racism. These factors contributed to making the foreign Jews' response uniquely different from that of the French Jews.

The exodus from Paris of June 1940 resulted in the total disintegration of communal activities within immigrant Jewry. The flight from Paris of leaders, members, and supporters of the former vast network of organizations affected each and every one of them. Even the Yiddish-speaking group of the French Communist party (PCF), which had been operating illegally since the PCF had been banned in September 1939, was affected.[1]

However, not all the Jews left Paris. It was from among the remaining immigrant leaders and communal activists that the first Jewish organization was reformed in Paris. What made this resumption of communal activities particularly significant was that it occurred as the German armies were marching into Paris on 15 June 1940. On their own initiative, without directive or guidance but moved by a sense of responsibility, this handful of individuals from various political movements and organizations had sought each other out. These people had sufficient experience in community affairs and a clear enough vision of what was ahead to know that the Jewish immigrant population would require much assistance once the exodus was over. That appreciation of the situation was not based on some broadly pessimistic view of the future, but on a close acquaintance with the situation in Paris before the exodus. Already a substantial number of families depended upon communal help: the refugees from Germany, Austria, and Central Europe, as well as the families of men in the army. The social dislocation resulting from the exodus could only compound the problems. These communal activists therefore knew that the need to reconstitute relief organizations was imperative, despite the presence of the German army.[2]

By the second day of the Occupation of Paris, 16 June, representatives of five organizations were already discussing the practical aspects of reopening welfare institutions: the Bund, Left Poale-Zion, the FSJF, the Right Poale-Zion, and activists from the Colonie Scolaire. Two considerations dominated the debates: how the Jewish population would be affected by the German Occupation and what would remain of the former organized immigrant community once the exodus ended. It was unanimously decided to begin modestly, and August was set as a target date for a general reopening of institutions. Meanwhile, all resources would be pooled. Four days after the arrival of the German armies four immigrant canteens were operative: the Bund and the Left Poale-Zion canteens had been kept open and the canteens of the Right Poale-Zion and the FSJF were reopened.[3]

Within the first week of the Occupation, these immigrant Jews had laid the foundation for a renewal of communal life. They formed a committee and selected an executive. It was chaired by Rubin Grinberg, the former chairman of the Banque Populaire Juive (Jewish People's Bank). Its treasurer was Léon Glaeser, a lawyer, and its secretary was Yehuda Jakoubowicz, a professional communal worker. No name was given to the committee but as it was meeting in the offices of the Colonie Scolaire situated in the rue Amelot, it became known as the Comité Amelot. A number of problems required immediate attention, and finance was one of them. The only resources available were the meager funds held by the various canteen managers. There was, however, a check for 200,000 francs which had been left by the FSJF with the Colonie Scolaire on the eve of the exodus. This check would have given the committee breathing space but it could not be cashed: all the banks in Paris were closed and no one knew when they would reopen.[4] The other problem facing Amelot was more serious. The press had published an official announcement stating that all French organizations were dissolved and that permission to function had to be applied for at the Prefecture of Police. Of all the various communal workers and organizations represented on the Amelot Committee the Bund was the only group that felt directly threatened because of its former connection with the French Socialist party. None of the others felt that their past activities could possibly attract the attention of the Gestapo or the French police. The Amelot Committee did not believe that the reason for the Bund's fear was likely to cause the committee embarrassment with either police force, however. It decided to disregard the order and proceed as if this police order did not affect relief activities.[5]

By August the decision to reactivate Jewish organizations led Amelot to approach known former activists of other organizations. Remaining representatives of OSE and ORT were asked to join but they declined, unwilling to act without prior approval from their respective leaderships which had left Paris during the exodus. The Amelot executive also considered approaching the Communist organization. But the Communists presented a political problem of a totally different nature. There was strong opposition within Amelot to their participation. The Bundists' representatives, adhering to their party's former policy, which had stated their refusal to belong to any committee on which Communists were represented, warned that they would withdraw from Amelot. Others at Amelot were concerned that the traditional activism of the Communists would attract police attention at a time when the PCF itself was banned. Conscious of the major troubles their presence might create, Amelot decided not to seek Communist participation.[6]

Meanwhile the Jewish Communist movement began to reorganize. Its first illegal news-sheet appeared in July 1940.[7] Members and supporters believed that the illegal Yiddish *Unzer Vort* (Our Opinion) would help reestablish the Communist presence. The organization was conscious of the dislocation caused by the exodus and viewed the news-sheet as a major step toward rebuilding popular support. It was to serve as a vehicle for the dissemination of Communist policies and above all act as an organizational tool.[8] Not all Jews viewed the reappearance of an illegal Yiddish publication in the same way. Some felt that it would have been safer for the Jewish population to avoid attracting attention from the authorities. Others saw the Jewish Communist press as provocative, inviting police attention. These reactions were understandable. Everybody feared the Gestapo, and its presence had already been felt by the Bund. On two occasions, Gestapo officers had enquired at the Bund's canteen for the whereabouts of some of its leaders in connection with their public utterances during the Grynspan trial before the war.[9] It was therefore no surprise that Amelot, though it hoped others would join in its efforts to reorganize relief activities, acted so cautiously.[10]

Amelot's desire to encourage all the activists who remained in Paris to assume their responsibility vis-à-vis their former organizations was based on a realistic appraisal of their own capacities to meet the immigrant population's needs. The central problem Amelot faced in July 1940 was to secure the necessary funds. The exodus had altered traditional sources of funding. The Joint, one of the major contributors to immigrant institutions, had also left Paris during the exodus. The other major source of financial support, the middle classes, were temporarily out of reach. Desperate for funds, Amelot decided to send an emissary to the Vichy Zone to contact the Joint. Mrs. Rina from the Bund succeeded in contacting Katzki, the Joint chief of operations in France, and obtained 180,000 francs.[11] The difficulties in establishing lines of communication in the weeks that followed the Armistice were compounded by the fact that none of the immigrant organizations in the Vichy Zone had yet reorganized. However, Mrs. Rina did succeed in establishing contacts with Bundist leaders in Toulouse and with some leaders from the FSJF.[12] By August 1940, a limited cash flow had been initiated. The Joint, through its connection with the Quakers' representatives in Paris, began to send modest amounts.[13]

During July 1940 welfare activities began. A children's clinic (Pour nos Enfants) reopened.[14] The OSE, under Dr. Minkowski, began functioning too.

Amelot formed a special children's commission, under Margaret Schachnowski, a non-Jewish Russian and wife of a Bundist activist. By August, immigrant relief activities in Paris began to regain something of their former scope.[15] The Communists reopened their own canteen and a clinic. The return of many immigrants, including some businessmen, from the exodus helped meet the daily budgetary difficulties. The OSE began receiving funds from the Vichy Zone. Moreover, the reopening of the *Comité de Bienfaisance* under the auspices of the Paris Consistory in September helped ease the pressure upon Amelot's resources.[16]

It was during August that David Rapoport, a former senior member of the FSJF, returned to Paris. He was to become the heart and soul of the Amelot Committee. His first step was to establish contact with Chief-Rabbi Julien Weill. Anticipating Amelot's need to develop links with the Paris Consistory, Rapoport offered his support. However, Dannecker had already made his presence felt, demanding that Weill establish a central Jewish representative organization. The Paris Consistory was then too concerned with the implications of such a demand to pursue Rapoport's offer.

The Communists, through their illegal newspaper, set about rebuilding their organization during July. They had been operating illegally since the outbreak of the war, but some of their institutions, because they were not legally part of the Communist movement, had remained open. Although such channels were valuable in terms of overcoming political isolation, the Jewish Communists labored under a major political handicap. Their movement was (and in the Jewish community was recognized as) an integral part of the French and international Communist movements committed to supporting and defending Soviet foreign policy. This close relationship worked against its acceptance. Immigrant Jewry judged the German-Soviet Non-Aggression Pact of 1939 as catastrophic and the Jewish Communists received public reprobation for their official support of the pact.[17] Although the majority view within the Jewish Communist membership opposed the pact and the Yiddish Communist daily, *Die Naie Presse* (The New Press), published their views, the movement nevertheless faced political isolation. The months between the pact and the arrival of the German armies witnessed a virtual disappearance of Communist influence among the immigrant Jews.

Yet this loss of public standing had not resulted in the collapse of the Communist organization. Around a core of dedicated members and faithful supporters who had seen political adversity in bygone days, it had survived. The German Occupation of Paris, with the resulting conditions, gave the movement new impetus. Internal problems explain best why they were slower than the Amelot Committee in regrouping. By August 1940 the Communist organization had carried out sufficient groundwork to allow the illegal leadership to review the situation created by the Occupation.[18]

The Communist leadership mapped out a policy designed to meet the new conditions. It took into account the current needs of the Jewish population and aimed at rebuilding popular support by articulating a policy directed toward meeting immediate material needs.[19] Furthermore, the absence of active Communist organizations had created a political vacuum which had been capitalized upon by the Bund and the Zionist organizations. The Communist leaders decided therefore to establish a new organization. It was to be called Solidarité (Solidarity) and would be based on local branches. The Communists had finally found a formula that would permit them to enter into a dialogue with other political organizations and, most importantly, from their political point of view, give them access to the Jewish population.

The problems in overcoming the material needs of the Jewish population went beyond simple questions of reopening canteens or finding resources. The most important problems were political. Until December 1940 two factors dominated the situation: a growing SD assertion of control over the Jewish organizations and its relentless pressure toward their centralization, and, on the other hand, the communal organizations' need for unifying and rationalizing their welfare activities. It was then only partially clear, but nevertheless clear enough, to the immigrant leaders from Amelot and to the Paris Consistory that there was a conflict of interest between those two factors. Although all feared Gestapo control, the overriding need for united relief action was crucial. The Paris Consistory still believed it could find protection in French law against the SD's more threatening demands. Amelot took its cue from the Consistory, while adhering to its own priorities.

By November 1940, under the pressures of communal needs and Dannecker's demands, the contact established earlier between Rapoport and Chief-Rabbi Weill began to develop. The Paris Consistory and Amelot decided to form a committee to coordinate their activities while retaining organizational independence. The problems governing the establishment of such a coordination committee were, however, more complex for Amelot than for the Consistory, because although Amelot was a collection of various political movements, it could not claim to represent the full spectrum of immigrant political opinion. Under the conditions arising from SD pressure to enforce controls over Jewish organizations, Amelot would have difficulties with immigrant public opinion in justifying its participation. Given the prevalence of anti-Nazi feelings in the immigrant population, failure to justify its actions would have been political suicide. The problem for Amelot, which was then convinced of the benefits that would accrue from a centralization of relief activities, was to find a way of working with the Communists.

The five organizations brought together in the Amelot Committee represented, in fact, two ideological blocs: the Bund was a Socialist group and the Left and Right Poale-Zion represented Zionist ideologies. For Amelot, therefore, political factors could surface in any dispute and had the potential to influence all decisions. The Bund and the Right Poale-Zion were opposed to any rapprochement with the Communists; the Left Poale-Zion, Marxist in orientation, wanted to bring the Communists into Amelot. Rapoport, from the FSJF, Amelot's acknowledged leader, consistently refused to introduce divisive political issues into what he held was Amelot's primary task: to dispense help to those in need regardless of political affiliation. It was under his direction in August 1940 that Amelot approached the Communist canteen which had just reopened and asked it to join. But, although the Communists saw political advantages in such recognition, they demanded appropriate representation on the executive of Amelot. A majority of that committee in turn decided to use this demand as justification for refusing to accept them, claiming that Amelot was not a political organization and that its executive was not elected on political criteria. Nevertheless, Amelot did not wish to seem biased against the Communists on political grounds, so it offered consideration of the demand, but only after the Communists had joined the committee. These negotiations lasted until December 1940 and culminated in the Communists' refusal to accept such a vague undertaking.

For the Communists Amelot's offer and Dannecker's continued pressure upon the Jewish organizations to centralize their activities presented serious political difficulties.[20] While Amelot offered a possibility of gaining access to Jewish political life, the implications of Dannecker's demands could not be evaluated. They had to weigh the political cost of participating without guarantees of political independence on a committee already threatened with Gestapo controls. The temptation for the Communists was great but so was the price. The political movements already affiliated with Amelot were well aware of the Communist dilemma but they were more interested in the gains to be had from an unconditional Communist participation than in encouraging a serious and deep examination of the reasons for the Communists' hesitations.

By November 1940, the Amelot Committee was already engaged in a range of activities that were to characterize its general field of activities until its demise in June 1943. It had committed itself to extend all necessary forms of relief within the immigrant community and at the same time to seek a working relationship with French Judaism. But at no time was it prepared to be bound by laws that would restrict its relief objectives. By November Amelot controlled four canteens, an orphanage, a children's welfare commission, a clinic, a special financial relief fund, and a legal department. Although its activities were still on a modest scale it was already fulfilling an important social function.

Economic activities in Occupied Paris had begun anew, yet the Jewish working population did not appear to benefit by it. The German purchasing commissions boosted the economy but the traditional Jewish trades did not improve significantly. These economic difficulties, as well as the many families whose breadwinners were prisoners of war or were still in the army in the Vichy Zone, were expressed in the number of people who resorted to soup kitchens. In November 1940 Amelot served 38,239 meals, of which 13,897 were provided free of charge.[21] By December 1940 the monthly figure increased to 39,960 meals.[22] If we include the number of meals served by the Communists, 13,000, and the ACIP, 12,904, we find that during December more than 65,000 meals had been dispensed. It was clear that more than 2,000 persons daily needed this basic communal help.[23]

It was in response to the material plight of the immigrant Jews that the immigrant organizations, other than the Communists, had reconstituted themselves. Political questions were bound to arise. Although none of them in the past had constituted effective political organizations in the immigrant community, they nevertheless represented political alternatives. The Bund, originating in Poland where it had been the largest Jewish working-class organization, had formed an independent organization in Paris in 1932.[24] Though there had been Bundist committees in France for decades they previously viewed themselves as local branches of the Polish Bund. The successive crises that bedeviled the international Communist movement during the 1930s, particularly the changes in the political line of the Comintern on the Jewish national question, and finally the string of political trials in the Soviet Union, had all benefitted the Bund by increasing disenchantment with the Communists. A number of Jewish Communists had left the party and joined the Bund in Paris, giving it the energy to create an organization concerned with local problems.[25] The Bundist-Communist relationship had always been uneasy. In France, in particular, it suffered from the vagaries of the Socialist-Communist relationship. Competition for support from the immigrant population and the presence of embittered former Communists in the ranks of the Bund never made for harmonious contacts. The political conflicts between Bund and Communists did not discourage personal contacts, however. For example, Dr. Ogus, president of the *Arbeiter Ring* (Workers' Alliance), had always maintained close ties with the Communists.[26] Therefore, hostility to any united activities or even to joint participation on any committee coexisted with close personal ties between members of both groups.[27]

The exodus of June 1940 especially affected the Bund in Paris. Many of its leading activists left, some for the south of France, others for the United States. The reduced leadership that remained continued to pursue the prewar strategy which took into account the Bund's limited forces and the need to ally with other immigrant organizations, save the Communists. That political line led to the Bund's participation in the Amelot Committee while seeking to build its own organization. The Bund had kept its canteen open throughout the days of the exodus and the arrival of the Germany army in June 1940. It soon reopened its lending library (Medem) and once more began holding political meetings in its canteen. Its prewar newspaper *Unzer Shtime* (Our Voice) no longer appeared; only Raphael Riba remained of the editorial staff.[28] The Bund's adherence to Amelot, though temporarily beneficial in that it received material help for its relief activities and also communal recognition, was no help in buttressing its political standing in the community. The Bund became an appendage to Amelot and lost a historical opportunity to assert its unique role with the immigrant population as a Marxist political alternative, independent from the Third International.

The Zionist movements, especially the Left and the Right Poale-Zion, although never mass political organizations were influential in that Zionism itself was then a growing political movement among the immigrants. In June 1940 these groups suffered the same fate as all the other organizations. Before the war their general activities had consisted in advocating the establishment of a Jewish national home in Palestine, disseminating news affecting the Zionist movements, collecting funds for the purchase of land and the establishment of settlements, and encouraging Jews to migrate to Palestine. The rise of Nazism in Germany and its anti-Jewish measures had stimulated public interest in Zionism. Zionists had been among the prime movers of a world boycott of Nazi Germany and when a Jewish Popular Front formed in Paris in 1936, they participated in it. But they never sought to constitute themselves on the highly structured Communist organizational model. The nearest they came was through the establishment of youth movements, but even then they could never claim to have been of significant size. Like the Bund and the Communists, it was through their canteens that they conducted their political activities. The other Zionist movement, the Revisionist Movement, led by Kadmi Cohen, stood outside the Zionist mainstream. It never entered into any alliance with the other Zionist organizations. It never attracted a following nor sought to proselytize through such channels as canteens. Early in 1942 Kadmi Cohen approached the Germans for permission to operate legally and publish his group's platform. This gained the movement little advantage. Both the Bund and the Communists attacked Kadmi Cohen for his attempted ingratiation.[29]

Besides these political formations there was also the FSJF. Although led by Zionists it did not express a distinctive political viewpoint. But in the final analysis, it was to play a more important political role than any of the strictly Zionist organizations. Its importance derived from its central position in immigrant activities. It was the structure around which small organizations gathered and as such the FSJF considered itself as representing majority immigrant opinion within and without the Jewish community.[30] Its role in the Amelot Committee was central. But the most significant aspect of immigrant organizational life during that period was not found in the role played by prewar communal activists but in the growing participation of people who had never formerly taken an active part in any organization.

The key to all the various relief activities in the early period, until the end of 1940, was the canteens. All the organizations affiliated with Amelot managed their own. The Bund and the Left Poale-Zion each managed their own party's canteen. Amelot had allocated the other two on the basis of each party being entitled to prove the value of its contribution by being given the opportunity to develop committees responsible for their management: a canteen to Karlzbach, of the Right Poale-Zion, and the fourth canteen to Aron Kremer and Hersz Zimmerman. The Amelot executive was responsible for ensuring the necessary support, financial or otherwise, and for working out general policy.[31]

Between August and November 1940, Amelot began to face problems other than general relief. During September Dannecker ordered Chief-Rabbi Weill to form a central organization[32] In October two German ordinances appeared: the census of the Jews and the registration of all Jewish-owned businesses, with the announcement that administrators would be appointed to them.[33] In November the Gestapo arrested a number of Zionists whose names it had found on prewar Zionist collection lists.[34] The apprehension caused by all those measures was further compounded by Vichy's own legislation and pronouncements.

The reactions of the various immigrant organizations to these political developments were indicative of the ways they tried to handle the difficult political issues throughout the war. The Communists were the only ones to advance an analysis that related the anti-Jewish measures to the general political situation. They concluded that Fascism was the enemy of the Jewish people, that Nazism was the worst expression of Fascism, and that Vichy was an antidemocratic state that would inevitably continue to take up positions hostile to the Jews.[35] This interpretation of events led the Communists to develop organizational structures that would engage the Jews in the struggle against Nazism and Vichy with those movements already committed to this struggle. The Jewish Communist leadership was convinced that the Jews as a people would find in these forces, when the time came, the necessary help. Accordingly, the destruction of Nazism, rather than the temporary conditions confronting the Jews, was the primary focus of their activities.

All the other organizations were only partly in agreement with the Communist interpretation and its consequent policies. They did not agree with the characterization of Vichy as an antidemocratic state that would inevitably continue on its anti-Jewish course. They viewed with apprehension Vichy's early xenophobic measures which began to assume ever more pronounced antisemitic proportions as temporary difficulties dictated by the political requirements of the negotiations of a peace treaty with Germany manifested themselves. They did not think Vichy would ever become a racist state nor did they believe it would take the racist measures adopted so far any further.

Such an analysis had two corollaries: that the Jewish position was not desperate and that the only real task facing Jewish organizations was to develop self-help institutions. This particular conclusion had its roots in a widespread attitude among the foreign Jews, an attitude that began to develop in the late 1930s. It resulted from what was seen as the West's inability to take a firm stand against Nazism in Germany and Austria and its failure to condemn German antisemitism. The mood of despair deepened with every Nazi success and led the Jewish population to feel abandoned by the "democracies."[36] The growing realization of vulnerability, the rise of antisemitism at home, and finally the German-Soviet Non-Aggression Pact of 1939, resulted in an inward-looking determination to seek defense and survival within the Jewish organizations themselves. The establishment of communal institutions to help Jews in need might seem a limited goal but the organizations felt it both necessary and within their capacity.

The two distinctive policies, the Communist and the Jewish nationalist, expressed themselves in organizational forms. Solidarity began to form committees in each *quartier*. To strengthen local leadership it obtained from the PCF the transfers of Jewish party members working in non-Jewish spheres.[37] It established clandestine printing presses; it created a laboratory for the manufacture of forged identity papers. There was a determined drive to organize the largest possible number of supporters in a complex of specialized activities: women's sections, youth groups, trade-union branches. By December 1940 Solidarity had formed 130 street committees, 50 women's groups, 20 trade-union branches, and youth sections that numbered hundreds of members. These clandestine structures were complemented by the legal activities of a canteen and a clinic. Although Solidarity aimed to develop relief activities, this objective was secondary to its political aims: the development of a political campaign within and without the Jewish community, seeking to alert Jewish and non-Jewish public opinion to the dangers of German antisemitism.[38]

The other immigrant organizations, those gathered around Amelot, directed their efforts to one end only: the establishment and sound management of relief institutions. They saw no need to establish organizational structures involving the largest possible number of people. The objective of self-help, although justifiable in its own terms, dealt only with the effect and not the cause. It resulted therefore in a failure to draw popular attention to the inherent dangers of the Jews' situation. Such an organizational conception, which assumed that these institutions would be permitted to continue to operate, left all those in need of their help permanently exposed to the risk of summary closure of those institutions. As a consequence, a massive sense of insecurity grew alongside the inevitable feelings of dependency in those who frequented the supporting institutions.

The increasing antisemitic propaganda, the anti-Jewish measures of the latter part of 1940, and the growing apprehension gave the question of unity renewed importance. The Communist organizations, already firmly established, were still suffering from political isolation. It had become imperative, in order to extend their influence, to find a common language with the other immigrant organizations.[39] Within Amelot, Left Poale-Zion was pressing for a rapprochement. It argued for the need to further strengthen relief work and believed that Solidarity needed to be drawn into Amelot. Some support for that view appeared to have developed; however, when the news of the negotiations being conducted between the Coordination Committee, to which Amelot belonged, and Dannecker, became known to the Communists, they decided to let all discussions lapse.

The establishment in December 1940 of the Coordination Committee (ACIP and Amelot) was recognized by the immigrant organizations as necessary. The immigrants, furthermore, saw the Coordination Committee achieving two purposes: it would extend general relief work and, more important, bring together French and foreign Jews. Dannecker's pressure tactics soon led some of Amelot's member organizations to question the wisdom of participating in the Coordination Committee. In March 1941, Judith Topcha, from the Left Poale-Zion, met with Solidarity's leadership and sought its views. The Bund, through its canteen administrator, Nathan Schachnowski, met Communist representatives over the same question. Amelot found itself divided over whether it should remain in the Coordination Committee.[40]

The Communists, confident of their political line, argued for nonparticipation in any Gestapo-controlled body.

The alternative to legally operating relief institutions, to which Amelot was committed, was none other than the Communist position of confrontation with the occupying authorities and if neccessary with the French police. But no member of the Amelot organizations was at this stage capable of adopting such a policy or even willing to consider it. The general conditions did not yet seem to them to warrant such a reaction nor did their past political experience in France equip them to undertake that role. The Left Poale-Zion and the Bund organization in Paris did not have the same fighting spirit as their parent organization in Poland; indeed some critics have even gone as far as to suggest that this was due to the corrupting effect of working closely with communal officialdom.[41] A more balanced judgment would perhaps look for an explanation in their existing leadership rather than in sociological causes. The Left Poale-Zion and the Bund, although in opposition to Amelot's continued participation in the Coordination Committee, decided to remain within Amelot and campaign for a change of policy.[42]

The period up to the May 1941 internment of foreign Jews witnessed a major growth in the activities of immigrant organizations. They overcame the early difficulties and successfully adapted themselves to the existing conditions. The Communist organizations were firmly implanted. Although bereft of a newspaper, the Bund was politically active, campaigning for Jewish national culture and for socialism. It conducted cultural and political meetings; it even held a May Day celebration attended by 150 people.[43]

The immigrant organizations' problems were external: the conciliatory stance of the Coordination Committee and Dannecker's determination to transform it into an instrument of his own policy. It was between the end of March and May 1941 that the intent of Dannecker's policy began to be apparent, when he brought to Paris the two Viennese Jews, and assigned them to the Coordination Committee as technical advisers. The manner in which Israelowicz and Biberstein asserted their presence at Coordination Committee meetings, with the authority conferred upon them by their patron, radically challenged all previously held assumptions about organizational independence. Even greater anxiety, however, ensued when the French police suddenly arrested 3,710 foreign Jews on 14 May.

Overnight the immigrant Jews who had already become accustomed to living under German rule were shown how insecure their position was. Overnight this event compounded, for the immigrant organizations, all previous problems. Yet although a totally unexpected measure, its effect on the population's morale was short-lived. Families lamented the loss of husbands and sons; others were grateful at having been spared. Jacques Biélinky, a well-placed and keen observer, noted in his diary, "It is believed, in Jewish circles, that there will not be any more massive arrests followed by internments."[44] Biélinky must have been reflecting the views of the Coordination Committee leadership, for in the ranks of Amelot and Solidarity there was much concern at the significance of the measure and the likelihood of a repetition.[45] The first reaction was to increase the level of activity. Solidarity was the only group, however, to point out the thread linking the internments, the German and Vichy laws and the Gestapo's control of the Coordination Committee.[46]

Shortly after these internments, Elie Danon, a representative from the Coordination Committee, called upon the Communist canteen to ask it to join the committee and to display staff recruitment posters for firms working for the Germans. The management's refusal led Danon to threaten calling in the German authorities.[47] The Communist leadership, taking the threat in all seriousness, decided to close the canteen rather than submit. Their clinic was also the object of a visit from a representative of the Coordination Committee. Again pressure was applied. The clinic president, Adolphe Ribozchad, was even called up to the Department for Jewish Affairs at the Prefecture of Police, and asked to sign a document placing the clinic under the control of the Coordination Committee. His refusal led to the arrest of the secretary of the clinic, Laska, and again the Communists closed the clinic rather than submit.[48]

The Communists were not the only ones to refuse to accept the control of the Coordination Committee. Amelot's representatives officially resigned and, expecting reprisals, took immediate steps to protect their organization. All activities were immediately decentralized. All the various commissions formerly operating from offices in the Colonie Scolaire immediately shifted premises. Its clinic became the center for illegal interviews and all financial help was dispensed at the homes of the claimants. This state of emergency lasted a number of weeks but as no reprisals occurred Amelot's leadership decided to call off the emergency measures and resume activities from its former office.[49]

The German invasion of the Soviet Union, on 22 June 1941, marked a political turning point in the activities of the Communist organizations. On 25 June a special edition of the illegal *Unzer Vort,* published in both Yiddish and French, warned that Jewish survival would be fought out on Soviet soil and that the outcome of the war was of "vital interest to the Jewish People."[50] Yet the poignancy of that appeal and the sense of a dramatic historical crisis was not reflected in the Communists' day-to-day activities. This same special edition also advanced a list of demands for those who had been interned in May: better food, humane treatment, the right to correspondence, the release of war veterans and sick men, the payment of family allowances, and rights to conjugal visits. The gulf between the historical evaluation of the significance of the invasion of the Soviet Union and the more mundane but necessary demands advanced for those interned reflects the tension between matters of high principle and the pressing demands of increasingly difficult daily life for the Jews in Paris in June 1941.

Of all the problems faced by the population and the immigrant organizations the need for information was becoming more and more important.

The collaborationist press and radio under the control of German and Vichy censorship blocked access, in Occupied France, to all news from afar. For the Jewish population, increasingly isolated, news became a psychological lifeline. The only external channels available were the broadcasts of the BBC and Radio Moscow beamed to France, but none of these stations especially concerned themselves with specific Jewish problems. No Jewish newspapers, not even censored ones, were published in Paris. The only uncensored news available was that disseminated by the illegal Jewish Communist press. It was no surprise that its publications were eagerly sought. The *Informations Juives,* a weekly publication, imposed by Dannecker upon the Coordination Committee in March 1941, did not meet the need. Dannecker had conceived it as a vehicle for the dissemination of legislation affecting Jews, and he did not intend to allow it to develop any other role.

The presentation and interpretation of events became a key issue for all the immigrant organizations as well as for the Communists. But the question proved difficult, indeed impossible, for the non-Communist groups to resolve. It required not only technical facilities but above all an organizational infrastructure for distributing the paper. Only Amelot, if it had pooled all the available resources of its member organizations, could have overcome all the obstacles. During the summer of 1941 Amelot examined the technical feasibility of publishing its own newspaper but concluded that it was beyond its capabilities.[51] Having considered itself primarily a relief committee and not having involved the immigrant population directly in its work, Amelot was now paying the price. Its constituent organizations were no more broadly based, and they also proved unable to publish. Only the Communists remained capable of regularly supplying the immigrant population with relevant news until the end of the war.[52]

The Amelot Committee, divided politically but committed to its common objectives, was held together by David Rapoport. He steered it through the difficulties arising from its status as a legal organization that needed to resort to illegal procedures. Amelot did eventually sever its connection with the Coordination Committee in May 1941, but this had not occurred suddenly.[53] Rapoport had tried once before to convince its leaders to disband but had failed. Amelot therefore found itself nominally a member of that committee while in practice it kept no contacts. To force the Coordination Committee to transform itself into a central organization, Dannecker had informed the French administration that the Coordination Committee was the only officially recognized Jewish organization. Amelot, which had formerly obtained the supplies for its canteens from the Secours National, was therefore forced to define its relationship with the Coordination Committee. Giving highest priority to keeping the canteens open, Amelot finally agreed to submit regular reports to the Coordination Committee on the number of meals it served. By this act all former protestations of independence were negated. Even the Bund, in spite of its earlier resignation from Amelot when faced with the choice of conforming or closing down its canteen and thereby penalizing the poor, had ended up accepting a form of control. Left Poale-Zion, which had also opposed Amelot's participation in the Coordination Committee, found itself having to compromise.

It was the ever-increasing hardship faced by an ever-growing number of immigrant families that forced Amelot to acknowledge the authority of the Coordination Committee. The May 1941 internment of 3,710 men placed added strain on the limited resources available.[54] Those interned, as well as those in breach of the law, came to swell the numbers of those who had been previously helped. The men sent to Beaune-La-Rolande and Pithiviers became the focus of all the immigrant organizations' relief efforts. The wretched conditions in the camps impelled the Amelot Committee, and its constituent organizations acting independently, to help, each immigrant group attempting to discover from its own interned members what was most needed.

The Communists took an even broader view of the scope of the aid necessary: they mobilized their organizations and launched a broad political campaign. On 20 May, their women's groups were at the camps' gates demanding the right to send food parcels.[55] The starving men on the inside and the women on the outside began attacking the barbed wire. The camp administration was compelled to accept the food parcels. The Communists were also the first to organize illegal committees within both camps.[56] The largest, in Pithiviers, numbered 300 from a camp population of more than 2,000. These committees set out to organize the internees and fight the camp administration. Within the first week the Communist organization in the camp had established contact with their leaders in Paris. In Beaune-La-Rolande, the Communist organization, although smaller, was also operating within the first week. The first objectives were to formulate a common policy based on the men's needs and to see that campaigns organized inside and outside the camps were synchronized. After four weeks of intensive campaigning they won from the camp administration substantial victories: food parcels were accepted, mail and visiting days were granted.

But gains were not taken for granted. By mid-June, Solidarity had organized another demonstration of 100 women outside Pithiviers to show the authorities their determination.[57] The Communist underground in the camps functioned at three levels: a clandestine political leadership, a semilegal committee of heads of barracks (semilegal in the sense that it had not been approved by the camp administration), and a cultural commission that functioned legally. An executive committee of twenty-five Communists in each camp supervised and controlled all these activities. In Pithiviers it published a handwritten bulletin, *Pithiviers Konzentrazionlager Zeitung* (Pithiviers Concentration Camp Newspaper); in Beaune-La-Rolande the bulletin appeared under the name *Unzer Lager* (Our Camp). Before their final deportation they had succeeded in producing fourteen issues of their respective bulletins as well as a number of leaflets.[58]

One of the main tasks the Communist camp organizations had set themselves was to develop total solidarity among the internees. They began their campaign around the most crucial question: food supplies. Although the right to food parcels had been won, many families could not afford to take advantage of that right. The Communists campaigned for all incoming parcels to be equally divided. All the other organizations contributed to assisting the internees as far as their own resources allowed, relying on their own members in the camps to participate in making the internment bearable. The members of the Bund, and especially those of Hashomer Hatzair, a Zionist youth organization connected with the Left Poale-Zion, actively participated in the mutual help movement.[59]

The Bund in Paris collected parcels for the men and persisted with this activity well after Dannecker had ordered that all Jewish relief be carried out under the aegis of the Coordination Committee. This breach of regulations by the Bund incurred a visit from Dannecker and the arrest of two of its leaders, Ika Richter and Nathan Schachnowski. Richter believed that as a woman she would have a better chance of avoiding reprisals, so she took full responsibility. She was incarcerated in the fortress of Romainville where she died on 5 October 1941. The German officer commanding the fortress ordered the guards to present arms as her body was taken out for burial and personally visited the Bund's canteen to pay his respects.[60]

Assisting internees and their families became the basis from which Solidarity launched a major political campaign. A spirit of confidence prevailed in its ranks. The confidence born of a broadly based network of commitees gave Solidarity good cause to believe it could mobilize substantial popular support. The general objective was to discredit the Coordination Committee by making demands it could not meet and thereby to lead the immigrant population to conclude that the Coordination Committee could not be trusted. The women's organization was directed to begin the campaign. Between 20 and 25 July 1941, continuous groups of women, numbering at times up to 500, filled its offices demanding the release of the men.[61] Solidarity knew that there was nothing the Coordination Committee could do and sought a public admission to that effect to show the population how powerless its official representatives were. The militancy of the women was remarkable. Despite a police presence they came back on five successive days. Although this particular campaign did not yield immediate results it provided Solidarity with an opportunity to gauge the extent of its popular support. On a different level the tactic achieved two further results: it showed the Coordination Committee that it lacked the confidence of all the immigrants and revealed to the immigrant population that it was not a genuine Jewish committee but that it functioned by the grace of the authorities.

An incident that occurred during one of the women's demonstrations caused much popular apprehension. Israelowicz happened to be present at the time and believing that he could pacify the women told them that "their husbands and sons were martyrs to the Jewish cause" and that their internment had been a "sacrifice by the Jewish population in order to avert a pogrom."[62] Israelowicz's statement achieved the opposite of what he had intended: instead of mollifying the women it generated a wave of speculative fear among the immigrants; it neither comforted those in the camps nor reassured the others. Furthermore, Israelowicz's conscious or inadvertent use of the word "pogrom," which every immigrant Jew understood well, assumed immediacy for some of them. The fear that this news generated found its way to the camps, even though these camps were under French control. The interned men began to consider their own position. As none of them sought to become martyrs, the question of escape became a dominant issue. The difficulty was not so much how to escape but what to do next. Those with families feared for their safety; the single men tried to assess what their own fate would be in case of recapture.[63]

For one group of men, the Communists, internment and escape presented special questions. As active militants their confinement had its own hardships; none of them until their arrests had seriously considered the question of leading a clandestine existence. Until May 1941, save for their leaders, all lived legally. Few of them were known to the French police, for before the war most of them had used assumed names in their political activities. To be found out by the French authorities would have meant serious risks which could result in deportation from France to their countries of origin.[64] The particular problems faced by the Communist activists in the camps were bound up with their own sense of organizational responsibility. In the first place they found themselves interned because their own leaders had not instructed them to avoid compliance with the French police order. Once in the camps these activists behaved as their own political experience had taught them, as well as according to the instructions they received from their movement. The Jewish Communist leadership then took the view that they were to remain where they were. In a few instances only, when certain individuals were required for special duties, were they instructed to escape. The question of the escape for the men interned on 14 May was therefore governed by fears and uncertainties in some cases and party discipline in others. This explains why throughout the thirteen months of their internment, until their deportation to Auschwitz, only 300 men, including Communists, escaped.[65] In May 1942, the Jewish Communist leadership finally gave the order to its members to "break out, to tear down the gates of the camps and escape." At last, the leadership took the view that "deportation was death," but the chances of escape from Pithiviers and Beaune-La-Rolande were by then lost.[66]

The immigrant organizations also devoted much energy to helping families in need. Amelot, with the Joint's financial support, was then the largest distributor of direct financial help. Solidarity's resources, collected locally from supporters, were more limited but nevertheless complemented Amelot's. To generate funds Solidarity printed special stamps which it gave as receipts to the donors.[67]

The difficulties faced by the immigrant organizations in the collection of funds came from the economic aryanization program. This program was affecting an ever-growing number of trades and preventing members of many professions from practicing. A number of skills were, however, still open to Jews and it was within these trades that Solidarity and Amelot found the donors. In the industries connected with knitwear, gloves, furs, and leather goods a significant number of skilled tradesmen and artisans still found employment. The demand in these trades came from the German purchases on the home market, and the invasion of the Soviet Union in June 1941 had strengthened the demand. The realization by the immigrant organizations that this production was of direct use to the Wehrmacht was to pose a dilemma that soon would become the object of a major campaign.

During June and July 1941 the demand for skilled tradesmen had not yet reached its highest levels. There were still many unemployed immigrants for whom little could be done and who posed problems neither immigrant organization could resolve. They represented a constant drain upon the limited resources as well as a potential source of political problems. The continuous outpouring of the collaborationist media relentlessly depicted the Jews as parasites and the purveyors of the "black market," accusations that caused much concern and gained more weight by the known existence of a considerable body of unemployed destitute Jews. It was during July 1941 that the unemployed Jews became a serious political question. Dannecker informed the Coordination Committee that he required it to supply 7,000 men and women for agricultural work in Northern France. This demand, coming only two months after the internment of 3,710 men who were held in camps without being assigned any work, was viewed by the immigrant organizations as a definite indication that worse measures were yet to come. Amelot informed the Coordination Committee that it was firmly opposed to any cooperation in the fulfillment of the order, irrespective of the consequences. The Coordination Committee itself refused to be directly involved in such a measure, but to prove to Dannecker that it was attempting to fulfill the order, used the *Informations Juives* to appeal for volunteers, claiming that "the work would ensure a peaceful life." It asked unemployed workers to "volunteer in large numbers, in their own interest, in the interest of their families and the community."[68] Dannecker's assurance that the German authorities would not arrest any more Jews if the required numbers were supplied did not alter Amelot's position; it refused to cooperate with the Coordination Committee in an examination of the question.

The broad campaign of the immigrant organizations against working for the Germans, as well as the general distrust by the immigrants of the Coordination Committee, resulted in an overall boycott of the appeal.[69] On 20 August 1941, Dannecker ordered the French police to arrest 4,232 Jews in the eleventh arrondissement. This time French Jews were among those arrested.[70] The men were taken to Drancy, a camp hitherto unknown. Again, the Jewish organizations needed to find resources to assist more families. The number of meals dispensed by the Amelot group of canteens, which had reached 65,000 in December 1940, had only fallen to 34,368 by September 1941, although 8,000 men had been interned in that period, an unknown number had left Paris for the Vichy Zone, and employment opportunities for tradesmen had improved.[71]

The deteriorating situation and the magnitude of the problems gave unity among the immigrant organizations new urgency. At the Amelot committee, the FSJF and the Right Poale-Zion finally supported the view that despite the risk of being unable to control the Communists unity had to be achieved.[72] The Bund was the only movement opposed to any unity agreement. The decision of the Communist leadership also to seek unity, after having previously decided not to proceed, was the result of a number of factors. In the first place it had become PCF policy to engage in a "national front" strategy and the Jewish Communists could not but have been influenced by the party line. Second, on 24 August 1941, Radio Moscow had broadcast an appeal to world Jewry from a Soviet Yiddish poet, David Bergelson, not only pleading for support for the Soviet Union, but above all warning world Jewry of the danger of the extermination of Polish and Russian Jewry: "The very question of the existence of the Jewish people presents itself in all its magnitude." Referring to the history of the Jews, Bergelson made a call to arms to all Jews which went beyond political and religious beliefs.[73] The Communist leadership in Paris transcribed the appeal and distributed copies by the thousands. Its impact upon the immigrant population was profound. A special meeting of the Solidarity leadership was held to plan a campaign for unity, as well as greater efforts at sabotage in industry and the armed struggle.[74] The combined factors of continued persecution, constant pauperization, the Soviet appeal, and a growing realization by the majority of the immigrant organizations of the need for a new approach led to the first unity meeting with the Communists on 30 August 1941.

The meeting brought together Rapoport from the FSJF, Judith Topcha from the Left Poale-Zion, Aron Kremer from the Right Poale-Zion, Shapiro, a representative of ORT, and Albert Youdine and Ydl Korman on behalf of the Communists.[75] The representatives unanimously decided to form a United Workers Parties Committee to combine all efforts in assisting and protecting the immigrant population. They decided furthermore to publish an illegal newspaper to announce the establishment of the committee and to present its views.[76] Solidarity supplied the technical facilities and the first issue appeared the following month. But this unity, which emerged so spontaneously and so rapidly, had not been thoroughly prepared. No program had been discussed and all the participants agreed that further discussions needed to be held to map out a charter and a course of action.[77]

Indeed, fundamental questions had to be discussed and agreed upon to translate the formal unity into a workable reality. All parties were aware of the earlier unity discussions and the reasons for their breakdown. It was clear to all that the differences did not come from conflicting conceptions of the immediate tasks but rather from different views of appropriate general strategy. Two fundamental approaches clashed: the Communists promoted a policy designed to draw the immigrants into an ever more active participation in the French Resistance, particularly that organized by their own party; Amelot's affiliates wanted to make the survival of the Jewish people their first priority. The failure to spell out these major differences doomed the uniting movement to a stillborn life. The unanimous desire to establish united committees in the localities did not yield the expected results. Solidarity's numerical dominance, together with the sectarian attitude of its local leaders who sought to direct these committees toward acceptance of Solidarity's policies, soon appeared to the others as threatening their independence. In retrospect this consequence was inevitable. Solidarity was a mass organization, highly structured and animated by a political conception of Jewish Resistance that could not accommodate narrower perspectives. The other participants were, in comparison, devoid of any structured popular support and led by individuals motivated by a single goal, the protection of the Jewish population. Inevitably, without having fully debated the aims and objectives of the United Committee, these fundamentally different conceptions proved to be the rock on which unity split.

The relationship between Solidarity's youth organization and Hashomer Hatzair exemplifies the demise of immigrant unity. Of all existing political groups in the Amelot Committee, Hashomer Hatzair was the organization with which the Communists could have reached a satisfactory agreement. This movement, affiliated to the Left Poale-Zion, had been formed before the war. Although it never boasted a large membership, under the leadership of Henri Bulawko during the Occupation it succeeded in becoming numerically as large an organization as the Communist youth movement.[78] Ideologically, it was even further to the left than its parent organization, Left Poale-Zion. The unity agreement of August 1941 found Hashomer Hatzair eager to participate in all forms of Jewish resistance. As a consequence of the agreement Hashomer Hatzair directed its membership to unite with local Communist youth committees.

The collapse of the united youth committees came when Solidarity's youth organization decided, in the spring of 1942, to shift the emphasis of the Jewish response to armed struggle. Although Hashomer Hatzair was in full agreement with the principle it had one reservation: it demanded autonomous groups.[79] Therein rested an essential difference between the Communists and all the others. The Jewish Communists viewed their membership as an integral part of the general Communist underground, and expected their newly found allies to accept unreservedly that position. Agreement with Hashomer Hatzair's demand could not be envisaged. Although Hashomer Hatzair had shown itself willing to join the anti-Nazi struggle, and was open to Communist help and guidance, its demand for autonomous groups was seen as detrimental to the overall Communist objective of controlling the general strategy of armed resistance. Hashomer Hatzair sought to retain independence of action, so that specifically Jewish objectives would not be dissolved into the much broader Communist aims. Individual Hashomer Hatzair members did join the Communist units but as an organization it refused to be absorbed.

The mass arrests of immigrants in July 1942, followed by Bulawko's own internment, led to the end of the organization in Paris. The Communists had not proven flexible and had shown a lack of political vision. By asking Hashomer Hatzair to surrender its independence on the question of the armed struggle, however justified the demand might have been from a military stand-

point, the Communists had failed to provide one of their few allies with the
assistance necessary for its survival even if it meant its growth. For even if, as
a consequence, Hashomer Hatzair would have grown in the process of com-
peting for the same popular support, it would have nevertheless contributed
to the overall development of resistance activities within the Jewish population. The same criticism can be leveled at the Jewish Communists in their relations with the other members of the newly formed coalition. In their impa-
tience to lift the general level of anti-Nazi Jewish resistance the Communists
bemoaned their allies' lack of militancy.[80] Their cardinal error was to under-
value the impact of the constantly deteriorating situation upon their partners.
The Communists' failure to show political understanding, and patience, was
the most important single factor that led to the disintegration of the unity
achieved in Paris in August 1941.

The difficulties facing the establishment of a truly united Jewish immigrant response did not mean that there were not issues that evoked united action. The fact of immigrants working in factories producing for the Wehrmacht was one issue on which there was total agreement. It not only helped
sustain for some time the fragile unity but helped stimulate new forms of Jewish resistance.

All the immigrant organizations consistently opposed any communal dealings with the Germans. Time and time again, their illegal publications and
oral propaganda warned of retaliation against anyone who dealt with the
Germans. All immigrant organizations supported the view that the Jews
should boycott all economic contacts. This view was directed not only at
Jewish traders but also at Jewish workers. There existed, however, a problem
that none of the parties could overcome by a blanket opposition. The whole
economy was controlled by and geared to the needs of the German army.
The home market, on account of the shortages of primary products, was too
limited to provide sufficient employment for immigrant skills. Moreover, the
Jews faced a program of economic aryanization which even further reduced
their opportunity for employment and trade. The early policy of economic
boycott therefore faced a conflicting economic reality. The German invasion
of the Soviet Union in June 1941 and the suddenly increased demand on local industries to assist the German war effort led the Jewish Communists to
call for sabotage of any production directly useful to the Wehrmacht. The
problem of the Jews working in German-controlled industries could no longer
be seen in strictly economic terms; it became a serious political question taken
up by all the other immigrant political organizations.

The early Communist campaign for a total boycott, coupled with the call
for the sabotage of production, had, however, run counter to the economic
reality. The majority of artisans and workers in the trades in demand by the
Germans could not find alternate employment. They faced an insoluble problem: they had to work in order to live but their labor was helping the Germans.[81] To further complicate the issue, there was real popular opposition
to the demand that the immigrants withhold their labor. The majority could
not accept that of all those in Occupied France who worked in industries es-

sential to the German war effort only they, the Jews, should be asked to refuse to continue.[82]

The problems faced by the boycott campaign were discussed at a special meeting of representatives from the various Jewish Communist organizations in September 1941.[83] The existence of the newly constituted United Workers Parties Committee had radically improved the possibility of developing a much broader campaign. The assembly set out to reexamine the strategic objective of harming the German war effort in the light of the new situation. The meeting recognized that the call for a boycott had not brought the expected results and so the group decided that an organized sabotage of production was the only avenue left to achieve their objective. The new strategy was to operate on three levels: a lowering of the level of production, a general sabotage of all finished products, and sabotage of the machinery. This, it was hoped, would overcome the earlier opposition to a general boycott. Furthermore, it was thought such activities would draw the Jewish working population into more advanced forms of anti-Nazi struggle. By then the PCF's foreign workers section, the Main d'Oeuvre Immigrée (Foreign Workers [MOI]) of which Solidarity was part, had already formed partisan units and a number of Jews were already actively involved.[84] But at this stage the Jewish Communist leadership believed that it ought to concentrate its main efforts in the economic field.

In order to begin the industrial struggle the Communists decided to concentrate all efforts upon a single sector of production, the glove industry.[85] The strike began in September; within days of the decision the special commission assigned to carry out the campaign had decided upon strike actions aimed at reducing production by 25 percent and the working week from six to four days. Representatives from the illegal trade-union leadership called upon each of the major factories and formed strike committees. By the end of the first week production had fallen by 10,000 pairs of gloves. The strike lasted until 7 December 1941, when it was finally called off. Some 160,000 pairs of gloves, destined for the Eastern Front, had been lost in production and the Jewish workers in that industry never went back to a full working week. The strikes had been supported by all the immigrant organizations: the United Workers Parties officially, the Bund unofficially. The success had shown that given an appropriate organization and the political support of all the various workers' movements, the Jewish tradesmen were prepared to support anti-German actions, even to accept a reduced working week.

Following the success of this campaign Solidarity decided to apply the same tactics to another industry. This time it selected the knitwear industry as its target.[86] The chance concentration of Bundists and Communists in that industry created favorable conditions for common boycott committees in a number of factories. Owing to the variety of articles manufactured by the knitters, different tactics were applied. Both Solidarity and Bundist workers agreed that the strike actions should apply only to men's wear. Such a concentrated effort, limited to a single branch of the industry, was to ensure the strikers the material support of the knitters in the other branches of the industry. The selection of men's wear was based on the assumption that only these articles were directed to the Eastern Front. But the strike committees soon realized that even women's garments were useful to the German war effort. The committees therefore decided to extend the strike to the other factories. As in the glove industry, the working week was reduced to four days. The strike which began in October went on until December 1941 and production fell by 375,000 garments. Attempts by some firms to break the strike made this campaign particularly complex and in some factories the strike did not end until January 1942. The Wehrmacht demand for these garments was such that in December it even offered to have knitters released from Drancy to replace the strikers.[87] But the strike committee, although faced with a moral dilemma, refused to consider the German offer.

Despite this success, Solidarity and the other movements recognized that such victories were transient. Sooner or later the Germans or some employers would succeed in resuming full production and it was doubtful whether Jewish workers in industry could sustain indefinite campaigns. Solidarity therefore decided to proceed to phase two of the campaigns planned in September: the sabotage of production. Solidarity's press began to advance the new slogan in December 1941. Still calling for an economic boycott, it also called for sabotage: "Jewish merchants, do not deal with the Germans! No one should willingly work for them; whenever forced to do so, sabotage production, work slowly, all means are to be used to counter the needs of the Fascists!"[88]

During the second half of 1941 the activities of the immigrant organizations not only increased greatly in number but changed in kind. It was the end of an epoch. Until then all the immigrant organizations' activities had been inward-looking and concerned with rebuilding themselves and extending help to those immigrants most in need. The new situation created by the various strikes and the open confrontation with the Germans heralded a new era. For Solidarity in particular, however, the question remained how much the successes so far indicated a rising popular militancy that would support their new slogans. When that militancy was expressed, it had occurred among groups and individuals who had traditionally supported left-wing causes. It was still open to question whether these sections of the immigrant population were prepared to advance along the path of the Resistance, and whether the others, the overwhelming majority, could be won to that strategy.

By December 1941 this silent majority of immigrants had been seriously affected by the various German measures. Close to 8,000 men were still interned, with a corresponding number of families affected; economically, a large number of the remaining Jews were paupers. The constantly deteriorating situation should have resulted in a much more somber appreciation by the immigrants as to what the future held. Yet the forecasters of doom went unheard. A number of unexpected measures helped sustain hope when fear should have prevailed. Of those arrested in May and August 1941 some were released: at Drancy, in October 1941, a German military commission ordered the release of over 900 sick men; soon after, the French administration also released 32 men from Beaune-La-Rolande.[89] At Beaune-La-Rolande and Pithiviers the French administration sent some men to work on various farms in the region.[90] In Paris, immigrants working in factories producing for the Wehrmacht had been assured by the management of the factories of protection from internment.[91] All these various measures had given ground for hope as well as sown confusion and uncertainty. Even the bombing of seven synagogues in October 1941 did not succeed in raising salutary fear.[92] No amount of propaganda on Solidarity's part could dispel these illusions.

Solidarity's failure did not dissuade it from pursuing its campaign. The release in November 1941 of the body of a man who had died at Drancy provided Solidarity with an opportunity to test its popular support. The Communist leadership decided to call upon the immigrant population to form a funeral procession, despite police bans. A thousand people came.[93] This success confirmed that while as yet only a limited number of people were prepared to take an active part in organized resistance there was wider support for actions designed to express immigrant solidarity.

Anti-Jewish propaganda, orchestrated by the Germans and expressed through the press, radio, and even a permanent exhibition, which opened on 5 September and finally closed on 11 January 1942, continued unabated in order to isolate the Jews.[94] In the opinion of such organizations as Solidarity those attacks had to be answered. Louis Gronowski, the general-secretary of the MOI and a Jewish Communist, prepared a special pamphlet, *L'Antisémitisme, le Racisme et la Question Juive*. Solidarity printed it, with the approval and in the name of the PCF, in a run of 25,000 copies. The aims of such a publication were twofold: to counter the recent propaganda and win popular support among the Gentile population, and to give the Jews themselves courage and confidence. It sought to show them that the PCF, at least, rejected antisemitism and more importantly was willing to help break the psychological isolation of the Jews.[95]

Within the immigrant organizations, the hopes that had burgeoned with the formation of the United Workers Parties Committee did not come to fruition. Admittedly, the original goodwill among the participants had neither vanished nor reverted to the earlier distrust. However, in factories and in the localities mutual understanding did not lead to the wider involvement of immigrants. Each organization tended to concentrate on the issues it felt competent to handle and which its members would support. The Communists and their supporters continued to concentrate on directing resistance activities such as the sabotage of production and preparations for the armed struggle. The others concentrated on communal self-help. Instead of a symbiosis the differences grew.

Amelot was directly assisting some 1,500 families. But the gap between the available resources and the ever-growing numbers requiring help could not be bridged. By the end of 1941 the budgetary allocation of 400,000 francs a month to assist the inmates of the camps and their families was already well below the actual requirements. Of the 705 inmates of Beaune-La-

Rolande who had applied, only 555 could be helped. Instead of the weekly food parcel necessary to sustain them, Amelot could only provide one parcel fortnightly.[96]

While the Communists never decried the work done by Amelot or the real need for mutual help, which they were also conducting, they believed that a meaningful response needed to extend from mutual help to active participation in the struggle against the Germans and Vichy. By the end of 1941 the issue of armed struggle, which had become the primary objective of the PCF, was requiring the Solidarity leadership's attention. As long as the anti-Jewish campaign had confined itself to propaganda and legislation and even as long as the anti-Jewish measures did not go any further than internment, the question of armed struggle against the Germans could not be raised within immigrant Jewry without great political risks. It would receive serious consideration from the general body of immigrant Jews only when it could be shown to be the only possible line of action. If that interpretation was not accepted, Solidarity ran the risk of being viewed either as a PCF front organization or as provoking German reprisals against the Jews. The internments of May and August 1941, the invasion of the Soviet Union, and the appeal of Bergelson in August 1941 had, without doubt, helped create psychological foundations upon which a campaign for such a course of action could be justified.

Until August 1941 the only active armed resistance group in Paris was the Organisation Spéciale (Special Organization [OS]). It had been formed by the PCF as a defense corps whose role was to protect party leaders and, less clearly, to execute those the PCF believed were traitors to the movement.[97] The German attack upon the Soviet Union in June led the PCF to send the OS into military confrontation with the Germans. On 15 August 1941, the illegal newspaper *Humanité* openly called for armed struggle against the invaders. This was the take-off stage of the policy of armed struggle.[98] Among the first units to be formed in Paris were the Bataillons de la Jeunesse (Youth Battalions). These armed detachments included a large number of Jews, the sons and daughters of immigrants. They came from the ranks of the Jeunesse Communiste (Communist youth organization), particularly from the "quartiers populaires."[99] Alongside the Youth Battalions, the PCF also ordered its immigrant organization, the MOI, to constitute its own units from among the various national and language groups. The foreign Communists in Paris, political refugees, many of whom had recently fought in the Spanish Civil War as volunteers for the Republic, not only proved a dedicated and experienced fighting force but also showed themselves to be dedicated as a body to a life or death struggle against Nazism.[100] The MOI became the major source of recruitment of volunteers for the Communist armed units.[101] The first units of immigrant partisans in Paris were composed of Rumanians and Hungarians, of whom 90 percent were Jews.[102]

No sooner had these units been sent into action against the Germans than the infernal circle of reprisals and counterreprisals began to operate. The German reprisals took the form of the execution of those caught or of hostages.[103] Every German announcement of executions included Jews. The black-rimmed posters, displayed by the thousands on the walls of Paris, were intended to intimidate the Resistance movement and bring public reprobation upon it by making it appear guilty of the execution of innocent hostages. By highlighting that those caught and executed were both Jews and Communists the German propaganda not only sought to alienate them from the population but to show that the execution of hostages was caused by foreigners and anti-French elements. For the immigrant population, a closely knit community, each Jewish name appearing on the posters was viewed with a deep sense of bereavement.

Solidarity's leadership, although committed organizationally through its membership in the MOI to support the partisan movement, decided to conduct an independent assessment of the efficacy of the policy. It had earlier committed itself to industrial sabotage as a preliminary stage; now the problem was how to manage the transition. For although there was support within the organization for the principle of armed struggle, there was also a broad debate over its merits.[104] The Communists needed a consensus to justify the human cost of German reprisals. The most often debated issue was the military value of acts of terror in relation to their overall military significance.[105] The belief prevailed among rank-and-file members that the Nazi war machine could only be defeated on the battlefields of Eastern Europe and not in Paris.[106] And then there were the ideological and moral arguments. Ideologically, Marxism had always been opposed to individual acts of terror. There was moral repulsion at killing a German soldier. Although the German uniform was seen as the symbol of oppression, and the German soldier donning it as contributing to its perpetuation, the view was also held that this soldier was himself an ultimate victim of Nazism. There was a humanistic abhorrence of acts of terror which could not be reconciled with the struggle against Nazism.*

The debates in the ranks of the Communist organizations went on until December 1941. Then the sudden announcement on 15 December of the execution of 100 hostages, of whom 53 were Jews, provided the psychological opportunity for the Solidarity leadership to overcome its supporters' hesitations. Until then few had realized that the selection of hostages to be shot was not simply the consequence of a connection with those guilty of terrorist acts. It suddenly became clear that the Jews were being singled out as hostages because they were Jews. The German executions, designed to stop the French Resistance, instead created the psychological climate among the Jews themselves to take up arms. The executions generated more political activities. Hundreds of illegal meetings were held in private homes, with attendances ranging from a handful to twenty people.[107] Members of Solidarity addressed thousands of people and exhorted them to join the organization or at least to help the bereaved families.[108] To channel popular support to these families Solidarity established a Fonds National de Vengeance et de Solidarité (National Fund for Vengeance and Solidarity). Collections for the fund were

---

* This same attitude continued to manifest itself until the Liberation of Paris. Indeed, to my knowledge, there is no report of any German soldier or officer being maltreated when taken prisoner during the Paris uprising in August 1944.

even conducted within the camps. At Beaune-La-Rolande the internees donated 30,000 francs.[109]

The lapsed United Workers Parties Committee was once more convened.
Solidarity approached Amelot to join in the appeal for funds to help the families, to glorify the hostages, and to mobilize the immigrant Jews into the ranks
of the Resistance. But Amelot was only prepared to participate in the relief
program.[110] The execution of the fifty-three Jewish hostages represented a
new stage in the evolution of the resistance spirit among the immigrants, yet
Solidarity proved unable to sway the United Workers Parties Committee. The
other members of that committee did not view the executions as specifically
directed at the Jewish population, they saw them as reprisals against the
French Resistance. The 100 women demonstrating in the offices of the Coordination Committee were told that "the executions were not directed against
the Jews but at the Communists."[111] No Jewish organization, other than the
Communists, was yet ready to accept that for the Germans the Jews were an
expendable commodity and that their fate was linked not only to the Communists but above all to the Resistance movements of the French people. The
psychological isolation of the immigrants from the non-Jewish population was
one of the major obstacles to the development of an internal, united Jewish
response.

The Solidarity leadership did not allow the setbacks in its pursuit of immigrant unity to affect its overall policy of active resistance. It continued to direct its main efforts at the industrial sector. The year 1941 had ended with
the strike among the knitwear workers; 1942 began with a major strike among
carpenters. Some 400 men in a number of enterprises downed their tools. Although the nominal demands were for better pay and conditions, the actual
components of the situation gave it a political character and made it a decidedly anti-German action. The organization of the strike and the popular
support it received helped sustain it until March.[112]

In the midst of executions and attempts by Solidarity to revive the collapsed United Workers Parties Committee came the crisis caused by the official establishment of the UGIF. Although it was generally opposed by all the
immigrant organizations, it nevertheless resulted in further divisions among
them, and those differences arose when the time came to articulate that opposition.

Solidarity maintained an unambiguous opposition. Hashomer Hatzair, the
Left Poale-Zion, and the Right Poale-Zion were opposed to any cooperation.
The Bund believed that all possible contacts with the UGIF should be
avoided.[113] Rapoport, and the FSJF, held a less clear-cut position. The prime
concern was to maintain Amelot in operation. Rapoport therefore argued that
although Amelot should not assist the UGIF leadership it was imperative that
Amelot remain legal and it was necessary to ensure that the UGIF did not interfere with Amelot's activities.[114] This approach led Rapoport to seek lines of
communication with the UGIF.

The establishment of the UGIF in 1942 had revived former differences among immigrant organizations, differences as complex and divisive as when the Coordination Committee had first come under Dannecker's control. The first deportations of 27 March marked the qualitative differences between the two periods. The deportations provided for those opposed to any form of co-operation the necessary argument for dispelling doubts about the projected role of the UGIF. Solidarity used the deportations as evidence in their anti-Nazi propaganda. Although the deportations had been announced as part of the December 1941 reprisals, Solidarity endeavored to warn the Jewish population of the anti-Jewish character of the measure.[115] But the immigrant population was not convinced that the connection was valid.

Although it was clear that the Jews were used to punish the Resistance it was not self-evident that this was a manifestation of German anti-Jewish policy. Solidarity, aware of the difficulties encountered by its propaganda, resorted to emphasizing the constant deterioration of the Jewish population's position, from the more innocuous measures such as identity controls in Jewish canteens to the continuing aryanization that was affecting the smallest Jewish establishment.[116] The latest measures of 7 February 1942, which forbade Jews to be out of their homes between 8 P.M. and 6 A.M. and which followed an earlier order to surrender radios and bicycles to local police stations, provided the Communist illegal press with arguments to convince its readers that worse was yet to come. It was therefore understandable that a note of urgency crept into Solidarity's propaganda when it could only watch with frustration Amelot's refusal to extend its activities from the necessary relief work to full-scale political resistance in general and open opposition to the UGIF in particular.

The deportations of March 1942 marked the beginning of a campaign of warning designed to explain to the Jewish population Solidarity's view of German and Vichy intentions toward the immigrant Jews. The campaign was at first cautious, not reaching a crescendo until the following deportations of May and those of June in particular. By then Solidarity was convinced that the issue of the deportation of the Jews from France had reached a high priority. Special illegal publications were directed to Beaune-La-Rolande and Pithiviers calling upon the internees to "Break down the gates of the camp! Do not let yourself be deported!"[117] If the Jews from Paris could not understand Solidarity's strident appeals, the inmates of Beaune-La-Rolande and Pithiviers took them much more seriously. They began to escape. Of the ninety-seven escapes from Pithiviers during the first six months of 1942, seventy-three occurred during April and May.[118] Solidarity's warning was directed not solely at those internees but at all the Jews. It was attempting to drive the point home that Nazism meant deportation and that deportation threatened everyone.

Simultaneously with the warning campaign, the Communist leadership took the decision during the spring of 1942 to fully commit Solidarity to the armed struggle by fielding its own Jewish units.[119] Until then, as we have seen with the Rumanian and Hungarian units, the Jewish volunteers or those assigned by Solidarity had been integrated into units based on countries of origin. In some cases they were even assigned to tasks nominated by the PCF. Already during the autumn of 1941 the PCF decided that it was politically necessary to carry out propaganda activities among the German troops, and addressed itself to the Jewish Communist organization to select from its ranks members linguistically equipped for this work. The Jewish leaders drew upon the German-speaking membership. Jewish women in particular were organized into special units to handle anti-Nazi propaganda. Their task was not only to distribute printed material to German soldiers but to organize anti-Nazi cells within the Wehrmacht.[120]

The decision to constitute specific Jewish units represented a fundamental change in former policy. By then Solidarity's membership and the Jewish volunteers for the armed struggle wanted to fight as Jews, and the Jewish Communist leadership itself supported such a position. Politically it corresponded to the need for Solidarity to be fully accepted as a Jewish organization by all those critics who had always claimed that it was a bridgehead designed to win Jews to "alien" causes. This long-standing attitude of other immigrant organizations toward the Jewish Communists had not been totally devoid of foundation, at least until the outbreak of the Second World War.[121] With the Occupation, the Jewish Communist leadership was led to redefine its former position in relation to the "Jewish national question." Without any doubt the formulation of the problem represented by Nazism, the war, and the Jews, as presented by Bergelson in his dramatic appeal to world Jewry, had been a major factor. Such an appeal coming from the Soviet Union, the fountainhead of Communism, had been the justification for the emergence of what formerly the Communist movement would have considered a nationalist deviation. Certainly it corresponded to the national sentiments espoused by the organization's membership as the anti-Jewish propaganda and measures increased.[122]

The first leaders of the Jewish partisan units were former members of the International Brigades who had fought in Spain.[123] The rank-and-file members were selected from Solidarity, and the units were officially recognized as Jewish partisan units. Simultaneously, Solidarity launched a major campaign of sabotage in industries working for the Wehrmacht, this time backed by Jewish partisans operating as full-time military units. The Bund also backed the call for sabotage of production. In April and May 1942, the Bund's illegal newsletter passionately appealed to Jewish workingmen to sabotage production and again sternly warned all who traded with the Germans.[124]

The May 1942 traditional working-class celebrations witnessed countless meetings in workshops and factories where speakers, protected by Jewish partisans, appealed for a slowing down of production and for sabotage. These meetings gave Communists the chance to recruit new members, distribute illegal publications, and collect funds. In the larger establishments existing permanent illegal committees set levies on salaries to boost the Fonds de Vengeance. At Grundel, the largest fur establishment in Paris, which employed 500 workers, the illegal shop committee deducted 2 percent of the workers' salaries for the Fonds. A report on illegal activities in this factory describes how they were carried out:

The Jewish foreman, on pay day of 21 April, 1942, called on each worker to give 2 percent of his salary for the Jewish internees. On 7 May another collection was made, without however insisting that non-Jewish workers also donate. Unusual happenings are taking place, sabotage in the form of parts from machinery are disappearing, furs are rendered useless by being cut. . . .[125]

Increasingly Solidarity was moving toward forms of resistance that made it unique among all the immigrant organizations. Its political perspectives led it to extend its field of activities outside the narrow confines of the immigrant population.

It was between the March 1942 deportations and July 1942 that immigrant organizations began to give more attention to informing the non-Jewish population of the plight of the Jews, the conditions in the Jewish camps, and the meaning of deportation.[126] The Bund, through its prewar contacts with the French Socialist party, set out to alert the French public. But it was Solidarity that proved most effective. By June 1942, the Jewish Communists had formed the Mouvement National Contre le Racisme (National Movement Against Racism [MNCR]). Although formally established then, the basis of such an organization had been laid in the spring of 1941, when a group of Jewish and non-Jewish intellectuals had begun publishing an illegal news-sheet which they had named *J'Accuse*. About the same time, but totally independent of them, another group of intellectuals who were concerned with antisemitism had also begun publishing a news-sheet named *Lumières* (Lights). It was on the basis of these two movements as well as a third group, Combat Medical (Medical Struggle), formed by medical men organized on professional lines, that the MNCR was formed.[127]

The four deportation convoys of June 1942 which emptied the camps alerted the Jewish Communists and the MNCR to the likelihood of new internments. On the eve of the July mass internment the MNCR had already established a list of some 200 Protestant and Catholic institutions likely to hide Jews.[128] By then a note of desperation had begun to show in the immigrant organizations. Even Amelot, which until then had chosen to limit its activities to relief work, also began seeking out friendly non-Jewish social workers to assist Jews in anticipation of further German measures. Although the previous internments had not involved women or children, the emptying of Beaune-La-Rolande, Pithiviers, and the Jewish camp at Compiègne was seen as ominous. The immigrant population grew restless. Economically, despite privileged groups employed in German industries, the situation had become grim. The number of families depending on communal help increased with each passing month. The Bund sent desperate appeals to its central leadership in Lyons: "the money we have left is insufficient to support our 80 families of comrades. We appeal to you with all our strength to send us help."[129]

The latest German ordinance, which appeared at the end of May 1942, requiring all Jews above the age of six to wear a Yellow Star of David contributed significantly to the immigrants' feeling of isolation and despair. The ninth and last German ordinance, of July 1942, completed the physical ostracism of the Jewish population: all public places were closed to them; in the Parisian Metro, Jews were allowed to use only the last wagon; purchases could only be made between 3 P.M. and 4 P.M., when most food stores were already sold out. The effect of this series of ordinances, though demoralizing, was not meekly accepted by the immigrant population.

The immigrant organizations reacted as forcefully as they could. Parallel with their attempt at developing ties with illegal non-Jewish organizations they tried to develop internal activities that would maintain a semblance of normalcy and sustain hope. Amelot canteens staged cultural activities. Solidarity formed a special organization for Jewish intellectuals which by June numbered some 200 members. Mounie Nadler, the prewar editor of the *Naie Presse,* helped the organization prepare the publication of a new illegal publication *Die Gele Late* (The Yellow Star). The issue was ready to go to press when the Gestapo uncovered the premises. Nadler's subsequent arrest and the seizure of the manuscript stopped the projected publication.[130]

The immigrant organizations' frenzied activities during June 1942 suggest a collective, unconscious premonition of what was shortly to take place. Early in July 1942 the Jewish Communist leadership received information from the PCF that mass internments were imminent. It immediately launched a major campaign of warning. A special leaflet was printed in thousands of copies. It urged Jews to take precautions:

> Do not passively wait in your homes. . . . Take steps to hide your families with non-Jews. If arrested, resist the police by all possible means: barricade your apartment, call for help, fight, do whatever you can to escape.[131]

As there had been no precise information on the form of the arrests, nor any precedents of arrests of anyone other than men of working age, Solidarity could not point to the particular dangers facing women, children, the old, and the sick. Solidarity could do little else but warn the immigrant population. It was beyond the resources of any single organization or even of all the immigrant organizations to hide even a fraction of that population. The call therefore to hide with non-Jews was the only realistic one. Even Solidarity, the largest of all the immigrant organizations, was incapable of doing more than warn the Jews. The only laboratory operated by Solidarity was so inadequately equipped that it could produce only four to five sets of false identity papers a day.[132] Their own members were not given such basic survival kits. They themselves, despite their political understanding of the dangers, lived astride two worlds: participating in an underground organization while living in their legal abodes.

Yet the warning had not been in vain: of the projected 22,000 to be arrested, French police found only 13,000.[133] The news of the planned arrests, coming from Solidarity, from friendly municipal policemen, transmitted orally, had partly succeeded in its objective. Nevertheless Parisian Jewry was never to recover, and never to be the same.

A historical period had passed between June 1940 and July 1942, during which immigrant organizations had taken up the Nazi and Vichy challenge.

During that period the two major immigrant groups, Solidarity and those centered around the Amelot Committee, defined the objectives to which they would dedicate themselves. Two main currents appeared: the Communists concluded that there was a life or death struggle for the Jewish people and carried the struggle to the enemy with all the consequences it entailed; the others, equally convinced that there was a specific war directed against the Jews, believed that survival would be achieved primarily through Jewish self-help.

Although the Communists' perspectives were a function of their ideological and organizational links with the PCF, these perspectives increasingly assumed Jewish national dimensions. Yet the Communists did not succeed in allaying the fears of the other organizations. Even in August 1941 when the non-Communist organizations were swayed by the Soviet Jewish call, enough suspicion of the Communists remained to affect that fragile unity. The fear that Solidarity was controlled by external forces, that its policies were not formulated solely by Jewish imperatives made nonsense of that unity. On another level, Communist perspectives, being political by definition, were not seen as directly relevant to the Jewish drama. The Zionists from the left to the right viewed the war in strictly Jewish terms. The Bund, rejecting the Communist as well as the Zionist analysis, had also taken up a position that posited Jewish survival first, although in many respects it found itself concurring with the Communists. All the organizations, save the Communists, acted on the assumption that Jewish survival could only be the concern of the Jews themselves. None of them, until the eve of July 1942, had considered a strategy that would include non-Jewish assistance. It was only after the indiscriminate mass arrests and deportations of July 1942 that the Communist position began to be considered by them. Only then, and despite the links with the PCF, were the Communists recognized as representing a genuine Jewish organization. Only then was a real working unity possible.

9

The Struggle for Survival:
August 1942 to August 1944

For the immigrant organizations the events of July 1942 marked the end of a historical period. Viewed in retrospect, the problems they had confronted until then were all within their capacity to overcome. But the new problems which they were to confront were totally unprecedented. From July 1942 until Liberation in August 1944, they would face a situation for which they were not prepared. In meeting that challenge these ill-equipped popular organizations not only succeeded, be it at enormous human costs, in maintaining their operations but they emerged strengthened and united.

The significance of the July 1942 arrests has been stressed throughout this book. These indiscriminate arrests of foreign Jews—men, women, and children, the old and the sick—which began on 16 July, shattered once and for all every popular misconception about the long-range significance of all previous anti-Jewish measures. On that day, throughout Paris, thousands of French municipal policemen, supported by the national gendarmerie and volunteers from French Fascist parties, particularly the *Parti Populaire Français,* received from the Paris Prefecture of Police precise lists of the names and addresses of those immigrant families to be arrested. The fear and grief of the families, escorted by the police, has been graphically shown in films and photographs, described in books, and verified by countless witnesses.[1] The arrests lasted until 18 July 1942. When they stopped, nearly 13,000 Parisian Jews were gone. The French police took families with children to the Vélodrome d'Hiver, and those without children to Drancy. But 10,000 Jews had succeeded in evading arrest, finding shelter with friends, French Jews or Gentiles, in attics, cellars, or unoccupied apartments.

The dissemination of the news about the projected police measure as well as the inability of the French police to carry out the arrests within one night had borne fruit. There is no doubt that getting the news out was decisive in warning the immigrant population. Solidarity's warning, carried by its members and supporters from door to door, had been the only organized and systematic attempt at informing the immigrants. The MOI military commanders even temporarily withdrew the Jewish partisans from military activities and directed them to "warn the Jews of Paris. . . . Knock on the door of every known Jewish family. Do away with the usual precautions. Every Jew must leave his home on the night of the fifteenth."[2] Of all the immigrant organizations only Solidarity had the membership and organizational strength to carry out such a vast campaign of warning. That campaign, which had begun a week before, was first received with skepticism by the immigrant population as well as by immigrant organizations. Everyone believed that the Communists' warning was a propaganda exercise. Even the Left Poale-Zion, which always took note of the Communists, found the news too incredible to be taken seriously.[3] When Amelot finally accepted that there were indeed some sinister preparations under way, it used its offices and canteens to pass the warning.[4]

Of all the Jewish organizations, the UGIF had been the first to obtain precise information of the police preparations. It knew of both the magnitude of the operation and its radically new character: the planned arrest of women and children. The UGIF had known about it as early as 8 July 1942.[5] The UGIF took its own steps to meet the expected contingencies: it readied accommodation for the children and prepared name-tags for the very young lest they became separated from their families.[6] It notified doctors to be on duty at the Vélodrome d'Hiver.[7] But it was not until 13 July 1942, that Baur and Stora informed Rapoport and Jakoubowicz of the projected measure.[8]

Baur's and Stora's renewed offer to have the Amelot personnel issued UGIF staff cards which would have protected them from internment had come too late. True, Amelot had earlier debated the question and decided to refuse Nazi protection. But in this instance, Baur's offer, even if accepted, could not protect Amelot: these documents were only validated by the SD during the first week of each month.

The July arrests therefore found Amelot, although a legal organization, totally paralyzed until it decided what to do regarding the UGIF staff cards.[9] Solidarity itself, while a clandestine organization and used to working in unauthorized ways, was also temporarily out of action. Half of immigrant Jewry had been affected: either arrested or in hiding. The July arrests therefore not only radically altered the lives of the immigrants but simultaneously disrupted, albeit temporarily, their organizations.

Solidarity maintained an organized, illegal leadership, but had lost many of its members and supporters. Local committees were in disarray.[10] The leadership began an immediate reorganization. The transition period was brief. On 18 July, Solidarity's women's committee organized 100 women to call upon the UGIF's offices demanding to know what it was going to do with the children the arrested parents had entrusted to the UGIF.[11] The same day another group of Jewish women, this time accompanied by non-Jews, were outside Drancy demanding the right to leave food parcels for the internees.[12] Solidarity found itself the sole immigrant group capable of organizing systematic help.[13] The Amelot committee had vanished, its doors were closed, and all its associated organizations were inoperative.[14]

The massive task of helping Jews who had escaped, children left without parents, and people in camps awaiting deportation led Amelot to reconsider its previous opposition to UGIF passes. In the first days of August its staff received UGIF accreditations and on 5 August 1942, it reopened its offices.[15] Some 10,000 foreign Jews who had avoided arrest needed help. None of them could return to their homes, as the police had sealed every apartment they visited. Living outside the law, these people did not dare call in person upon legal organizations. They could not ask help of the UGIF, for its relief centers required them to give their addresses so that its social workers could examine their situation. For frightened people, acceding to such a demand was unthinkable. Therefore, until Amelot reopened, Solidarity was the only organization dispensing help without such formalities.

The most pressing single problem resulting from the 16 July measure was caring for children left behind by their families. Many had been left to their own devices, others in the care of neighbors or friendly concierges. The UGIF's *Bulletin d'Information* appealed to the remaining Jewish population to inform the UGIF of such children's whereabouts.[16] The UGIF established a register of these abandoned children.[17] Solidarity also directed attention to this problem: it organized the placement of some children with non-Jewish families or institutions.[18] The MNCR took others in groups out of Paris to be placed in Christian institutions. Solidarity would pay half of their board and sponsors were found to meet the balance. The MNCR recruited non-Jewish social workers to regularly visit the children and ensure that their board was paid. In order to protect the children, Solidarity set up a special laboratory for the manufacture of forged ration books and identity papers.[19] The support provided to the MNCR by the PCF was particularly valuable in the search for helpful municipalities and mayors to hide the children.

As soon as Amelot had resumed operations, it also established a special commission, headed by Henri Bulawko, from Hashomer Hatzair, to deal with the question of supplying forged documents.[20] It too, with the assistance of non-Jewish social workers, began placing children with non-Jewish families. But it was in Amelot's direct financial assistance to the immigrants that it distinguished itself. Rapoport, assuming full responsibility, set aside all bureaucratic procedures and distributed help without asking for addresses or referring the claimants to social workers for the usual inquiries. Even the UGIF, which until July 1942 had not sought to extend its relief activities, was galvanized into action. The reports it had received from its personnel and through Baur's own visit to the "Vélodrome d'Hiver" had acted as catalysts upon its relief work.[21]

Although all communal organizations now directed their efforts to relief work, there remained one group of unfortunate immigrants left to their own devices: those who had evaded arrest. These people had a limited number of possibilities; they could either cross into the Vichy Zone, find hiding places with non-Jews in Paris or in the countryside, seek protected employment, or assume non-Jewish identities. Large numbers of foreign Jews began leaving Paris for the Vichy Zone. Though in the Vichy Zone foreign Jews who could not show that they had sufficient financial resources or that they held a job were either interned or conscripted into Compagnies de Travailleurs Etrangers (Foreign Workers Battalions, later renamed Compagnies Palestiniennes), no deportations had yet occurred from there.[22]

The second possibility, finding permanent hiding places with non-Jews, proved more difficult. Though many Christian families were willing to help, hiding entire families did present serious difficulties. Only in major cities such as Paris was it possible to find accommodation for whole families. In fact, owing to the exodus there were a large number of empty apartments in Paris which could provide shelter. But even this form of survival entailed certain prerequisites. In the first place there had to be a friendly "concierge," prepared to let a Jewish family in. Then there had to be friendly neighbors who would not inform the police. Assuming a non-Jewish identity was equally risky: false papers had to withstand police examination and the bearer had to be fluent in the appropriate language. Not many immigrants were fluent in any language other than their own.

The simplest, easiest, and least dangerous means of protection was to find employment with the UGIF or in a factory working for the Wehrmacht. But the numbers seeking this kind of protection were such that it quickly proved unobtainable. Large sums of money exchanged hands with employers in order to obtain the privilege of working in these factories.[23] The UGIF positions with their protective passes became commodities in themselves. Survival for the immigrants became a function of their personal wealth. Even the well-off immigrants needed help from Amelot and Solidarity. Admittedly they did not need material help; what they needed could not be bought—advice and above all contacts with trustworthy people who could help them. Such help was unobtainable from the UGIF for it refused to be party to any activities that did not correspond to its charter or that could be viewed as illegal by the authorities.

Amelot, which was operating legally, was naturally the more accessible source of help. Its staff, immigrants themselves, had understanding and compassion. Everyone was welcome, whether they were legal residents of Paris or not. Rapoport had seen to it that all available means were to be used to help. Anyone seeking the name of a trustworthy smuggler into the Vichy Zone, a set of false identity papers, a hiding place, or a non-Jewish family willing to take in a Jewish child was assisted.[24] Amelot used its legal standing to guide, advise, and help, and it never departed from this policy.

Solidarity was more limited in the numbers it could assist and in the type of help it could dispense. It never had Amelot's resources so the financial aid it could distribute was more modest. Being a political organization, it did not consider relief work its primary task but a component of its overall spectrum of activities. Relief work was a means rather than the end in itself. Solidarity viewed all questions through a complex political grid; all its policies were formulated on the basis of the PCF's general political line. Inevitably, Solidarity directed its human and material resources in accordance with its political imperatives and not according to what it viewed as the temporary material needs of the population. The conflicting priorities be-tween party responsibilities and the needs of the immigrant population did not mean that the Solidarity leadership and the rank-and-file members were less responsive to the specific Jewish problems. But they chose political solu-tions rather than relief. As far as they were concerned only the defeat of Nazism could resolve the problems. Therefore, they consistently advocated the path of active struggle against Nazism.

The July 1942 events led Solidarity to draw the only conclusion consis-tent with its political analysis: the armed struggle must intensify. All other considerations, such as diverting people and resources to the amelioration of hardship, became secondary. In fact the July events did generate, besides fear, a new motivation for struggle. Immigrants who had been reluctant to participate now joined the ranks, animated by grief and anger and seeking revenge. Jewish youth, in particular, responded to this call for an armed struggle.

The first Jewish partisan units, which had begun operating in May 1942, suffered many losses and by July 1942 had to be reorganized. The Jewish units, operating as the MOI's Second Detachment, led by Myer List, Gilbert Weisberg, and Joseph Davidowicz, were then reinforced by scores of these new volunteers who had been motivated by the July events. A tremendous upsurge of military activities followed. Between August and October 1942, the Second Detachment carried out thirty-one operations against military objectives in Paris.[25]

Although the post-July period was characterized by a desperation that found expression in armed resistance, this new emphasis did not mean that Solidarity had stopped giving attention to the political aspects of its activi-ties within the immigrant population. On 18 September 1942, Solidarity or-ganized a demonstration of wives of prisoners of war demanding Vichy's protection from internment.[26] Through its illegal publications Solidarity con-stantly urged the Jews to demand human rights. The aim of such campaigns was not an unrealistic hope of forcing the German authorities to alter their anti-Jewish policy but rather to inform non-Jews of what was occurring. Solidarity was convinced that only with the assistance of non-Jews was sur-vival conceivable. This was why it chose to mobilize all its members and supporters when the PCF called for a public demonstration, on 20 Septem-ber 1942, to commemorate the defeat of the Prussians at Valmy in 1792. Solidarity issued 5,000 leaflets urging the Jews to join in.[27] While, doubt-lessly, the Jewish Communists wanted to support their party and show that the Jewish population heeded its call, Solidarity's appeal to the Jewish popu-lation was hardly realistic. The imposition of a curfew by the German mili-tary governor aborted the planned demonstration. And, although Solidarity was not then able to assess the degree of support its campaign could gener-ate, it also highlighted the fundamental differences of emphasis between Solidarity and all the other Jewish organizations.

Solidarity's persistent appeals to Amelot to direct its activities toward close liaison with non-Jewish organizations began to have an impact after the July arrests. Only then were the merits of these appeals recognized by the Amelot Committee, and then only gradually. Only then did it agree that Jewish survival depended upon the support of non-Jews. Amelot was still reluctant to place the necessary confidence in such a possibility. The FSJF, the driving force of Amelot, continued to seek solutions within the Jewish community itself. Jarblum, the FSJF leader in the Vichy Zone, pleaded in vain with the Central Consistory for that help.[28] In Paris, Amelot continued to believe that if only the French Jews could be won over succor would be within reach. But the response of the leaders of the Central Consistory, concerned as they were about the survival of French Judaism, failed to meet the immigrants' expectations. Between 16 July and the end of September 1942, 28,930 immigrant Jews were deported, of whom 9,000 were taken from the Vichy Zone.[29] After July 1942, twenty-nine convoys left Drancy for Auschwitz and the rate of transportation did not seem to be slackening. By October 1942, the number of foreign Jews still in Paris had considerably diminished, the latest population count showing 7,926 immigrant families from an estimated 25,646 at the October 1940 census.[30]

The steady fall in the number of immigrant Jews in Paris affected Solidarity in particular, for it was from among their ranks that it replenished its membership. Yet from October 1942 to September 1943 Solidarity was most effective in its resistance activities. Its certitude that salvation could only come with the military defeat of Nazism and with the assistance of the French population made it pursue these twin objectives with renewed vigor. Solidarity's military activities, in particular, were relentlessly pursued. During October 1942, the Jewish partisans carried out twenty military operations in Paris. By January 1943, the Second Detachment had become so active that it was carrying out half of all the partisans' operations conducted in Paris.[31] Even after the sudden arrest by the Gestapo of twenty partisans from the Rumanian-Hungarian units, of whom 90 percent were Jews, the Second Detachment continued to function. Its activities were so effective that German troops in Paris only dared march in fighting formations. During February 1943, the Jewish partisans were responsible for eleven attacks out of the twenty-one that took place in Paris.[32]

But it was in the propaganda war, in the winning of the hearts of the non-Jewish population, that Solidarity applied itself most strongly. It was through *J'Accuse,* published by the MNCR, that Solidarity pursued this campaign. The first issue of *J'Accuse* had appeared in April 1942, but police discovery of the printing presses and the arrest of a number of Solidarity members had interrupted publication. The next issue appeared in October 1942.[33] Because the MNCR addressed itself only to intellectuals and professionals the volume of publication was never large, and unlike Solidarity's other publications *J'Accuse* was never for general distribution. *J'Accuse* was posted under sealed envelopes, and the names of the recipients were obtained by the editors from telephone directories. Although a very primitive mode of distribution and questionable as to its immediate value, it nevertheless indicated both the paucity of contacts and the blind faith that sooner or later, the unknown readers' humanity would express itself in favor of Jews. This war of propaganda carried out by Solidarity, with its obvious limitations, aimed at creating sympathy and compassion which, Solidarity hoped, would soon find expression.

The critical question was whether Solidarity would be able to ensure the continued functioning of the illegal presses. In Paris there were ten such illegal printing centers at one time or another.[34] Each one of these centers required technical expertise and a distribution organization. The tremendous energy and human resources required to maintain them was justified by a real belief in their value. It was an article of faith for Solidarity's leaders and for its members that the information thus disseminated, though its impact was not measurable, would ultimately bear fruit. There was a romantic faith in the printed word, a faith for which countless men and women sacrificed their lives. There were also calculated political considerations. The Communists viewed the press as an organizing medium, as the only means available to reach the population under existing conditions. It served a dual purpose: it informed readers of events not otherwise widely known and it presented the movement's policies.

The press proved its value with its reporting of the mass extermination of the Jews of Eastern Europe. Solidarity received a report in November 1942, from a Polish Communist, a former member of the International Brigades, who had just returned from Krakow. He informed Solidarity's leadership that the Jews were being exterminated by gas, and that during his stay in Krakow 11,000 men, women, and children had been thus killed in Auschwitz.[35] The Communist leadership, despite its own oft-repeated references to the German war of extermination of the Jews in Eastern Europe hesitated before publishing the report. They decided to release the news but to emphasize the numbers killed[36] rather than the use of gas.[37] Solidarity was swayed by the political necessity of presenting the fate of the Jews in the deportation camps in all its ghastliness not only to alert the Jewish population but in order to convince the non-Jews. The Jewish population itself received the news with skepticism. The Amelot Committee considered that Solidarity had engaged in a propaganda exercise and refused to accept the veracity of the information. At the Central Consistory, which had known since August 1942 that mass extermination was taking place in these camps, there was total silence. Not wanting to attract attention to itself, it neither denied nor confirmed the information. In Paris, the UGIF leadership remained silent, as if this issue was outside its concern. The illegal Communist press was therefore more than a political platform from which party policy was announced. It helped to convey information that other organizations suppressed. However, certain factors limited its influence: the political isolation of the movement, the political presentation of the information, and the reluctance of many readers to accept the news that it brought to them.

Solidarity's increased activities, particularly in areas where it confronted the repressive forces of the Gestapo, German and French, and the French police, inevitably caused large losses. In the military field, losses sustained during the second quarter of 1942, had been very serious. An accidental explosion at the end of April 1942, which occurred as two men (Hersz Zimmerman, a former member of the International Brigades, and Saul Bot, a violin student) were manufacturing a bomb, led to the arrest of Mounie Nadler, in charge of propaganda, Joseph Bursztyn, who organized the Jewish intellectuals, and many others.[38] A few weeks later Sivek Kirszenbaum, military commander in charge of coordination between the leaders of the various units and recruitment, disappeared. During June, a number of experienced fighters, Léon Pakin, Aron Wallach, Charles Feld, and Maurice Feferman, were killed in action.[39] The losses were bitter but not fatal. Like a phoenix rising from its ashes, Solidarity doggedly rebuilt its organization.

All the other immigrant organizations also suffered losses, but until the more militant period initiated by the July 1942 arrests none of the setbacks grew directly out of the organizations' activities. July 1942 was a watershed. By the end of 1942 Amelot had only a few leaders left of its original committee. The overwhelming majority were no longer in Paris; some had been arrested and deported while others had gone to the Vichy Zone. The leader of the Left Poale-Zion, Judith Topcha, was arrested during the July 1942 days, as was Motie Dobin, from the Bund. Kremer, who represented the Right Poale-Zion at the unity talks of August 1941, was caught at the demarcation line and deported. Glaeser and Grinberg left Paris for the Vichy Zone. Shapiro, an American citizen, was interned in a special camp for enemy aliens.[40] Only Rapoport and Jakoubowicz were left from the old guard, and new people, such as Abraham Alperine, were called upon to assist the committee.[41] The changes in personnel in the various immigrant organizations resulted from vastly different causes: Solidarity's losses stemmed directly from its policies, all the others' from causes extending from the general internment measures affecting all the Jews to more personal reasons such as attempts to gain individual safety. These differences characterize most clearly the fundamental differences between Solidarity and the others. Apart from the Communists, they all viewed themselves as voluntary workers, and as such were guided by ethical principles. The Communists, leaders and rank and file alike, considered themselves soldiers under orders.

By the end of 1942 two specific styles of work characterized the immigrant organizations. Amelot, protected by the UGIF, could operate free from the daily anxiety of arrest. As part of the UGIF organization it received help for its canteens and was therefore in a position to assist the immigrants materially. Its affiliation with the UGIF did not stop its leaders from conducting parallel illegal assistance. A special commission consisting of Rapoport, David Oks, and Mrs. Esther Greenberg, with the assistance of Musnik, one of the UGIF's leaders, established a clandestine workshop for the manufacture of false identity papers. Contacts with town hall employees ensured a regular supply of food ration tickets. Immigrants who were wanted by the police knew that Amelot was a source of help.[42] Funds for its activities either arrived from the Vichy Zone by courier or were borrowed from individuals with the Joint's guarantee. But as the constant internments of foreign

Jews increased, the numbers seeking help to escape from Paris generated corresponding pressures upon Amelot. The result was an even larger involvement in illegal practices. Inevitably, the security problems, coupled with the organizational difficulties created by the never-ending demand for forged identities were not given the necessary attention by Amelot. The failure to anticipate the danger of police action was to bring, by mid-1943, catastrophic consequences.

Solidarity had a much more flexible mode of operation. It could and did adapt to the changing situation. It was above all permanently conscious of the problem of security.[43] Until July 1942, the members of the organization gave little attention to the issue of protecting themselves, and the organization, from Gestapo surveillance. Supporters met in homes as in earlier days. But as police repression intensified, as the organization's activities began to attract the attention of the Gestapo, the Communist leadership imposed strict security rules. The majority of activists had become "illegals," keeping away from their former associates and former neighborhoods.[44] Thus the organization could minimize the permanent dangers faced in maintaining an illegal organization. The only Solidarity members still residing in their registered homes were those directed by the organization to work in industry in order to organize the work force. Accordingly, all activities centered on the factories, whether the activity was recruitment, distribution of illegal literature, or fund raising. The essential policy of Solidarity remained what it had always been, resistance to the Germans, but now it had a new field of activities where resistance work could be carried out with less risks of Gestapo surveillance.

The immigrants who worked in these factories were well aware of the protection resulting from their employment. The Gestapo had issued the workers documents ensuring security for themselves and their families. Ironically, the distribution of these *Ausweise* to Jews who were "economically useful" had taken place after the 16 July events. As the sudden internment of a large number of skilled artisans had seriously affected production, the manufacturers asked the German authorities for their workers' protection.[45] By September 1942 some twenty-two major factories directly employed immigrants and supplied work to many hundreds of small workshops.[46] The largest firms were either German or formerly Jewish now under the control of administrators. The fur industry employed the largest number, its products needed for the Eastern Front. At the beginning of 1943, nearly 3,000 Jews were employed and received an *Ausweis*.[47] The possessors of these documents were undoubtedly protected against the worst evils threatening their fellow Jews. Any accidental internment brought an immediate release order from the Germans. The files of the UGIF's Liaison Department, which was in charge of such representation to the German authorities, show that until February 1943 possession of such a document did indeed guarantee release.[48] After that date there was much popular uncertainty about their value and the numbers seeking such employment fell.

Although the majority of immigrants in Paris depended upon such protected work, a significant number still depended upon communal help. Some had remained unaffected for unaccountable reasons and were still living in their homes; others belonged to national groups which for German foreign policy reasons had been left undisturbed. Others were the families of prisoners of war who were nominally exempt from arrest. Members of all these immigrant groups received help from Amelot and from the UGIF. Of all the direct help distributed by Amelot its canteens were the most useful. They saved the poor from starvation; furthermore, as they had done prior to July 1942, they remained a meeting place where immigrants found kindred souls with whom to share their anxiety. The canteens were unique as providers of moral support. But by 1943 they had become even more dangerous than before to those who relied upon them.[49] Frequent police controls resulted in the arrests of many unfortunate illegal poor who depended on the daily canteen meal for survival. Dr. E. Minkowski, an OSE leader who worked closely with Amelot, recalled some years later,

> More than once we asked ourselves whether it was not preferable to close them [canteens] as the Gestapo had shown itself on a number of occasions. I recall the opinion of one of the canteen managers, "Without a doubt prudence requires that we close our establishment, but my clients, especially the older ones, having nowhere to live, helpless, have told me that if we were to close they would voluntarily present themselves at Drancy."[50]

The Communists continually appealed to people not to be tempted by the availability of free or cheap meals. They campaigned for the closure of the canteens on the grounds that they were a permanent threat to the poor. This opposition was in line with the overall Communist position regarding legal activities. It was on the issue of relief, which was in fact a political question, that the major differences between the Communists, Amelot, and the UGIF revealed themselves. There were three positions: the Communists absolutely opposed any form of legal activity; the UGIF's leadership were just as opposed to any illegal activity; Amelot had a more supple policy, favoring use of both legal and illegal means to help those most at risk. Nevertheless, because the Communists were so adamant that they would not take part in any legal relief activity, by the beginning of 1943 the gulf widened between the Communists and the other two groups. Dialogue between them remained impossible.

The fundamental rift between the UGIF and the immigrants, over whether political wisdom required that they always act within the law, resulted from the different conditions affecting the two communities. Until the beginning of 1943 the UGIF leadership saw no reason to believe that the French Jews would not continue to benefit from Vichy's "protection." The leaders did not need to consider alternate forms of operation. The French Jews who resorted to communal help were satisfied with the UGIF's relief policy. The others, the foreign Jews, although benefiting from the UGIF's existence, did not hold out any serious hope of avoiding internment. It was therefore inevitable that immigrant organizations developed such a pessimistic outlook and were so highly critical of the UGIF. Even Amelot, which was determined to use any available legal channels, refused to place its faith in continued legal existence.

The conflict between the Communists and Amelot was more complex. The Communist argument rested on the view that Amelot's opportunism was also harmful, for its continued legal operation lulled the immigrant Jews into believing that the Germans would continue to tolerate the Jews. The Communists' premise that the Germans could impose an overnight closure of all existing institutions and in that event the population would be immediately and totally deprived, was as irrefutable as was their conclusion, that it was imperative to place all relief activities upon an illegal footing before it was too late. Such divergent views could not but be a stumbling block to a united policy.

The differences between the policies followed by the UGIF and the immigrant organizations were not only due to their own conflicting analyses. The Nazis themselves needed to keep these schisms alive. Nazi actions were governed by a policy of gradualism in the application of anti-Jewish measures. That policy was expressed in limiting anti-Jewish actions to specific nationalities at any single moment and allowing such reassuring devices as the protection of UGIF personnel or the *Ausweis*. This technique of eliminating one group of Jews at a time stimulated hopes in those who remained that they would not be the next victims. In the field of relief the presence of two groups, those currently protected and those without protection, resulted in different needs and varying degrees of urgency.

The three strategies were also the outcome of each organization's specific experiences. The UGIF leadership at all times had to face the SD. This situation made these leaders cautious and fearful. They were confronted with ruthlessness. The use of terror and force by the SD consistently led the UGIF leaders to underestimate their own capacity to resist. Amelot, sheltered by the UGIF from direct confrontation with the SD, could, as a consequence, take a much broader view of the problem. It was thus more reckless in its work. The justification of the Communist position resided in the worsening situation of the immigrants, and each new measure against the Jews further strengthened their argument.

Solidarity's prime commitment to armed resistance never meant that it failed to give direct assistance to the population. That need became even more marked in February 1943 when arrests, internments, and deportations began anew. On 11 February, new massive arrests occurred, directed this time more specifically at the old and the sick. Foreign Jews in the Rothschild Hospital and Old People's Home were the first victims. Children were taken from the UGIF homes.[51] In the deportations of 9, 11, and 13 February, the age composition of the victims was quite different from the earlier ones. The convoy of 13 February comprised 689 persons over the age of sixty and 150 children under eighteen.[52] Solidarity and Amelot produced forged identity papers on a mass scale, and the Jewish partisans supplied ration coupons to the organizations to assist the families who had avoided arrest.[53] But the most complex problem encountered was the protection of the children, including both those left "at large" in Paris without parents, those belonging to families wanting to hide them, as well as those held in the UGIF institutions. Solidarity considered this last group as the most exposed; particularly those who had been handed over by the SD to the UGIF and whose names and places of residence were at all times subject to SD control. These children were permanently vulnerable to an SD deportation order. Following the 11 February deportation of some of them, Solidarity and Amelot were constantly aware of their degree of exposure.

On 16 February 1943, Solidarity's children's commission received a warning from the PCF that the Germans were about to take a number of children back to Drancy for deportation. The commission called upon Suzanne Spaak of the MNCR; with Pastor Vergueras she organized a network of Christian families willing to hide them. Fifteen Jewish and twenty-five non-Jewish women called on the UGIF's "homes" and took sixty-three children out as though for an afternoon's outing and thus placed them in safe houses.[54]

The whole issue of the protection of children was, however, very complex. Even the UGIF policy regarding their protection, a policy Amelot rejected, had succeeded in saving a large number. As far as the UGIF was concerned, the care of the children was part of its overall relief. Special help could only be extended as long as it did not jeopardize the whole enterprise. The UGIF even organized special means to take some children to the southern zone to hide them with farmers. The cost of their upkeep was met by secret funds, so it cannot be said that the UGIF was callous or ineffective; it was cautious.

The UGIF was not willing, early in 1943, to risk all for the sake of the children who had been entrusted to it by the SD. Too many institutions and too many individuals were at risk to attempt to hide them. This fear originated from the strict control imposed upon the UGIF; whenever the SD requested information on the number of people in institutions the UGIF had to comply. In December 1942 the SD had asked Baur to supply a list of addresses of all the children's homes. The SD, knowing of the UGIF's constant reorganization of its homes, wanted to be sure that it was kept fully informed at all times.[55] The CGQJ itself was not far behind, and during 1943 it became concerned with the number of children the UGIF supported outside its official institutions.[56] The CGQJ wanted above all to ensure that the UGIF did not disperse them and especially that the children not be placed with non-Jews. It was at this stage that the UGIF began to consider the illegal placement of children, the cost to be borne by illegal funds.[57]

The immigrant organizations in Paris, as well as the OSE, considered all the children maintained under such conditions permanently threatened. They therefore never encouraged immigrant families to entrust their children to the UGIF. Amelot was at first reluctant to place children with Christian families or institutions, but the July 1942 events compelled it to reconsider the question. Once Amelot decided to follow this alternative it rapidly established an appropriate organization. The difficulties were indeed serious. Parents had to be prepared for the eventuality that they might not have access to their children. A service had to be created that would ensure regular payment and the records of true and false identities and addresses had to be carefully maintained and protected. A special system for correspondence between families and children had to be organized. The Amelot Committee created just such a complex organization with the assistance of Mrs. Lucie Chevalley, then chief social worker for immigrants of the Seine department.[58] The cost of this placement service rose between October 1942 and December 1942 from 50,000 to 200,000 francs.[59] The sums required by Amelot for its general operations reached the monthly amount of a million francs during the first semester of 1943. Financed by the FSJF, Amelot even helped Solidarity meet its obligations when it ran short of funds.[60]

Until March 1943, most of the remaining "legal" immigrants in Paris owed their safety to their employment in protected industries. But the German defeat at Stalingrad suddenly altered that work force's usefulness. The SD in Paris decided to reduce their number by a third, and in March 1943 Röthke ordered the French police to proceed with their arrest.[61] Simultaneously, Röthke reduced the immigrant component of the UGIF personnel. These unprecedented measures affecting those considered until then "superprivileged" produced a new panic among the immigrants. There was a wave of departures from Paris.

One island of security remained for those who feared arrest: the Italian Zone of Occupation. Although this zone had resulted from France's defeat in June 1940, the area occupied by Italy had been limited at first to a small enclave. However, the landing of the Allied armies in North Africa in November 1942 had led to a major extension of Italy's Zone of Occupation. It extended as far west as the Rhône River. The significance of the enlarged zone for the Jews was that Italy, unlike Germany or Vichy, took a different view of the Jewish Question. True, it had introduced racial laws at home, but it had never taken steps leading to the physical elimination of the Jewish population from its territories.[62] The Italian authorities had introduced a similar policy in the French territories it occupied. The Jews there were effectively protected by the Italian military administration from Vichy's anti-Jewish measures. The extension of the Italian Zone of Occupation resulted in a major influx of Jews from the rest of France.[63] The news even reached Paris, and all those fearing arrest and having the necessary means considered making the journey.

The immigrant organizations disagreed on the significance of this unheard-of situation and on the advice they should give to the Jews. The Amelot Committee took a pragmatic view: if the Italian Zone of Occupation offered safety then advantage should be taken of it, for time was essential to survival. Of course, Amelot was aware that the SD would not tolerate such a situation and would exert pressure upon the Italians for a reversal of policy, but the chance had to be taken.[64] The Communists conducted a strong campaign against acceptance by the Jews of the notion that Italy would continue to protect them. From their point of view Italy was a Fascist state and would inevitably surrender to Nazi pressure. The Communists' major concern was the conviction that the Jews courted disaster by concentrating in any particular areas. But the attraction of even temporary protection was too strong for a terrorized population to withstand. In spite of a campaign of warning from Solidarity, thousands of Jews from all parts of France, including Paris, made their way to the Italian Zone of Occupation during the first half of 1943.[65]

It was during that period that the Jewish Communist leadership began to reexamine its positions. The changes that had taken place in the lives of that population since July 1942, and the consequences of these changes upon Communist policies and organizational structures as they had evolved since Solidarity had been formed in August 1940, needed to be appraised. The conditions as well as the political line to which the organization had been committed had resulted in increased isolation of the movement. It was clear that this isolation was not solely due to the specific conditions affecting the Jewish population in Paris. The reexamination of policy was all the more necessary when considered in the light of what was taking place within the non-Jewish Resistance. The PCF's "national front" policy, toward which it had been working since May 1941, had helped overcome some of its isolation from the mainstream of the Resistance. The establishment of the Conseil National de la Résistance (National Resistance Council [CNR]) in May 1943, was probably the decisive external factor that influenced the Jewish Communists in their policy review.[66] They began to seek new political formulations which would renew a dialogue with the various Jewish organizations and lead to national unity.

It was in the Southern Zone, in December 1942, that the first steps toward a dialogue between immigrant organizations took place.[67] The Vichy promulgation of a new law ordering the stamping of the Jews' identity cards had created the opportunity for a meeting between Communist representatives, including Jacques Ravine, the former leader of Solidarity in Paris, Léon Gordon, the former leader of the Communist organization at Pithiviers, and representatives of the coordinating committee of the immigrant organizations in the Southern Zone.[68] All agreed about the need to exchange opinions on the significance of this measure as well as the need to reach an agreement on how to advise the immigrant population. The Communist representatives argued for a campaign of boycott.[69] They believed that the legislation was a preparatory step to deportations and that all the Jewish organizations should campaign for the Jews not to present themselves for the stamping.[70] The other immigrant organizations felt, however, that the Jewish population would not follow such advice. The Communists' argument, though based upon the experience of the Occupied Zone, did not convince the others. Although the discussions resulted neither in a united decision nor in any agreement about the value of regular consultations, a dialogue had nevertheless begun.

At the end of April 1943 a national conference of the Jewish Communist leadership took place in Paris to discuss general problems. High on the agenda was the question of unity.[71] There was unanimous agreement on the urgent need to bring about a national union of all the Jewish organizations. To create the necessary preconditions for such a campaign the national conference decided to broaden Solidarity's platform by redefining its objectives and, to indicate the nature of the changes, to rename the organization. Solidarity would henceforth be called the Union des Juifs pour la Résistance et l'Entr'aide (Union of the Jews for the Resistance and Mutual Aid [UJRE]). Solidarity had served its purpose; a new name was to symbolize the new objectives which corresponded to the new situation. Solidarity's former organizations, Union des Femmes Juives, Union de la Jeunesse Juive, Solidarité in Paris, Secours Populaire in the south, La Commission Intersyndicale, and all the armed units in the north as well as in the south, were now merged into the single new organization, the UJRE.

It would be an oversimplification to believe that the renaming of Solidarity was motivated purely by political opportunism, that is, by a desire to hide the Communist character of the organization. From as early as August 1942 the Communists' illegal publications had begun to reflect changed attitudes. Although their writings still articulated general Communist policies there had been a shift of emphasis toward Jewish issues. An affirmation of national pride began to appear; previously it had been subordinated to ideological positions which had defined Jewish nationalism as a bourgeois phenomenon. A number of factors brought about this gradual change. The Jewish persecutions were certainly the determining factor, and they significantly contributed to the growth of national consciousness. The post-July 1942 recruits had joined as a response to the persecutions. By 1943 Solidarity's overall membership had qualitatively altered the general character of the organization. Most of the former immigrant left-wing members and supporters had either been killed or deported or had left Paris for the south. New elements had joined to whom Communist ideology was secondary to the anti-Nazi struggle.[72] Although UJRE remained a Communist organization, led and inspired by Communists, its leader took note of these changes in the formulation of new policies. By doing so they were building a bridge that would give the movement access to a new section of the Jewish population and to other organizations. The UJRE's first statement of position made the changes clear:

> The propaganda and the anti-Jewish persecutions are directed against all the Jews. . . . No distinctions are made in their extermination. . . . Workers or bourgeois, Zionists or Communists, believers or atheists, they are all Jews.[73]

It was on the basis of such a formulation that the national conference adopted a new and concrete program, articulated around three issues. The first point addressed mutual help, calling for the development of local committees that would be financed by collections and that would assist every Jew who asked for help. The UJRE would establish social services to take care of the children, the old, and the sick. It would form an identity card service to assist every Jew to go underground. The second part of the program called for a major campaign to develop all forms of resistance and the establishment of fighting units. Third, it was proposed that a central Jewish representation be established and that it represent all Jews in any negotiations with the CNR and the French provisional government.

The program was clearly designed to present to the other immigrant organizations and the Jewish population UJRE's firm commitment to the principle of self-help. This emphasis was a recognition of the popular demand for such assistance. It was also an admission of the isolation in which Solidarity had found itself due to its former policy of concentrating all efforts toward active resistance. By relegating the call for the establishment of armed units to the second position on its program the UJRE sought to allay fears that the Communists were still adhering to former positions and would make participation in the anti-Nazi struggle a precondition of any unity. Lastly, the program sought to promote the widest possible unity by anticipating, through reference to a national representation, the participation of the Central Consistory.

It was while the Communist national conference was in progress that news of an uprising in the Warsaw Ghetto arrived. The historical significance of the event was immediately seen by the assembly as a vindication of Communist strategy, as an answer to all those who had previously rejected such a policy as of no significance to Jewish survival. Although information about the scope of the uprising was scanty, Solidarity's leadership nevertheless decided to give the event immediate publicity.[74]

The Communist organizations had just concluded their May Day campaign. Activists had addressed the workers in most major factories but, although there had been a high level of activities, recent arrests had seriously depleted the forces of trade-union committees and the youth organizations.[75] Nevertheless the organization succeeded in publishing an issue of *Unzer Vort* on 15 May.[76] The lack of details about the Warsaw Ghetto Uprising led Solidarity to present it as a battle fought by the Jews against the Nazis. From 15 May onward detailed news reached Paris and Solidarity launched a major political propaganda campaign. Three appeals, in Yiddish, appeared during the remainder of May: an appeal from the Jewish Communists, an appeal from the Jewish trade-union organization, and a general appeal to Brider Yiden (Jewish Brothers), the Jewish population.[77] Not until 1 June 1943, did an issue of *Unzer Vort,* which appeared in the French language, present details of what had taken place in Warsaw.[78] The Communist leadership ordered each of its organizations to set aside 3 June as a commemorative day. Solidarity ordered the units of the Second Detachment to launch a special offensive against the Germans to mark the uprising.[79] It dispatched activists to the factories to address the work forces and many workers donated a day's pay to support the UJRE.[80]

While the Communist leadership had already formulated its new political line, it nevertheless believed that the significance of the Warsaw Ghetto Uprising needed to be linked to the policy of armed struggle. All the Communist publications therefore emphasized the connection between mass extermination and the need to struggle in order to ensure the survival of the Jews.

Shortly after this campaign the immigrant organizations in Paris were themselves fighting for survival. Yet the UJRE underground propaganda never publicly acknowledged that its existence in Paris was poised on the edge of destruction. Nor did Amelot inform the immigrant population that its various centers were threatened with overnight closure.

Amelot suffered several blows that immediately affected a large number of immigrants in Paris. The general-secretary, Jakoubowicz, had to flee in May to the Southern Zone. On 1 June 1943, Rapoport, Amelot's leader, was arrested on a charge of distributing forged identity cards.[81] Upon his arrest, the remaining leaders decided to close Amelot and warned the personnel of the situation. A small group of workers decided to remain at their posts. A week later the police raided Amelot and the remaining immigrant employees were arrested and sent to Drancy.[82] On 28 June the CGQJ formally dissolved Amelot and its network of institutions were handed over to the UGIF to operate as it saw fit.[83] The sudden increase in the numbers calling upon its own facilities led the UGIF to immediately reopen Amelot with the remaining French personnel. Alperine and Joseph Byl the last two leading activists, took over the responsibility of directing Amelot under the UGIF's control.[84] The June crisis, which had begun with Rapoport's arrest, did not lead to Amelot's permanent closure but it did mark the end of a line of communal workers whose efforts to assist the poor immigrants had cost them their lives.

For the newly formed UJRE in Paris, July proved the most critical period of its existence. By then the local Jewish Communist organizations had passed their zenith. The ever-decreasing Jewish population could no longer be counted upon as a reservoir of new forces by the UJRE. Fewer and fewer immigrants worked in factories. Successive arrests had further weakened their operational capacity. The general policies of Solidarity, shaped by its PCF affiliation, as well as the anti-Jewish measures, had gradually transformed the whole organization. In order to survive it had to plunge deeper underground. The concentrated efforts of the Gestapo and the French police to stamp out resistance compelled most of Solidarity's members to cut off personal contacts with the Jewish population.

The authorities directed much of their effort to uncovering the Jewish organizations because of the high proportion of Jews active in Communist-led Resistance attacks upon the German army. The Jewish Communist organizations became a particular target of the police. The PCF's immigrant organization, the MOI, which was particularly active in the armed resistance, was Solidarity's connection to the PCF's organizations. These links were all the more significant when we consider that two of the three MOI leaders were former Solidarity activists.[85] Furthermore, Solidarity's contribution to the armed units of the MOI was inordinately high, and the PCF's appeal to all its affiliated bodies to transfer 10 percent of their memberships to the partisan movement had resulted in an even larger Jewish participation.[86] Between January and May 1943, these Jewish units were carrying out at least two major military operations a week.[87]

In March 1943 the Gestapo finally succeeded in tracking down some of their members and a number of arrests were made. In the eleventh arrondissement alone the youth organization lost thirty-six members. Among them was Henri Krasucky, then in charge of all youth activities in Paris.[88] The Jewish Communist leadership now faced serious problems, for there were close links between the youth organization and the Second Detachment and through this detachment the whole of MOI was endangered. The problem was even more serious as the MOI was directly attached to the PCF central leadership.[89] The arrests of Solidarity youth members actually threatened the whole Communist movement in France. The Jewish leaders took drastic steps to contain the danger. It ordered the Second Detachment to stop all activities, and dispersed the units out of Paris until the extent of Gestapo penetration could be assessed.[90] These measures succeeded temporarily in blocking any further arrests and, after some weeks, the leaders decided to bring the Second Detachment back to Paris. But from then on they no longer operated as Jewish units. Out of the fear that the Gestapo might still be on the trail of some Solidarity members connected with the partisan organization, the MOI leaders dispersed the Jewish partisans into other MOI units. The crisis affecting the Jewish Communist organization had only been temporarily averted.

In July 1943 new massive arrests took place, affecting the youth organization in particular and endangering the whole clandestine leadership. The earlier measures, quarantining the Jewish units and ruthlessly imposing security measures, had not succeeded in averting the arrests. The Gestapo, fearing that it might lose its grip on the situation through a voluntary dismantling of the organization, decided to proceed with the arrest of 140 youth and adult members.[91] This sudden police operation temporarily paralyzed the whole network. The Jewish leaders sent out of Paris members it believed were known to the Gestapo and appointed new members to lead the Paris organization: Paulette Rapoport and Gaston Gruner. Furthermore, the leadership ordered all local and factory branches to cease operations. The UJRE in Paris was paralyzed and needed time to rebuild itself along new organizational lines which would not be known to the Gestapo. This was the task assigned to the incoming leadership.[92]

The most important cause of the collapse of the UJRE organization in Paris had been due to the relentless demands placed upon it by the MOI. The Jewish Communists had never questioned these orders, particularly when they consisted in directing Jewish efforts to the armed struggle. The tremendous losses sustained by the Jewish organizations were not only due to the very high concentration of anti-Resistance repressive forces in Paris. Nor were they due solely to the high level of activities of the Second Detachment, nor even to the close personal connections between the partisans and the youth organization.

The collapse of the UJRE, with terrible human losses, was the consequence of political decisions. The MOI leadership had refused to view the problems of Solidarity/UJRE in terms of its specific needs and obligations as a Jewish organization. The arrests, which had begun in March, were avoidable had Solidarity been allowed by the MOI to make the organizational changes it had demanded.[93] Solidarity's demand for permission to transfer some of its personnel to other towns had been rejected by the MOI. The MOI took the view that the PCF's overall objectives had to be supported despite the human costs. The subordination of the particular interests of the Jewish organization and the Jewish fighters to the PCF's general policy of armed struggle proved ruinous to the pursuit of an independent Jewish Communist policy in Paris. As a consequence, hundreds of Solidarity members were sacrificed and the Jewish immigrant population was deprived of one of the few organizations it possessed. Nevertheless the Jewish Communist leadership, obedient and faithful to party decisions, carried out the orders.[94]

The arrests during June and July 1943 of members and leaders of the UJRE and of the Amelot Committee seriously affected their activities. The UGIF itself, for different reasons, saw its Vice-President Baur and most of its Parisian leaders arrested during the same period (see Chapter 8). All the organizations were in the throes of the most severe crisis they had ever encountered. The day-to-day situation of the remaining Jews in Paris was constantly worsening. The streets of Paris, long unsafe for those wearing the Yellow Star, had become even more dangerous. Any Jew could be arrested at any time. The remaining 2,000 Jews working in industry under the protection of the *Ausweis* were not spared when the Jewish population was once more the victim of internment measures during July 1943.[95] Their only distinction lay in being taken by trucks to Drancy from their place of work.[96] Those Jews remaining in Paris were predominantly French, with a small number of immigrants who had so far not been sought by the police and a mass of immigrants who lived illegally. Amelot, which resumed activities once it had overcome the problems created by the police raids, continued to care for the immigrants, especially those without legal status. The reformed UGIF leadership, knowing of Amelot's illegal assistance, asked only that aid not be rendered in its offices.[97] Amelot continued to be funded by the FSJF from the Vichy Zone. For the remainder of 1943 Amelot received 600,000 francs a month and that amount was continued until 1944.[98]

While the depleted immigrant organizations in Paris suffered from arrests and deportations and constant Gestapo attention, the immigrant organizations in the Southern Zone were firmly established by mid-1943. The constant stream of Jews arriving from Paris significantly contributed to their strengthening. The Franco-Jewish organizations in the south had also, by then, overcome the divisions that resulted from the earlier conflicts arising from the establishment of the UGIF. When the Wehrmacht, and the SD, marched into the Vichy Zone on 11 November 1942, the Jewish organizations were prepared. The non-Jewish population itself did not panic as it did in the north during July 1940; civil administration and communal structures continued to function, a situation which was to prove useful to the Jewish population. No sooner had the SD installed itself than it ordered the application of anti-Jewish measures. In December 1942 the SD instructed the French police to order the Jews to present themselves to the local police stations to have their identity cards stamped. Although uncertain about what to do, the immigrant organizations were nevertheless considering the issue in an organized fashion.

From January 1943 onward, when the SD began to assert its authority in matters of anti-Jewish policy in the Southern Zone, the immigrant organizations began, hesitantly at first, to direct their attention to the issue of united Jewish response. The arrests during January in Marseille, of French Jews and immigrants heralded the new era. The following month, in Lyon, a UGIF branch office that catered to immigrants was raided by the SD and all personnel were arrested. The Jewish scouting movement, which had been functioning until then, was disbanded on Vichy orders.[99] The mounting pressure upon the Jewish population in the Vichy Zone generated a communal response. Gamzon, a UGIF board member, who was in charge of youth activities, began to direct the banned scouting organizations to illegal relief activities. The ORT stopped financing agricultural projects.[100] The OSE, which had already begun to develop illegal networks to hide children, committed itself wholly to this course of action.[101] These developments, unconnected as they were, created the basis from which united action between organizations could emerge. As far as the immigrant organizations themselves were concerned, it was the news of the Warsaw Ghetto Uprising that finally persuaded them to take the necessary steps toward establishing a united committee that could map out a collective survival strategy.

During that period, in July 1943, a majority of the southern coordinating committee of immigrant organizations in Lyon finally decided to meet representatives of the UJRE to discuss common problems.[102] The UJRE immediately recognized the importance of the invitation. Two issues dominated the talks: assistance and protection of the Jewish population and armed resistance.[103] There was immediate and full agreement on the need to develop relief activities. It was over the question of Jewish armed struggle that the old differences reemerged. The FSJF refused to accept the UJRE's thesis. Even the terms of disagreement were not new. The UJRE, like Solidarity in August 1941, argued that the question of survival was inseparable from the armed struggle, that Jewish survival could only be conceived in terms of the speediest defeat of Nazi Germany; Jewish participation in that struggle being understood as necessary not only to assert national dignity but also to show the people of France that the Jews were participating in the battle for the Liberation of France.[104]

The FSJF and the other organizations that participated in the discussions, the Bund and the various Zionist groups, took a different position. They agreed in general terms with the Communists, that it was important for Jewish national reasons to make it known that Jews fought, but this was as far as the community of view extended. The divisions emerged over the military significance, in the overall world struggle, of the Jewish contribution in France to the defeat of Nazism. This, the non-Communist organizations believed, had to justify the sacrifice of human and material resources. The aim of the Jewish organizations, they argued, was to ensure the survival of the largest number of Jews. Jewish armed struggle could only provoke further measures against the Jewish population and possibly alienate some sections of the non-Jewish population.[105] The Communists' argument that the Nazis had not required any pretext to deport or kill Jewish families and that, if only out of national pride, such a struggle should be pursued, did not overcome the differences and convince the others.

Despite fundamentally differing views over an issue that the UJRE considered central to its policy and over which the other organizations were united, a compromise was reached. Both sides were too conscious of the critical problems facing immigrant Jewry to accept the responsibility for rejecting unity. The immigrant coordinating committee and the UJRE joined to form the Comité Général de Défense des Juifs (General Jewish Defense Committee [CGD]) in which they would share resources to assist the population. A compromise was reached on the issue of armed resistance: the coordinating committee agreed that although the armed groups would not be permitted to operate as part of the CGD they would nevertheless receive financial subsidies.

From the Communist point of view, the agreement, though limited, was a major success. It marked the acceptance of the movement into the national Jewish political scene. And, unlike the previous unity agreement reached during August 1941 in Paris, it offered much broader possibilities, for it was in the Southern Zone that the national leaderships of all the Jewish organizations resided. The aim of the Communists, to achieve a national representation that would include French Judaism, was therefore a step closer to realization. Even though the principle of armed resistance had not been accepted, the offer of financial help represented in itself a form of commitment that did not preclude a reexamination of the question. The Communists had good reason to feel satisfied at the outcome of the agreement.

The other immigrant organizations also greeted the formation of the CGD as a major political achievement. It had transformed the loose coordinating committee into a representative organ which gave it the necessary standing within immigrant Jewry and allowed it to address French Judaism from an authoritative position. One problem remained: the likelihood of political problems arising from the UJRE's presence. But the non-Communist organizations took the view that they would be able to steer the committee on the desired course.[106] Generally, all parties to the agreement were satisfied that they had gained a clear political advantage, and this ensured the unity of the CGD. All recognized, however, that it was only the first step toward a united national representation, for which the Central Consistory's support had to be won.

The political developments achieved in the south took some time to find expression in Paris. The disarray of the immigrant organizations, the problems faced by the remaining leaders in the regrouping of their diminished forces, hindered, at the time, the establishment of a similar committee in Paris.

For the UJRE in Paris the second half of 1943 was a period of stagnation. The youth organization, the spearhead of sabotage and the armed struggle, was temporarily out of action. The trade-union activists still in the factories found themselves without political direction. The illegal presses operated only spasmodically. The women's organization, because of its responsibility for the children in hiding, was the only UJRE organization that continued to operate without interruption. And so did the Jewish partisans who had avoided arrest, although they no longer maintained contacts with the UJRE members once they had been transferred to MOI units.[107] They had carried out their last operation as a Jewish unit on 19 July 1943. After this, they carried on as part of a special unit attached to the general staff of the MOI, led by the Armenian poet Missak Manouchian.[108] This unit of twenty-three fighters, including twelve Jews, one a woman, carried out the most spectacular operations against the Germans in Paris until its final destruction by the Gestapo in November 1943. Among its most important military actions was the execution of Julius Ritter, Fritz-Ernest Sauckel's representative, whom the National French Military Committee had condemned to death.[109] These twenty-three fighters became the protagonists, in February 1944, of the most famous public trial of immigrant fighters staged by the Germans. The German military court condemned them all to death.[110] According to Abraham Lissner, who had been closely associated with all the armed groups in which Jews had volunteered, between March 1942 and November 1943, they had participated in 459 military actions. These included blowing up ten military trains, destroying antiaircraft batteries, bombing hotels housing German personnel, and attacking countless other military objectives.[111]

The arrest in November 1943 of the last Jewish fighters in Paris, together with another 108 members of the UJRE, and the resulting fear that the Gestapo still kept other activists under observation, further held back the UJRE leadership from rebuilding its organization.[112] The relentless Gestapo pressure upon the Communist organization during 1943, which resulted in executions and deportation of hundreds of their members, was a possibility each individual member had been prepared to accept. But none of them had ever envisaged being so ruthlessly sacrificed.

The Jewish Communists have been seen by some as expendable for the PCF because they were foreigners. Claude Lévy, in his book *Les Parias de la Résistance,* chose to call them the "pariahs" not only because they have remained to this day the unknown heroes of the French Resistance but because they were so readily sacrificed. As the widow of Manouchian, who headed the famous special unit, wrote, quoting her husband's remarks on the eve of his arrest: "I effectively believe that they [our leaders] want to send us to our death."[113]

Although the UJRE had not been allowed by the PCF to save its fighters, it nevertheless took the appropriate steps to rebuild its organization. It proceeded, during October and November 1943, to relocate its leaders: the old leadership was sent out of Paris and new people brought in.[114] The reconstituted UJRE leadership screened every remaining member of the organization and formed new local committees. By December 1943, fifteen new groups, divided into three sectors, were once more operative in Paris.[115] The UJRE installed a new printing press and established a laboratory for the manufacture of forged identity papers. The organization was once more on its feet.[116]

The new leaders who arrived from the south fresh from the experience of the newly formed CGD set to work establishing a similar united defense committee in Paris. By early 1944 the UJRE was fully operational there, but conditions had vastly changed. The number of workers in protected industries had considerably diminished.[117] The immigrants were less and less accessible. There were still enough of them living legally in Paris to be seen by the UJRE as warranting another appeal to "Hold on, be vigilant, once and for all abandon your registered apartments and do not return to them under any conditions." The same appeal addressed those in hiding:

> Be discreet in your illegal lodgings; do not just invite anyone; do not carry your real identity card stamped "Jew"; if you possess false identification as well do not carry both; be wary of people who talk too much; do not walk the streets unnecessarily; do not speak Yiddish in the streets.[118]

Such appeals, coupled with the caution exercised by the majority of illegal residents, although designed to ensure their survival, did not help the UJRE extend its membership. Contacts with the illegals were difficult. The organization's mass basis among the immigrants was, for all intents and purposes, nonexistent.

The final mass arrests of immigrants in Paris took place in February 1944.[119] It was the last house-to-house arrest on such a scale. From then on, until Liberation in August 1944, the SD found the numbers required to fill the convoys through permanent street identity controls. The only sizable group of Jews left in Paris were the French, and the UJRE increasingly directed its appeals in their direction.[120]

In January 1944, following the establishment of the CGD in the South, a United Defense Committee—the Comité d'Union et des Défense des Juifs—was formed in Paris.[121] It included individuals who worked in a number of institutions: Alperine of the Amelot Committee; Dr. Minkowski from OSE; Toni Stern, a member of the Paris UGIF board; Rabinowicz, employed in the UGIF's legal department; Gruner from the UJRE. Its president was Alperine and its general-secretary Albert Akerberg, from the scouting movement. An emissary from the south, Simon Levitte, had drawn all these individuals together and helped negotiate the establishment of the committee. The funds for its operation came from the CGD in the south, itself financed by the FSJF.[122]

The Parisian United Defense Committee proceeded to organize its activities on the same basis as the southern CGD. It assisted both illegal and legal Jews. It ensured that the children were protected. It worked toward an understanding with the UGIF leadership in order to realize these objectives. The presence of a UGIF board member, although helpful in maintaining channels of communication, did not prove sufficient to win the UGIF leadership to the view that there should be a close working relationship. Serious political differences needed to be overcome before the question of cooperation could begin to be considered by both sides. The committee was firmly opposed to the continued existence of the UGIF. The UGIF leadership was equally convinced that the Jewish population needed its services. When in February 1944 Alperine, on behalf of the United Defense Committee, suggested to Edinger that the UGIF should prepare its own scuttling, it was no surprise that Edinger rejected the proposal.[123]

By then whether or not the UGIF had been of benefit to the Jewish population was no longer a political question. All along the Eastern Front the German armies were in retreat. The Allied armies were progressing in Italy. Everyone was convinced that 1944 was the year of the "Second Front." Liberation seemed at hand. The United Defense Committee was firmly convinced that the nearer the end the greater the danger of desperate anti-Jewish measures by the SD. The committee saw the UGIF's continued existence as a source of danger to all those who depended upon its services. The poor Jews obtaining their meals in the UGIF canteens, the children in the homes, the residents of the Old People's Home and the Rothschild Hospital, all were permanent hostages, unless, as the committee demanded, the UGIF immediately proceeded to disperse and hide them.

Furthermore, news had reached Paris that in the provinces the SD was arresting the UGIF representatives and thus closing all the UGIF branches. It seemed to the United Defense Committee that the Germans had concluded that the UGIF had reached the end of its usefulness. Edinger, on behalf of the UGIF, agreed that the situation was indeed serious, but he opposed the sudden closure. Such a plan, Edinger believed, did not take into account the complexity of the situation. There were thousands of Jews held in various camps in and around Paris who would be immediately exposed to reprisals, there were still more than 20,000 Jews living legally in their homes and all those in the institutions could not be hidden overnight. The Paris UGIF leadership refused to assume such a responsibility, without a serious examination of its consequences.

A nationwide debate between the immigrant committee supported by some elements from the UGIF in Paris and in the south and the respective UGIF leaderships began under the aegis of the Conseil Représentatif des Juifs de France. A national council, CRIF was agreed to, in principle, in January 1944 by immigrants and representatives of French Judaism, and was by its representative character the decisive force in the Jewish community. The debate between the contending parties on the future of the UGIF was pursued until the Liberation of Paris in August 1944 and agreement was never reached. The CRIF had formed a commission, chaired by Léon Meiss, president of CRIF, and also acting president of the Central Consistory, to adjudicate the issue. It was then in Meiss's power to pronounce the ultimate decision, but he refused to assume responsibility for the UGIF's closure. Mindful of the consequences of such a decision, Meiss was not convinced that the immigrants' proposals were practical, that it was indeed possible to hide and disperse such large numbers of people or that the immigrants would be able to guarantee their protection.[124]

In February 1944, on the basis of directives from the PCF, the UJRE, began organizing units of Milices Patriotiques.[125] At the UJRE's proposal the United Defense Committee formed a military commission, headed by Gruner and Rabinowicz, with the task of representing the Jewish forces with the Forces Française de l'Intérieure (French Forces of the Interior). It was the UJRE's responsibility to recruit, train, and form the Jewish units. Through its contact with the MOI, the UJRE arranged for technical personnel to prepare these units for combat. The units armed themselves in the same primitive manner as in the early days of the armed struggle in 1941. Sometimes using their wits and sometimes such primitive weapons as hammers, these groups disarmed French municipal police guarding public installations and attacked isolated German soldiers.[126] By April 1944 the United Defense Committee had arranged a contact between its military commission and the Armée Juive (sometimes called Organisation Juive de Combat [AJ or OJC]) which had then established headquarters in Paris. But these contacts did not lead to a unified military resistance. The ideological differences separating the UJRE and the OJC were so serious that they could not be bridged. The UJRE emphasized the anti-Nazi character of its activities while the OJC stressed its Zionist ideals.[127] Two distinct views of the function of a Jewish resistance operated within the Jewish community and the differences were such that they were not overcome. Ideological factors continued to hinder the development of a united armed resistance.

The landing of the Allied armies in Normandy on 6 June 1944, gave the committee new perspectives. The appeal of the CNR to the French Resistance to prepare for the *Insurrection Nationale* prompted the committee to define its own objectives in the event of an insurrection in Paris. One of the major political problems faced by the committee remained the UGIF. On the question whether the UGIF would or would not decide at the last moment to close its institutions depended the fate of thousands. The United Defense Committee's examination of the situation led it to conclude that of all those directly dependent upon the UGIF, those least able to protect themselves and who could immediately be saved were the children. The committee met with Edinger a number of times to impress upon him the danger faced by the children. But the committee failed to convince him of the necessity of immediate action.

One more deportation convoy left Drancy destined for Auschwitz during July 1944, and that convoy included the children from the UGIF homes which had been raided on direct orders from Brunner. And this deportation took place less than three weeks before Paris was freed.

The question remains, therefore, why the United Defense Committee, faced with Edinger's refusal to act, and convinced that the children were effectively in danger, did not undertake, under its own responsibility, the necessary actions to save them. Undoubtedly the issue of hiding the children was an integral part of the debate over the closure of the UGIF. The committee, faced with the Central Consistory's refusal to support such a move, refrained from taking a step, which in the likely event of SD reprisals, might have jeopardized the unity they had only just established. The immigrant organizations did not want to have to answer charges of irresponsibility or of refusing to accept the ruling of the president of the CRIF. So the Germans took the children from the UGIF homes and deported them to Auschwitz.

Although these children were the innocent victims of the UGIF strategy, the United Defense Committee, paralyzed because of its concern for communal unity, must equally share the blame for their deaths. For if it was certain that they were in danger and that the UGIF had been criminally negligent in failing to hide them, then the failure of the committee to act was just as criminal.

The Wehrmacht began withdrawing from Paris on 9 August 1944. The battle for Paris between insurgents and the German army began on 17 August. It ended with the arrival of the Leclerc Division from the Free French Forces on 25 August, when the remaining German forces surrendered. Meanwhile the Jewish activists had not been idle. The UJRE organized 60 fighting groups. The Union de la Jeunesse Juive contributed 150 members and the Jewish militia 250 fighting men.[128] The United Defense Committee's military commission had a simple plan of action directed at its Jewish opponents as well as at the Germans: to participate in the general struggle and to occupy the UGIF offices and institutions. In the confusion and excitement of the preparations for the battle for Liberation, the United Defense Committee and the UJRE forgot the men and women at Drancy. The Jewish resistance did not open the gates of Drancy. It was the local French Forces of the Interior with the participation of Drancy's own resistance organization which liberated the internees on 18 August. It took place without bloodshed. Aloïs Brunner, on the eve of his departure from Drancy had ordered the gendarmes to guard the inmates until his return. But Liberation came too late for a group of forty Jewish resistance fighters in the camp. In exchange for pigs bred at Drancy, Brunner succeeded in obtaining permission from the retreating Wehrmacht to attach one wagon to the last departing train.[129]

For the UJRE the Liberation of Paris did not mark the end of the war. Committed to the goal of the total defeat of Nazi Germany, it appealed to the Jews to join the reconstituted French army and carry on the struggle. During and shortly after the battle for Paris it formed two units, the Rayman and the Markus companies, named after two outstanding Jewish partisans who had fallen in the struggle. These two units became part of the MOI's own contribution of foreign volunteers to the new French army (Bataillon 51/22, Premier Régiment de Paris).

The Liberation which came with the uprising did not bring to all Jews the joy and relief they had prayed for. For too many of the survivors, particularly the immigrants, life could never be the same. Old Paris could never again exist for them. Thousands of families had filled the deportation trains to the camps of Eastern Europe, thousands of others had lost at least one relative, thousands of children had been orphaned. The broken lives of the survivors needed mending. The immediate tasks of the immigrant organizations were enormous. They threw themselves into rebuilding their community. The immigrants had emerged from their hiding places without homes to go to or resources with which to build a new life. Workmen lacked the tools of their trade. Businessmen had been dispossessed. The process of returning to their rightful owners the proceeds of aryanization, of housing the homeless, of finding accommodation for all those who made their way back to Paris, of tracing the children left with Christian families and institutions, became the new challenges of organized Jewry.

The immigrant organizations' contempt for the UGIF had been further compounded by the UGIF's refusal to disband itself on the eve of the Liberation as well as by its failure to save some of the children in its care. The settlement of accounts between wartime opponents which raked liberated France did not take place in the Jewish community. But the bitterness and the divided opinions over whether the UGIF had been a collaborationist organization were never truly resolved. Too many leading French Jews had committed too many errors of judgment during the war to support an open, public debate. The Central Consistory would have had to acknowledge having held for some time xenophobic positions and this it could not do. It would have had to acknowledge the times it had chosen to remain silent when its voice could have significantly helped prepare the Jews for the dangers facing them. The Central Consistory chose to bury the evidence of four years of history rather than risk communal judgment.

Conclusion: Strategies for Survival

During the four years of Occupation the Jewish organizations in Paris sought in vain to formulate policies that would ensure the survival of the Jewish population. In the final analysis they could only claim limited success in their attempt at foiling the Nazi deportation policy. The choice of policies finally adopted by the Jewish organizations to counter the German and Vichy challenges can only be understood if we examine the reasons that led them to follow such a course of action. It is to these reasons that we need to address ourselves in conclusion. It is clear that from the various strategies the Jewish organizations adopted, the Communist strategy was the only one that would have best succeeded in frustrating the murderous Nazi plan. This does not mean, however, that if all the Jewish organizations had adopted such a strategy that the Nazi Final Solution, as applied in France, would have been rendered ineffective, nor that the alternative strategies did not have, at one stage or another, some merits. Rather, of all the possible strategies the Communist was the only one which, if generally implemented, could have ensured the survival of the largest number of Jews both French and foreign.

As late as August 1944, three distinct and necessarily contending policies for survival endured. Neither the unification of the immigrant organizations in July 1943, nor the subsequent extension of the movement toward unity by the participation of the Central Consistory in a national representative committee, helped consolidate the different analyses that underpinned the various strategies. Only agreements of a general character were achieved which, although originally understood by all parties as anticipating unified policies, nevertheless failed to bring them to fruition. The promise of unity, among the immigrants themselves and with French Judaism, never materialized.

The official strategy, as formulated by French Judaism and expressed in Paris as early as September 1940, then in the decisions of the Coordination Committee and lastly in those of the UGIF, affected the greatest number of Jews. As its first priority that strategy strove to ensure the continued existence of French Judaism—and that objective did not include the foreign Jews. The Central Consistory clearly assumed that the immigrant Jews represented a liability in regard to its own survival and that the fate of these foreign Jews, however regrettable, had to be seen as secondary to the central problem. This

223

premise resulted in efforts to first assist and protect the French, even though the immigrants were more vulnerable.

The second assumption of the leaders of French Judaism was that an understanding could be reached with Vichy which would provide recognition of the French Jews' rights. Underlying that assumption was the belief that Vichy would maintain the legal distinctions between French Jews and the others, the stateless, the refugees, and the immigrants. Vichy's own legislation showed the fallacy of this assumption. Although that legislation took into account past services rendered to the country, it did not, in principle, distinguish between French Jews and the others. To uphold the comforting view that Vichy would maintain, in practice, such a distinction, French Judaism argued that although certain elements of the traditional French Right, which viewed the Jewish Question in racist terms, were influential at Vichy, the dominant forces there viewed the Jewish issue as a *Question d'Etat.* French Judaism understood this to mean the foreign Jews: they were too numerous and there was no employment for them. There is no doubt that French Judaism agreed with Vichy that these foreign Jews were socially and politically undesirable.

Although the racist and the political expressions of antisemitism were equally dangerous to all Jews, including French Judaism, it is clear that the Central Consistory believed that from a long-range point of view the latter position, racism as a *Question d'Etat,* represented a lesser threat. The serious internal and external difficulties faced by France contributed to the interpretation that once these problems were resolved the Jewish Question would recede. The critical economic situation arising from the Occupation of over half of the country, the industrial north, had caused a crisis in employment and brought to the fore the problem of the foreign work force. Inevitably, therefore, the Central Consistory accepted that the foreign Jews were also a surplus in the national economy.

Within the spectrum of reasons for Vichy's state antisemitism, the Central Consistory recognized that France's urgent need to proceed with peace negotions with Germany also had a bearing upon the question. The Central Consistory was not unaware of Vichy's need to develop political preconditions to advance the negotiations, and that the Jewish Question was seen by Vichy as useful in gaining goodwill from Germany. The view therefore prevailed that state antisemitism, arising from specific conditions, would soon resolve itself once Germany and Vichy France signed a peace treaty. The foreign Jews might have to return to their countries of origin but then the Central Consistory also believed that their existing numbers had contributed to the Vichy legislation. Once peace was achieved, the remaining French Jews would no longer present an economic or a political issue and all would be well again.

The Central Consistory's early appreciation of the situation was not as unrealistic as it subsequently appeared. Indeed, until August 1942 a number of French Jews had benefited by dispensations from the laws affecting Jews.[1] Darlan's instructions to Vallat and Pétain's own inner circle of advisers supported the Central Consistory's analysis. Yet this interpretation of Vichy's effective Jewish policy could not be reconciled with the ever-harsher anti-Jewish measures originating from Vichy in which the expected mitigations in favor of French Jews failed to materialize.

In the final analysis, official Judaism proceeded from wishful thinking. The vague words of comfort from Pétain's staff were interpreted as grounds for hope even though they proved totally ineffectual. The Central Consistory completely failed to take into account the Nazi capacity to bring Vichy into line with its own policies; just as it failed to take into account France's own foreign policy requirements which made Vichy ever more compliant with Nazi demands.

French Judaism's strategy did succeed in gaining time, but at the price of abandoning the foreign Jews to a fate which in the end the French themselves shared. The only area in which French Judaism redeemed itself was in its relief work, and even then there were limitations. They always sought to carry out their relief activities in such a manner that they were seen by Vichy as expressions of charity and never as open solidarity. Vichy for its part supported such activities as they complemented its own policies. It would be wrong to belittle the importance of aid, any aid, to the desperate foreign Jews, but the value of such help was questionable. Given the context of the persecution of the Jews, concentration upon relief led French Jews to participate, despite verbal opposition, in the imposed representation of the UGIF which had long been sought by the SD and was clearly designed as a mechanism to achieve the Jews' isolation.

Official Judaism was aware, from the beginning, of the intended role of the UGIF. In Paris the view prevailed that only with its participation could the interests of French Jewry be defended. Its leadership, despite earlier experience, failed to evaluate correctly the calculating manner in which the Nazis set about applying their racial policy. The Nazis' gradual procedure, first directed at the foreign Jews, was not perceived by French Judaism as directed at all the Jews. French Judaism's connection with Vichy led to confuse desire with reality. While the Nazis, with Vichy's assistance, ruthlessly deported the foreign Jews, official Judaism chose to be seen publicly accepting the Vichy press reports of Jewish "settlements" in Eastern Europe. Yet let there be no mistake about it, the Franco-Jewish leadership knew, as the Central Consistory's letter to Pétain of August 1942 shows, that the so-called resettlements were far more sinister. They chose public silence in order not to attract attention to themselves.

Official Judaism remained unable, for too long, to evaluate correctly Vichy's Jewish policy and its connection with Nazi racism. Such a failure raises several questions. Why did French Judaism persist in adhering, in the face of accumulating evidence, to a patently incorrect interpretation of events? Did it consider the forces confronting Jews so powerful as to cancel any available alternative? Did it fear that conflict with Vichy would result in the loss of the limited protection thus far obtained without commensurate prospect of improving the chances of survival? Were the leaders themselves at fault?

The dominant factor affecting the official Jewish leadership's choice of a course of action was outside of the unfolding drama. It was determined and shaped by the image French Judaism had of itself and the general attitudes and values of the social class it represented. It refused to consider itself as anything but French, only distinguishing itself from the rest of the French community by its religious principles. This age-old attitude continued even while the legislation which effectively reduced the French Jews to a status of foreigners in their own land was challenging that self-image.

This leadership belonged to the upper bourgeoisie and had that class's respect for government and legal conventions. Because it was respectful of the established order it could never consider engaging in the uncertainties of illegal opposition. That leadership's former social and political integration in French society carried certain consequences. The choice of policies was shaped by the multiplicity of ties connecting it with Vichy. Helbronner, the president of the Central Consistory, was a long-standing friend of Maréchal Pétain, and they continued to meet while anti-Jewish laws were promulgated and signed by Pétain. This connection was only one of many that bound official Judaism to the Vichy ruling circles, making it all the harder to adopt oppositional attitudes. Even when it became unmistakably clear that Vichy was irreversibly committed to an antisemitic course which would engulf them, French Jews still could do no more than express, by letters, their anguish at being rejected from the polity. As late as December 1942, when all previous efforts had failed, when even Vichy had lost its limited independence through its own occupation by the Wehrmacht, the leadership of French Judaism was still unable to bring itself to oppose the law of the land. Vichy had then passed a law that ordered Jews to present themselves to their local police stations in order to have their identity cards stamped. Georges Wormser, a leading member of the Central Consistory, placed a resolution before its general assembly calling upon it to urge the Jewish population not to present itself to the police. The results of the vote on the resolution confirm the view that official Judaism was fundamentally conservative: from an assembly of forty-five members only the mover voted for its support; there were four blank votes and forty members voted for compliance with the law.[2] The Central Consistory, as earlier, refused to countenance opposition to authority, however unjust it felt the measure to be.

Unwilling to wage a political struggle against Vichy or against the Nazis for that matter, the Central Consistory devoted itself to the pursuit of relief activities. But even such a goal could not be abstracted from the political context within which it was being pursued. There again the Central Consistory was found wanting in its claim to represent the French Jews. Some French Jews, in their commitment to relief work, had broken away from the leadership's conservatism. The OSE exemplifies this changing allegiance. By the end of 1942 the OSE was firmly committed to developing illegal channels of assistance, which at the time were directed at helping the immigrant Jews. The arrests and deportations of French Jews which began early in 1943 certainly challenged the Central Consistory's policy of "legalism." The immigrant organizations had shown that organizational structures could be formed. By taking advantage of all legal possibilities including working within the UGIF, as was possible in the Vichy Zone, it could provide effective alternatives to police-controlled assistance.

But neither the OSE's example nor the immigrants' could sway the Central Consistory, or the UGIF leaders, from their strategy. They refused to accept the view that the recipient of legal relief from the UGIF, however much that help was needed in the short term, was made dependent upon an organization that was actually established to better control that population. The majority of the Central Consistory never accepted the view that "legalism" was not tenable as a survival strategy. Neither the deportation by the Nazis of half the immigrant population nor the rising number of French Jews also being deported could convince French Judaism's leadership that the survival of the remaining Jews required primarily the need to overcome the dependency of thousands upon the UGIF. Not until Helbronner's arrest, in October 1943, was a serious reevaluation of its strategy effectively made.

The other strategies, those followed by the immigrant organizations, evolved from different conditions and premises. And precisely because they were rooted in the reality of persecution, they reflected more closely the limits and conditions under which survival was possible.

In the first place the foreign Jews held no illusions about the political conditions they confronted. Their former experience of state antisemitism led them to recognize the signs as they manifested themselves. They knew, from the prewar days, how exposed foreigners were in France. They had no illusions, therefore, about the significance of Vichy's early xenophobic legislation and pronouncements nor did they take comfort from the German authorities' early public silence on the Jewish Question. They knew too well how racial policies had been expressed in Germany after Hitler's advent to power to expect Nazi law in France to be any different. The immigrant organizations were therefore psychologically and politically better prepared than was French Judaism. The immigrant organizations, attuned to the question of state antisemitism, were more conscious of the need to achieve a communal unity of views, among themselves and with French Judaism, concerning the dangers and the need to arrive at a common resolve in the struggle for the protection of the Jewish population. The main problem persisted. In spite of such an understanding of the necessity of achieving communal unity, in spite of Amelot and Solidarity being equally convinced of the catastrophic dangers facing the Jews, political differences hampered that unity.

Amelot, by applying the criterion of national identity to its analysis of the situation, continued, throughout the war, to adhere to the position that the only way to meet the crisis was for the Jews themselves to mobilize their human and material resources and that in the final analysis the Jews could only depend upon themselves.

Solidarity's analysis, based on specific political criteria, only concurred partially with Amelot's. It also consistently emphasized the necessity to seek within the Jewish population forces to meet the crisis. Furthermore, it claimed that Jewish survival in France was inconceivable without the help of non-Jews. Solidarity therefore called for the Jews to join the ranks of those French organizations that fought the Germans in order to justify its call for help. More importantly, Solidarity distinguished itself from Amelot by demanding that all Jewish efforts be directed not only at overcoming the consequences of the anti-Jewish laws but at fighting the root cause of the evil: Nazism.

Although there were many areas of agreement between Amelot and Solidarity, differences in political analysis had precluded an early unity. Amelot posited a policy of self-help based on communal unity within which the problems faced by the Jewish population were internalized. Amelot accepted as a cornerstone of its general strategy the isolation of the Jews from the rest of the population. Solidarity, on the other hand, because it possessed the confidence of a movement linked to the non-Jewish population through its ideological and organizational connections with the PCF, consistently refused to imagine that the French people might not come to the Jews' assistance. It was therefore inevitable that Solidarity, and later UJRE, would want to draw the immigrant organizations into the struggle of those French organizations fighting the German occupiers and Vichy in order to show the PCF that the Jews were also participants in the anti-Nazi struggle. Solidarity's strategy based on political and ideological concepts continually ran the risk of being misunderstood by a majority of the Jewish population because the solution it advocated appeared so removed from the immediacy of the difficulties experienced by that population.

These divergent perspectives were not solely due to varying interpretations of the situation and of what needed to be done. They also had their roots in organizational differences. Amelot was a committee constituted of representatives of various political movements as well as communal workers not affiliated to any political parties. Amelot was therefore always prey to internal divisions. Its policies were always the outcome of compromises, but its basis for internal harmony rested in the mutual acceptance of a specific national-cultural identity which helped override political differences, an identity which under siege bound them together precisely because it was threatened. And, last but not least, Amelot never controlled a political machine capable of organizing supporters. It was never in a position to conduct campaigns in depth for the popular support of its policies. Amelot could only rely on the goodwill of associated organizations or highly motivated activists. Nevertheless, the absence of a political machine supported by a membership relieved Amelot from direct political accountability and also gave it greater maneuverability.

Solidarity, on the other hand, was a monolithic organization with substantial support. As a political movement it had a centralized leadership, a disciplined membership, and an impressive array of technical resources. It could therefore plan and sustain campaigns without resorting to compromise. But it faced one major difficulty: as a Communist organization it had to adapt

PCF policy into policies that would be relevant to the Jewish population, its supporters, and its members, and therefore would be accepted by them.

The differences between Amelot and Solidarity had one further dimension that should be emphasized; namely, a qualitatively different kind of popular support. Solidarity's strength was above all the product of a unique leadership and membership. Unlike other Jewish organizations whose effectiveness depended in the final analysis upon a nucleus of devoted members, Solidarity's leaders and members viewed themselves as soldiers. Other organizations allowed their members to make individual decisions about their personal safety; for example, some of the remaining Bundist leaders in Paris left in 1941, and a number of them took refuge in Switzerland; so did FSJF and Zionist leaders. None of these people ever believed that they were abandoning their organizations or that they were abdicating their responsibilities when they sought personal safety.

Solidarity, and later the UJRE activists, never allowed themselves such freedom. The immigrant Communists' dedication and self-imposed discipline were shaped by an ideological commitment to a cause as well as to the organization. In Pithiviers, Beaune-La-Rolande, and Drancy they formed themselves into Communist cells.[3] They consistently continued to act as disciplined members. The last message sent from the leadership, on the eve of their departure from the camps for Auschwitz was "organize, organize until your death."[4] Even in the extermination camps, the Parisian Communist immigrant Jews organized.[5] They formed and headed the underground organization which took and sent out from Auschwitz the first photographs of the camp. They organized and led the fighting groups that blew up the crematoria in Auschwitz with dynamite smuggled into the camp by immigrant Communist women also from the Paris organization.[6] These people were dedicated to the destruction of Nazism and to the building of a new society. It was therefore to be expected that such strong political commitment would influence not only general Jewish Communist strategy but also interorganizational relationships. Yet despite the vastly different styles of work that distinguished the organizations, the process of anti-Jewish persecution helped bring about a consensus. The objective need to overcome their differences helped bring together disparate movements. More than any single event, it was the news, in June 1943, of the Warsaw Ghetto Uprising, following on months of continuous deportations, which led the immigrant organizations to recognize that survival and unity were closely linked.

But immigrant consensus was but one aspect of the overall question of uniting all forces to ensure the survival of the remaining Jews in France: French Judaism needed to be won over to that conclusion. The task was complicated by the issue of the UGIF. The immigrant organizations firmly opposed participation in the UGIF, and the participation of French Jews had reinforced a longstanding schism. Official Judaism, although allowed by Vichy after the UGIF's estblishment to maintain its own corporate existence, had been linked to it. Indeed, the Central Consistory remained in reality its ultimate authority: the Central Consistory led the UGIF, and the UGIF never made any major decision without prior consultation with the Consistory. The task faced by the immigrants' United Defense Committee was to win the Central Consistory over to the view that the UGIF's existence was no longer compatible with the interests of the Jewish population.

The rapprochement between immigrants and French Jews began in earnest in October 1943. By January 1944 a broad agreement had taken place over the question of a national representation of all the Jews of France, though in the interest of that agreement the immigrants had set aside the UGIF issue. This agreement was a unique event in the contemporary history of the Jews of France, for it was the first time that French Judaism accepted and conceded equality to the immigrant Jews.[7] The uniqueness of this event was even more remarkable because of the presence of Communist representatives. It was the first time that Communists and anti-Communist Jews had found ground for agreement and, consequently, showed how far both the immigrant Communists and the conservatives of the Central Consistory had moved from their traditional positions. The Communists had recognized as worthy partners those forces which not so long ago had represented the enemy class. Official Judaism had shifted from its age-old position of an exclusively religious representation to recognition of the need for political representation; it had come to accept the concept of secular Jewish identity. The process of change was directly related to the Jewish persecutions and French Judaism's growing recognition of its own isolation within persecuted Jewry.

The first phase of that change began with the German Occupation of the Vichy Zone in November 1942. Until then French Judaism never sought organizational links with foreign Jews. However, in day-to-day activities, the rabbinical corps and its chaplaincy were closely involved in relief activities which inevitably brought them into contact with immigrant Jews and their organizations. But at all times those contacts were never more than expressions of charitable concern. It was from 1943 onward, as the impact of the German Occupation began to be felt, that these contacts changed character. In April 1943, on the initiative of Isaac Schneersohn, representatives from various organizations decided to establish an illegal documentation center.[8] The aim was to centralize all information pertaining to the persecution of the Jews. The Central Consistory agreed to participate in this work. Its participation and that of various immigrant organizations in this center did not yet mean that these contacts would ultimately lead to wider developments but they represented nevertheless an extension of existing contacts.

Nevertheless, the immigrant organizations had always hoped to achieve unity with the French Jews. Yet, differences between these two major groups were so profound that, despite various contacts, such a possibility seemed remote. It was owing to Joseph Fisher that the first step was made to begin a dialogue. He was the only East European member of the Central Consistory. As such, and also as the president of the French Zionist Federation and as a trustee of the Joint, he was eminently suited to act as mediator.

The debate leading up to the CRIF charter and the terms of the charter that was finally adopted in 1944 throw a great deal of light on the issues in dispute between French Judaism and the immigrants' organizations.[9] Three major questions dominated the debate: the position of the new representative body on Jewish resistance, the evaluation of the UGIF's role, and the claim to a National Home in Palestine. To these central issues, complex enough in themselves, were added such difficulties as the Central Consistory's basic reluctance to cooperate with the Communists, which endangered the recently established immigrant unity. The Communists for their part had already anticipated this problem when, in July 1943, they transformed themselves into the UJRE. Fisher had then met a Communist representative, Abraham Rayski, and the issue was discussed.[10] To answer Fisher's questions and to anticipate the Central Consistory's objections, the Communists issued a statement that emphasized the necessity for a national representation that would include all political and social groups.[11] The subsequent meeting between Communist representatives and Fisher took place in the context of a conference with the newly formed CGD.

Fisher's objective, as Zionist leader, was that French Jewry support the postwar Zionist claim to the establishment of a national home in Palestine. It was therefore important to ensure that the national representation he sought would endorse this proposition. The first stage in this campaign was to win the immigrant organizations to this view; Fisher needed to overcome the well-known Bundist and Communist opposition to Zionism. Not until this was achieved could Fisher hope to win the Central Consistory to this program.

Fisher began his campaign by directing his attention to the Communists. He was well aware that the Communists sought participation in a national representation, just as the Communists were well aware that they were needed to achieve a majority support within the CGD for Zionism. Communist support for Zionism was necessary not only to win over the immigrant committee but also to forestall Central Consistory objections. Fisher's gravest concern remained, until the issue was resolved, that the national representation under the influence of the Central Consistory might decide to take a neutral position on the Zionist issue.[12]

The arrest of Helbronner in October 1943, and his replacement by Léon Meiss, resulted in greater flexibility in the policies of the Central Consistory. Fisher succeeded in bringing Abraham Rayski and Meiss together, to offer both parties an opportunity to exchange views and more particularly to allow the Central Consistory to meet Communists. As Meiss himself observed, it was the first time he had ever met a Communist face to face. At this stage of the negotiations the psychological factors assumed a decisive role.[13] The Communist leaders' choice of Rayski to carry through the negotiations proved apt. He showed himself capable of convincing Meiss of his party's sincere desire to participate fully in the projected national representation by abiding by majority decisions.

The CGD formed a commission to draft a proposed charter for the new body to be submitted to the Central Consistory. The commission consisted of

Grinberg from the FSJF, Glaeser from the CGD, Adam Braun from the UJRE, and Fisher on behalf of the Zionist organizations. By then all the parties concerned had accepted the principle of a unified representation; all that remained was to find an approved formula.

The first draft was completed by April 1944.[14] The commission considered that it would satisfy every shade of opinion. It supported the Zionist claim on Palestine and the immigrant organizations' policy that all possible action be taken to protect the remaining Jews. As a postwar objective the representation was to seek from the government the restitution of civic rights and confiscated properties. On the issue of organizational structures, the draft proposed that, while a provisional committee of nine members would assume management, the future leadership would be elected on the democratic principle of organizational representation.

In spite of the broad nature of the proposals the draft met objections. The Bund rejected the clause dealing with the projected support for the Zionist claims to Palestine. The Communists, although supporting the Zionist demand, asked for a reformulation of that clause in the sense that it should also embody the principle that Palestine would be a democratic state where Jews and Arabs would have equal rights. The Central Consistory was concerned that its support for Zionism might be seen as recognizing and demanding for Jews a duality of national allegiances. The final draft paragraph dealing with this issue must surely have been prepared by the Central Consistory, for it read:

> It is understood that the national status of the Jews in Palestine will in no manner whatsoever affect the status of the Jews in other countries and the ties which bind them to their fatherland.[15]

The Bund and the Communists, anxious to participate in a national representation rather than remain isolated, withdrew their objections. The Central Consistory's amendment had not met their particular demands but as it at least ensured that support for Zionism would not be unconditional the Bund and the UJRE supported it.

The immigrant organizations, and the Zionists, had made what they believed were all the necessary concessions in order to arrive at the unity of the Jews of France. No one had envisaged that the Central Consistory would raise procedural questions that would overturn all that had been agreed to so far. The immigrants had assumed that the national representation would be constituted on democratic principles, at first representing the various cosigning parties and then, after the war, elected according to democratic procedures which would have to be debated.

The Central Consistory was not prepared, however, to enter into any agreement without first being guaranteed its independence. As the Central Consistory represented only part of the Jewish population, there was indeed a serious problem. By sheer weight of numbers the immigrants did have it in their power to threaten the equilibrium and compel the Central Consistory to support issues it did not approve. Furthermore, each immigrant organization could also raise similar objections. The final compromise is indicative of the immigrants' sense of historical responsibility and of the Central Consistory's apprehension at the steps it had already taken. It was agreed that Léon Meiss would be the new body's first president and that the committee be enlarged from nine to thirteen members: six seats were to go to the Central Consistory, of the remaining seven seats, five were allocated to the United Defense Committee, one to the Zionist organization and one to a youth representative. The Central Consistory, through its control of the presidency, was thereby assured not only of its independence but also of the votes necessary to block policies it opposed. The Conseil Représentatif des Juifs de France became the Central Consistory's prisoner. In May 1944 all parties finally accepted the official charter.[16] All the various ideological and political positions were at last consolidated and embodied in a compromise formulation.

The CRIF, conceived as a representative body, never became during the Occupation an organizational or a political factor; it was never more than a preliminary meeting ground for contending political forces. It heralded a new era in communal relationships, however. Its role was to act as representative for the Jews in France to the Conseil National de la Résistance and the French provisional government to present the Jewish case as plans were drawn for the France that would emerge after Liberation. The CRIF had been formed at a time when the future of the Jews in France was no longer threatened, whatever the fate of individual Jews might prove to be. But the CRIF could never claim to have directly contributed to the survival of the Jewish people. Its impact was achieved in the political arena: it helped in the short term to sustain the morale of the immigrant organizations and their political unity. If only for this, it was worthwhile.

This study has primarily centered on the Jews in Paris. It has sought to show how a population of 150,000 in October 1940, half of the total Jewish population of France, reacted to attacks by the combined might of the German and Vichy authorities. Paris, although important because it represented the largest concentration of Jews in any French city, was but an example of how throughout France local and national committees sought suitable forms of communal responses to meet the problems. The experience of the Jews of Paris has special interest for historians because the particularly complex and difficult conditions Jews encountered epitomized the worst aspects of Nazi and Vichy policies. It also affords a case study of organized Jewish responses, enabling us to explore and to judge the merits of the various strategies adopted. But the situation in Paris cannot be divorced from the conditions in the rest of France. This is evident whether one examines the development of movements for unity, the debate at the time of the establishment of the UGIF, or the development of specific forms of resistance.

The armed struggle, for instance, to which the Communists devoted so much energy in Paris was influenced by their experience and provided the personnel for similar such activities in all the major cities in France.[17] And such influences were not always in only one direction: a Zionist resistance movement, first formed in Toulouse in 1940, only made its appearance in

Paris as late as April 1944. This study, although primarily concerned with the examination of the manifold Jewish responses to both the Nazi and Vichy anti-Jewish measures, has of necessity taken into account internal communal conflicts. The nature of these conflicts needs to be stressed; they were, although serious and divisive, never the primary threat to Jewish survival, but the product of conflicting evaluations of a situation always outside their control. The immigrants were pained at the indifference of French Jewry to their plight, an indifference they believed was underpinned by xenophobia. They knew quite well that the French Jews were the fortunate holders of a different status and that their failure to respond to the foreigners' drama arose in part from this position. They understood and, broadly speaking, accepted this.

What grieved the immigrants was that French Judaism's search for a survival strategy did not include them and was based, at least until the end of 1942, on compliance with Vichy's demands. French Judaism's actions, even those most questionable, were the outcome of their own dilemma. Thus when some members of the Catholic hierarchy appealed to Cardinal Pierre Gerlier, the *Primate des Gaules,* to protest the treatment of the foreign Jews, Helbronner pleaded that no such step be taken lest this action endanger the French Jews.[18] The establishment of the CRIF, that is, the first recognition by French Judaism of the immigrants' claim to an equal share in the representation of the Jews in France, did not in any fundamental way alter the situation. Internal divisions between French Jews and immigrants continued throughout the war, even when the German Occupation of the Vichy Zone propelled the French Jews into the position faced by the immigrants since 1940. The French administration continued to favor the French Jews and this situation did not help overcome communal divisions. This difference in treatment led the foreigners and the French Jews to develop quite divergent notions of such matters as the urgency of the situation, the priority to be given to rescue activities, and the appropriate view to be taken toward the UGIF.

Although the major internal conflict was between the French and the foreign Jews, with the immigrant leaders generally having a clearer view of what needed to be done, there were also serious differences among the immigrant organizations themselves. That between the Communists and the others was particularly marked and like the division between the French and foreign Jews remained a factor to be reckoned with throughout the war.

When from July 1943 onward the Communists altered their general strategy so that the question of helping fellow Jews became a primary objective, they nevertheless did not mean to relegate armed resistance to a minor position. The CGD had pledged itself, as the price for unity with the Communists, to support Jewish armed groups. The UJRE continually demanded that this agreement be honored. It asked for financial assistance and also for an active policy that would stimulate the development of the armed struggle. This insistence soon gave rise to a debate. Those of the CGD in favor of directing all efforts and resources first to self-help took the view that it was conceivable that, in the process of the struggle to defeat Nazism, the extermination of the Jews could reach such proportions that the outcome of the war would no longer be relevant to the Jews as a people. There would not be any Jews left to celebrate victory. They further argued that in the final analysis the shedding of Jewish blood did not guarantee that peace would automatically restore human rights to Jews. These arguments were not advanced in order to deny the significance and importance of the armed struggle policy but rather to stress the need for the development of an armed struggle policy that would posit the survival of the Jewish people as its central objective.

The debate became public in December 1943 when the Jewish Communists issued a statement in reply to a document then circulating in Zionist circles titled "The Jews and the War." This Zionist paper criticized the Soviet Union. It followed an announcement of a book by Ilya Ehrenburg publicizing the number of Jewish soldiers who had died as "Heroes of the Soviet Union." The Zionist paper demanded that the Soviet Union should clearly stigmatize the senseless murder of Jews, and further stated that unless this was done it would be tantamount to denying these heroes their Jewish national identity. The Communists chose to view the document as an attack on the Soviet Union where, they believed, the Jewish Question had been resolved. Furthermore, they viewed the document not only as a challenge to one of their most firmly held assumptions but also as a denial of the Soviet contribution to the defeat of Nazism. They could therefore only conclude that it was an attempt to introduce divisions within the CGD by suggesting that the Communists were not truly committed to the recognition of the Jews as a people.[19]

The Communists' public rebuke, eloquent in its own justifications of the need for Jewish participation in the war, could not fail to raise questions about their own strategy. The crisis of July 1943, when their own organizations, decimated by the Gestapo, were paralyzed, demonstrates the problem. Their acceptance of the PCF's overriding political line had led to their destruction in Paris. Their acceptance of party discipline had cost them a terrible price and, as a result, had deprived the Jewish population of yet another source of organized support. As a consequence of having made their participation in the French Resistance as expressed by the PCF their first priority, they found themselves isolated from the Jewish population. Resistance, conceived by the Jewish Communists as a national struggle, as a struggle for survival, had not posited its objectives primarily in Jewish terms, but rather in terms of much broader political objectives. The Jewish Communists' armed units in Paris never undertook objectives that mattered directly to the Jewish population. They attacked German lines of communication, not the trains taking Jews to the camps of Eastern Europe. They shot German officers but no attempt was ever made to kill the *Judenreferenten* for France. Even during the final struggle for the Liberation of Paris in August

1944, their efforts were not aimed at liberating the Jews from Drancy or from the other more minor camps. At all times, the Communist leadership acted as part of the French Communist Resistance.

Although the Resistance's objective, the speediest defeat of Nazi Germany, was in the final analysis the only way to ensure Jewish survival, it caused major problems in the Communists' relationship with the other organizations. It can even be said that it placed in question their own claim to be acting as a Jewish organization. The tension between a political analysis which demanded that all efforts be directed to the destruction of Nazism and a specific Jewish view which stressed the short-term needs of the Jewish population could not be resolved as long as the Jewish Communists were an organic part of the French Communist movement. Yet in spite of the opposition they consistently encountered because of their affiliation to the PCF, the other immigrant organizations and the Central Consistory did accept them as a genuinely Jewish political organization. The general opposition they met earlier gave way to the recognition that they nevertheless represented a significant sector of the Jewish population.

For non-Jews, resistance had been a deliberate choice, political, patriotic, and for some moral, but at all times an act of free will. For each of these reasons for joining the Resistance the Jews had further reasons. For some, their persecution evoked a spirit of revenge for their martyred families, for others it was an affirmation of their Jewish national pride. But above all the determining justification for the majority was the situation confronted by the Jewish population. In the early period, that is, until July 1942, some Jews had hesitated before condemning Vichy but no Jewish organization ever tried to justify ideological "collaboration" with the Germans, nor were they tempted, unlike some French organizations, by the rewards promised for such "collaboration." It was clear to them that in a Europe under Nazi hegemony there would be no place for them. There prevailed within the Jewish population—French and immigrant—a particular climate of ideas that predisposed them to resistance, passive or active.

Central to the Jews was the problem of survival. Inevitably, each Jewish family, the immigrant sooner than the French, faced the question of evading the laws and the repressive measures. That struggle for survival imposed its own imperatives in which the fearsome world of illegal existence became the only viable alternative. Given that only two options were available to Jews, to either await one's fate or to hide, Jews, as a group, were already receptive to ideas that could provide explanations and solutions: to participate in active resistance was one of them. Since they were psychologically conditioned to accept radical measures in order to evade their situation or to make a stand, it was not surprising to discover a disproportionately large number of Jews participating in the work of the Resistance organizations. Thus Philippe Henriot, later to become secretary for information and propaganda in the Vichy government, claimed in June 1942 that "the police have established that 80 percent of the attacks on the German army in the Parisian region are committed by Jews." David Knout, in his study of Jews in the

Resistance in France, concluded that the Jews were in the forefront of the armed resistance and in the establishment of many Resistance organizations."[20]

Any mention of Jews in the historiography of the French Resistance has always been understood as referring to a specific immigrant group. The French Jews were never seen as belonging to that group; they were French without any qualifications. A closer examination of the question of the Jewish participation in the Resistance shows, however, that during the course of the war differences between French and foreign Jews underwent changes of such magnitude that, in a significant number of Jewish organizations, it was no longer accurate, in the Jewish context, to maintain such a distinction. The question of the Jews in the Resistance raises a further question in the Jewish historiography of the period: whether there had been a "Jewish resistance" or a "Jewish contribution" to the French national Resistance. Whenever that question arises, some historians reject the view of a separate Jewish resistance on the ground that the Jewish organizations were part of the common struggle to free France from its German occupants. The Jewish organizations, it is suggested, although distinguishable by their specific field of operation, constituted in the final analysis but a separate sector of the national Resistance.[21]

Underlying this assertion is a denial of the existence of the Jewish community in France with which a majority of Jews either identified or tacitly recognized some links. This position stems from an analysis based on the social and cultural fragmentation that characterized the Jewish population in the interwar period as well as a major degree of assimilation of the overwhelming majority of the French Jews. Many French Jews had never looked to Judaism as a personal point of reference and never accepted the racist or religious definitions that suddenly recast their human condition as Jewish.[22] The participation of such "Jews," it is therefore claimed, was never the direct result of that imposed social distinction, but an act of patriotism. Diamant, a historian of Jewish immigrant resistance, chose to reject the thesis of a specific Jewish resistance by emphasizing that the Resistance was *une et indivisible,* that the Jews were but one of the "spiritual" families that participated in it. In order to integrate the foreign Jews into the French Resistance, Diamant asserted that "the Jews fought as much as Jews as Frenchmen . . . that even the non-naturalized immigrant considered himself French."[23]

The case for a distinct "Jewish resistance" has been presented by Léon Poliakov.[24] The examination of the various criteria by which a Jewish resistance could define itself, be it its ideology, its personnel, or its objectives, led Poliakov to conclude that it was historically accurate to refer to a Jewish resistance. Indeed, viewed in its own terms, the underlying ideological premises that dominated not only the rhetoric of all Jewish organizations that came to constitute that resistance but also the basic assumptions underlining their actions were deeply embedded in a historical Jewish national consciousness. All the Jewish organizations, from the immigrant groups to French Judaism, sooner or later concluded that there was more than a legislation of exception and a community of fate binding these disparate groups of people. It was, as Fisher claimed, a dormant national consciousness, arising from the persecution, which came to sustain, encourage, and define the struggle of the Jews to survive as a people.[25]

Our study of the varied Jewish reactions, as complex as the process of their elimination from France and as varied as their own self-perception of identity is not intended to be a comparative examination of Jewish and non-Jewish reactions to the German Occupation or to Vichy's rule. As for claims supporting the existence of a Jewish resistance, which in the light of this book are justified, the argument rests on the development by Jews, for Jews, of defense structures well before the appearance of an organized French resistance. Even if these defense structures proved too weak, or on an erroneous path, they were nevertheless specific and unique attempts at defending a population, apart from what France as a nation was to do. When, without a doubt, France was still unreservedly behind Pétain and Vichy, these ill-equipped and often ineffectual Jewish defense mechanisms had already formed and were operative. Indeed, it is reasonable to assume that even if the French Resistance had never materialized the Jewish organizations would have continued to pursue and develop these defense activities and would have continued to function as a "Jewish resistance" in the struggle for Jewish survival.

In conclusion, it remains to emphasize that in order to understand the strategies of the various Jewish organizations in their chronological development, it is essential to view them in their precise context. The strategies were at all times reactions to governmental policies whose timetables and natures were unpredictable. These organizations constantly needed to adapt themselves to German decisions as well as to the degree of cooperation, no less than the "autonomous" nature, of Vichy's own anti-Jewish policies. And, lastly, their strategies were also highly affected by the general situation.

Of all these factors, German policy was the determinant. It is no longer necessary to establish that the Nazis used all available means to hide from the victims, and from the Jewish organizations, the ultimate fate of the deportees. But it needs to be stated anew: the decision to exterminate the Jews was a state secret. When the camps were finally liberated, the general public was struck with horror as the magnitude of the massacres became known.

The manner in which the Nazis pursued their "deception" policy in France was different than in Eastern Europe. In Eastern Europe the Nazis used the *Judenräte*—the imposed Jewish councils—to supply people for the so-called labor camps, when in fact they were sent to extermination camps. In France, the UGIF was never asked to supply manpower for these camps, although the Coordination Committee had been asked, in 1941, to provide workers for farms in Northern France and in 1943 to establish manufacturing industries. But these orders were never pursued with the same determination as similar orders had been in Eastern Europe. From the very beginning, Jews were led to believe that they would be sent to some mythical Jewish colony in the east. It is clear that the "deception" covering the deportations had been conceived to lessen any backlash among those about to be deported no less than among those not yet affected. Unlike the Jewish communities in Eastern Europe,

France was too far away from the extermination camps to obtain information about what was taking place, and in France the Nazis never resorted to the methods they applied in the east.

The Jewish organizations were never able to evaluate fully the significance of the menace, even when the evidence about the fate of the Jewish population was becoming increasingly available. A number of key elements were never at their disposal. Thus even if they did not need to know of the existence of a *Judenreferat,* they never knew the real extent of the powers, and limitations of these powers, held by the *Judenreferenten,* Dannecker and Röthke. For even when these men finally received MBF approval for the execution of certain measures, the MBF always evaluated these measures in terms of other considerations; moreover, they always needed approval from Berlin. It may appear that the Jews in France might have benefited from the limited manpower available to the *Judenreferat,* although the same limited manpower never hampered mass extermination in Eastern Europe. It remains that Röthke's failure to establish a ghetto in Paris in 1943, and his determination to proceed with the arrest of the French Jews in the same year, were not rejected by the MBF on the grounds of limited police forces.

The Nazi capacity to pursue their anti-Jewish policy depended, in the final analysis, upon political factors. Political considerations arising from the need to sustain a policy of "collaboration" with Vichy which would protect the broad interests of the Third Reich and the occupation forces governed all German decisions. Accordingly the German authorities sought at all times to have Vichy carry out the anti-Jewish measures. This is why three quarters of French Jewry survived. The *Judenreferenten,* though determined to maintain from 1942 onward the momentum of deportations, never obtained from Höherer SS-und-Polizeiführer, SS Brigadeführer Karl Albrecht Oberg, nor from the MBF, the level of priority they sought.

The Jewish organizations' dilemma was also the outcome of factors beyond the measures taken against the Jewish population or even the aims of the *Judenreferat.* Their permanent confrontation with the Germans was complicated by Vichy policies. Having begun with xenophobic antisemitic policies, Vichy found itself compelled to define the thrust of its policies in terms of German decisions and desires as well as in terms of internal political factors. Although Vichy had adopted its own brand of anti-Jewish policies, it was also motivated by the desire not to enter into conflict with Germany over the Jewish Question in its quest for a peace settlement. Its need to maintain administrative control of the country led Vichy to adopt policies that would not run counter to Nazi aims, stated or unstated. Furthermore, as the developments in the second half of 1942 showed, Vichy could be forced, given sufficient broad popular opposition, to reconsider certain elements of its collaboration with the Nazis on the Jewish Question. Such a political situation could not help but have some bearing upon the Jewish organizations' strategies. The broad xenophobic components of Vichy's actions which had been directed at the foreign Jews did provide temporary protection to the French Jews, but it proved disastrous for the others.

The existence of these two policies, German and Vichy, which although distinctive, nevertheless complimented each other and could only reinforce the different evaluations of the situation by the various organizations. It certainly did not assist in the evolution of a consensus on the dangers confronting the population; for too long it maintained existing divisions.

This book has examined the positions adopted by the Jewish organizations toward Vichy and the Nazis, and more particularly their different perceptions. Its main theme is the study of the behavior of a community fighting for its very survival. It deals therefore with the forms and the nature of resistance, at times widely different, at times in manifest opposition to each other. We must remember, however, that the tragedy confronting the Jews cannot be separated from the overall situation affecting France. The French were also forced to respond to the German and Vichy measures. Each French citizen who witnessed the arrest of Jews had to find justification in his or her conscience. It is in this sense that this book can be read as a contribution to the study of individual and collective behavior in confrontation with totalitarian regimes.

Notes

Chapter 1. Population and Survival

1. Vichy's view was clearly expressed in an official statement issued at the eve of the publication of the first Statut des Juifs. See Lubetzki, *La Condition des Juifs*, pp. 11–12.

2. Grayzel, *A History of the Jews*, pp. 138, 490; Roth, *History of the Jews*, p. 212.

3. Roblin, *Les Juifs de Paris*, pp. 35–40.

4. Roblin, p. 51; Hertzberg, *The Enlightenment and the Jews*, p. 133; Marrus, *Les Juifs de France à l'époque de l'affaire Dreyfus*, p. 47.

5. Mendel, "Die Yidn in Frankraich," p. 628; Roblin, pp. 72–74.

6. Hersch, "Yiddishe emigratie fun die letste undert yor," pp. 441–82.

7. According to Robert Byrnes, the Jewish population of Alsace-Lorraine fell by more than 10,000; see *Antisemitism in Modern France*, p. 95.

8. Weinberg, *Les Juifs à Paris*, pp. 25–26.

9. The Alliance Israélite Universelle was established in 1860 in order to combat the persecution of Jews in North Africa and the Middle East. As the situation of the Jewish communities in these areas stabilized the AIU did not, however, deem it necessary to abandon them or to relax its attention in the event of a renewal of anti-Semitic incidents. Continued peace led the AIU to devote its efforts to educational programs. For a history of the organization, see Chouraqui, *L'Alliance Israélite Universelle et la renaissance juive contemporaine*.

10. For their numbers, see Roblin, pp. 67–68; for their relationship with the Ashkenazim, see Weinberg, p. 21.

11. Patrick Girard quotes a government census that shows a Jewish population count of 89,047 and a Central Consistory count of 92,321. *Les Juifs de France de 1789 à 1860*, p. 101.

12. Ruppin, *The Jews in the Modern World*, p. 45.

13. Weinberg, p. 18.

14. The German and Austrian Jews constituted the largest group of refugees, but there were also substantial numbers of Central and East European Jews. See Friedländer, *When Memory Comes*, pp. 37–41. There are, however, no figures available on the numbers of refugees from the different nationalities. See Roblin, p. 71; see also Tartakower and Grossman, *The Jewish Refugees*, pp. 130–33. For a bibliography of the question and comments on the problems faced by historians, see Weinberg, pp. 19–21.

15. Weinberg, p. 20; Roblin, pp. 76–77; for an excellent study of the Consistories in France during the nineteenth century, see Albert, *The Modernization of French Jewry.*

16. Weinberg did not have access to wartime census returns in his evaluation of the geographical distribution of the immigrant population in Paris. The October 1940 census, despite obvious changes due to the exodus, could not have substantially affected the residential patterns. The census results are available at the Department of Demography, Institute of Contemporary Jewry, Jerusalem University (hereafter Department of Demography, Jerusalem); for the geographical dispersion of the Jewish population at the eve of the war, see Roblin, pp. 75–86.

17. For an interesting collection of excerpts of articles that appeared in the Jewish press during that period regarding the uneasy relationship between French and foreign Jews, see Rajsfus, *Sois Juif et tais-toi!* chap. 3, "La France aux Français"; Roland, *Du Ghetto à l'Occident,* pp. 231–32.

18. Alfred Grant describes the general atmosphere that prevailed in the Jewish districts and how thousands of Jews took to the roads or waited at the railway stations for the elusive trains; see *Paris a Shtot fun Front,* chap. 1. Other observers confirmed Grant's observations, see Mintz, *In die Yorn fun Yiddishn Umkum un Vidershtant in Frankraikh,* p. 56; the *Bulletin Officiel de la Ville de Paris* 317, no. 7 (July 1940), states that the population of the city of Paris was then 1,051,506. The 1936 population census shows that Paris numbered 2,829,746. *Annuaire Statistique de la ville de Paris,* secretariat général de la préfecture de la Seine, Paris, 1943. The population of Paris had fallen by two thirds; it could therefore be assumed that the Jewish population would have been reduced by the same proportions and can be estimated to be between 50,000 and 70,000.

19. For the period from July to September 1940, see the *Bulletin Officiel de la Ville de Paris* 319, no. 9 (September 1940).

20. The German criterion was based upon a religious criterion of two or more Jewish grandparents. Vichy's Status des Juifs deemed a Jew to be a person of the Jewish race with three or more grandparents of the Jewish race. Two elements, race and religion, determined the status of the person concerned; for the legislation see *Les Juifs sous l'Occupation,* pp. 18–21.

21. Department of Demography, Jerusalem; Report of the Prefect of Police to the Chief of the German Military Administration, 26 October 1940, Centre de Documentation Juive Contemporaine (hereafter CDJC), LXXIXa-10. To these numbers must be added 9,507 Jews in various camps in the Vichy Zone by mid-1941 (CDJC, DXLIV-47) as well as those who did not register. There were therefore more than 300,000 Jews then in France. For the number of Jews in the Vichy Zone, see CDJC, B-16390, 2 vols.; see also note 30.

22. According to David Knout the Ligue Internationale Contre le Racisme had opened recruitment centers at the outbreak of the war for immigrant Jews and 12,000 men had enrolled. Other immigrant Jews had joined a Polish division which was formed on French soil by the Polish government, while yet other immigrant Jews had joined the French Foreign Legion. To these volunteers must be added the French Jews who upon call-up were incorporated into French army units. *Contribution à l'histoire de la Résistance Juive en France,* p. 79. Roblin asserts that the number of Jewish prisoners of war ranged between 10,000 and 15,000; p. 78, n. 4. Roblin's evidence is based upon a report that claimed the Jewish contingent in all units operating on French territories was on the order of 60,000 men; see *Contemporary Jewish Record* (New York: American Jewish Committee,

1939), p. 65. Israel Cohen, however, claims that the number of Jews in the army in France was 40,000, of whom 15,000 were Germans or Austrians, the majority of whom were sent to North Africa; *The Jews in the War,* pp. 65–66. According to Joseph Fridman, president of the Engagés Volontaires et Anciens Combattants Juifs, the number of Jews, French and foreign, in the French army would have been in the vicinity of 40,000, excluding all those sent to North Africa. These estimates are based upon the numbers of special regiments for foreigners which included a majority of Jews. Accordingly, the likely number of Jewish prisoners of war would correspond to the national average and would number between 7,000 and 10,000 men. Fridman, interview, Paris, 10 August 1978.

23. The HICEM was an organization that helped Jews to migrate. It was formed as a result of a merger between the HIAS, the Hebrew Immigrant Aid and Sheltering Society, the Jewish Colonization Association, and Emigdirect, a former German organization which only helped German Jewish migrants. The HICEM records show that 1,352 Jews left France through its offices during 1940. How many more did leave Europe until the Armistice could not have been significant as all seafaring traffic was restricted on account of the hostilities and the requirements of the British expeditionary forces in France. The following sources give some indications of the minimum numbers known: CDJC, CDXIV-54, tableau IV, 1941: January, 154; February, 110; March, 190; April, 187; May, 474; June, 132; these sources give us a total of 1,247 persons. Another source, CDJC, XXXI-113, a letter from the HICEM to the Vichy Ministry of the Interior, 31 December 1942, states that for 1940 it had handled the departure of 105 persons. Another source, the American Jewish Committee, reports that 3,000 applications had been received and of these 28 percent arrived during the war. Dr. Max Gottschalk, American Jewish Committee, archives, foreign countries, file: France, 1940–45. The leader of HICEM (France), W. Schah, indicates in another report that 7,000 Jews left France between October 1940 and November 1942; Schah to Edinger, November 1942, YIVO, UGIF, CIV, 19,045. Another source, J. Dijour, "Jewish Emigration from Europe in the Present War," *YIVO Bleter* no. 2 (March–April 1942): 145–56, states that 1,607 Jews arrived in the United States from France during 1940 and 3,730 during 1942.

24. Blanke, from the German military administration, reported that Xavier Vallat, the Vichy commissioner for Jewish affairs, would have stated that as many as 8 to 10 percent of the Jews had refused to register; CDJC, LXXV-59. Another source, Inspection Générale des Services de Renseignements Généraux, Vichy, 10 July 1941, stated:

> It must be noted that there prevails among the Jews a definite refusal to register as ordered. A real conspiracy is taking place toward a boycott of the census. It must also be noted that since the last decree a number of conversions to Catholicism, although very badly viewed in Jewish circles, have taken place. (CDJC, LXI-38)

Pierre Paraf takes a different view of the question: "The overwhelming majority has declared itself in a twin assertion of pride and excessive legalism." *Israel dans le monde,* p. 151. André Weil-Curiel's personal experience would seem to confirm the view that the Jews did register:

> I was faced with delicate problems. Must I declare myself as a Jew? I was not of the opinion of the quasi totality of the French Jews who, in the fear

of sanctions, had precipitated themselves, like sheep to the slaughter, to the police stations where they were ordered to fill out the forms." *Le Temps de la honte,* 3:56).

All translations in this study are my own.

25. No French government ever encouraged immigrants to adopt French names, not even to simplify the spelling which always gave rise to bureaucratic difficulties. The legal costs and the delays were such that few foreigners ever attempted it. Furthermore, to ensure that no Jew be tempted to use such a tactic to avoid detection, Vichy passed a law, 10 February 1942, forbidding Jews to use pseudonyms. *Journal Officiel (JO),* 27 March 1942.

26. Roland, pp. 277–78; there were 7,373 mixed marriages; October 1940 census, Department of Demography, Jerusalem.

27. According to Raul Hilberg, 6,300 Jews from Baden and 1,150 from the Saarland had been expelled from Germany to France; see *The Destruction of the European Jews,* p. 392. Another version states that only 6,000 Jews were expelled to France; see *Trial of War Criminals before the Nuremberg International Military Tribunals,* vol. 13, case no. 10, Ernest von Weizsaecker, NG-4934, pp. 164–65. Hilberg's figures, which include both the Saarland and Baden, are no longer questioned, cf. Marrus and Paxton, *Vichy et les Juifs,* p. 24.

28. "Rapport du Gouvernement Belge sur la persécution des Juifs en Belgique durant l'Occupation Allemande," in *La Persécution des Juifs en France et des autres Pays de l'Ouest, presentée par la France à Nuremberg,* pp. 202–28, doc. 47 (UK 47) (hereinafter *La Persécution des Juifs).* The Jews from Belgium did not figure in the census as originating from there. The overwhelming majority were in fact former refugees from Germany or foreign nationals living in Belgium. Some of them returned to Belgium after the Armistice while others chose to remain in France; see Jewish Telegraphic Agency (JTA), 29 September 1940: "4,000 to 5,000 Belgian Jews from Antwerp and Brussels are held at Saint Cyprien (Dordogne), many have returned to Belgium out of sheer despair" *(YIVO).* There were still some Belgian Jews in Paris in November 1940 who needed to be helped by the Jewish organizations. "I have just had a call from some foreign Jews, mostly Polish, who had left Belgium in May [1940] who have just arrived from the Vichy Zone where those originating from Belgium and unable to return are interned in camps. They are seeking to return to Belgium where they have their homes. Until now it had been relatively easy but it is no longer so and there are a few hundred of them in a truly tragic situation." Jakoubowicz to Rabinowicz, 13 November 1940, YIVO, Amelot, 1–2, 09.

29. *Le Journal de Paris,* 1 April 1941, quoted in Lubetzki, p. 13.

30. This figure is based on a study of the census of the Jews in the Vichy Zone held in July 1941, made accessible to me by Claude Lévy from the Institut National d'Etudes Démographiques, Paris. The census shows that 60 percent of the Jews there were French, but it must be borne in mind that the total number of Jews registered included a large percentage of refugees from Belgium, Holland, and Luxemburg. According to my calculations the percentage of French Jews in relation to the prewar Jewish population would be 75 percent. This census is now at the CDJC, B-16390, 2 vols.

31. For a sociological study of immigrant Jewry in Paris see Roland.

32. For a study of the camps in which these men were interned, see Diamant, *Le Billet vert.*

33. For a description of the arrest of the French Jews and their reactions, see Bernard, *Le Camp de la mort lente;* Wellers, *De Drancy à Auschwitz,* pp. 219–21; for a breakdown of the men's ages and professions, see CDJC, IV-177.

34. *Les Juifs sous l'occupation,* p. 106.

35. Sixth German Ordinance, 7 February 1942. *Verordnungsblatt des Militärbefehlshabers in Frankreich (VOBIF).*

36. *VOBIF,* 1 June 1942.

37. There were then in Paris 46,442 French Jews, and 46,322 foreign Jews, as well as 15,322 French and 2,106 foreign children over the age of six. From the immigrant population, 9,837 were not required at the time to wear the star; CDJC, XLIXa-109. For the background to the introduction of the Yellow Star in France and the reasons for the exemptions, see Poliakov, *L'Etoile jaune.*

38. Poliakov, p. 42.

39. Dannecker, note, 1 July 1942, Paris, in *La Persécution des Juifs,* pp. 189–91, doc. no. 40.

40. Röthke, report to IV J-SA, Berlin, 18 July 1942, CDJC, XLIX-67; see also Jean Leguay's deposition in *France under the German Occupation,* 3:1155–59.

41. On the number of Jews thought to still be in France during that period, see CDJC, I-54. This report gives the following figures: Paris: 60,000; Italian Zone of Occupation: 50,000; Lyon: 40,000; Marseille: 30,000; and Toulouse: 20,000.

42. Klarsfeld, *Le Mémorial de la Déportation,* tableau chronologique des convois de déportation.

43. For the repatriation figures until March 1943, see Röthke "La situation actuelle de la question juive en France," 6 March 1943, CDJC, XXVc-214; for Sweden, see CDJC, XXV-56; for the Soviet Jews, see Biélinky, diary, 5 June 1941, Biélinky Collection, YIVO (hereafter Biélinky, diary); for Denmark, see CDJC, XXV-20, 27; Italy; CDJC, XXVI-209; Hungary: CDJC, CLXXXIX-5 and Yad Vashem Archives (hereafter YVA) 09/8(2); Turkey: YVA, 09/8(4), 09/27; Switzerland: YIVO, UGIF, XXVII-11, 076.

44. For a description of the personal problems faced in such cases, see Grant, chap. 10.

45. The number of deaths has been calculated from the burial lists held at the Institut Maurice Thorez (IMT), UGIF, beta, 10, 73.

46. Dossier du control de la population juive de la Seine, CDJC, XXVc-252.

47. There are no authoritative sources as to the number of Jews still in Paris by 1944. Jacob Kaplan held that there were 30,000 declared Jews while an equal number lived illegally; "French Jewry under the Occupation," p. 75. One report from September 1944 tells of 15,825 people being helped by the Immigrant's Unity Committee; IMT, Comité Général de Défense des Juifs Collection (hereafter CGD), alpha, 7, 164. Another source claims that by the summer of 1944 there were only 20,000 Jews wearing the Yellow Star, a figure likely to be based on UGIF sources; see *L'Activité des organisations juives,* p. 218.

Chapter 2. The Politics of Expropriation

1. For the Madagascar Plan, see Hilberg, *The Destruction of the European Jews,* pp. 259–61; Memorandum, special report addressed to the French Foreign Ministry, May 1937, YIVO, HIAS-HICEM Collection, séries II, France Second World War, 29; JTA, Stockholm, 29 April 1941. Besides Madagascar, other places had been considered as territorial solutions to the European refugee problem,

meaning the Jews. Indochina was thought to be a likely place to settle the Jewish refugees; see Marrus and Paxton, *Vichy et les Juifs*, pp. 67–68; L. Yahil, "Madagascar–Phantom of a Solution for the Jewish Question," in Vago and Mosse, *Jews and Non-Jews in Eastern Europe, 1918–1945.*

2. For the Lublin Project, see Reitlinger, *The Final Solution*, pp. 50–51.

3. *Le Temps*, 17 October 1940.

4. *JO*, 18 October 1940.

5. Statut des Juifs, Articles 3 and 4, *JO*, 18 October 1940.

6. The following figures are from a press release issued by Xavier Vallat, *Le Figaro*, 13 April 1941. The original evidence is no longer in existence. However, a comparison with the existing census results does establish the veracity of Vallat's figures. The same press release reveals that of a total of 2,395 pharmacists in Paris there were only 25 Jews. In the medical profession of a total of 5,890 medical practitioners there were 557 French Jews and 184 Polish and Rumanian, that is, 12.5 percent; of the 2,430 dentists 225 were Jews, 9.2 percent. No other comparative figures are available for the other professions. Some results are, however, of general interest. There were 400 Jewish, French, and foreign, stage performers, of whom 122 were musicians; but there were only two Jewish conductors, one French and one of Persian origin. Among the small traders there were 2,522 second-hand dealers and stall holders at market places. In the various occupations related to the clothing industry there were 1,473 cap makers, 1,457 ladies' tailors, 1,280 men's tailors. Of the 2,796 Jewish commercial companies, 421 manufactured clothing, 216 furs and fancy goods, and 11 agricultural implements. Department of Demography, file FR021.

7. Figures extracted and calculated from the economic census returns, Department of Demography, Jerusalem.

8. Ibid.

9. *La Géographie juive, Marseille*, 11 April 1941, YIVO, UGIF, CXII, 16, 05.

10. Marrus and Paxton, *Vichy et les Juifs*, p. 62. Some 3,000 were expelled from France.

11. Général de La Laurencie to the Prefects in the Occupied Zone, 5 November 1940, *Les Juifs sous l'Occupation*, pp. 28–29.

12. MBF, General Administratif Staff, Instructions pour les commissaires-gérants d'entreprises juives, 12 November 1940, *Les Juifs sous l'Occupation*, pp. 29–30.

13. *Bekanntmachung*, 12 December 1940, *VOBIF*, 26 January 1941.

14. Général de La Laurencie to the Prefects in the Occupied Zone, 15 December 1940, *Les Juifs sous l'Occupation*, pp. 32–34.

15. Commission de la Production Industrielle, 11 December 1940, Paris to Vichy: "Krupp has established itself and is now acting under its own name and not as Austin's successor. The 'Production Industrielle' is seeking ways of stopping Krupp from continuing." CDJC, XXIX-149, 151.

16. Decree of 16 January 1941, *JO*, 17 January 1941.

17. For the establishment of the Commissariat Général aux Questions Juives, see notes of the Darlan-Schleier meeting, 23 April 1941, CDJC, V-83; for an excellent study, and so far the only one, see Billig, *Le Commissariat Général aux Questions Juives.*

18. Law of 11 April 1941, *JO*, 30 April 1941; law of 26 April 1941, "permettant le blocage de certains comptes en banques," *JO*, 21 May 1941.

19. *VOBIF,* 5 May 1941.

20. Circulaire de l'Union Syndicale des Banquiers, 23 May 1941, quoted in *Les Juifs sous l'Occupation,* p. 47; *Bekanntmachung,* 7 May 1941, *VOBIF,* 25 May 1941.

21. *VOBIF,* 28 May 1941, 10 June 1941; the SCAP was established in October 1940 by the Ministry of Industrial Production. Its first director was Pierre-Eugène Fournier, former director of the Bank of France; Billig, *Le Commissariat Général aux Questions Juives,* 1:38.

22. Law of 2 June 1941, second Statut des Juifs, replacing the earlier statut, *JO,* 14 June 1941.

23. SCAP to provisional administrators, 9 June 1941, *Les Juifs sous l'Occupation,* pp. 53–54.

24. Communiqué de la Préfecture de Police, *Le Matin,* 15 June 1941.

25. Law of 22 July 1941, "relatif aux entreprises, biens et valeurs appartenant aux Juifs," *JO,* 26 August 1941.

26. CGQJ, note, 13 October 1941, *Les Juifs sous l'Occupation,* p. 88.

27. G. Ripert, Le Secrétariat d'Etat à l'Instruction Publique et à la Jeunesse, à MM. les Recteurs, et à MM. les Inspecteurs d'Académie, 21 October 1940, *Les Juifs sous l'Occupation,* pp. 25–27.

28. Decree of 16 July 1941, "réglementant, en ce qui concerne les Juifs, la profession d'avocat," *JO,* 17 July 1941.

29. Antignac, CGQJ, to Röthke, 15 March 1943, CDJC, XXIII-17b.

30. MBF to Association Professionnelle des Banques, 22 December 1941, *Les Juifs sous l'Occupation,* p. 109.

31. CGQJ to Caisse des Dépôts et Consignations (hereafter Caisse), 2 January 1942, CDJC, XXVIIIa-262. Vichy, in its haste to proceed with the sales of Jewish assets, also sold assets belonging to "enemy aliens," Jews, naturally. The German authorities, in their fear that such sales were arranged between willing parties, did not view them with favor. We find the German foreign office criticizing the MBF (Paris) for having allowed Vichy to proceed with these sales, see Billig, *Le Commissariat Général aux Questions Juives,* 3:220–25.

32. *VOBIF,* 27 September 1943.

33. CGQJ to MBF, rapport sur l'élimination des Juifs de l'administration, CDJC, CXCIII-108.

34. CGQJ, note, 3 June 1942, CDJC, XXIII-66; CDJC, CXV-39.

35. Darquier de Pellepoix to Zeitschel, German Embassy, Paris, 17 October 1942, in reply to a complaint as to the delay in dismissal of Jews from the administration by Vichy, CDJC, CXV-77.

36. Antignac, CGQJ, to Röthke, 15 March 1943, CDJC, XXIII-17b.

37. The Friendly Association's appeal reached Fernand de Brinon, Vichy's ambassador in Paris, who proceeded to inform the CGQJ of its claim on 15 May 1941. This Friendly Association was supported by 1,500 doctors; CDJC, CVIII-34; for the text of the appeal, see CDJC, IIIa-3/4.

38. Groupement Corporatif Sanitaire Français to CGQJ, 19 July 1942, CDJC, XXIII-12.

39. Antignac to Röthke, 15 March 1943, CDJC, XXIII-17b.

40. For the pharmacists see Assistance Publique to CGQJ, May 1943, CDJC, CVIII-54 and 57; for the midwives see Bureau d'Hygiene de la Préfecture de Police to Antignac, 16 March 1943, CDJC, XXIII-18.

41. List of dentists allowed to practice, April 1943, CDJC, CVIII-49.
42. Vallat to MBF, 16 January 1942, CDJC, CVIII-7.
43. Le Bâtonnier de Paris to Antignac, 7 April 1943, CDJC, CVIII-15.
44. See Billig, *Le Commissariat Général aux Questions Juives*, 3:27–28.
45. Artists were affected by the first and second Statut des Juifs. A Vichy decree, 6 June 1942, finally closed all public venues; for the SEC, see Billig, *Le Commissariat Général aux Questions Juives*, 1:294–309; 2:63–142.
46. At the Salon d'Automne of 1942, painters had to present their identity cards if there was doubt about their non-Jewish racial status; CDJC, XXI-7.
47. Blanke to Ministry of Industrial Production, 7 February 1941, CDJC, XXXIV-2.
48. It was in November 1941 that Vallat was informed of the German military administration's economic policy. It was then that Vallat was informed that the Germans viewed them as potentially dangerous. Blanke to Vallat, November 1941, CDJC, LXXV-59.
49. Stenger to SCAP, 15 December 1941, CDJC, XXIII-48.
50. Darlan to Vallat, 8 January 1942, CDJC, XXIII-78.
51. Military Administration, note, 1 January 1943, CDJC, XXIII-56.
52. Prefecture of Police, report, November 1940, CDJC, LXXIXa-10.
53. Compte rendu de la conférence des délégués des Comités d'organisations professionelles, 7 April 1941, CDJC, XXIX-70/71.
54. May 1941, CDJC, XXIX-137.
55. Vallat to Blanke, 8 December 1941, CDJC, LXXV-63.
56. Each successive Statut des Juifs added new classes of Jews to those so defined by the laws. There were, however, instances when individuals and groups of individuals applied to the Germans and had their claims of not being Jewish upheld. In these cases their properties were freed from the controls of the appointed administrators; see Lévi Eligulashvili, "How the Jews of Gruziya in Occupied France Were Saved," and Asaf Atchildi, "Rescue of Jews of Bukharan, Iranian and Afghan Origin in Occupied France," in *Yad Vashem Studies* 6 (1967): 251–81.
57. Consultative Committee, 8 December 1941, CDJC, CX-170.
58. CGQJ, statistical report, May 1944, CDJC, CXIXa-7.
59. Ibid., June 1944, CDJC, CXIXa-112.
60. Direction de l'aryanisation, CGQJ, to Stenger, MBF, 12 September 1942, CDJC, LXXV-262.
61. Blanke to CGQJ, 15 July 1944, CDJC, LXXV-263.
62. Billig, *Le Commissariat Général aux Questions Juives*, 3:298.
63. Dienstelle Western, 8 August 1944, CDJC, XIXa-42. Another source states that 38,000 Jewish apartments' contents had been sent to Germany; report from Von Behr, Action M, Paris, 8 August 1944, CDJC, XIII-47. Vichy had made numerous representations to the German armistice commission on the illegality of these actions; Vichy to the President des Services de la Délégation Française auprès de la Commission Allemande, Vichy 11 November 1943, CDJC, CCXLVIII-1.
64. *La Persécution raciale*, pp. 34–36. According to Amouroux the Jewish-owned works of art could have amounted to two billion francs; *La Vie des Français sous l'Occupation*, p. 323.
65. Comité Général de Défense des Juifs, CDJC, CCXXI-10.
66. Vallat to Blanke, 16 December 1941, CDJC, LXXV-63.
67. Quoted in Lubetzki, *La Condition des Juifs*, p. 16.

Chapter 3. Life under the Occupation

1. The decision to begin preparations for the deportations from France was taken in Berlin on 11 June 1942. At a conference of all the Western European SD representatives, Adolph Eichmann informed them that the RSHA had made the decision to proceed with the Final Solution. Dannecker was informed that the target for France was set at 100,000 people. It was decided that the French government would not only assume the transportation costs but also supply those to be deported with equipment and food for fifteen days. Furthermore, the French government would need to pass a law that would strip those deported of French citizenship as soon as they had left French territory. *La Persécution des Juifs*, pp. 126–27.

2. Wellers, *De Drancy à Auschwitz*, pp. 32–33; Simon Zaidov, interview, Melbourne, 15 April 1982.

3. For some of the letters from the men at Pithiviers and Beaune-La-Rolande about to be deported, particularly J. Roussak, and also the leaflet produced by the underground organization in Pithiviers which was distributed on the eve of their deportation on 14 May 1942, see Diamant, *Le Billet vert*, pp. 274–76.

4. For examples of the comments from the collaborationist press, see *Paris-Soir*, 15 May 1942, and *Aujourd'hui*, 16 May 1941.

5. Broszat, "Hitler and the Genesis of the 'Final Solution.' "

6. Dannecker to MBF, CDJC, V-63; law of 4 October 1940, which was specifically directed at the immigrant Jews; Dannecker to Befehlshaber des Sicherheitspolizei, Brussels, 9 July 1942, CDJC, XXVb-56.

7. A full chronological list of the 400 or so laws, decrees, and regulations applying to Jews which were issued by Vichy are to be found in Lubetzki, *La Condition des Juifs*, pp. 219–57.

8. Aron, *The Vichy Regime, 1940–1944*, p. 12.

9. ". . . Informed by our friends in the government we had, at the end of May 1940, taken the necessary measures," "Le Dernier interview de R. A. Olchanski," *Journal des Communautés* 403 (27 October 1957); Compte-rendu du Grand-Rabbin de France sur son activité depuis Juin 1940, Jewish Theological Seminary of America (JTS), box 13, file Vichy, p. 1.

10. May, *Paris en 1,591 jours*, p. 5.

11. Geissmann, "Le Rabbinat consistorial sous l'occupation."

12. Bernard, *Le Camp de la mort lente*, p. 32.

13. Grant, *Paris a Schtot fun Front*, pp. 28–29; Israel, *Heureux comme Dieu en France*, pp. 69–73.

14. Grant, p. 37; Israel, p. 241.

15. Note from Hans Speidel, 20 September 1940, CDJC, LXXV-73 to 80; Steinberg, *Les Allemands en France, 1940–1944*, p. 209.

16. Korenhandler, *Brieven fun Lectoure*, p. 17.

17. Henri Bulawko, interview, Paris, 10 July 1978.

18. For the lure of profits as a motive, see Henri Sindler, report, D. Moshowitch Collection, sheet 21434, YIVO; Mintz, pp. 56, 93.

19. Jacques Biélinky, diary, 11 October 1940, "more than 6,000 people attended the Yom Kippour services"; 12 October 1940, "I have visited synagogues in the 4th. arrondissement and there are large numbers of 'Polacks' . . . posters, in Yiddish and in French, forbid political discussions inside the synagogues and gatherings outside. . . ."

20. *JO,* 23 July 1940.

21. Israel, p. 93.

22. For a list of the major meeting places where immigrant businessmen met, see Grant, p. 75.

23. For the number of people thought to be in need of communal help, particularly among immigrants and refugees, see YIVO, Amelot, I-5.

24. For the committee formed on 14 June 1940, see Jakoubowicz, *Rue Amelot;* for the Jewish Communists, see Aron Beckerman, diary, manuscript at IMT, Union des Juifs pour la Résistance et l'Entr'aide (UJRE), Collection. Excerpts have been published in *Dos Vort fun Vidershtant un Zeig,* pp. 31–37.

25. Biélinky, diary, 20, 27 July 1940, 17 August 1940.

26. Ibid., 3 September 1940; Jakoubowicz, *Rue Amelot,* chap. 1.

27. *La Persécution raciale,* p. 22. Some Jewish shopkeepers did not display the shield and were prosecuted. Military Administration to German Military Tribunal, 1 July 1941, CDJC, LXXVII-23.

28. Bulawko, *Les Jeux de la mort et de l'espoir,* p. 35; Lévy and Tillard, *La Grande rafle du Vel d'Hiv,* p. 235.

29. Steinberg, *Les Allemands en France,* p. 209; Bulawko, interview.

30. Israel, p. 241; Samuel Radzinski, interview, Paris, 10 March 1978.

31. Grant, p. 42; Bulawko, "Les Premiers internments Juifs à la Caserne des Tourelles."

32. Grant, pp. 68ff.

33. Simultaneously with the general arrests, 52 Jewish lawyers were also interned. No evidence is available for the motives that led Dannecker to order the measure; we can only infer that he acted on the same principle that the SD acted on in all the occupied countries, to physically eliminate any and all potential source of anti-German leadership. *La Persécution raciale,* p. 120.

34. Grant, pp. 82–84; Georges Tachnoff, interview, Paris, 2 July 1978.

35. According to my calculations, based on the records held at the Secrétariat d'Etat des Anciens Combattants, 1,086 men were released between September and December 1941, 160 in October, and 926 in November. Access to these files has been made possible by the personal assistance of Alphonse Grisoni, Sous-Directeur des Statuts de Combattants et de Victimes de Guerre, June 1978; cf. Jakoubowicz, *Rue Amelot,* p. 87.

36. Ydel Korman, interview, Paris, 15 March 1978; cf. Wellers, *De Drancy à Auschwitz,* p. 23.

37. M. Waiszbrot, interview, Paris: 2 March 1978, Broniek Ezerowicz, interview, Melbourne, 15 November 1977.

38. Ory, *Les Collaborateurs, 1940–1945,* pp. 153–58: Osgood, "The Antisemitism of the French Collaborationist Press," pp. 51–56; Miller, "En feuilletant les archives du CGQJ," 2:63–102.

39. The bombings of the synagogues in Paris were not isolated incidents. Such incidents occurred during the same period in the Vichy Zone as well. For Jewish protests, see YIVO, Geographical Collection: France 1940–44 (hereafter France, II WW, Generalities), box 2, folder 28; Cardinal Gerlier to Chief-Rabbi, 5 December 1941, YVA, 0-9/25. Florin Du Bois de la Villerabel to Chief-Rabbi, 15 December 1941: "We have faith in the wisdom of the Maréchal [Pétain] not to allow acts so contrary to our compatriots' character." YVA, 0-9/25.

40. Delpech, "La Persécution des Juifs et l'Amitié Chrétienne," pp. 161–62; Geissmann, "Il y a 25 ans."

41. Reports from the Prefecture of Police, 2–4 October 1941, CDJC, LXXV-268; for Stülpnagel's indignation at the bombings, see CDJC, I-24; German Propaganda-Abteilung, n.d., but certainly written at the end of 1941 or early 1942, CDJC, LXXV-236.

42. Biélinky, diary, 1940, 8 December 1941; Guéhenno, *Journal des années noires (1940–1944)*, p. 188.

43. Eighth Ordinance, 19 May 1942, *VOBIF*, 1 June 1942. The introduction of the compulsory wearing of the Yellow Star was the object of extended discussions between the military administration, Stülpnagel, the RSHA of all the Western European countries, Abetz, and the Ministry of Foreign Affairs in Berlin. It was finally introduced in France when the Ministry of Foreign Affairs gave it the seal of approval on 22 May 1942. According to the evidence it appears that Stülpnagel did press for its imposition, as part of a number of other anti-Jewish measures, quite likely on account of reports of the high incidence of Jews who had been involved in attacks upon German army personnel: see CDJC, IV-205. Abetz, according to Zeitschel, was opposed to the introduction of the Yellow Star in France; CDJC, LXXI-73. For the Ministry of Foreign Affairs approval, see CDJC, XLIXa-56. Each Jew over the age of six was entitled to three Yellow Stars in exchange for one textile coupon; *Les Juifs sous l'Occupation*, p. 155.

44. CDJC, XXVb-80. Those arrested numbered 3,031 men, 5,802 women, and 4,051 children; *La Persécution des Juifs*, doc. 45, RF 1233, p. 197. According to Steinberg the number of Jews arrested then numbered 14,189; *Les Allemands en France*, p. 219.

45. The effects of these measures will be discussed in Chapter 7 for French Judaism and in Chapter 9 for the immigrant organizations. The grave fears caused by the July 1942 events led the UGIF leaders to write to Maréchal Pétain and express their gratitude for having been spared. See André Baur to Pétain, 21 August 1942, YVA, 0-9/6-1.

46. According to Lévy and Tillard, there were 106 cases of suicide and 24 cases of death among those arrested; pp. 39, 44–45.

47. There was also a high incidence of children who had nowhere to go. Ezerowicz, interview; Jacques Adler, personal recollections.

48. Schrager, *Oifn rund fun tzwei tkoufes (zechroines)*, p. 140. For the difficulties in finding a trustworthy smuggler, see Korenhandler, p. 21; for the treatment of the immigrant Jews if caught by the French gendarmes, see p. 31; see also a UGIF note on the internment procedure, report, 23 August 1942, CDJC, CCXIII-59. For the immigrants with money, see Korenhandler, p. 72. The immigrant Jews in the Vichy Zone were subject to the law of 27 July 1940, which established the principle of their incorporation into special work units under the authority of the Secretariat for Industrial Production and Labor. The law was subsequently modified in such a way as to place them under police controls. By December 1941 the compulsory incorporation was modified to allow those foreign Jews who could show sufficient resources to be assigned, instead, to confined residence. *JO*, 31 January 1942.

49. For Marseille, YIVO, UGIF, XCIV, 10, 029; Limoges, children without parents, YIVO, UGIF, CI, 8, 029, CDJC, CCXIII-59; Lyon, 12 August 1942, YVA, 0-9/24; Toulouse, 27 August 1942, YIVO, UGIF, XCIII, 7, 027.

50. The relevant sources are to be found at the CDJC, see Steinberg, *Les Autorités allemandes en France*, pp. 176–91.

51. Dr. Kurt Schendel, "Rapport sur le service de liaison et mon activité dans ce service," 2 September 1944, CDJC, CCXXI-26, p. 2; Tachnoff, interview.

52. Each major underground organization possessed its own technical facilities, certain individuals such as Maurice Loebenberg were recognized experts; he was subsequently recruited into a non-Jewish resistance organization; see CDJC, CDLXIX-24.

53. Grant describes vividly the problems and difficulties attached to becoming an illegal, although in his particular case he was one of the leaders of an underground organization; see Grant, chap. 6.

54. Report, Comité Général de Défense, September 1944, IMT, Joint, alpha, 2, 56.

55. For the Italian Zone of Occupation, see Poliakov and Sabille, *Jews under the Italian Occupation.*

56. Klarsfeld, *Le Mémorial de la Déportation,* convoy no. 48.

57. On 25 February 1943, there were in Paris 543 Italian and 2,076 Hungarian Jews; CDJC, XXV-100. There were also 7 Swedes and 3 Danes who, according to the German Foreign Ministry, were due to be repatriated by June 1943; CDJC, XXV-20, 22, 23. There were also other nationalities in Paris then, such as Turkish Jews, but the Germans did not seem particularly concerned about their repatriation.

58. Wellers, *De Drancy à Auschwitz,* p. 71. An earlier letter, dated 7 May 1942, had reached the UGIF offices in Paris from Oswiecim (as Auschwitz was known when it was still a Polish town); YIVO, UGIF, CXI, 102, 010; the *Bulletin de l'Union Général des Israélites de France* had informed its readers of the arrival of a number of letters, no. 52, 15 January 1943. Letters continued to arrive in Paris until November 1943; YIVO, UGIF, IV, 29, 088.

59. Korenhandler, p. 59ff.; my family had also received such news, and had also sent help to Poland.

60. Wellers, *De Drancy à Auschwitz,* pp. 25–26; Zaidov, interview.

61. Wellers, *De Drancy à Auschwitz,* pp. 69–70; Bulawko, interview.

62. Wellers, *De Drancy à Auschwitz,* p. 70; Adler, recollections.

63. Le Consistoire Israélite de France au Chef du Gouvernement, 25 August 1942, CDJC, CCXII-15. See also Dr. J. Weill's deposition, 27 June 1974, CDJC, DXLXI-37.

64. Rayski, "Les Origines et le rôle de la presse clandestine antiraciste en France" (hereafter *La Presse antiraciste*), pp. 15–21; cf. Grant, p. 163.

65. On the German use of euphemisms see a circular telex from the MBF, 12 May 1942, forbidding the use of expressions such as "deportation" and "toward the East." The MBF ordered that only the expression "sent to hard labor" be used in official communications; CDJC, XXVI-21. The UGIF itself also used such a coded language, see *Bulletin de l'UGIF,* 62, 26 March 1943.

66. Edinger to Goetschel, 2 April 1943, CDJC, CDXXIV-25.

67. Based on an examination of the published lists of recipients of letters printed in the *Bulletin de l'UGIF.*

68. André Tulard was head of a department at the Prefecture of Police of Paris, in charge of the organization and permanent control of the Jewish population card index. As a technical officer, Tulard participated in the preparations for the July 1942 mass arrests. Dannecker, note, 8 July 1942, doc. 17, in *La Persécution des Juifs,* pp. 142–45. Tulard's card index was used in each and every operation against the Jewish population. The index appears to have disappeared following the Liberation of Paris.

69. For a summary presentation of the case against the French police, which cooperated and participated to the execution of German orders, see Commission Rogatoire, Judge Zousman, 18 May 1948, CDJC, XI-I. It would appear, according to Judge Zousman, that after June 1943 (that is, after the arrival of Aloïs Brunner's SD unit) the French police had been asked by Department IV B4, RSHA, to assume initiatives in the arrest of Jews. According to Zousman, the French police, which had previously always acted on instructions, refused to initiate arrests. Between 25 November 1943 and 3 February 1944, only 1,000 Jews were arrested as against several thousand who should have been.

70. *La Persécution raciale,* Annexes I, pp. 285–86.

71. André Radzinski, interview, Paris, 9 March 1978; Emile Somer, interview, Paris, 14 March 1978.

72. Klarsfeld, *Le Mémorial de la Déportation,* tableau chronologique des convois de déportations, convoy nos. 76 and 77.

73. Tachnoff, interview; Bernard Borenstein, interview, Paris, 5 May 1978.

74. The CDJC has a substantial collection of letters of denunciations addressed to the French police, the CGQJ, and the Gestapo. The motives are surprisingly honest, and in overwhelming majority based on greed. The informers would always ask for the Jew's apartment or his property. For the fate of the children left behind by their families, two moving books convey the depth of the tragedy: Friedländer, *When Memory Comes;* and Vegh, *Je ne lui ai pas dit au revoir.*

Chapter 4. The Coordination Committee of Jewish Relief Organizations: September 1940 to November 1941

1. For two excellent studies of the period and the perception by the Jewish organizations and their leaders of the problems facing the Jews in France, see Weinberg, *Les Juifs à Paris,* and Hyman, *From Dreyfus to Vichy.* For a collection of articles that appeared in various Jewish journals during that period, see Rajsfus, *Sois Juif et tais-toi!*

2. Tcherikower, *Yidn in Frankraikh;* vol. 2 is devoted to the interwar period.

3. Helbronner's reply, on behalf of the Central Consistory, to the invitation by the government of the day is indicative of a range of attitudes that were expressed during the Occupation. "It is at the invitation of the [French] government that I allow myself to inform you that French Judaism has been set into motion. It has taken us a long time to do so. It is because the French Israelites are French before being Jewish that it has been hard for us to forget what the German Jews did during the war [1914–18]." Comité de Secours aux Refugiés Allemands, Leo Baeck Institute (LBI), West European Collection, II, Frankreich, AR-C 1638–4099; R. Thalman, "L'Emigration du IIIe Reich en France de 1933 à 1939," *Le Monde Juif* No. 96 (Oct.–Dec. 1979):127–39.

4. The Croix de Feu was a major right-wing organization during the integration period; for right-wing movements, see Anderson, *Conservative Politics in France.* For the relationship between the ACIP and the Croix de Feu see Weinberg, pp. 105–6; Hyman, pp. 226–28; for a selection of articles that appeared then about the issue, see Rajsfus, pp. 189–268; for a list of Jewish-owned banks that financed Doriot, see Wolf, *Doriot; du communisme à la collaboration,* pp. 211–12.

5. Weinberg, pp. 101–2.

6. Ibid., chap. 7; Hyman, chap. 8.

7. Debré, *L'Honneur de vivre. Témoignage,* p. 214. "Compte rendu du Grand-

Rabbin de France sur son activité depuis juin 1940," YVA 0-9/28-3, p. 3. Wormser, "Notre organisation après la défaite de 1940."

8. *JO*, 30 August 1940.

9. For biographical data on the Jewish experts in France, see Klarsfeld, *Le Mémorial de la Déportation*, and Billig, *La Solution Finale et la Question Juive*. For Dannecker's arrival in France, see Marrus and Paxton, *Vichy et les Juifs*, pp. 19, 81–82.

10. For biographical data, see Billig, *La Solution Finale de la Question Juive*; Klarsfeld. *Le Mémorial de la Déportation*.

11. Billig, *La Solution Finale de la Question Juive*, p. 189.

12. For the freedom of operation of the RSHA in Eastern Europe, see Poliakov, *Harvest of Hate*, chaps. 6–8; Hilberg, *The Destruction of the European Jews*, chaps. 7, 8. In Western Europe, and in France in particular, the RSHA never had a free rein until early 1942. An explanation for this situation needs to be sought in the complex Wehrmacht Ministry of Foreign Affairs and RSHA power struggle, which was not resolved until 1942.

13. Among the institutions visited where archives were confiscated was the AIU; report, 6 December 1940, Department of State, Washington, D.C., to S. Edelman, American Jewish Committee, file France, 59-241155-F; among the personalities interviewed were Kadmi Cohen, Dr. Reichman and Biélinky. They were asked the whereabouts of Baron de Rothschild and Marc Jarblum, president of the FSJF; see Jakoubowicz, "Unter die Koulissn fun Deutschen Yidn Politik in Frankraikh," p. 12; see also Dannecker, "La Question Juive et son traitement, 1 July 1941," in *La Persécution des Juifs*, p. 84; cf. p. 91. Biélinky, diary, 1940, 17 August 1940, September 1940, p. 10; Jakoubowicz, *Rue Amelot*, p. 24.

14. Biélinky, diary, September 1940, p. 10.

15. Trunk, *Judenrat*, p. 2.

16. Marrus and Paxton, p. 19. For reference to Abetz's special instructions from the Führer, see Best, note, 30 August 1940, CDJC, LXXV-72, XXIV-5.

17. Biélinky, diary, 1940–41, 15 September 1940; Jakoubowicz, *Rue Amelot*, p. 25.

18. According to one source, Gestapo representatives had called at the Prefecture of Police on 15 June 1940, see Bourdrel, *Histoire des Juifs de France*, p. 343. The Jewish section at the Prefecture of Police was established in November 1940; Dannecker, "La Question Juive en France," in *La Persécution des Juifs*, p. 104. CDJC, LXXV-72.

19. Dannecker, "La Question Juive en France," p. 98.

20. For a discussion of this question, and more particularly the application of the policy of prodding Vichy into becoming committed to such a course of action, see Marrus and Paxton, pp. 82–83.

21. Jakoubowicz, "Unter die Koulissn fun Deutschen Yidn Politik in Frankraikh," Part II; Biélinky, diary, 1940–41, p. 12.

22. Jakoubowicz, "Unter die Koulissn fun Deutschen Yidn Politik in Frankraikh," Part II.

23. *VOBIF*, 30 September 1940.

24. Note, October 1940, not signed, no source, in German, Z. Szajkowski; Jakoubowicz, *Rue Amelot*, pp. 24–26; CDJC, CCXVII-4(90-97).

25. Jakoubowicz, *Rue Amelot*, p. 27.

26. Ibid. "Note concernant les rapports entre l'ACIP et les autorités alle-

mandes" appears to have been drafted in April or May 1941; YIVO, Amelot, 1–3, 013–016. Biélinky, diary, 1940–41, p. 14.

27. YIVO, France, Second World War, Generalities (hereafter France, II WW, Generalities), 3–33, 01–02. "Note concernant les rapports entre l'ACIP et les autorités allemandes," YIVO, Amelot, 1–3, 014.

28. ACIP, 30 November 1940, YIVO, Amelot, 1–3, 011.

29. Jakoubowicz, *Rue Amelot,* p. 27; Jakoubowicz, "Unter die Koulissn fun Deutschen Yidn Politik in Frankraikh," Part III; Biélinky, diary, 1940–41, p. 14.

30. Jakoubowicz, "Unter die Koulissn fun Deutschen Yidn Politik in Frankraikh," part III.

31. Biélinky, diary, 1940–41, p. 14.

32. "Note concernant les rapports entre l'ACIP et les autorités allemandes," YIVO, Amelot, 1–3, 014.

33. Ibid.

34. Jakoubowicz, *Rue Amelot,* p. 24.

35. Amelot Committee to Dr. Minkowski, 18 September 1940, YIVO, Amelot, 1–7, 039. "Plans were drawn up to centralize even further our activities," Jakoubowicz, *Rue Amelot,* p. 31.

36. Jakoubowicz, *Rue Amelot,* pp. 26–27.

37. Ibid., p. 30. "Note concernant les rapports entre l'ACIP et les autorités allemandes," YIVO, Amelot, 1–3, 014.

38. Le Comité de Bienfaisance à la Colonie Scolaire, 20 January 1941, YIVO, Amelot, 1–2, 0016; Jakoubowicz, *Rue Amelot,* p. 28.

39. Jakoubowicz, *Rue Amelot,* p. 31; Relation entre les Juifs et les autorités allemandes, diary, author unknown, YIVO, France, II WW, Generalities, 3–41, 001; Le Comité de Coordination, 30 January 1941, YIVO, Amelot, 1–8, 005.

40. Jakoubowicz, *Rue Amelot,* pp. 30–31; Procès verbal de la séance du Comité de Coordination, 4 February 1941, YIVO, Amelot, 1–8, 06–07.

41. Zeitschel, 21 January 1941, CDJC, V-59; Zeitschel to Dr. Thomas, 14 February 1941, CDJC, V-60.

42. Jakoubowicz, *Rue Amelot,* p. 32; author unknown, March 1941, YIVO, France, II WW, Generalities, 3–41; 04; Biélinky, Diary, 1940–41, p. 16; for the text of the form prepared by Dannecker, see YIVO, UGIF, 1–1.

43. For the choice of personalities to lead the Central Jewish Office, and the difficulties encountered in its establishment, and which was subsequently named the CGQJ, see CDJC, V-65. By 20 March 1941, Dannecker was still expressing concern at the delays in its establishment; see note from Nostiz, CDJC, V-83.

44. "Note concernant les rapports entre l'ACIP et les autorités allemandes," YIVO, Amelot, 1–3, 014.

45. Coordination Committee, cash book, entry, 18 March 1941, YVA, 0-9/34(7). According to Maurice Rajsfus, they would have been sent to Paris on Eichmann's orders. Biberstein brought along with him his father and a few employees from the Vienna *Judenrat.* No surviving members of the Coordination Committee, nor of the UGIF, were able to confirm that some Viennese *Judenrat* employees had also arrived, besides immediate family. Rajsfus, *Des Juifs dans la collaboration,* p. 266, Israelowicz brought to Paris his mother, and in September 1941 he married a woman from Vienna. The wedding took place at the ACIP main synagogue, rue de la Victoire. Chief-Rabbi Julien Weill was the officiating minister. *Informations Juives* (19 September 1941), CDJC, YIVO

46. I. Israelowicz, "Paroles explicatives," synagogue rue Pavée, 3 May 1941, *Informations Juives* 8 (6 June 1941).

47. Comité de Coordination, séance du 27 Mars 1941, YIVO, Amelot, 1–8, 019; Jakoubowicz, *Rue Amelot*, pp. 33–34.

48. Ibid., p. 34; Comité de Coordination, séance du 27 Mars 1941, YIVO, Amelot, 1–8, 1–19; for the declaration adopted, see YIVO, Amelot, 1–8, 1–20.

49. YVA, 0-9/25. Jakoubowicz, *Rue Amelot*, p. 34.

50. Projet d'un status, CDJC, CCXVII-4; Bericht uber die Besprechung vom 1 April 1941, Sachs and Dannecker, YIVO, UGIF, 1–7; Statutes, draft, YIVO, Amelot, 1–8, 024–025.

51. "Propositions en vue de la création d'un journal pour la communauté israélite de Paris," YIVO, UGIF, X, I, 001–003.

52. "Note sur le projet d'un journal pour la communauté de Paris," 26 Mars 1941, YIVO, UGIF, X, I, 04–05.

53. Sachs to Dannecker, 27 March 1941, YIVO, UGIF, 1–7.

54. Bericht über die Besprechung, Sachs and Dannecker, 28 March 1941, YIVO, UGIF, 1–7.

55. Jakoubowicz, *Rue Amelot*, pp. 34–35; Biélinky, diary, 1940–41, 18 April 1941.

56. YVA, Jarblum Collection, 7/14. Jakoubowicz, *Rue Amelot*, p. 35; ACIP, YIVO, UGIF, X, I, 0015; *Informations Juives*.

57. Jakoubowicz, *Rue Amelot*, p. 35.

58. Ibid., p. 51.

59. Comité de Cordination to Comité de Bienfaisance, 7 April 1941, CDJC, CCXVII-4.

60. Comité de Coordination, 27 April 1941, JTS, box 13, file Vichy.

61. Comité de Coordination, membres payant et non-payant, Mai–Juin 1941, YIVO, UGIF, 1–29, 03–04; YVA, 09/11–3. For Dannecker's declaration, which was to be signed by D. Rapoport, see Jakoubowicz, *Rue Amelot*, p. 36.

62. No copies of the leaflets have remained. According to surviving Communist activists, at least two were printed in thousands of copies, Y. Korman, interview, Paris, 15 March 1978; G. Tachnoff, interview, Paris, 2 July 1978; Henri Bulawko, interview, Paris, 10 July 1978; B. Ezerowicz, interview, Melbourne, 15 November 1977.

63. Jakoubowicz, *Rue Amelot*, p. 37. Jakoubowicz to Sachs, 12 May 1941, YIVO, UGIF, 1–8, 039.

64. 23 April 1941, CDJC, CCXVII-4.

65. Biélinky, diary, 1940–41, p. 19.

66. "Note concernant les rapports entre l'ACIP et les autorités allemandes," YIVO, Amelot, 1–3, 015.

67. Biélinky, diary, 1940–41, p. 24.

68. David Szlamowicz, interview, Melbourne, 15 March 1981.

69. Elie Krouker, curriculum vitae, YIVO, UGIF, 1–19; Biélinky, diary, 1940–41, p. 19.

70. See Knochen (initialed by Dannecker) to MBF, 28 January 1941, in which it is already envisaged using the Vichy law of 4 October 1940, for the internment of foreign Jews; CDJC, V-64; Report, MBF, 7 March 1941, anticipating the internment of 100,000 to 120,000 foreign Jews, CDJC, LXXIXa-14; Ingram to CGQJ, 6 June 1941, CDJC, CXI-1.

71. Biélinky, diary, 1940–41, p. 20; Krouker to Dannecker, 13 June 1941,

YIVO, UGIF, 1–9, 005; Weill was arrested on 6 June 1941; Jakoubowicz, p. 39; CDJC, CDXXX-41, p. 6.

72. Jakoubowicz, *Rue Amelot*, pp. 32–33; Biélinky, diary, 1940–41, p. 18.

73. Jakoubowicz, *Rue Amelot*, p. 40.

74. Ibid., pp. 40–41; Biélinky, diary, 1940–41, p. 22.

75. Jakoubowicz, *Rue Amelot*, pp. 40–41.

76. Undated, unsigned, CDJC, CCXVII-4(124).

77. Biélinky, diary, 1940–41, pp. 22–23.

78. Jakoubowicz, *Rue Amelot*, pp. 41–42. General opposition within the committee is but one aspect of the question, for it leaves open the question of Dannecker's own views on the issue. I have found no source that permits me to ellucidate the problem.

79. Le secrétaire-général du Comité de Coordination à Mr. l'Obersturmfuhrer Dannecker, 30 June 1941, YIVO, UGIF, 1–9, 06–07.

80. *Informations Juives,* 4 July 1941; Ezerowicz, interview.

81. Grant, *Paris a Schtot fun Front,* p. 75.

82. "Note concernant les rapports entre l'ACIP et les autorités allemandes," YIVO, Amelot, 1–3, 016. Jakoubowicz, *Rue Amelot,* pp. 33, 42.

83. Procès verbal de la séance du bureau du Comité de Coordination, 18 August 1941, YIVO, UGIF, 1–9, 019–020.

84. Déclaration du Consistoire Central addressée à Xavier Vallat, 21 April 1941, CDJC, XXXI-41. X. Vallat to Helbronner, President of the Central Consistory, CDJC, CCXIII-3.

85. Grant, p. 75.

86. CGQJ au Comité de Coordination, 10 July 1941, YIVO, UGIF, XLIV-1, 04. Secrétariat d'Etat au Travail au Comité de Coordination, 18 July 1941, YIVO, UGIF, XLIV-1, 06. *Informations Juives,* 29 August 1941.

87. Actually this was the situation in the Vichy Zone rather than in the Occupied Zone. Bloch's informant must have alluded to it, for no such labor camps existed in the Occupied Zone. "Rapport concernant le placement agricole," Georges Bloch, 29 July 1941, YIVO, UGIF, XLIV-2.

88. Procès-verbal de la séance du bureau du Comité de Coordination, 18 August 1941, YIVO, UGIF, 1–9, 019.

89. Note du Comité de Coordination à Dannecker, n.d., YIVO, UGIF, 1–9, 010.

90. Georges Bloch, "Les Juifs et l'agriculture," YIVO, UGIF, XLIV-1, 02–03; see also the appeal published in *Informations Juives,* 29 August 1941.

91. MBF, report, 25 September 1941, CDJC, LXXV-98.

92. "Appel à tous les Juifs," Comité de Coordination, August 1941, YIVO, Amelot, 1–8, 069.

93. "Rapport sur l'activité du Comité de Coordination," August–September 1941, YIVO, UGIF, 1–9, 023–027. Edinger, note, n.d., YIVO, UGIF, 1–22, 31.

94. "Situation de la caisse," Edinger, notes manuscriptes, n.d., YIVO, UGIF, 1–22.

95. Dépenses pour le mois d'Août 1941: 243,651 francs, YIVO, Amelot, 1–15, 081, September: 240,647 francs, YIVO, Amelot, 1–15, 087.

96. Tachnoff, interview; Jacques Adler, recollections.

97. "Note sur les manifestations des femmes des internés civils, 20–31 Juillet 1941," YIVO, UGIF, 1–13.

98. Note, 8 August 1941, YIVO, UGIF, 1–9, 08; Baur to Ditte (CGQJ), 7 August 1941, YIVO, UGIF, CVIII-1.

99. A collection of such letters is to be found at YIVO, UGIF, 1–20. A typical letter received by the Coordination Committee reads: "If you want money for your organization, and your welfare activities, ask Mr. X who has been interned at Pithiviers for four months and who has never received any aid." YIVO, Amelot, 1–8, 069.

100. "Note d'acceptance conditionnelle de l'ACIP," 4 August 1941, YIVO, UGIF, 1–9, 013. ACIP to Coordination Committee, 8 August 1941, YVA, 0-9/25.

101. Le Comité de Coordination à l'ACIP, 16 September 1941, YIVO, UGIF, 1–8, 040.

102. Acceptances sent to the ACIP, YVA, 0-9/25.

103. Listes d'associations affiliées, YVA, 0-9/11-3.

104. *Informations Juives,* 1 May 1941.

105. For membership figures, see YIVO, UGIF, 1–29, 03–04; YVA, 0-9/11-3.

106. "Personnel du Comité de Coordination," 9 October 1941, YVA, 0-9/11-3.

107. Folder I on personnel includes also biographical information, YIVO, UGIF, 1–16.

108. Comité de Coordination to Vybert, Prefecture of Police, 26 August 1941, YIVO, UGIF, 1–10, 07.

109. Coordination Committee to Mr. Benaroya, 26 August 1941, YIVO, UGIF, 1–8, 026.

110. Vallat to Blanke, Military Administration, MBF, 24 September 1941, CDJC, LXXVI-16.

111. Confirmation of Dannecker's order, 10 October 1941, YIVO, UGIF, 1–9, 015; Coordination Committee's appeal to an ACIP local branch, Lilas, to seek volunteers, 13 October 1941, YIVO, UGIF, 1–8, 021.

112. Marrus and Paxton, pp. 333–39.

Chapter 5. The Establishment of the Union Général des Israélites de France: September 1941 to January 1942

1. For a discussion of the crisis generated within French Judaism by the Dreyfus Affair, see Marrus, *Les Juifs de France à l'époque de l'Affaire Dreyfus;* Rabi, *Anatomie du Judaisme français,* pp. 72–77.

2. Best to Vallat, 29 August 1941, CDJC, LXXVI-16.

3. Report, Administrative General Staff, on a conference attended by Dannecker, from the SD; Zeitschel from the embassy; Blanke, on behalf of the military administration, Paris, 10 June 1941, CDJC, LXXVI-16.

4. Best to Vallat, Paris, 29 August 1941, CDJC, LXXVI-16.

5. Vallat to Best, Vichy, 6 September 1941, CDJC, LXXVI-16.

6. "In the attitude of the Government [French] there is no antisemitism but simply the application of State policy." Vallat to Rabbi J. Kaplan, 5 August 1941, YVA, 09/6-1. "Germany was never at the origin of the anti-Jewish legislation of Vichy. This legislation was . . . spontaneous and indigenous." Vallat, *Le Nez de Cléopâtre,* p. 238.

7. Consistoire Central à Vallat, 21 April 1941, CDJC, XXXI-41; CGQJ au Consistoire Central, 29 April 1941, CDJC, XXXI-42.

8. Note, René Mayer à Vallat, "HICEM," 17 November 1941, in Raymond

Raoul Lambert, "Compte rendu de mes voyages à Vichy" (20 Septembre 1941–9 Janvier 1942): YIVO, UGIF, II, 1 (hereafter RRL, "Voyages à Vichy").

9. Marrus and Paxton, *Vichy et les Juifs,* pp. 86–87.

10. Réunion du 11 Mars 1942, pour l'audition de Mr. X venu de Paris," document made available for consultation by Zosa Szajkowski, New York, 1978. Also reprinted in part in Szajkowski, *Analytical Franco-Jewish Gazetter,* p. 49, n. 211a, p. 57, n. 250. According to Richard Cohen, Institute of Contemporary Jewry, Hebrew University, Jerusalem, Mr. X. was Marcel Stora.

11. Letter of protest from the Central Consistory to Maréchal Pétain, 1 July 1941, CDJC, LXXII-2; CGQJ to Central Consistory, 29 April 1941, CDJC, XXXI-42.

12. *Contribution à l'histoire de l'UGIF,* Part II, CDJC, CCXIII-33.

13. Chief-Rabbi Liber, meeting of the Association des Rabbins Français, extrait du procès verbal de la séance du Conseil d'administration, 7 December 1941, YVA, 0-9/28-2.

14. "Note sur les rapports du Consistoire Central et la Commission Centrale des Oeuvres Juives d'Assistance," quoted in Szajkowski, *Analytical Franco-Jewish Gazetteer,* pp. 53–54, n. 229.

15. For a list of all the official letters of protest sent by the Central Consistory to Maréchal Pétain and Laval, see YIVO, France, II WW, Generalities, Documents Confidentiels, série 4, no. I; see also "Le Consistoire Central," in *L'Activité des organisations juives,* pp. 19–31.

16. Paraf, *Israel dans le Monde,* pp. 161, 187; René Mayer to R. R. Lambert, 2 December 1941, RRL, "Voyages à Vichy."

17. Weinberg, *Les Juifs à Paris,* pp. 105–9; Hyman, *From Dreyfus to Vichy,* pp. 226–27; Rajsfus, *Sois Juif et tais-toi!* chap. 5.

18. For Oualid's prewar attitudes about immigrant Jewry, see Weinberg, p. 65n; although a vice-president of the Central Consistory, Oualid worked closely with the Commission Central d'Oeuvres Juives d'Assistance (CCOJA) due to his interest in the Organisation pour la Reconstruction et le Travail (ORT). Oualid's refusal to endorse fully the French *Israélites'* nationalism stemmed from his close association with immigrant organizations and in particular his close relationship with Marc Jarblum, the president of the FSJF.

19. *Arche* 62 (October 1962): 62; Paraf, pp. 187–88; see also P. Vidal-Naquet in Marrus, *Les Juifs à l'époque de l'Affaire Dreyfus,* pp. i–xvii.

20. For a list of the participating organizations in the CCOJA and the history of the committee, see Szajkowski, *Analytical Franco-Jewish Gazetteer,* pp. 44–45.

21. "Réunion du bureau du CCOJA," Marseille, 24 October 1941, CDJC, CCXIII-73.

22. Jarblum, "Zu die Geschichte fun UGIF," pp. 13, 25.

23. MBF, 14 December 1941. The imposition of the fine was never publicly announced. The Parisian daily press only informed its readers of the executions and future deportations to labor camps. The fine was recorded in *VOBIF,* 20 December 1941.

24. Jarblum; see also Albert Lévy's statement made at the meeting of the Central Consistory's executive, 28 February 1942, document communicated by Z. Szajkowski, excerpts in Szajkowski, *Analytical Franco-Jewish Gazetteer,* pp. 131–32.

25. *Unzer Vort* 36 (6 December 1941), in *Dos Vort fun Vidershtant,* pp. 65–67.

26. Mintz, *In die yorn Fun Yiddish Umkum un Vidershtant,* p. 132.

27. *Unzer Kampf,* May 1942, Bund Archives, Atran Center, New York.

28. Access to the Central Consistory's archives would elucidate the precise date when Vallat first discussed the draft UGIF constitution with Helbronner. The *Contribution à l'histoire de l'UGIF* places Helbronner's first view of the draft in early October. The date would most likely be toward 20 September, that is, before the expiration of the German military administration's ultimatum and probably before Lambert's first meeting with Vallat. But then the *Contribution à l'histoire de l'UGIF* was prepared by the Central Consistory in order to justify its actions.

29. Vallat asserts in his memoirs that he had considered offering Helbronner the presidency of the UGIF; Vallat, p. 204.

30. "In the event that the desired legislation establishing the organization would meet with obstacles I envisage to have the necessary ordinance issued." Best to Vallat, 29 August 1941, CDJC, LXXVI-16.

31. YIVO, UGIF, IX, I, 019–020.

32. Vallat to Best, 24 September 1941; Best to Vallat, 25 September 1941, CDJC, LXXVI-16.

33. "Note concernant le projet, contre-projet de loi," 15 October 1941, CDJC, CCXIII-6.

34. For an excellent study of the man and his activities during the Occupation, see Richard Cohen's introduction and notes to Raymond Raoul Lambert, *Carnet d'un témoin; Encyclopedia Judaica,* 1972 ed., s.v. "R. R. Lambert"; *L'Activité des organisations juives,* p. 113; Rajfus, *Sois-Juif et tais-toi!* p. 308.

35. RRL, "Voyages à Vichy."

36. Ibid., p. 4; for a study of the conditions in these camps, see Weill, *Contribution à l'histoire des camps d'internement dans l'Anti-France.*

37. RRL, "Voyages à Vichy," p. 5.

38. Contre-projet de loi presenté à Vallat, 15 October 1941, CDJC, CCXIII-6; *Contribution à l'histoire de l'UGIF,* Part I.

39. Ibid.

40. Resolution adopted by the CCOJA, 22 October 1941, CDJC, CCXIII-72.

41. Lavagne headed Pétain's personal Cabinet; he was also a Maitre des Requêtes at the Conseil d'Etat. For his note to Helbronner, see JTS, box 15, file Consistoire Israélite de France.

42. For the resolution, see YVA, 09/25; for the Central Consistory's position, see *Contribution à l'histoire de l'UGIF,* Part IV.

43. RRL, "Voyages à Vichy, p. 2; R. R. Lambert, compte rendu de mon entretien avec Vallat, 7 November 1941, confidentiel, CDJC, CCXIX-15.

44. According to one source, a meeting between Pétain and the Holy See's representative in France, Archbishop Valerio Valeri, had taken place on 26 September 1941, at which meeting Valeri gave a note to Pétain pointing out, from the religious point of view, the grave problems resulting from the existing anti-Jewish legislation. This might well have been the reason for Vallat's concession on that issue; see Morley, *Vatican Diplomacy and the Jews during the Holocaust,* pp. 52–53; RRL, "Voyages à Vichy," p. 2.

45. Vallat, *Le Nez de Cléopatre,* pp. 219–68.

46. Note on the German position regarding granting approval to the proposed legislation, MBF, Paris, 28 November 1941, CDJC, LXXVII-25.

47. *Contribution à l'histoire de l'UGIF,* p. 4.

48. Maurice Lagrange was also on Pétain's staff. CDJC, CCXIII-9; Louis Noguères in *Le Véritable procès du Maréchal Pétain,* pp. 277–88, has presented

extracts of correspondence between Helbronner and Pétain's secretariat. Noguères is mistaken in the presentation of some of the correspondence, however. There were a number of draft constitutions for the UGIF. There was the German outline, handed to Vallat during September, Vallat's own which he forwarded to Helbronner, then Helbronner's amended draft, and the final draft which appeared in the *Journal Officiel.*

49. Marrus and Paxton, p. 87. According to one document Helbronner stated that until July 1941 he had met Pétain twenty-seven times, "Réunion pour l'audition de Mr. X." Weil-Curiel, *Le Temps de la Honte,* 3, pp. 169–70. Delpech, *La Persécution des Juifs, et l'Amitié Chrétienne,* p. 161.

50. Gyges, *Les Israélites dans la société française,* p. 238; Martin du Gard, *La Chronique de Vichy, 1940–1944,* p. 64.

51. RRL, "Voyages à Vichy," p. 6; *Contribution à l'histoire de l'UGIF,* Part V.

52. RRL, "Voyages à Vichy," p. 5.

53. The law appeared in the *Journal Officiel* on 2 December 1941. The final text of the law was remarkably close to Helbronner's own draft.

54. *Contribution à l'histoire de l'UGIF,* section IX–1.

55. RRL, "Voyages à Vichy," p. 10.

56. Three members of the CAR were in fact nominated by Vallat to be on the proposed board: Lambert, Kahn, and Albert Lévy. Lambert was to be the general-secretary and Lévy the national president. Yet there were seventeen organizations that could claim representation on the future board.

57. RRL, "Voyages à Vichy," p. 8.

58. CDJC, CCXIII-21.

59. *Contribution à l'histoire de l'UGIF,* Part XI-7; Consistoire Central, secrétariat permanent et les delegués du CCOJA, 7 December 1941, CDJC, CCXIII-10.

60. "Extrait du procès verbal de la séance du conseil d'administration de l'Association des Rabbins Français," 7 December 1941, YVA, 0-9/28-2.

61. RRL, "Voyages à Vichy," doc. no. 7, p. 30.

62. Ibid.

63. Ibid., p. 10; *Contribution à l'histoire de l'UGIF,* Part XIII.

64. For a biography of Robert Gamzon, see Pougatch, *Un Bâtisseur, Robert Gamzon, dit "Castor soucieux";* RRL, "Voyages à Vichy," p. 10.

65. R. R. Lambert à Oualid, 13 December 1941, in RRL, "Voyages à Vichy," doc. no. 8, p. 32.

66. Ibid., doc. no. 9, p. 35; *Contribution à l'histoire de l'UGIF,* Part XIV.

67. Olmer, Oualid, Jarblum, Lévy, Gamzon, Millner, Mayer, and Lambert. RRL, "Voyages à Vichy," p. 11; *Contribution à l'histoire de l'UGIF,* Part X.

68. RRL, "Voyages à Vichy," doc. no. 11; *Contribution à l'histoire de l'UGIF,* Part XVI, p. 10.

69. Note sur l'entretien de Joseph Millner et R. R. Lambert avec Vallat, 30 December 1941, in RRL, "Voyages à Vichy," doc. no. 12; telegraphic confirmation of acceptance, 2 January 1942, doc. no. 13.

70. In fact, Vallat was never short of personalities on whom he could call. The final list of board members reveals names of individuals who had never been previously mentioned. The final meeting of the eight nominated candidates took place on 4 January 1942. Millner, Lévy, and Lambert had already wired Vallat their acceptance, and Gamzon was ready to send his. Jarblum was definitely opposed. Oualid hesitated, and Olmer was still seeking another meeting with Vallat to

elucidate various points. Mayer had nominated someone else in his stead. RRL, "Voyages à Vichy," doc. no. 140.

71. *Contribution à l'histoire de l'UGIF,* Part XIX.

72. *JO,* 9 January 1942.

73. Verbatim report of a meeting held between the UGIF leadership and Amelot representatives which was also attended by Dr. Eugène Minkowski from the OSE, 29 January 1942, YVA, Jarblum, 7/8.

74. *L'Activité des organisations juives,* p. 204.

75. CDJC, CDXXX-41, Part II, chap. 2, p. 6.

76. The two Austrian Jews brought to Paris by Dannecker, I. Israelowicz, and W. Biberstein. CDJC CCXIII-48.

77. X. Vallat, trial, CDJC, LXXIV-7, p. 11.

78. "Compte rendu de la séance de travail du conseil d'administration de l'UGIF," 11 January 1942, Paris," YIVO, UGIF, IV, 4, 01.

Chapter 6. The UGIF and Its Functions: January 1942 to December 1942

1. For Heydrich's order concerning the establishment of *Judenräte* in the occupied territories, see Trunk, *Judenrat,* pp. 2–4.

2. Of all the measures taken during December 1941, the execution of 53 Jews was the only measure over which communal disagreements as to the significance of their execution were manifested. According to S. Klarsfeld, 42 of the men had former association with Jewish left-wing organizations, see *Le Livre des otages,* pp. 36–44. The majority of these men were already interned at Drancy when the Germans made the decision to execute hostages, the others were taken from various jails in Paris. The list of Jewish hostages would have been compiled by Inspecteur Eugène Sadoski, Service des Renseignements Généraux, French Police; see *La Persécution raciale,* pp. 242–43.

3. Lucienne Scheid-Haas, interview in Rajsfus, *Des Juifs dans la collaboration,* pp. 345–48.

4. *JO,* 2 December 1941, Article 2.

5. Edinger à Lévy-Risser, 16 February 1942, YIVO, UGIF, XXXI-26, 05–07.

6. Edinger à Julien Lévy, n.d. (probably March 1942), YIVO, UGIF, XXXI-26, 017.

7. Ordinance, MBF, 17 December 1941, CDJC, XXVIIIa-11.

8. Dr. Michel to Ministry of Finances, 15 December 1941, Paris, CDJC, XXVIIIa-10.

9. "Note sur l'amende du milliard," CDJC, LVIII-11.

10. Ministry of the National Economy to the President of the Comité d'Organisation Professionelle des Banques, 13 January 1942, YIVO, UGIF, V, I, 04–06.

11. *JO,* 16 January 1942.

12. YIVO, UGIF, V, I, 010.

13. Sale of shares and bonds belonging to Jews, Yves Bouthilliers, 10 January 1942, *JO,* 9 February 1942.

14. UGIF, board meeting, 18 January 1942, YIVO, UGIF, IV, 4, 04.

15. Baur to Dannecker, Paris, 29 January 1942, YIVO, UGIF, V, I, 023.

16. UGIF, financial commission, Paris, 29 January 1942, YIVO, UGIF, IV, 3, 010–011.

17. The final cost of the fine was 1,001,644,943 francs: 855,996,433 francs

came from the *Caisse* and 145,648,510 francs were drawn from private bank accounts. CDJC, LVIII-11.

18. "Note sur l'amende du milliard," CDJC, LVIII-11.

19. "Réunion pour l'audition de Mr. X."

20. YIVO, UGIF, IV, 3, 09; 04.

21. UGIF-Paris, board meeting, 25 January 1942, YIVO, UGIF, IV, 09.

22. UGIF-Paris, financial commission, 29 January 1942, YIVO, UGIF, IV, 3.

23. Ibid., XXXII, 33, 01.

24. Report to Dannecker, YIVO, UGIF, V, I, 023.

25. Dannecker, report, 22 February 1942, Paris, CDJC, XXVI-80.

26. Marrus and Paxton, *Vichy et les Juifs,* pp. 114–17.

27. UGIF-Paris, board meeting, 3 March 1942, YIVO, UGIF, IV, 3, 017.

28. CGQJ, financial control, report on the UGIF's financial operations, 1 March 1942, CDJC, XXVIII-16.

29. YIVO, Amelot, 1–8, 028.

30. 24 June 1941, YIVO, UGIF, 1–8, 05.

31. Order from Dannecker to the Coordination Committee to proceed with the integration of the ACIP onto its committee, YIVO, UGIF, 1–8, 011; note from the Coordination Committee to all religious institutions informing them of the order to affiliate with the ACIP, 16 August 1941, YIVO, UGIF, 1–8, 040. For a list of organizations that joined the Coordination Committee, YIVO, UGIF, 1–9, 01.

32. Coordination Committee to Vybert, Prefecture of Police, 26 August 1941, requesting the stamping of Elie Danon's identity card and a note indicating that he was not to be affected by the current arrests of foreign Jews, YIVO, UGIF, 1–10, 07.

33. 9 October 1941, YIVO, UGIF, 1–16.

34. "Réunion pour l'audition de Mr. X."

35. I May 1942, CDJC, CDXIX-10. For a presentation of the UGIF's administrative structure, see Szajkowski, "Glimpses on the History of Jews in Occupied France," pp. 133–49.

36. Katz to all UGIF services, Paris, 18 November 1942 (document in Z. Szajkowski's possession).

37. Note from Baur, 22 January 1942, inviting the Amelot Committee to a meeting, YIVO, UGIF, IV, 9, 06; verbatim report of the meeting which took place on 28 January 1942, YVA, P.7/8.

38. An average of 2,800 parcels were transported by the French Red Cross. *Bulletin de l'UGIF,* 30 January 1942. This situation arose from Dannecker's order to the French administration that the Coordination Committee was the only Jewish organization officially accredited.

39. For a history of Compiègne, see Rutkowski, "Le Camp de Royallieu à Compiègne (1941–1944)."

40. "The camps of Antony at Drancy are occupied by 2,000 prisoners of war." in Langeron, *Paris, Juin 1940,* p. 127.

41. According to S. Klarsfeld the overwhelming majority of the Jews deported from France to the extermination camps of Eastern Europe had left via Drancy. The choice of this particular site can only be attributed to its proximity to Paris and its access to the railway lines leading to the east. See *Le Mémorial de la Déportation.*

42. According to Samy Halfon, director of the Rothschild Hospital, some 900

men, including 100 who were very sick, had been released from Drancy; *La Persécution raciale,* p. 124; cf. Chapter 3, note 35.

43. UGIF, board meeting, 24 March 1942, YIVO, UGIF, IV, 3, 027.

44. Robinson, *And the Crooked Shall Be Made Straight,* chap. 4.

45. Dannecker to MBF, 18 April 1942, CDJC, LXV-11.

46. Hilberg places their number at 2,500 to 3,000 men; *The Destruction of the European Jews,* p. 407. Other sources bring their number up to 6,000 by including the Geheime Fieldpolizei; Bourdrel, *Histoire des Juifs en France,* p. 340. S. Klarsfeld has published a number of documents establishing René Bousquet's role—as the secretary of the French Police—in the arrests of Jews; see *Vichy-Auschwitz,* vol. 1, chaps. 3–6.

47. UGIF-Paris, board meeting, 17 March 1942, YIVO, UGIF, IV, 3, 024.

48. *Bulletin de l'UGIF,* 20 March 1942.

49. Dannecker to MBF, 1 April 1942, CDJC, LXXV-196; Baur to CGQJ, 26 March 1942, YIVO, UGIF, CVIII-8, 028–029.

50. Billig, *Le Commissariat Général aux Questions Juives,* 3:179; see also CDJC, LXXV-196.

51. Baur to CGQJ, 26 March 1942, CDJC, XXVIII-23.

52. CGQJ to Baur, 31 March 1942, YIVO, UGIF, XC, 6, 013–14. Stora, report on the results of the discussions between Dannecker and the CGQJ, 31 March 1942, YIVO, UGIF, IV, 3, 30. The first deportation from France took place on 27 March 1942, and was personally escorted by Dannecker. It was the only convoy that traveled in third-class carriages. The convoy left Paris fully equipped by the UGIF. It arrived at Auschwitz on 30 March 1942. CDJC, XXVb-20. Of the 1,112 men who had left, 19 survived. For the evidence regarding the organization and composition of the convoy, see Klarsfeld, *Le Mémorial de la Déportation,* convoy no. 1.

53. There were 1,000 pairs of shoes, 1,200 blankets, 1,100 mess tins, 1,150 tin cups, 35 belly pots. YVA, 0–9/5(2).

54. UGIF-Paris, board meeting, 17 May 1942, YIVO, UGIF, XC, I, 05–06.

55. UGIF-Paris, Supply Commission, 21 May 1942, YIVO, UGIF, XC, I, 07, 011.

56. Baur to Dannecker, 2 June 1942, YIVO, UGIF, XI, 20, 04. UGIF-Paris, Supply Commission, 4 June 1942, YIVO, UGIF, XC, I, 020–021.

57. Ibid., 15 June 1942, YIVO, UGIF, XC, 3, 022.

58. Klarsfeld, *Le Mémorial de la Déportation,* chronology of deportation.

59. Ibid., notes, techniques et statistiques.

60. Reitlinger, *The Final Solution,* p. 126.

61. Dannecker to Knochen, note, 15 June 1942, in *La Persécution des Juifs,* pp. 126–27.

62. 26 June 1942, CDJC, XXVI-33; German Embassy, Paris, 27 June 1942, CDJC, XIXa-25a.

63. For a discussion of Laval's role, see Marrus, "Vichy et les enfants Juifs," pp. 6–15; see also Klarsfeld, *Vichy-Auschwitz,* 1:122–25.

64. Laval presented his demand to Knochen on 4 July 1942, and two days later Dannecker telexed to Berlin to Eichmann for instructions and recommending that children under the age of sixteen be included in the convoys to Auschwitz. Dannecker to Eichmann, CDJC, XXVI-46.

65. CGQJ to Baur, 1 July 1942, YVA, 0–9/6; CDJC, XXVIII-30.

66. Baur to CGQJ, 6 July 1942, YVA, 0–9/6.

67. CGQJ to Baur, YIVO, UGIF, CVIII, 9, 029; CGQJ to UGIF, 15 July 1942, CDJC, XXVIII-37.

68. Baur to CGQJ, 9 February 1943, YIVO, UGIF, IV, 4, 029–30; UGIF, board meeting, CDJC, vol. III, not classified.

69. Note to the CGQJ's Director of Cabinet, "List of premises available, orally communicated by Baur," 13 July 1942, CDJC, XXVIII-36.

70. 8 July 1942, CDJC, XXXVIII-36.

71. Wellers, *De Drancy à Auschwitz*, p. 46. Beaune-La-Rolande, CDJC, XXVb-102; Pithiviers, CDJC, XXVb-40.

72. Jakoubowicz, *Rue Amelot*, p. 95.

73. Dannecker, note, re meeting with Vichy representatives, 8 July 1942, CDJC, XXVb-55.

74. Berthe Libers, deposition, X. Vallat, trial, audience of 6 December 1947, CDJC, LXXIV-12, pp. 100–104. Katz to CGQJ, 16 July 1942, YIVO, UGIF, CVIII, 9, 037.

75. Lévy and Tillard, *La Grande rafle du Vel d'Hiv*.

76. CDJC, CCXIX-125; cf. Klarsfeld, *Vichy-Auschwitz*, 1:126.

77. Dannecker, note, 21 July 1942, in *La Persécution des Juifs*, pp. 197–98.

78. CDJC, XLIX-13.

79. Wellers, *De Drancy à Auschwitz*, pp. 55–58; Klarsfeld, *Le Mémorial de la Déportation*, convoy nos. 19 to 22 inclusive.

80. YIVO, UGIF, CVIII, 2, 01.

81. Note to Group II (Finances), 14 December 1942, YIVO, UGIF, XXXI, I.

82. Baur to CGQJ, YIVO, UGIF, CVIII, 2, 01–02.

83. CDJC, LVIII-8.

84. Ecole de Travail, rue des Rosiers, July 1942, YIVO, UGIF, XLVIII, I.

85. Syngalowski to R. R. Lambert, 20 April 1942, YIVO, UGIF, XCVIII, 4,021.

86. For the student population pre-July 1942, see YIVO, UGIF, L, 2, 02–04; October 1942, see socio-medical commission, 17 September 1942, YIVO, UGIF, LIX, I, 010.

87. YIVO, UGIF, LIX, 5.

88. Morley, *Vatican Diplomacy and the Jews during the Holocaust*, p. 55; Friedländer, *Pie XII et le IIIe Reich*, pp. 109–15; Marrus and Paxton, pp. 191–94.

89. For the text of the agreement, see Szajkowski, "The French Central Consistory," p. 196, n. 8.

90. Debré, *L'Honneur de vivre*, p. 229.

91. *Le Temps*, 28 November 1941.

92. For a general history of the camp and satellite establishments, see Garlinski, "The Underground Movement in Auschwitz Concentration Camp." See also Langbein, *La Résistance dans les camps de concentrations nationaux-socialistes*.

93. Baur to French Red Cross, French Red Cross to Baur, YIVO, UGIF, IV, 02–04.

94. For a discussion of the International Red Cross, see Dworzecki, "The International Red Cross and its Policy Vis-à-Vis the Jews in the Ghettos and Concentration Camps in Nazi Occupied Europe."

95. Baur to Pétain, 21 August 1942, YVA, 0–9/6–1.

96. Tableau recapitulatif des secours payés, Paris, 1 November 1942, YIVO, UGIF, XXXXII, 33, 02; 31 December 1942, YIVO, UGIF, XVI, 12, 018.

97. Klarsfeld, *Le Mémorial de la Déportation*, tableau chronologique.

98. Report on the activities of Department 14, for the year 1942, IMT, beta, 3.

99. Klarsfeld, *Le Mémorial de la Déportation*, tableau chronologique.

100. Examination of the files of those released from Drancy from August 1941 until the Liberation, in August 1944, shows that 2,399 men, women, and children were effectively freed. Of these there were 253 children, 458 women, and 1,688 men. From these 360 were rearrested and deported, 18 repatriated, 16 died subsequently, 30 were non- Jews, 17 were non-Jews interned for having helped Jews, or for having worn the Yellow Star as a mark of sympathy. Archives of the Ministère des Anciens Combattants.

101. Vichy law of 28 August 1942, *JO,* 5 September 1942.

102. UGIF, financial commission, 14 September 1942, YIVO, UGIF, XX, 1, 04–09.

103. Ibid., 05.

104. Baur to CGQJ, 18 September 1942, CDJC, CDXXIII-25.

105. CGQJ to Baur, 23 September 1942, YIVO, UGIF, CVIII, 11, 025–026.

106. Ibid., 13 November 1942, YIVO, UGIF, CVIII, 12, 03.

107. Baur to CGQJ, 21 October 1942, YIVO, UGIF, CVIII, 11, 038.

108. Ibid., 23 September 1942, YIVO, UGIF, CVIII, 15, 23.

109. General-secretariat to Department 14, 26 November 1942, YIVO, UGIF, XI, 96, 043.

Chapter 7. The UGIF in Conflict: January 1943 to August 1944

1. Klarsfeld, *Le Mémorial de la Déportation*, notes, convoy no. 45; Marrus and Paxton, *Vichy et les Juifs,* pp. 252–59. Klarsfeld holds, however, that it had been due primarily to the protests of the churches rather than to the lack of trains; see *Vichy-Auschwitz,* 1:152–56.

2. R. R. Lambert to UGIF-South, Marseille, 30 September 1942, YIVO, UGIF, XCII, 4, 024; Secrétariat général to service 14, 26 November 1942, XI, 96, 043.

3. Convoy no. 71, 13 April 1944, in Klarsfeld, *Le Mémorial de la Déportation.*

4. Chief-Rabbi Paul Hagenauer to Baur, 4 February 1942, YIVO, UGIF, XXVII, 1, 01.

5. UGIF-Paris, control commission to Edinger, 25 March 1943, YIVO, UGIF, LXXXIII-24, 058.

6. Baur to Mrs. X., 13 November 1942, YIVO, UGIF, IV, 8, 066.

7. Baur to R. R. Lambert, 23 December 1942, YIVO, UGIF, XXI-62, 195.

8. CGQJ to A. Lévy, president, UGIF, Marseille, 22 October 1942, YVA, 0–9/6–1.

9. There were 282 from a total of 815. Stora to CGQJ, 24 December 1942, YIVO, UGIF, CVIII, 1, 032.

10. CGQJ to Baur, 28 January 1943, YIVO, UGIF, IV, 4, 016.

11. UGIF-Paris, board meeting, 2 February 1943, YIVO, UGIF, IV, 4, 019–020.

12. Baur to CGQJ, 9 February 1943, YIVO, UGIF, IV, 4, 021; UGIF-Paris board meeting, 9 February 1943, YIVO, UGIF, IV, 4, 023.

13. UGIF-Paris, board meeting, 16 February 1943, YIVO, UGIF, IV, 4, 027; Klarsfeld, *Le Mémorial de la Déportation,* convoy nos. 46, 47, and 48.

14. UGIF-Paris, extraordinary board meetings, 22–23 February 1943, YIVO, UGIF, IV, 4, 027.

15. Ibid.
16. UGIF-Paris, board meeting, 26 February 1943, YIVO, UGIF, IV, 4, 037–038.
17. Ibid., 2 March 1943, YIVO, UGIF, IV, 4, 039–041.
18. UGIF-Paris, board meeting, 9 March 1943, YIVO, UGIF, IV, 4, 042.
19. Baur to R. R. Lambert, 4 March 1943, YIVO, France, II WW, Generalities, III, 14, 09.
20. UGIF-Paris, board meeting, 9 March 1943, YIVO, UGIF, IV, 4, 042.
21. "Le personnel de l'UGIF aux collègues étrangers," 10 March 1943, YIVO, UGIF, IV, 4, 045.
22. For photocopy of document, see Wellers, *De Drancy à Auschwitz*, p. 80; see also Röthke's comments about the UGIF-Paris having warned the immigrant employees; 25 April 1943, CDJC, XXVI-72.
23. UGIF-Paris, board meeting, 16 March 1943, YIVO, UGIF, IV, 4, 047–050.
24. "Réunion pour l'audition de Mr. X."
25. CGQJ to Baur, 13 January 1943, YIVO, UGIF, CVIII, 10, 03.
26. UGIF-Paris, board meeting, 26 January 1943, YIVO, UGIF, IV, 4, 011.
27. Ibid., 2 February 1943, YIVO, UGIF, IV, 4, 019.
28. UGIF-Paris, extraordinary board meetings, 22–23 February 1943, YIVO, UGIF, IV, 4, 031–033.
29. Lambert, *Carnet d'un témoin*, entry 1, February 1943.
30. YIVO, UGIF, XCII, 12, 02.
31. UGIF-South, board meeting, 15 February 1943, YIVO, UGIF, XCII, 12, 03–011.
32. Ibid., 01–06.
33. Ibid.
34. Baur to CGQJ, 3 March 1943, YIVO, UGIF, CVIII, 3, 03–05.
35. The Parisian delegation consisted of Stora, Musnik, and Weill-Hallé, UGIF-South, board meeting, 29 March 1943, YIVO, UGIF, XCII, 12, 013–023.
36. Lambert, *Carnet d'un témoin*, 21 March 1943.
37. UGIF-South, board meeting, 29 March 1943, CDJC, DXLIV-49.
38. Ibid., 13 April 1943, YIVO, UGIF, IV, 4, 062.
39. "My President—no one must know—has left Annecy for Switzerland. *Geste sans élégance* which leaves me to face heavy responsibilities." Lambert, *Carnet d'un témoin*, 3 January 1943.
40. UGIF-South, note, board meeting, 29 March 1943, CDJC, DXLIV-49.
41. UGIF-Paris, board meeting, 4 May 1943, YIVO, UGIF, IV, 4, 071.
42. Jules Jefroykin, interview no. 61(1), Oral History Division, the Institute of Contemporary Jewry, the Hebrew University of Jerusalem (hereafter deposition, Jerusalem).
43. CDJC, CDX-3.
44. UGIF-South, board meeting, 16 June 1943, YIVO, UGIF, XCII, 13, 01–06.
45. R. R. Lambert to André Lazard, 7 July 1943, YIVO, UGIF, XCII, 61, 04–05.
46. Ibid.
47. Cf. UGIF-Paris, board meeting, 2 June 1943, YIVO, UGIF, IV, 4, 0101–0103 and 0105–0106.
48. Jefroykin, deposition, Jerusalem, p. 10.

49. "L'American Joint Distribution Committee," in *L'Activité des organisations juives,* pp. 15–18.

50. Grant, *Paris a Schtot fun Front,* p. 39.

51. *Unzer Tsait,* 8 May 1942, YIVO, France, II WW, Generalities, 1–10, 072.

52. Dr. Joseph Schwartz, interview no. 19(47), 24 May 1968, deposition, Jerusalem.

53. The Joint had also considered appointing R. R. Lambert as their representative for France. Such a suggestion is indicative of the Joint's attitude to the UGIF; see Lambert, *Carnet d'un témoin,* 29 November 1942.

54. See Jefroykin, deposition, Jerusalem; Latour, *La Résistance Juive, 1940–1944,* p. 122.

55. See Schwartz, interview no. 19(47), 24 October 1967, p. 16, deposition, Jerusalem.

56. "The French Committee was borrowing US$140,000 a month until the end of 1943," Joint, 29th annual meeting, 5 December 1943, Joint Archives, New York: D. Rapoport to M.M., "1,000 dollars to be reimbursed 3 months after the end of the hostilities," Paris, 7 March 1943, YIVO, Amelot, 1–12, 043.

57. Schwartz, 24 October 1967, p. 15, deposition, Jerusalem; Latour, p. 123.

58. "Rapport sur la situation générale en France de Novembre 1942 à juin 1944," Barcelona, August 1944, YVA, 0–9/32. Although this report is unsigned it would appear to have been drawn up by J. Jefroykin who was then in Spain; see also "Rapport sur l'activité du Mouvement de Jeunesse Zioniste de France, 28 August 1944," Barcelona, Central Zionist Archives, 26–1538.

59. Lattès to Helbronner, 4 August 1943, YIVO, France, II WW, Generalities, 2–25, 013–016.

60. Darquier de Pellepoix to Baur, 23 January 1943, *Les Juifs sous l'Occupation,* pp. 173–74; YIVO, UGIF, CVIII, 15, 032.

61. CGQJ to Baur, 23 January 1943, in *Les Juifs sous l'Occupation,* pp. 173–74.

62. CGQJ to Baur, 30 April 1943, CDJC, XXVIIIc-58.

63. UGIF-Paris, board meeting, 4 May 1943, YIVO, UGIF, IV, 4, 072.

64. Report of meeting of financial commission and control commission, UGIF-Paris, 5 May 1943, YIVO, UGIF, XXIII-1.

65. UGIF-Paris, meeting of board and financial commission, 11 May 1943, YIVO, UGIF, IV, 4, 075.

66. UGIF-Paris, board meeting, 6 June 1943, YIVO, UGIF, IV, 4, 091.

67. Ibid., 15 June 1943, YIVO, UGIF, IV, 4, 097.

68. Ibid., 29 June 1943, YIVO, UGIF, IV, 4, 0108.

69. UGIF-Paris, report of the financial commission, 18 June 1943, YIVO, UGIF, XXIII-1, 028–031.

70. Ibid., 9 July 1943, YIVO, UGIF, XXIII-1, 032–034.

71. "Projet d'emprunt à la Caisse des Dépôts et Consignations," 9 July 1943, YIVO, UGIF, XXIII-1, 033; UGIF-Paris, board meeting, 6 July 1943, YIVO, UGIF, IV, 4, 118.

72. UGIF-Paris, report of the financial commission, 9 July 1943, YIVO, UGIF, XXIII-1, 033.

73. UGIF-Paris, board meeting, 13 July 1943, YIVO, UGIF, IV, 4, 0121–0123; 20 July 1943, YIVO, UGIF, IV, 4, 0125.

74. Baur to Lambert, 1 June 1943, YIVO, UGIF, IV, 11, 002; "Inform Dyka [Jefroykin] that I believe that this measure might interest potential lenders."

75. UGIF-Paris, board meeting, 20 July 1943, YIVO, UGIF, IV, 4, 125.

76. CGQJ, Paris, 30 August 1943, YIVO, UGIF, CVIII, 5, 047.

77. CGQJ, 18 August 1943, YIVO, UGIF, CVIII, 6, 011; list of private bank accounts holding over 200,000 francs each which totaled 46 million francs, YIVO, UGIF, CVIII, 6, 012.

78. UGIF-Paris, report of the financial commission, 13 December 1943, YIVO, UGIF, XXIII-1, 038–039.

79. Ibid., 7 July 1944, YIVO, UGIF, XXIII-1, 040–041.

80. UGIF-Paris, board meeting, 8 June 1943, YIVO, UGIF, IV, 4, 091–093; the question of how to make the Jews productive should be seen in the context of Germany's need for manpower for its industry as well as in relation to the Service du Travail Obligatoire which Laval had introduced in France; for the general lines of the issue, see Azéma, *De Munich à la Libération, 1938–1944,* pp. 210–13; Paxton, *Vichy France. Old Guard and New Order, 1940–1944,* pp. 368–70. For the specific problem faced by Jews throughout Occupied Europe, and in particular the policies adopted by the various *Judenräte* to the question of "labor" in relation to the possibilities it offered for survival, see Gutman, "The Concept of Labor in Judenrat Policy."

81. UGIF-Paris, board meeting, 22 June 1943, YIVO, UGIF, IV, 4, 0101–0106.

82. Ibid., 29 June 1943, YIVO, UGIF, IV, 4, 0108.

83. Hilberg, p. 392; Marrus and Paxton, pp. 303–4.

84. Present at the meeting were SS Hauptsturmführer Aloïs Brunner, SS Hauptscharführer Brückler, Baur, and Israelowicz; verbatim report of the meeting of 30 June 1943, YIVO, UGIF, IV, 4, 0111–0113.

85. UGIF-Paris, board meeting, 6 July 1943, YIVO, UGIF, IV, 4, 0116–0119.

86. Krausnick and Broszat, *Anatomy of the SS State,* pp. 165–217.

87. UGIF-Paris, board meeting, 6 July 1943, YIVO, UGIF, IV, 4, 0116–0119.

88. Ibid., 15 June 1943, YIVO, UGIF, IV, 4, 096.

89. Wellers, *De Drancy à Auschwitz,* pp. 102–8.

90. Ibid., pp. 93–98; UGIF-Paris, board meeting, 6 July 1943, YIVO, UGIF, IV, 4, 0116–0119.

91. Wellers, *De Drancy à Auschwitz,* p. 101.

92. In November 1943 an attempt to dig a tunnel to escape from Drancy was uncovered by Brunner; see Rutkowski, *La Lutte des Juifs en France à l'époque de l'occupation,* doc. 148, pp. 212–14; Wellers, *De Drancy à Auschwitz,* pp. 118–19.

93. By November 1942 the UGIF had to constitute its own police force; see YIVO, UGIF, XI, 71,04. The new police took over in July 1943; Rothschild Hospital to Baur, 9 July 1943, YIVO, UGIF, LXXII-6, 021.

94. Wellers, *De Drancy à Auschwitz,* p. 101. The chief of the Jewish police at Drancy, Oscar Reich, was a former Austrian footballer, who had been made honorary "Aryan" by the SD. He was the only Jew in France who was shot after the war for collaboration. Joint, file 32, France.

95. UGIF-Paris, board meeting, 13 July 1943, YIVO, UGIF, IV, 4, 0121. Helbronner and the chief-rabbi of France also wrote to Laval; 13 July 1943, JTS, box 13, file Vichy.

96. Helbronner and the chief-rabbi to Laval, 2 August 1943, JTS, box 13, file Vichy; secret CGQJ report to Röthke, 30 July 1943, CDJC, XXVIII-182.

97. Verbatim report of meeting at Drancy, 30 July 1943, UGIF, board meeting, in CDJC Board Meetings Register, vol. IV, nonclassified.

98. UGIF-Paris, board meeting, 10 August 1943, Board Meetings Register, CDJC, vol. IV, unclassified.

99. Edinger to Lambert, 2 August 1943, YIVO, UGIF, IV, 11, 13.

100. Edinger to Manuel, general-secretary, Central Consistory, 2 August 1943, YVA, 0–9/9(3).

101. Lambert to Edinger, 7 August 1943, YIVO, UGIF, XCII, 26, 0158.

102. Edinger to Central Consistory, 5 August 1943, YIVO, UGIF, IV, 29, 072.

103. *L'Activité des organisations juives,* p. 216; UGIF-Paris, board meeting, 6 August 1943, Board Meetings Register, CDJC, vol. IV, nonclassified.

104. Baur to Garde des Sceaux, 2 August 1943, CDJC, XXVIII-183. "It is the survival of French Judaism which is at stake." 6 August 1943, CDJC, Board Meetings Register, vol. IV, nonclassified.

105. CDJC, XXVIII-200.

106. Edinger and Stora felt it necessary to defend themselves against accusations of not having done enough to ensure Baur's release; UGIF-Paris, board meeting, 9 August 1943, YIVO, UGIF, IV, 38, 08; Kurt Schendel, "Rapport sur le service de liaison et mon activité dans ce service," 3 September 1944, CDJC, CCXXI-26. They were all deported in convoy no. 63, 17 December 1943; Klarsfeld, *Le Mémorial de la Déportation.* None returned after Liberation.

107. Duquesnel, CGQJ, CDJC, XXVIII-219.

108. Report, Röthke, 14 August 1943, CDJC, XXVII-36.

109. UGIF-Paris, board meeting, 3 September 1943, Board Meetings Register, vol. IV, nonclassified.

110. *L'Activité des organisations juives,* pp. 231–33. See also Lambert, *Carnet d'un témoin,* p. 259, n. 117.

111. Combined board meeting, 25 October 1943, Paris, CDJC, Board Meetings Register, vol. V, nonclassified; YIVO, UGIF, III, 1, 01–05.

112. CDJC, XXVII-219.

113. CDJC, XXVIII-242.

114. UGIF-Paris, report of the financial commission, 4 February 1943, YIVO, UGIF, XXIII-1, 20–22. During March 1943, the UGIF was ordered by the CGQJ to set aside a reserve of 5 million francs to meet the deficits of Jewish enterprises and expenses incurred by administrators; 5 May 1943, YIVO, UGIF, XXIII-1, 025–027.

115. Beaune-La-Rolande had been emptied in June 1942, then used once again for the children arrested in July 1942, who then were deported to Auschwitz during August 1942. Diamant, *Le Billet vert,* pp. 214–17. On 21 September 1942, 1,000 French Jews were transferred from Drancy to Pithiviers. YIVO, UGIF, XI, 78, 09.

116. Baur to CGQJ, 11 March 1943. There were 270 such people; YIVO, UGIF, CVIII, 3, 014.

117. Katz to service 14, 6 March 1943, YIVO, UGIF, XI, 6, 028; Katz to service 14, 13 May 1943; Drancy: 1,950; Beaune-La-Rolande: 675; Rothschild Hospital and Old People's Home: 450; Ecrouves: 200; Marignac: 400; Poitiers: 150; Compiègne: 300, YIVO, UGIF, XI, 6, 028.

118. Edinger to Central Consistory, 24 September 1943, YIVO, UGIF, XCII, 96, 029.

119. UGIF-Paris, board meeting, 19 April 1943, YIVO, UGIF, IV, 4, 066.

120. For the escapes, 27 April 1943, YIVO, UGIF, IV, 4, 068; release: 8 May 1943, YIVO, UGIF, IV, 4, 068; tightening of controls: YIVO, UGIF, IV, 4, 075.

121. YIVO, UGIF, XI, 77, 02 and 05.

122. Report, 31 January 1944, YIVO, UGIF, IV, 37, 012.

123. 31 January 1944, YIVO, UGIF, LXXIV, 5, 013.

124. Baur to CGQJ, 5 January 1943, YIVO, UGIF, CVIII-2, 01.

125. UGIF, service 14 to Prefecture of Police, 15 February 1943, YIVO, UGIF, XC, 7, 020.

126. YIVO, UGIF, LIII, 09–026.

127. UGIF-Paris, board meeting, 26 January 1943, Board Meetings Register, CDJC.

128. For February 1943, see board meeting, 16 February 1943, YIVO, UGIF, IV, 4, 027; for July 1943, see Charles Reine, *Sous le signe de l'étoile,* quoted in *La Persécution raciale,* p. 61.

129. IMT, CGD, alpha, 4, 77.

130. CGQJ to Percepteur des Finances, agence-comptable de l'UGIF, 15 April 1943, YIVO, UGIF, IV, 4, 065.

131. YVA, 0–9/5–1(6).

132. CDJC, LXXIV-12, pp. 100–104.

133. "Operations générales d'arrestations ordonnées à Paris par les autorités allemandes," in *La Persécution raciale,* Annexes I, p. 285.

134. Klarsfeld, *Le Mémorial de la Déportation,* tableau chronologique.

135. *La Persécution raciale,* Annexes I, p. 285.

136. Léah Raich, "La Wizo sous l'occupation," in *La Terre Retrouvée,* 5(156), ns (1 February 1945); Ariel, "Jewish Self-Defense and Resistance in France During World War II," p. 230.

137. Ariel, p. 230; Rajsfus, *Des Juifs dans la collaboration,* pp. 328–29.

138. CGQJ to Röthke, 11 May 1943, CDJC, XXVIIIb-72.

139. Latour, pp. 43–44.

140. Kurt Schendel to UGIF, 18 April 1944, CDJC, CDXXIV-7.

141. Albert Akerberg, interview, in Rajsfus, *Des Juifs dans la collaboration,* p. 338.

142. YIVO, UGIF, IV, 34, 050.

143. Frédéric Léon, interview, in Rajsfus, *Les Juifs dans la collaboration,* pp. 258–59.

144. Kurt Schendel, report, 31 August 1944, CDJC, CCXXI-27. Klarsfeld, *Le Mémorial de la Déportation,* convoy no. 77; see also Klarsfeld, *Vichy-Auschwitz,* 2:174–77.

145. Frédéric Léon deposition, May 1945, IMT, alpha 7; B. Aronson, in *Naie Presse,* 9 March 1945, quoted in Rajsfus, *Les Juifs dans la collaboration,* p. 256.

146. G. Tachnoff, interview, Paris, 2 July 1978; J. Adler, recollections.

147. CRIF, minutes, 22 October 1946, archives. I am indebted to Pierre Kaufman for permission to consult the CRIF archives.

148. Lubetzki, *La Condition des Juifs,* p. 192.

149. CRIF, minutes, 2 June 1947.

150. The organizations were the following: Association des Anciens Deportés, Association des Juifs Polonais, Eclaireurs Israélites, Unzer Shtime, Agence Télégraphique Juive, Artisans Juifs, Societé de Koulish, Presse Nouvelle, Sionistes Généraux, Unzer Weg, UJRE, Anciens de Varsovie, and the Bund; see CRIF, minutes, 17 June 1947.

Chapter 8. From Self-Help to Resistance: June 1940 to July 1942

1. Ravine, *La Résistance organisée des Juifs en France,* p. 27.
2. Jakoubowicz, *Rue Amelot,* p. 10; Biélinky, diary, Colonie Scolaire, 1940–41, 15 June 1940.
3. Jakoubowicz, *Rue Amelot,* p. 8; Biélinky, diary, 15 June 1940.
4. Jakoubowicz, *Rue Amelot,* p. 10; Léon Glaeser was one of the foremost immigrant leaders until his murder by the Milice in July 1944; see Tchoubinski, *Léon Glaeser, Der Kulturtuer un Freiheit-kampfer.*
5. Jakoubowicz, *Rue Amelot,* p. 11.
6. Korman, interview, Paris, 15 March 1978.
7. *La Presse antiraciste,* p. 15.
8. Korman, interview; David Diamant, interview, Paris, 2 June 1978.
9. On 7 November 1938, Herschel Grynspan, a young Polish Jew from Germany, shot Ernst vom Rath, third secretary at the German embassy in Paris. It was followed in Germany by the "Crystal Night" on 10–11 November 1938. Following the Armistice, Vichy handed over Grynspan to the German authorities; Schrager, interview, Paris, 2 May 1978; Weinberg, *Les Juifs à Paris,* pp. 228–31.
10. Jakoubowicz, *Rue Amelot,* pp. 10–11.
11. Ibid., p. 60; Schrager, interview.
12. Mintz, *In die yorn fun Yiddishn Umkum un Vidershtant,* p. 94.
13. Jakoubowicz, *Rue Amelot,* p. 60.
14. Ibid., p. 67; Biélinky, diary, 19 July 1940.
15. Biélinky, diary, Colonie Scolaire, 1940–41, p. 5; Grant, *Paris a Schtot fun Front,* p. 38.
16. Biélinky, diary, Amelot, 3 September 1940.
17. Weinberg, pp. 256–57.
18. Local branches had been reestablished, a technical department formed, a trade-union commission established, a youth organization formed, the Association of Artisans reactivated, a women's committee established, and a canteen and a clinic reopened; see Diamant, *Les Juifs dans la Résistance,* pp. 53–54; Grant, chap. 4.
19. Ravine, p. 28.
20. Grant, p. 52.
21. Number of meals distributed by each Amelot canteen during November 1940: Richer—7,477; Béranger—8,532; Vieille du Temple—16,802; Elzévir—5,428; YIVO, Amelot, 1–5, 037.
22. Number of meals distributed by the same canteens during December 1940: Richer—7,795; Béranger—8,832; Vieille du Temple—17,790; Elzévier—5,543; YIVO, Amelot, 1–5, 052.
23. Restaurant Populaire, Restaurant à bon marché, Fourneaux alimentaires, 120 boulevard de Belleville; YVA, 09/30–4.
24. Riba, "Yiddisher Socialistisher Farband, 'Bund,' in Frankraich."
25. Schrager is a notable example, see *Oifn rund fun tzwei tkoufes;* see also Weinberg, passim.
26. Grant, p. 149.
27. Mintz, p. 106.
28. M. Waiszbrot, interview, Paris, 2 March 1978.
29. Grant, p. 110; Marrus and Paxton, *Vichy et les Juifs,* pp. 286–90. On the

boycott of German goods, see M. Gottlieb, "Boycott, anti-Nazi," *Encyclopedia Judaïca,* 4:1280–82.

30. Hyman, *From Dreyfus to Vichy,* pp. 208–9, 214–16; Weinberg, pp. 250–54.

31. Jakoubowicz, *Rue Amelot,* pp. 63–66.

32. "Etude sur la situation des Juifs en zone occupée," n.d., n.a., YVA, 09/24, folder M20/108.

33. MBF, Ordinance nos. 1 and 2, in *Les Juifs sous l'Occupation,* pp. 18, 23–24.

34. Diamant, *Les Juifs dans la Résistance,* p. 96; Bulawko, *Les jeux de la mort,* p. 38; Bulawko, "Un anniversaire oublié: Les premiers internements Juifs à la Caserne des Tourelles."

35. Aron Beckerman, Diary, 22 October 1940, IMT, CGD file.

36. Weinberg, chap. 8.

37. Robert Endewelt, interview, Paris, 10 April 1978; Samuel Radzinski, interview, Paris, 10 March 1978.

38. Ravine, chap. 2; Korman, interview.

39. Diamant, *Les Juifs dans la Résistance,* pp. 95–96; Grant, pp. 51–52.

40. Grant, pp. 50–51; Korman, interview.

41. Grant, p. 51.

42. Jakoubowicz, *Rue Amelot,* p. 51.

43. Ibid., pp. 61–62; Waiszbrot, interview.

44. Biélinky, diary, 20 May 1941.

45. Korman, interview; Waiszbrot, interview.

46. Grant, p. 70; Korman, interview.

47. Grant, p. 75.

48. Ibid., pp. 74–75.

49. Jakoubowicz, *Rue Amelot,* pp. 51–52.

50. *Notre Parole,* édition speciale, Paris, 25 June 1941, in *La Presse anti-raciste,* pp. 29–30.

51. Jakoubowicz, "Fun 'aristocrat' tzu a konspirator," pp. 34–38.

52. The two collections of illegal publications, *La Presse anti-raciste* and *Dos Vort fun Vidershtant,* represent but a part of the material published during the whole period, but what has survived is in itself remarkable.

53. Jakoubowicz, *Rue Amelot,* p. 42.

54. The Joint was then transferring 250,000 francs monthly to Amelot; financial report, March to August 1941, YIVO, Amelot, 17, 6, 04; CDJC, LXXVII-12.

55. Diamant, *Les Juifs dans la Résistance,* p. 76.

56. Diamant, *Le Billet vert,* p. 201; H. Bulawko, interview, Paris, 10 July 1978.

57. Diamant, *Le Billet vert,* p. 43; Jacques Adler, recollections.

58. Diamant, *Le Billet vert,* pp. 84–86.

59. Bulawko, interview.

60. Most probably an officer from the old school who, it appears, was impressed by her personality; see Jakoubowicz, *Rue Amelot,* pp. 64, 78–79; Schrager, pp. 136–37.

61. German police report, CDJC, LXXV-238, pp. 3–5; YVA, 0–9/7(1); YIVO, UGIF, 1–13, 011–015.

62. Biélinky, diary, 1 August 1941; report of the Coordination Committee on the demonstration of wives of interned Jews, 20–31 July 1941, YIVO, UGIF, 1–13.

63. Albert Rozemblum, interview, Paris, 15 May 1978; Adler, recollections.

64. Ravine, p. 53; Gronowski-Brunot, *Le Dernier grand soir. Un Juif de Pologne*, p. 95; Zalcman, *Histoire véridique de Moshé*, pp. 50–52; Israel, *Heureux comme Dieu en France*, p. 77.

65. Diamant, *Le Billet vert*, p. 272; Perrault, *L'Orchestre rouge*, pp. 114–16.

66. "Solidarité," no. 4, May 1942, in *Dos Vort fun Vidershtant*, p. 91.

67. Grant, p. 38; S. Radzinski, interview.

68. *Informations Juives*, 20 August 1941, YIVO, UGIF, CXII, 26, 09.

69. Kaufman, *Unter die Deutsche occupatsie in Frankraikh*, p. 35.

70. MBF, Rapport sur la situation politique en France, September 1941, CDJC, LXXV-98; see also, Klarsfeld, *Vichy-Auschwitz*, 1:25–28.

71. During September 1941 the Amelot canteens served the following number of meals: Richer—10,124; Béranger—7,332; Vieille du Temple—11,696; Elzévir—5,316; YIVO, Amelot, 1–15, 084.

72. Bulawko, interview.

73. "Far dem nationaln kyoum fun Yiddishn folk, einheit fun alle Yidn tsum kampf kegn hitlerism," in *Dos Vort fun Vidershtant*, pp. 51–52; *Notre Parole*, numero spécial, 1 September 1941, in *La Presse antiraciste*, pp. 31–32.

74. Korman, interview.

75. Diamant, *Les Juifs dans la Résistance*, pp. 82–83. Korman, interview.

76. None of the surviving members of the committee or of the existing Solidarity leadership were able to recall whether more than one issue of *Yiddishe Shtime* ever appeared, nor was I able to locate any such issues; *Die Yiddishe Shtime* in *Dos Vort fun Vidershtant*, p. 59.

77. Korman, interview.

78. Henri Bulawko occupies a leading position in today's Zionist movement in France. Bulawko, *Les Jeux de la mort*, p. 42.

79. Diamant, *Les Juifs dans la Résistance*, pp. 96–97.

80. Korman, interview; G. Tachnoff, interview, Paris, 2 July 1978.

81. *Unzer Tsait*, n.d., YIVO, France, II WW, Generalities, 1–10, 070–075.

82. Jean-Claude Schwartz, interview, Paris, 5 April 1973; Tachnoff, interview.

83. Besserman, "Der Kampf fun die Yiddishe arbeiter in die yorn fun krieg un facism," pp. 73–84; Ravine, p. 80.

84. Diamant, *Les Juifs dans la Résistance*, p. 31; Tachnoff, S. Radzinski, interviews.

85. Besserman, p. 79; Diamant, *Les Juifs dans la Résistance*, p. 80; Schwartz, interview.

86. *Unzer Tsait*, n.d., YIVO, France, II WW, Generalities, 1–10, 073; Besserman, p. 80; Diamant, *Les Juifs dans la Résistance*, pp. 79–81.

87. Korman, Diamant, interviews.

88. *Unzer Tsait*, n.d., YIVO, France, II WW, Generalities, 1–9, 05–09; *Unzer Vort*, 6 December 1941, in *Dos Vort fun Vidershtant*, pp. 65–67.

89. *La Persécution raciale*, chap. 3, n. 35. YIVO, Amelot, 3–37, 043.

90. Diamant, *Le Billet vert*, pp. 61–65; Adler, recollections.

91. *Unzer Tsait*, n.d., YIVO, France, II WW, Generalities, 1–10, 073.

92. Robert Geismann, "Il y a 25 ans," pp. 2–3; CDJC, CXX-18.

93. *Die Yiddishe Shtime*, 29 November 1941, in *Dos Vort fun Vidershtant*, p. 59.

94. The Institut d'Etude des Questions Juives was to serve as an adjunct to the

CGQJ and assume the responsibility for anti-Jewish propaganda, but it never became the instrument Dannecker desired; see Billig, *L'Institut d'Etude des Questions Juives*. Sézille to Vallat, 31 January 1942, CDJC, XIc-661.

95. A. Krigel, without quoting her sources, has attributed the pamphlet to Georges Politzer; Krigel, "Résistants Communistes et Juifs persecutés," pp. 93–123, 97–98. J. Ravine, a former leader of the Solidarity organization in Paris maintained, however, that the pamphlet was written by Lerman (Louis Gronowski-Brunot), p. 78. Gronowski himself has set the story straight in his memoirs by explaining how Politzer came to be in possession of the manuscript; see Gronowski-Brunot, pp. 164–65.

96. Journal, author unknown, 1 May 1942, YIVO, France, II WW, Generalities, 1–10, 040.

97. Tillon, *Les F.T.P.: La guerilla en France*, p. 85n.

98. Courtois, *Le PCF dans la Guerre*, p. 221.

99. Ouzoulias, *Les Bataillons de la jeunesse*, pp. 89–91. According to another source the first group that was formed numbered nine people, of whom eight were Jews; Amouroux, *Le Peuple Reveillé*, pp. 316–17. The most authoritative study of the Communist armed groups remains Tillon.

100. "These immigrants have played an important role. Without them Communist resistance would have been different, less violent, less physically committed to direct action." Amouroux, pp. 342–43.

101. It is regrettable that Laroche died before completing his study of the contribution of the immigrants to the French Resistance. It might not have helped to answer the implied attack of such historians as Amouroux, but it would have certainly shown to those who held that Nazism had to be fought that the immigrants, and the Jews in particular, did not sit the war out. Despite limitations of the Laroche study it is still the most extensive account; Laroche, *On les nommait des étrangers*.

102. Diamant, *Les Juifs dans la Résistance*, p. 73.

103. See Steinberg, *Les Allemands en France*, chap. 10; for a discussion of German policy in France on the issue of hostages, see Klarsfeld, *Le Livre des otages*. The execution of hostages was made at the fortress of Mont Valerien. Between August 1941 and June 1944, 929 were executed, 117 of them were Jews (12.5 percent); list of hostages obtained from the Secrétariat d'Etat aux Anciens Combattants, Paris.

104. Rayski, "Les Immigrés dans la Résistance."

105. Tachnoff, Schwartz, interviews.

106. B. Borenstein, interview, Paris, 5 May 1978; J. Adler, recollections.

107. Ravine, p. 73; Schwartz, interviews.

108. "Kovet die Yiddishe Umgekomene Korbones," in *Dos Vort fun Vidershtant*, pp. 69–70.

109. Ravine, p. 73; Adler, recollections.

110. Grant, p. 108.

111. Ibid., p. 99; Schwartz, interview.

112. Besserman, p. 81; Ravine, p. 82.

113. Nathan to Central Leadership, Lyon, in Mintz, p. 131.

114. Bulawko, interview.

115. "Tsu die Yiddishe Arbeiter un Folkmassn," April 1942, in *Dos Vort fun Vidershtant*, pp. 89–90; Ravine, p. 83.

116. YIVO, France, II WW, Generalities, 1–10, 06–010. During March 1942 it issued four different appeals in Yiddish; see *Dos Vort fun Vidershtant*, pp. 81–88.

117. Ravine, p. 85; *Pithiviers Konzentrazionlager Zeitung*, no. 6(11), June 1942, in *Dos Vort fun Vidershtant*, pp. 101–4.

118. For a chronological list of escapes from Pithiviers, see Diamant, *Le Billet vert*, p. 272. Until March 1942, twenty-nine Jews had escaped from Drancy; see Rutkowski, *La Lutte des Juifs en France*, doc. no. 36, pp. 88–90.

119. Lissner, *Un Franc-tireur juif raconte*, p. 21.

120. Knout, *Contribution à l'histoire de la Résistance*, pp. 99–103; Steinberg, *Les Allemands en France*, pp. 66–67; Diamant, *Les Juifs dans la Résistance*, pp. 106–10; Gronowski-Brunot, p. 155.

121. See Weinberg, chap. 8.

122. Abraham Rayski, interview, Paris, 17 June 1978; Korman, interview.

123. Thousands of Jews fought in the ranks of the International Brigades on behalf of the Spanish Republic during the Civil War; see Diamant, *Combattants Juifs dans l'Armée républicaine espagnole*. According to one source 1,000 Jews would have joined in France; *In Kampf for Freiheit*, p. vi, French part. Until the evidence for such a figure is presented I find such a number excessive, unless the volunteers from Palestine and other countries who did not field their own units had joined in France are included.

124. *Unzer Kampf*, no. 1, May 1942, YIVO, France, II WW, Generalities, 1–1, 057–060; YIVO, France, II WW, Generalities, 1–9, 05–09.

125. R. Eloy, Front National du Travail to Dr. Gross, German Embassy, Paris, 22 April 1942, 9 May 1942, YVA, 09/4–3.

126. *Unzer Tsait*, 8 May 1942, YIVO, France, II WW, Generalities, 1–10, 070.

127. Rayski, "Paris face à la grande rafle," pp. 10–11.

128. Ibid.

129. *Unzer Tsait*, 8 May 1942, YIVO, France, II WW, Generalities, 1–10, 070.

130. Szajkowski, "The Jewish Press in France, 1940–1946."

131. See the special appeal to the Jewish population warning of imminent mass arrests, in Yiddish, June 1942, in *Dos Vort fun Vidershtant*, pp. 105–6. Though dated June, this warning effectively reached the Jewish population early in July 1942.

132. Raysky, "Paris face à la grande rafle," p. 9.

133. Steinberg has advanced much higher figures than previously accepted: 14,189, in *Les Allemands en France*, p. 219. One likely explanation might reside in his use of sources that would have included Jews arrested at a later date.

Chapter 9. The Struggle for Survival: August 1942 to August 1944

1. Besides Lévy and Tillard, *La Grande rafle du Vel d'Hiv*, which is, to date, the most exhaustive study, see also Boussinot, *Les Guichets du Louvre;* Klarsfeld, *Vichy-Auschwitz*, 1:110–28 (for the instructions given to the French police, see pp. 250–56).

2. Israel, *Heureux comme Dieu en France*, p. 125; G. Tachnoff, interview, Paris, 2 July 1978; Jacques Adler, recollections.

3. Grant, *Paris a Schtot fun Front*, p. 125; H. Bulawko interview, Paris, 10 July 1978.

4. Jakoubowicz, *Rue Amelot*, p. 94.

5. Note au Directeur du Cabinet, CGQJ, 13 July 1942, CDJC, XXVIII-36.

6. CDJC, LXXIV-11, pp. 101–2.

7. Dr. Benjamin Ginsbourg, interview, in Rajsfus, *Des Juifs dans la collaboration*, pp. 352–53.

8. Jakoubowicz, *Rue Amelot*, p. 95.

9. Ibid., p. 96.

10. Diamant, *Les Juifs dans la Résistance*, p. 135; Y. Korman, J. C. Schwartz, interviews, Paris, 15 March 1978, and 5 April 1978.

11. Diamant, *Les Juifs dans la Résistance*, p. 128. Pierre Smolinski, interview, Paris, 7 April 1978.

12. Diamant, *Les Juifs dans la Résistance*, p. 135; Korman, interview.

13. Grant, *Paris a Schtot fun Front*, chap. 9.

14. Jakoubowicz, *Rue Amelot*, pp. 95–96.

15. E. Somer, interview, Paris, 14 March 1978; Adler, recollections; Jakoubowicz, *Rue Amelot*, p. 96.

16. *Bulletin de l'UGIF* 24 (27 July 1942).

17. Smolinski, interview; Adler, recollections.

18. Diamant, *Les Juifs dans la Résistance*, p. 135. Grant, p. 137.

19. Grant, p. 137; Korman, interview.

20. Bulawko, *Les Jeux de la mort*, pp. 38–40.

21. Lévy and Tillard, pp. 77–78.

22. For a study of the Vichy concentration camp network and conditions, see Weill, *Contribution à l'histoire des camps d'internement;* for the "Compagnies de Travailleurs étrangers," see Lubetzki. *La Condition des Juifs*, pp. 209–14.

23. Kurt Schendel, report on the liaison department of the UGIF [Department 14], 4 September 1944, CDJC, CCXXI-26.

24. Bulawko, interview.

25. Diamant, *Les Juifs dans la Résistance*, pp. 139–42; Besserman, "Der Kampf fun die yiddishe arbeiter in die yorn fun krieg un fascism," p. 91.

26. Diamant, *Les Juifs dans la Résistance*, p. 130.

27. Grant, p. 145; R. Endewelt, interview, Paris, 10 August 1978.

28. Jarblum to the Central Consistory, Lyons, 18 August 1942, CDJC, CCXIV-2.

29. Klarsfeld. *Le Mémorial de la Déportation;* CDJC, XXVI-60, 61.

30. CDJC, XXVb-130.

31. Lissner, *Un Franc-tireur Juif raconte*, pp. 42–44.

32. Ibid., p. 51.

33. Ravine, *La Résistance organisée des Juifs en France*, pp. 104–10; Diamant, *Les Juifs dans la Résistance*, pp. 130–31.

34. For a full list of the locations of the illegal printing presses, see Diamant, *Les Juifs dans la Résistance*, p. 155.

35. "Appeal to the Jewish Population," *Unzer Vort* 50 (November 1942), in *Dos Vort fun Vidershtant*, pp. 143–44; CDJC, XLIX-13.

36. Grant, pp. 163–64.

37. Rayski, "Les Origines et le rôle de la presse clandestine," p. 17.

38. Diamant, *Les Juifs dans la Résistance*, pp. 98–99, dates the explosion at 22 March; Lissner, pp. 22–23, dates it at 27 April. According to R. Endewelt, April is the more likely date; interview. A German police report dates it at 25 April, CDJC, LXXV-275.

39. Diamant, *Les Juifs dans la Résistance*, p. 140; Lissner, p. 33.

40. Jakoubowicz, *Rue Amelot,* pp. 54–55.

41. Alperine, in *L'Un des Trente-six,* p. 3.

42. Bulawko, *Les Jeux de la mort,* p. 39; Jakoubowicz, *Rue Amelot,* p. 99.

43. For the code of conduct of partisans, see Diamant, *Les Juifs dans la Résistance,* p. 105. The rules by which partisans, as well as every member of the organization were to behave were the object of constant reminders, written and verbal. Instances even occurred when members' failures to observe them were considered grounds for expulsion. Adler, recollections.

44. Tachnoff, Schwartz, interviews.

45. "It is necessary to give the furriers the necesary protection in the event of their internment," 16 and 17 July 1942, CDJC, LXXV-65, 66.

46. YIVO, UGIF, IX, 3, 4, 5 series.

47. The precise number of Jews employed in these factories cannot be established, nor can we establish the number of *Ausweise* given out by the German authorities. A. Rayski held that some 3,000 men and women were working in these establishments or for them at home; see Rayski, "La Résistance en France et le soulèvement du Ghetto de Varsovie," pp. 56–62. The UGIF sources support such an estimate; YIVO, UGIF, IX, 3, 4.

48. Service de liaison, see YIVO, UGIF, XI.

49. Grant, p. 175; Dr. E. Minkowski, in *L'Un des Trente-six,* p. 46.

50. Minkowski, *L'Un des Trente-six,* p. 46.

51. List of eleven children taken from the Guy Patin Children's Home, YIVO, UGIF, LXIII, 3, folios not numbered.

52. Klarsfeld, *Le Mémorial de la Déportation,* convoy no. 48; CDJC, CCXV-28.

53. Grant, pp. 175–76; Schwartz, interview.

54. Ravine, p. 111; Trepper, *The Great Game,* p. 285 and passim; Perrault, *L'Orchestre rouge,* p. 500.

55. Lists of 249 "controlled" children in the UGIF homes, IMT, CGD, alpha, 4, 77.

56. Baur to CGQJ, 5 January 1943, YIVO, UGIF, CVIII, 2, 01.

57. Report on UGIF activities, n.d., n.a., CDJC, CDLXIX-53.

58. Jakoubowicz, *Rue Amelot,* pp. 106–7.

59. Ibid.

60. Ravine, p. 110.

61. Röthke to Prefecture of Police, 15 March 1943, CDJC, XXVI-72.

62. For a study of the Jewish response in Italy, see Katz, *Black Sabbath;* Michaelis, *Mussolini and the Jews.*

63. Poliakov and Sabille, *Jews under the Italian Occupation,* pp. 39–44.

64. Regarding the difficulties encountered by the French police in rounding up the Jews in the Italian Zone, see Hagen to Knochen, 9 January 1943, CDJC, XXVa-253, 318; Italian Military Commander to Prefect of Haute-Savoie, ordering him to stop arresting Jews, 15 March 1943, CDJC, XXVa-286.

65. *Notre Voix,* 1 June 1943, *La Presse antiraciste,* pp. 89–90; Rayski, "La Résistance en France et le soulèvement du Ghetto de Varsovie," p. 60.

66. Michel, *Histoire de la Résistance,* p. 48.

67. Rayski, "Le Comité Juif de Défense"; pp. 29–35; Ravine, p. 146.

68. *JO,* 13 December 1942.

69. Joseph Fridman, F. Schrager, interviews, Paris, 10 August 1978, and 2 May 1978.

70. Special appeal by Solidarity, "Unité-Résistance-Action!" n.d., *La Presse antiraciste,* pp. 79–80.

71. Diamant, *Les Juifs dans la Résistance,* pp. 174–75; Youdine, "Union—Die rumfule yiddishe vidershtant organizatsie"; Korman, interview.

72. Tachnoff, Schwartz, interviews.

73. "L'UJRE, son action, ses buts," *La Presse antiraciste,* pp. 155–60.

74. Diamant, *Les Juifs dans la Résistance,* p. 178. Besserman, p. 97; Rayski, "La Résistance en France et le soulèvement du ghetto de Varsovie," pp. 57–58.

75. Besserman, p. 97.

76. *La Presse antiraciste,* p. 87.

77. See *Dos Vort fun Vidershtant,* pp. 162–63.

78. *Notre Voix, La Presse antiraciste,* pp. 89–90: CDJC, CDLXXI-41.

79. Diamant, *Les Juifs dans la Résistance,* p. 180; Besserman, p. 101.

80. Schwartz, Tachnoff, interviews.

81. Minkowski, *L'Un des Trente-six,* pp. 27–35; Jakoubowicz, *Rue Amelot,* pp. 117–18.

82. YIVO, UGIF, IV, 4, 101–2.

83. CGQJ to UGIF, 18 June 1943, YIVO, UGIF, CVIII, 5, 023.

84. *L'Activité des organizations juives,* p. 195.

85. They were Louis Gronowski and Jacques Kaminski; see Gillot and Gillot, *Un couple dans la Résistance,* p. 201; Gronowski-Brunot, *Le Dernier grand soir,* p. 137.

86. Grant, p. 175; *Dos Vort fun Vidershtant,* pp. 153–56; Gillot and Gillot, p. 238.

87. Diamant, *Les Juifs dans la Résistance,* pp. 157–59; Ravine, pp. 159–67; Grant, pp. 136–37.

88. Rayski, "Gestapo contre résistants Juifs à Paris," p. 18; Diamant, *Les Juifs dans la Résistance,* pp. 163–67; Henri Krasucky is today one of the leaders of the Confédération Générale du Travail, CGT.

89. Gronowski-Brunot, pp. 136–37, 172–73.

90. Lissner, p. 59.

91. Ibid.; Adler, recollections.

92. Endewelt, Schwartz, interviews; Adler, recollections.

93. Rayski is one of the few surviving leaders of the organization who has publicly admitted the source of the UJRE destruction; see Rayski, "Les Immigrés dans la Résistance," p. 16.

94. For a view on the PCF's attitude toward the Jews, see Kriegel. Gronowski-Brunot's memoirs do, however, show that the whole question of Jewish Communists-PCF relationship is far more complex than Kriegel argues.

95. Besserman lists the following factories that employed Jews and gave out *Ausweise:* Grundel employed 700; Pilon, 350, Toutmain, 220; Avlon, 150; Franco-canadienne, 100. Besserman, p. 101. Schwartz, interview. *La Persécution raciale,* Annexes I, p. 285.

96. Somer, interview; Adler, recollections.

97. Jakoubowicz, *Rue Amelot,* pp. 126–27.

98. YIVO, Amelot, 11–87, 024.

99. The Eclaireurs Israélites de France (EIF) were officially dissolved on 5 January 1943. CGQJ to UGIF, YIVO, UGIF, XCII, 97, 023; "Rapport provisoire du mouvement de jeunesse sioniste de France," n.d., n.a., CDJC, CCXIV-117.

100. See *L'Activité des organisations juives,* p. 107; see also Schah, "L'Activité de L'ORT sous l'occupation."

101. *L'Activité des organisations juives,* pp. 158–62.

102. For a Bundist view of the question of establishing a unitary committee with the Communists, see Schrager, *Oifn rund fun tzwei tkoufes;* pp. 168–74; Fridman, interview.

103. Schrager, chap. 15; Ravine, p. 154; Rayski, "Le Comité Juif de Défense."

104. Rayski; Fridman, interview.

105. Schrager, chap. 15; Fridman, interview.

106. Schrager, Fridman, interviews.

107. Lissner, pp. 69–79; Schwartz, interview.

108. Laroche, *On les nommait des étrangers,* p. 110; see also Manouchian, *Manouchian.*

109. Manouchian, p. 111.

110. They were judged by a military tribunal in Paris on 17–18 February 1944, and executed on 21 February 1944. CDJC, CCXVI-72. For biographical data, see Rutkowski, *La Lutte des Juifs,* pp. 233–34. For the famous "Affiche Rouge" under which name the trial has entered into the history of the armed struggle in France, see Ganier-Raymond, *L'Affiche Rouge.*

111. Lissner, p. 120.

112. Diamant, *Les Juifs dans la Résistance,* p. 274; Schwartz, Endewelt, interviews.

113. Had they been sacrificed by the PCF because they were foreigners, and therefore expendable? Had their sacrifice been due to xenophobic currents from which, irrespective of PCF policy on the Jewish question, some of its military leaders may not have been immune? Claude Lévy, basing his writing upon his experience in Toulouse, maintains that they had been sacrificed precisely because they were foreigners; see Lévy, *Les Parias de la Résistance.* A 1985 television documentary, *Les Terroristes à la retraite,* shown on Anterre 2, sought, through interviews of surviving members of these units, to elucidate the question and concluded that xenophobism was the issue. A wide-ranging debate among historians has finally settled the question, concluding that although there was the betrayal of one of the leaders of these units, the real issue was the policy of the PCF. A false political strategy which had posited relentless partisan warfare in the capital in order to gain political standing in the French Resistance had led to a false appreciation of the military nature of partisan warfare. See Manouchian, p. 117; Rayski's interview, in *L'Histoire* 81 (September 1985): 98.

114. Ravine, p. 213; Adler, recollections.

115. Diamant, *Les Juifs dans la Résistance,* p. 284, states that there were nine groups operating; Ravine, refers to twelve youth committees; according to Schwartz, and Adler, recollections, there were fifteen groups.

116. Tachnoff, interview; B. Borenstein, interview, Paris, 5 May 1978.

117. Besserman, pp. 104–8; Somer, interview.

118. In *La Presse antiraciste,* p. 136.

119. *Droit et Liberté,* no. 3, March 1944, CDJC, XXII-3; *La Persécution raciale,* Annexes I.

120. *La Presse antiraciste,* pp. 136ff.

121. "Le Comité d'unité de Paris," procès-verbaux, 11 October 1944, IMT, CGD, alpha, 1, 52.

122. "Rapport sur l'activité du Comité Général de Défense," 18 October 1944, IMT, CGD, alpha, 2, 56; Budgets, IMT, alpha, 16.

123. Gaston, Gruner, report, 11 October 1944, IMT, CGD, alpha, 1, 52, p. 2.

124. "Procès-verbal des discussions de la commission Meiss-Greenberg-Adamovitch, Geissmann," JTS, box 15, file Consistoire Israélite, pp. 88–90.

125. Gronowski-Brunot, p. 187; *Notre Voix,* March 1944, *La Presse antiraciste,* pp. 139–42.

126. Schwartz, Endewelt, interviews.

127. Rapport 506, Armée Juive, Paris, 25 June 1944, Betty Knout to Armée Juive, CDJC, CDLXIX-49; Smolinski, interview, Adler, recollections; Jefroykin, "L'Organisation Juive de Combat."

128. J. Tancerman, interview, Paris, 12 July 1978; Schwartz, interview.

129. "La Libération de Drancy," n.d., n.a., CDJC, CCXVII-26; Lazarus, *Juifs au Combat,* pp. 147ff.

Conclusion: Strategies for Survival

1. CGQJ, note, five lists of individuals, numbering fifty people, dispensed by special Vichy decrees, CDJC, XVIIa-42(206).

2. Georges Wormser, "Allocution."

3. Diamant, *Les Juifs dans la Résistance,* p. 133.

4. Vilner, "An Oifshtant in Birkenau."

5. Ibid.; S. Radzinski, interview, Paris, 10 March 1978.

6. *Yiddishe Kultur,* 4 April 1962; Diamant, *Les Juifs dans la Résistance,* p. 220; Suhl, *They Fought Back,* pp. 189–95.

7. Rayski, "La Fondation du Comité Représentatif des Juifs de France," pp. 32–37; *Conseil Représentatif des Juifs de France.*

8. Hertz, "Historique du CRIF," pp. 58–62.

9. IMT, file CRIF, alpha, 15.

10. Rayski, "La Fondation du Comité Répresentatif des Juifs de France"; J. Fridman, interview, Paris, 10 August 1978.

11. "Far an emesdike representatie fun die ydn in Frankraikh," Paris, 1943, in *Dos Vort fun Vidershtant,* pp. 211–15.

12. Schrager, interview, Paris, 2 May 1978; Fridman, interview.

13. Rayski, "La Fondation du Comité Répresentatif des Juifs de France."

14. IMT, file CRIF, contains three versions of the proposed charter.

15. IMT, file CRIF; Schrager, Fridman, interviews.

16. IMT, file CRIF.

17. Diamant, *Les Juifs dans la Résistance,* pp. 166ff; Ravine, *La Résistance Organisée des Juifs en France,* p. 137.

18. Abbé Glasberg in *Eglises et Chrétiens dans la II Guerre Mondiale,* p. 203.

19. "Les Juifs dans la guerre contre le fascisme," in *La Presse antiraciste,* pp. 125–28.

20. "Gringoire," 5 June 1942, quoted in Knout, *Contribution à l'histoire de la Résistance,* p. 82; see also pp. 82–90.

21. Steinberg, *La Révolte des Justes,* pp. 144–45.

22. Marc Bloch, the famed historian of medieval France, who had been permitted by Vichy to continue teaching, and was subsequently killed for his participation in the French Resistance, represents a significant example of such Jews: see

his concluding testament in *L'Etrange défaite,* in which he articulated, without ambiguities, his relationship to Judaism; see also Bernard, *Le Camp de la mort lente,* for other such examples.

23. Diamant, *Les Juifs dans la Résistance,* p. 19.

24. Poliakov, "Les Différentes Formes de la Résistance Juive en France."

25. Ariel, "Jewish Self-Defense and Resistance in France During World War II," p. 247; on the issue of whether the Jewish Communist organizations were an integral part of the Jewish resistance, see Rayski, "Diversité et unité de la Résistance Juive."

Bibliography

Archival Sources

United States of America

American Jewish Committee (New York).
 France: antisemitism: 1936–58; file France: AIU. Collection of oral depositions.
American Jewish Joint Distribution Committee (Joint) (New York).
 French Collection: nonclassified.
  Budget: 1940–45.
  Correspondence: 1940–45.
  Saly Mayer Files: France: 32, 1941–43.
Atran Center (New York).
 Bund Archives: France: nonclassified; collection of Bundist illegal publications.
Jewish Theological Seminary of America (New York).
 France: Consistoire Israélite, box: 13–14–15.
Leo Baeck Institute (New York).
 Konzentrazionslagers, Frankreich, 1940–44, AR 1584, 3987.
 West European Collection, II, IX.
YIVO Institute for Jewish Research (New York).
 Amelot Collection:
  2. Correspondence with Coordination Committee.
  3. Coordination Committee's relations with SD.
  5. Report of activities, 1940.
  6. Report of activities, 1940–41.
  7. Y. Jakoubowicz: personal files, June 1940–February 1941.
  8. Y. Jakoubowicz: personal files, Coordination Committee, 1941.
  10. Amelot: reports of activities, 1940–44.
  16. Reports of activities, financial reports.
  22–27, 32, 33. Camps, Occupied France, 1940–43.
  30. Letters from internees.
  38. List of names of senders of letters from camps in Eastern Europe.
  46. Lists of names of internees to whom food parcels were sent.
  57–58. Index cards of applicants for assistance, 1941–43.
  99–1 to 99–16. Index cards of 4,164 applicants for assistance, 1941–42.
  100. Index cards of applicants for help, 1939–41.

101. Secret index cards of available foster parents, 1942–43.
102. Index cards of children sent to foster parents, 1942–43.
116. General reports, canteens, 1940–42.

Biélinky Collection: Diaries, 1940–41, 1941, 1942.

Geographical Collection: France 1940–44.
Illegal publications, 1–1; 1–9; 1–10.
Jewish police, 3–31.

HIAS-HICEM, Série II, France II.
General correspondence with UGIF: boxes 29, 65–74.
Administration and finance, financial reports: box 257.

D. Moshowitch Collection: 21434, H. Sindler, report.

UGIF Collection:
Coordination Committee of the Relief Organizations in Paris: I-1 to I-34.
Setting up of UGIF: II-1 to II-2.
General material from UGIF, both zones: III, III-2 to IV-38.
The milliard francs fine: V-1.
Census: VI-2.
Department XIV, liaison with the SD: XI, XIV.
Liaison with the Prefecture of Police: XVI.
Control commissions: XVII.
Finance commission: XXXIII.
Treasury: XX.
Personnel: XXI.
Isolated children: XXXVII.
Youth welfare: XL.
Youth work: XLII.
Youth control: XLV.
Homes for girls: XLIX, XVII.
Schools, ORT: XLVIII.
ORT: L.
Guardianship: LI.
Schools: LII, LIV, LVIII.
Homes for children: LVIII, LXII, LXVII, LXIX, LXXI.
Camps: CXI.
Correspondence with the CGQJ and Vichy government: CVIII.

France

Centre de Documentation Juive Contemporaine (Paris)
Censuses: XI; XX; XXV; XXVIII; XXXV; LXI; LXXII; LXXV; LXXIX; CII; CV; CXI; CXIV; CXV; CXIX; CCIII; CCXIII; CCXIV; CCXVI; CCXX; CCXXVI; CCXL; CDXI; CDXIV; CDXXIII; DX; DXLIV.

Economic Situation: II; IV–VI; VIII–XI; XIII; XIV; XVII–XXI; XXIV; XXVI; XXVIII–XXXI; XXXIV; XXXVI; XLVI; XLVII; XCVI; LVIII; LXI; LXIV–LXVI; LXXI–LXXIII; LXXV–LXXVII; LXXIX; LXXXIX; CII; CIV–CVIII; CX; CXIII–CXX; CXIV; CXXIV; CXXV; CXXXII; CXL; CXLIII; CL; CLXXIV; CXLIII; CXCIII; CXCV; CCXI; CCXIII–CCXVII; CCXIX–CCXXI; CCXXXV; CCXXIX; CCXLVI; CCXLVIII; CCLVIII; CCCXXVI; CCCLXII; CCCLXIX–CCCLXXI; CCCXCV; CDXIV; CDXXX; CDLVIII; DXLIV.

Minutes of UGIF (Paris) board meetings: nonclassified: Volumes I and II missing, volume III, 24 December 1942–25 May 1943; volume IV, 27 May 1943–16 September 1943; volume V, 27 September 1943–30 November 1943.

Meetings of the two boards of the UGIF: DXLIII; DXLIV.

Aide Médicale: XXVIII; XXXI.

Ardennes: CDXXVII.

Armée Juive (OJC): CCXIV; CCXV; CDLXIX; CDLXXI; CDLXXVI; DXXX.

Colonie Scolarie: XXVIII; CDXXIII; CDXXVI; CDXXIX.

Comité de Bienfaisance: LXXVI; CDXI.

Comité de Coordination: XXXI; CXCIII; LXXVI; CCXIII; CCXVI; CCXVII; CDXIV; CDXVII; CDXVIII; CDXXV; CDXXVI; DXLIV.

Conseil Représentatif des Juifs de France: CCXVI.

Consistoire de Paris: XXVIII.

Consistoire Central: LXXII; CCXIX; CCXX; CCLXXVI; CCCLXIII; CCCLXVI; CCCLXXIII; CCCLXXIX; CCCLXXXIV; CDXXIII; CDLXXII.

Eclaireurs Israélites de France: XXVIII; XXXI; LXXII; CCXIII; CCXV; DXLIV.

Fédération des Sociétés Juives de France: XI; XXVIII; XXXI; CCXIII; CCXIV; CCXVIII; CCXIX; CDXV; CDLXXII.

Union Générale des Israélites de France: V; X; XI; XXIV; XXVIII; XLVI; LVIII; LXXIV; LXXVI; LXXVII; XCVI; CX; CCXIII; CCXIV; CCXVII; CCXXI; CCXXXVIII; CCXXIX; CDX–CDXII; CDXV; CDXXII; CDXXIII; CDXXVI.

Incorporation of organizations: XXVIII; XXXI; CDXI; CDXV; CDXVI; CDXXIII.

Bulletin d'Information; Bulletin de l'UGIF: XLVII.

WIZO: CCXVII.

Youth centers and services: XXVIII; XXXI; XXXVI; CCXIII; CCXV; CCCXXIX; CDVIII; CDXVI–CDXIX; CDXXII; CDXXIV–CDXXVII; CDXXIX.

Mouvement National Contre le Racisme: CDLVIII.

Organizations: Résistance: XXII; LXXVII; LXXIX; LXXXIX; CCXVI; CCLXIII; CCCLXXIV; CDXXI; CDLXVII–CDLXX.

Raymond Raoul Lambert, Journal, 29 November 1942–20 August 1943, microfilm, nonclassified.

Eclaireurs Israélites de France (Paris)
Archives: nonclassified.

Conseil Représentatif des Juifs de France (Paris)
Archives: nonclassified.

Institut Maurice Thorez (Paris)
Collections: *Comité Général de Défense des Juifs:* série alpha. *Union Générale des Israélites de France:* série beta. *Union des Juifs pour la Résistance et l'Entr'aide:* série delta, zeta.

Bibliothèque Medem (Paris).
Collection: Unzer Shtime.

Secrétariat d'Etat aux Anciens Combattants. Statut de Combattants et de Victimes de Guerre (Paris), nonclassified.

Index cards of Internees at Pithiviers, Beaune-La-Rolande, Compiègne, Drancy.
Lists of individuals executed by the German authorities.

Israel

Central Zionist Archives (Jerusalem).

S26–1452.	Situation of the Jews in France.
Z4–15189.	Deportation of children.
S5 811.	Correspondence with Zionist organizations in France (1941–45).
S6 4565.	Letters from France.
L22 151.	General reports: France to Switzerland.
S26 1538.	J. Jefroykin, Rapport sur l'activité du MJS de France, Barcelona, 28 August 1944.

The Hebrew University of Jerusalem, *Institute of Contemporary Jewry.*

Department of Demography:
France: Jews, population, census; nonclassified.
France: economic census, FR 0201.

Oral History Division: Interviews:
Apenceler, Uri. 299:55(1).
Garel, Georges. 302:64(1).
Lambert, Anne Marie. 306:46(1).
Loinger, Georges. 30762(1).
Schwartz, Joseph J. 243:19(47); 291:10(2).
Jefroykin, Jules. 275:61(1).

Yad Vashem Archives
France: série 0/9.

0–9/3. Illegal publications.
0–9/4. Letters to Maréchal Pétain.
0–9/5, 6, 8, 9, 25–30. UGIF.
0–9/7. Drancy, camps.
0–9/31. Oberg-Knochen, protocols of trial.
0–9/34. Coordination Committee of the Jewish Relief Organizations of Paris.

Jarblum Collection: Série P 7/3.
Oral depositions:
Wiener Library Collection: statements and memoirs.
Série 02–03.
Charles Wittenberg Collection.

Published Documents

Die Endlösung der Judenfrage in Frankreich. German Documents 1941–44. Edited by Serge Klarsfeld. Paris: Beate and Serge Klarsfeld, Dokumentationszentrum für judische Zeitgeschichte CDJC Paris, 1977.

Les Juifs sous l'Occupation. Collection of French and German laws 1940–44. Introduction by R. Sarraute and P. Tager. Paris: CDJC, 1945, reed., postface S. Klarsfeld, Paris: CDJC and FFDJF, 1982.

Klarsfeld, Serge. *Le Mémorial de la Déportation des Juifs de France.* Paris: Beate and Serge Klarsfeld, 1978.

————. *Additif au Mémorial de la Déportation des Juifs de France.* Paris: Serge et Beate Klarsfeld, 1980.

————. *Vichy-Auschwitz. Le role de Vichy dans la solution finale de la question juive en France, 1942.* Vol. 1. Paris: Fayard, 1983.

————. *Vichy-Auschwitz.* Vol. 2 Paris: Fayard, 1985.

"Listes chronologique [*sic*] et analytique [*sic*] des textes intéressant directement ou indirectement les Israélites de France, Mai 1940–Juin 1944." In J. Lubetzki, *La Condition des Juifs en France sous l'occupation allemande 1940–1944. La Législation raciale.* Preface by Justin Godart, pp. 219–57. Paris: CDJC, 1945.

La Persécution des Juifs en France et dans les autres pays de l'Ouest présentée par la France à Nuremberg. Centre de Documentation Juive Contemporaine. Série "Documents," no. 2. Published under the direction of Henri Monneray. Preface by René Cassin. Introduction by Edgar Faure. Paris: Editions du Centre, 1947.

La Persécution raciale. Crimes ennemis en France. [Roger Berg.] Preface by Jacques Billiet. Paris: Service d'informations des crimes de guerre, Office français d'édition, 1947.

La Presse anti-raciste sous l'occupation hitlérienne. Collection of illegal Jewish publications, 1940–44. Preface by Abraham Rayski. Introduction by Me. Charles Lederman. Mimeographed. Paris: Centre de Documentation de l'Union des Juifs pour la Résistance et l'Entr'aide, 1950.

Rutkowski, Adam, ed. *La Lutte des Juifs en France à l'époque de l'occupation (1940–1944).* Collection of documents. Introduction by Georges Wellers. Paris: CDJC, 1975.

Steinberg, Lucien. *Les Autorités allemandes en France occupée.* Annotated inventory of the CDJC collection of documents originating from the archives of the German embassy, the military administration in France, and the Gestapo in France. Foreword by Isaac Schneersohn. Preface by Jacques Delarue. Les inventaires des archives du Centre de Documentation Juive Contemporaine. Vol. 2. Paris: CDJC, 1966.

Trial of War Criminals before the Nuremberg Military International Tribunals under Control Council Law no. 10. Washington, D.C.: Government Printing Office, 1951–52, 15 vols.

Dos Vort fun Vidershtant un Zieg. Collection of illegal Yiddish publications, 1940–44. Introduction by Abraham Rayski. Mimeographed. Paris: Centre de Documentation de l'Union des Juifs pour la Résistance et l'Entre'aide, 1949.

Primary and Secondary Sources

Articles and Books

L'Activité des organisations juives en France sous l'occupation. Centre de Documentation Juive Contemporaine. Série "Etudes et monographies," no. 4. Paris: Editions du Centre, 1947; reed., pref. G. Wellers, 1983.

Albert, Phyllis Cohen. *The Modernization of French Jewry: Consistory and Com-*

munity in the Nineteenth Century. Hanover, N.H.: Brandeis University Press, 1977.

Amouroux, Henri. *La Vie des Français sous l'Occupation*. Paris: Fayard, 1961.

————. *Le Peuple reveillé*. Juin 1940–Février 1942. Paris: Robert Laffont, 1979.

Anderson, Malcolm. *Conservative Politics in France*. London: Allen & Unwin, 1974.

Ariel, Joseph [Fisher]. "Jewish Self-Defense and Resistance in France During World War II." *Yad Vashem Studies* 6 (1967): 221–50.

Aron, Robert. *The Vichy Regime, 1940–1944*. In collaboration with Georgette Elgey. Translated by Humphrey Hare. *Histoire de Vichy 1940–1944*. Paris: Fayard, 1954; Boston: Beacon Press, 1969.

Azéma, Jean Pierre. *De Munich à la Libération, 1938–1944*. Paris: Editions du Seuil, 1979.

Bernard, Jean Jacques. *Le Camp de la mort lente (Compiègne, 1941–1942)*. Paris: Albin Michel, 1944.

Besserman, Alfred. "Der Kampf fun die yiddishe arbeiter in die yorn fun krieg un fascism." In *In Kampf far Freiheit* (Yiddish and French), pp. 55–121. Published by the Commission Intersyndicale Juive auprès de la CGT. Paris: Farlag Oifsnei, 1948.

Billig, Joseph. *Le Commissariat Général aux Questions Juives (1941–1944)*. 3 vols. Preface by Edmond Vermeil. Paris: Editions du Centre, 1955–60.

————. *L'Institut d'Etude des Questions Juives: Officine française des autorités nazies en France. Les inventaires des archives du Centre de Documentation Juive Contemporaine*. Paris: CDJC, 1974.

————. *La Solution Finale de la Question Juive: Essai sur ses principes dans le IIIᵉ Reich et en France sous l'occupation*. With biographical studies of the Nazi personnel in charge of the "Final Solution" in France by Me. Serge Klarsfeld. Paris: Beate Klarsfeld, Serge Klarsfeld, and CDJC, 1977.

Bloch, Marc. *L'Etrange défaite*. Paris: Albin Michel, 1957.

Bourdrel, Phillipe. *Histoire des Juifs en France*. Paris: Albin Michel, 1974.

Boussinot, Roger. *Les Guichets du Louvre*. Paris: Editions Denoël, 1960.

Broszat, Martin. "Hitler and the Genesis of the 'Final Solution': An assessment of David Irving's Theses." *Yad Vashem Studies* 13 (1979): 73–125.

Bulawko, Henri. *Les Jeux de la mort et de l'espoir. Auschwitz/Joworzno*. Preface by Vladimir Jankelevitch. 2d ed. Paris: Encres. Recherches, 1980.

————. "Un anniversaire oublié. Les Premiers internements Juifs à la Caserne des Tourelles." *Le Monde Juif* 97, ns (January–March 1980): 36–37.

Byrnes, Robert. *Antisemitism in Modern France: The Prologue to the Dreyfus Affair*. Vol. 1. 2d ed. New Brunswick, N.J.: Rutgers University Press, 1961.

Cohen, Israel. *The Jews and the War*. London: Frederick Miller, 1943.

Cohen, Yerachmiel (Richard). "A Jewish Leader in Vichy France, 1940–1943: The Diary of Raymond Raoul Lambert." *Jewish Social Studies* 3–4 (Summer–Autumn 1981): 291–310.

————. "French Jewry's Dilemma on the Orientation of its Leadership: From Polemics to Conciliation, 1942–1944." *Yad Vashem Studies* 14 (1981): 167–204.

————. Introduction and annotation. In R. R. Lambert, *Carnet d'un témoin*. Paris: Fayard, 1984.

Chouraqui, André. *L'Alliance Israélite Universelle et la renaissance juive contem-*

poraine. Cent ans d'histoire (1860–1960). Preface by René Cassin. Paris: Presse Universitaire de France, 1965.

Conseil Représentatif des Juifs de France (fondé dans la clandestinité en 1943). Vingt-cinq années d'activités, ed. Maurice Moch. Historique du CRIF, 1944–69. Paris: CRIF, 1970.

Courtois, Stéphane. *Le PCF dans la guerre: De Gaulle, la Résistance, Staline*. . . . Paris: Editions Ramsay, 1980.

Debré, Robert. *L'Honneur de vivre. Témoignage*. Paris: Stock-Hermann, 1974.

Delpech, François. "La Persécution des Juifs et l'Amitié Chrétienne." In *Eglises et Chrétiens dans la IIe guerre mondiale. La région Rhône-Alpes*. Proceedings of a symposium held at Grenoble, 7–9 October 1976, pp. 143–79. Published under the direction of Xavier de Montclos, Monique Luirard, François Delpech, Pierre Bolle. Lyon: Presse Universitaire de Lyon, 1978.

Diamant, David. *Les Juifs dans la Résistance française, 1940–1944 (avec ou sans armes)*. Preface by Albert Ouzoulias. Postface by Charles Lederman. Paris: Roger Maria, Le Pavillon, 1971.

———. *Le Billet vert. La Vie et la résistance à Pithiviers et Beaune-La-Rolande. Camps pour Juifs, camps pour chrétiens, camps pour patriotes*. Preface by Marcel Paul and Olga Wormser-Pigot. Postface by Henri Bulawko. Paris: Edition Renouveau, 1977.

———. *Combattants juifs dans l'armée républicaine espagnole, 1936–1939*. Paris: Renouveau, 1979.

Dworzecki, Meir. "The International Red Cross and its Policy Vis-à-Vis the Jews in the Ghettos and Concentration Camps in Nazi Occupied Europe." In *Rescue Attempts during the Holocaust*. Proceedings of the Second Yad-Vashem International Historical Conference. Jerusalem, 8–11 April 1974, pp. 71–110. Jerusalem: Yad Vashem, 1977.

Eglises et Chrétiens dans la II Guerre Mondiale. La région Rhône-Alpes. Proceedings of a symposium held at Grenoble, 7–9 October 1976. Published under the direction of Xavier de Montclos, Monique Luirard, François Delpech, Pierre Bolle. Lyon: Presse Universitaire de Lyon, 1978.

France under the German Occupation, 1940–1944. 3 vols. A collection of 292 statements on the government of Maréchal Pétain and Pierre Laval. Translated by Philip W. Whitcomb. Stanford, Calif.: Stanford University Press for the Hoover Institute on War, Revolution and Peace, 1958–1959.

Friedländer, Saul. *When Memory Comes*. Translated by Helen R. Lane. Quand vient le souvenir. . . . Paris: Editions du Seuil, 1978; New York: Avon, 1980.

———. *Pie XII et le IIIe Reich*. Documents. Postface by Alfred Grosser. Paris: Editions du Seuil, 1964.

Ganier-Raymond, Philipe. *L'Affiche rouge*. Paris. Fayard, 1975.

Garlinski, Joseph. "The Underground Movement in Auschwitz Concentration Camp." In *Resistance in Europe, 1939–1945*, ed. Stephen Hawes and Ralph White. Based on a symposium held at the University of Salford, March 1973, pp. 55–76. London: Allen Lane, 1975; Penguin, 1976.

Geissmann, Robert. "Il y a 25 ans: Les attentats nazis contre les synagogues parisiennes." *Journal des communautés* 382 (9 December 1966).

———. "Le Rabbinat consistorial sous l'occupation." *Journal des communautés* 393 (28 April 1967).

Gillot, Auguste, and Gillot, Simone. *Un couple dans la Résistance.* 2d ed. Paris: Editions Sociales, 1976.

Girard, Patrick. *Les Juifs de France de 1789 à 1860. De l'émancipation à l'égalité.* Paris: Calmann-Lévy, 1976.

Grant, Alfred. *Paris a Schtot fun Front.* Paris: Farlag Oifsnei, 1958.

Grayzel, Salomon. *A History of the Jews.* 2d ed. New York: Mentor, 1968.

Gronowski-Brunot, Louis. *Le Dernier grand soir. Un Juif de Pologne.* In collaboration with Nina Kehayan. Paris: Editions du Seuil, 1980.

Guéhenno, Jean. *Journal des années noires (1940–1944).* Paris: NRF, Gallimard, 1947; 1973.

Gutman, Yisrael. "The Concept of Labor in Judenrat Policy." In *Patterns of Jewish Leadership in Nazi Europe, 1933–1945.* Proceedings of the Third Yad Vashem International Historical Conference. Jerusalem, 4–7 April 1977, pp. 151–80. Jerusalem: Yad Vashem, 1979.

Gyges. *Les Israélites dans la société française.* Témoignages et documents. Paris: La Librairie Française, 1965.

Hersch, L. "Yiddishe emigratie fun die letste undert yor." In *Algemeine Entsiklopedie,* Vol. "Yidn A," pp. 441–82. New York: Dubnow Fund and CYCO, 1950.

Hertz, Henri. "Historique du CRIF." In *Les Juifs en Europe (1939–1945).* Reports presented at the first European conference of historical commissions and Jewish documentation centres, pp. 58–63. Série "Etudes et monographies," no. 8. Paris: Editions du Centre, 1949.

Hertzberg, Arthur. *The Enlightenment and the Jews.* New York: Columbia University Press, 1968.

Hilberg, Raul. *The Destruction of the European Jews.* Chicago: Quadrangle Books, 1961; Harper Colophon, 1979.

Hyman, Paula. *From Dreyfus to Vichy. The Remaking of French Jewry, 1906–1939.* New York: Columbia University Press, 1979.

Israel, Gérard. *Heureux comme Dieu en France.* Paris: Laffont, 1975.

Jakoubowicz, Yehuda. "Unter die Koulissn fun Deutschen Yidn Politik in Frankraikh." In *Unzer Shtime,* 19 (6 December 1944); "Unter die Koulissn fun Deutschen Yidn Politik in Frankraikh." II, 29 (9 December 1944); "Unter die Koulissn fun Deutschen Yidn Politik in Frankraikh," III, no. 22 (16 December 1944).

―――. "Fun 'aristocrat' tzu a konspirator." In *Léon Glaeser. Der Kulturtuer un Freiheit-kampfer,* ed. C. Tchoubinski. Paris: Comité Général de Défense des Juifs, 1947.

―――. *Rue Amelot. Hilf un Vidershtant.* With a contribution by I. Bil. Paris: Colonie Scolaire, 1948.

Jarblum, Marc. "Zu die Geschichte fun UGIF." *Illustrierte Folksbleter* 2 (March–April 1945): 13, 25.

Jefroykin, Jules. "L'Organisation Juive de Combat. Le refus." *Les Nouveaux Cahiers* 37 (Summer 1974): 18–24.

Les Juifs dans la résistance et la libération. Histoire, témoignages, débats. R.H.I.C.O.J. (eds.). Paris: Editions du Scribe, 1985.

Les Juifs en Europe (1939–1945). Reports presented at the first European conference of historical commissions and Jewish documentation centres. Série "Etudes et monographies," no. 8. Paris: Editions du Centre, 1949.

Kaplan, Jacob. "French Jewry under the Occupation." *American Jewish Yearbook* 5706 (1945–46): 71–118.

Katz, Robert. *Black Sabbath. The Politics of Annihilation. The Harrowing Story of the Jews of Rome, 1943.* London: Arthur Barker, 1969.

Kaufman, Hersch. *Unter die Deutsche occupatsie in Frankraikh.* Paris: Hersch Kaufman, 1964.

Klarsfeld, Serge. *Le Livre des otages.* Preface by Marie-Claude Vaillant Couturier. Paris: Editeurs Français Réunis, 1979.

Knout, David. *Contribution à l'histoire de la Résistance Juive en France, 1940–1944.* Centre de Documentation Juive Contemporaine. Série "Etudes et monographies," no. 3. Preface by Louis Saillant. Paris: Editions du Centre, 1947.

Korenhandler, Chaskiel. *Briven fun Lectoure.* Paris: Oifgang Farlag, 1947.

Krausnick, Helmut, and Broszat, Martin. *Anatomy of the SS State.* Translated by Dorothy Long and Marian Jackson. *Anatomie des SS-Staates.* London: Paladin, 1970.

Kriegel, Annie. "Résistants communistes et Juifs persécutés." *H-Histoire* 3 (November 1970): 99–123.

Lambert, Raymond Raoul. *Carnet d'un témoin (1940–1943).* Introduction and annotation by Richard Cohen. Paris. Fayard, 1985.

Langbein, Herman. *La Résistance dans les camps de concentration nationaux-socialistes, 1938–1945.* Paris: Fayard, 1981.

Langeron, Roger. *Paris, Juin 1940.* Paris: Flammarion, 1946.

Laroche, Gaston (Boris Matline, Colonel FTPF). *On les nommait des étrangers. Les Immigrés dans la Résistance.* Paris: Editeurs Français Réunis, 1965.

Latour, Annie. *La Résistance Juive en France, 1940–1944.* Paris: Stock, 1970.

Lazarus, Jacques (Capitaine Jacquel). *Juifs au Combat.* Témoignage sur l'activité d'un mouvement de résistance. Preface by Henri Hertz. Série "Etudes et monographies," no. 9. Paris: Editions du Centre, 1947.

Lévy, Claude. *Les Parias de la Résistance.* Paris: Calmann-Lévy, 1970.

Lévy, Claude, and Tillard, Paul. *La Grande rafle du Vel d'Hiv (16 Juillet 1942).* Preface by Joseph Kessel. Paris: Robert Laffont, 1967.

Lissner, Abraham. *Un Franc-tireur Juif raconte. . . .* Presented by Joseph Fridman. Preface by Henri Roll-Tanguy. 3d ed. Paris: Abraham Lissner, 1977.

Lubetzki. J. *La Condition des Juifs en France sous l'occupation allemande, 1940–1944. La Législation raciale.* Preface by Justin Godart. Paris: CDJC, 1945.

Manouchian, Melinée. *Manouchian.* Paris: Editeurs Français Réunis, 1974.

Marrus, Michael R. *Les Juifs de France à l'époque de l'affaire Dreyfus. L'Assimilation à l'épreuve.* Translated by Micheline Legras. *The Politics of Assimilation.* Preface by Pierre Vidal-Naquet. Paris: Calmann-Lévy, 1972.

———. "Vichy et les enfants Juifs." *L'Histoire* 22 (April 1980): 6–15.

Marrus, Michael R., and Paxton, Robert O. *Vichy et les Juifs.* Translated by Marguerite Delmotte. Paris: Calmann-Lévy, 1981.

Martin du Gard, Maurice. *La Chronique de Vichy, 1940–1944.* Paris: Flammarion, 1948; reedited by Claire Roussel-Martin du Gard, Flammarion, 1975.

May, Jacques. *Paris en 1.591 jours.* Paris: Jacques May, 1947.

Mendel, Arnold. "Die Yidn in Frankraikh." *Algemeine Entsiklopedie.* Vol. 4, p. 628. New York: Dubnow Fund and CYCO, 1950.

Michaelis, Meir. *Mussolini and the Jews. German-Italian Relations and the Jewish Question in Italy, 1921–1945*. London: Institute for Jewish Affairs, Oxford: Clarendon Press, 1978.

Michel, Henri. *Histoire de la Résistance*. 7th ed. Paris: Presse Universitaire de France, 1975.

Miller, Gerard. "En feuilletant les archives du CGQJ." In *Elements pour une analyse du fascisme*. 2 vols. Séminaire de Maria-A. Macciochi. Paris VIII-Vincennes. 1:63–102. Paris: Editions 10/18, 1976.

Mintz, Pinkas (Alexander). *In die Yorn fun Yiddishn Umkum un Vidershtant in Frankraikh (persendleche zechoines)*. Buenos Aires: Farlag Yidbuch, 1956.

Morley, John F. *Vatican Diplomacy and the Jews during the Holocaust, 1939–1943*. New York: Ktav, 1980.

Noguères, Louis. *Le Véritable procès du Maréchal Pétain*. Paris: Fayard, 1955.

Ory, Pascal. *Les Collaborateurs, 1940–1945*. Paris: Editions du Seuil, 1976.

Osgood, Samuel M. "The Antisemitism of the French Collaborationist Press." *Wiener Library Bulletin* 23, nos. 2–3, ns, nos. 15–16 (1969): 51–56.

Ouzoulias, Albert (Colonel André). *Les Bataillons de la jeunesse*. Paris: Editions Sociales, 1972.

Paraf, Pierre. *Israel dans le monde*. Paris: Flammarion, 1947.

Patterns of Jewish Leadership in Nazi Europe, 1933–1945. Proceedings of the Third Yad Vashem International Historical Conference. Jerusalem, 4–7 April 1977. Edited by Yisrael Gutman and Cynthia J. Haft. Jerusalem: Yad Vashem, 1979.

Paxton, Robert O. *Vichy France. Old Guard and New Order, 1940–1944*. London: Barrie and Jenkins, 1972; New York: Norton, 1975.

Perrault, Giles. *L'Orchestre rouge*. Paris: Fayard, 1967.

Poliakov, Léon. *L'Etoile jaune*. Preface by Justin Godart. Centre de Documentation Juive Contemporaine. Série "Etudes et monographies," no. 2. Paris: Editions du Centre, 1949.

———. *Harvest of Hate*. Introduced by Lord Russell of Liverpool. Forewords by François Mauriac and Reinhold Neibuhr. London: Elek Books, 1956.

———. "Les Différentes Formes de la Résistance Juive en France." In *Jewish Resistance during the Holocaust*. Proceedings of the Conference on Manifestations of Jewish Resistance. Jerusalem, 7–11 April 1968, pp. 524–532. Jerusalem: Yad Vashem, 1971.

Poliakov, Léon, and Sabille, Jacques. *Jews under the Italian Occupation*. Foreword by Justin Godart. Paris: Editions du Centre, 1955.

Pougatch, Isaac. *Un Bâtisseur, Robert Gamzon, dit "Castor soucieux," 1905–1961*. Foreword by M. J. Kaplan. Preface by Robert Munnich. Paris: Service technique pour l'education, FSJU, 1971.

Rabi, Wladimir. *Anatomie du judaïsme français*. Paris: Editions de Minuit, 1962.

Rajsfus, Maurice. *Des Juifs dans la collaboration. L'UGIF (1941–1944)*. Preceded by a short study on the Jews in France in 1939. Preface by Pierre Vidal-Naquet. Paris: Etudes et documentations internationales, 1980.

———. *Sois Juif et tais-toi! 1930–1940. Les Français "Israélites" face au Nazisme*. Paris: Etudes et documentations internationales, 1981.

Ravine, Jacques. *Le Résistance organisée des Juifs en France (1940–1944)*. Preface by Vladimir Pozer. Paris: Julliard, 1973.

Rayski, Abraham. "Les Origines et le rôle de la presse clandestine antiraciste en France." Preface to *La Presse antiraciste sous l'occupation hitlérienne*. Collection of illegal Jewish publications, 1940–44, pp. 15–21. Introduction by Me. Charles Lederman. Mimeographed. Paris: Centre de Documentation de l'union des Juifs pour la Résistance et l'Entr'aide, 1950.

————. "Paris face à la grande rafle. Comment plus de 12,000 Juifs ont pu échapper à la mort." A. Rayski and G. Wellers, "Les Rafles des 16–17 Juillet 1942." *Le Monde Juif,* supplement, 12 (46): 1–13.

————. "La Résistance en France et le soulèvement du Ghetto de Varsovie." *Le Monde Juif* 49, ns (January–March 1968): 56–62.

————. "La Fondation du Comité Représentatif des Juifs de France." *Le Monde Juif* 51, ns (July–September 1968): 32–37.

————. "Le Comité Juif de Défense: Son rôle dans la Résistance Juive en France." *Le Monde Juif* 52, ns (October–December 1968): 29–35.

————. "Gestapo contre résistants Juifs à Paris. Le front invisible (II)." *Le Monde Juif* 55 (July–September 1969): 11–20.

————. "Les Immigrés dans la Résistance." *Les Nouveaux Cahiers* 37 (Summer 1974): 10–17.

————. "Diversité et unité de la Résistance Juive." In *Les Juifs dans la résistance et la libération. Histoire, témoignages, débats.* R.I.C.J.H. (eds.), pp. 165–68. Paris: Editions du Scribe, 1985.

Reitlinger, Gerald. *The Final Solution: The Attempt to Exterminate the Jews of of Europe, 1939–1945.* New York: Beechhurst Press, 1953; London: Sphere Books, 1971.

Rescue Attempts during the Holocaust. Proceedings of the Second Yad Vashem International Historical Conference. Jerusalem, 8–11 April 1974. Jerusalem: Yad Vashem, 1977.

Riba, Raphael. "Yiddisher Socialistisher Farband 'Bund,' in Frankraikh." *Unzer Tsait* 3–4 (November–December 1947).

Robinson, Jacob. *And the Crooked Shall Be Made Straight: The Eichmann Trial, the Jewish Catastrophe, and Hannah Arendt's Narrative.* New York: Macmillan, 1965.

Roblin, Michel. *Les Juifs de Paris: Démographie-Economie-Culture.* Paris: Editions A. et J. Picard, 1952.

Roland, Charlotte. *Du Ghetto à l'Occident (deux générations yiddishes en France).* Preface by Louis Chevalier. Paris: Editions de Minuit, 1962.

Roth, Cecil. *History of the Jews.* New York: Schocken Books, n.d.

Ruppin, Arthur. *The Jews in the Modern World.* London: Macmillan, 1934.

Rutkowski, Adam. "Le Camp de Royallieu à Compiègne (1941–1944)." *Le Monde Juif* 104, ns (October–December 1981): 121–50.

Schah, Eugène. "L'Activité de l'ORT sous l'occupation." In *Les Juifs en Europe (1939–1945).* Reports presented at the first European conference of historical commissions and Jewish documentation centers. Série "Etudes et monographies," no. 8, pp. 228–34. Paris: Editions du Centre, 1949.

Schrager, F. *Oifn rund fun tzwei tkoufes (zechroines).* Paris: F. Schrager, 1976.

Steinberg, Lucien. *La Révolte des Justes: Les Juifs contre Hitler, 1933–1945.* Paris: Fayard, 1970.

————. *Les Allemands en France, 1940–1944.* In collaboration with Jean-Marie Fitère. Paris: Albin Michel, 1980.

Suhl, Yuri. *They Fought Back: The Story of the Jewish Resistance in Nazi Europe.* New York: Crown, 1967.

Szajkowski, Zosa. "The Jewish Press in France, 1940–1946." *YIVO Bleter* 27 (Summer 1946): 388–401.

———. "Glimpses on the History of the Jews in Occupied France." *Yad Vashem Studies* 2 (1958): 133–57.

———. "The Organization of the 'UGIF' in Nazi-Occupied France." *Jewish Social Studies* 9 (July 1947): 239–56.

———. "The French Central Consistory." *Yad Vashem Studies* 3 (1959): 187–202.

———. *Analytical Franco-Jewish Gazetteer, 1939–1945. With an Introduction to Some Problems in Writing the History of the Jews in France During World War II.* New York: Zosa Szajkowski, 1966.

Tartokower, Arieh, and Grossman, Kurt. *The Jewish Refugees.* New York: New York Institute of Jewish Affairs of the American Jewish Congress and the World Jewish Congress, 1944.

Tcherikower, E., ed. *Yidn in Frankraikh.* 2 vols. New York: YIVO, 1942.

Tchoubinski, C., ed. *Léon Glaeser: Der Kulturtuer un Freiheit-kampfer.* Paris: Comité Général de Défense des Juifs, 1947.

Tillon, Charles. *Les F.T.P.: La guérilla en France.* 2d ed. Paris: Julliard, 1967.

Trepper, Léopold. *The Great Game: The Story of the Red Orchestra.* Written in collaboration with Patrick Rotman. Translated. *Le Grand Jeu.* Paris: Albin Michel, 1975; London: Sphere Books, 1979.

Trunk, Isaiah. *Judenrat. The Jewish Councils in Eastern Europe under Nazi Occupation.* Introduction by Jacob Robinson. New York: Macmillan, 1972; Stein and Day, 1977.

L'Un des Trente-six. A la mémoire de David Rapoport, 1883–1944. With contributions by A. Alperine, R. Grinberg, Dr. H. Baruk, L. Chevalley-Sabatier, J. Jakoubowicz, M. Jarblum, Dr. E. Minkowski, Serge Stern, and Rachel Tsoutsoulkovsky. Paris: Editions Kyoum, 1946.

Vago, Bela, and Mosse, George L., eds. *Jews and Non-Jews in Eastern Europe, 1918–1945.* New York: Wiley, 1974.

Vallat, Xavier. *Le Nez de Cléopâtre. Souvenir d'un homme de droite, 1918–1945.* Preface by Charles Maurras. Paris: Les Quatre fils Aymon, 1957.

Vegh, Claudine. *Je ne lui ai pas dit au revoir. Des enfants de deportés parlent.* Entretiens avec Claudine Vegh. Postface by Bruno Bettleheim. Paris: NRF, Gallimard, 1979.

Vilner, David. "An Oifshtant in Birkenau." In *In Kampf far Freiheit* (Yiddish and French), pp. 253–57. Published by the Commission Intersyndicale Juive auprès de la CGT. Paris: Farlag Oifsnei, 1948.

Weill, Joseph. *Contribution à l'histoire des camps d'internement dans l'Anti-France.* Centre de Documentation Juive Contemporaine. Série "Etudes et monographies," no. 5. Paris: Editions du Centre, 1946.

Weil-Curiel, André. *Le Temps de la honte.* 3 vols. Paris: Editions du Myrte, 1945–47.

Weinberg, David H. *Les Juifs à Paris de 1933 à 1939.* Translated by Micheline Pouteau. *A Community on Trial: The Jews of Paris in the 1930s.* Paris: Clamann-Lévy, 1974.

Wellers, Georges. *De Drancy à Auschwitz.* Centre de Documentation Juive Contemporaine. Série "Etudes et monographies," no. 6. Paris: Editions du Centre, 1946.

————. *L'Etoile jaune à l'heure de Vichy: De Drancy à Auschwitz.* Preface by J. Delarue. Postface by R. P. Riquet. Paris: Fayard. 1973.

Wolf, Dieter. *Doriot; du communisme à la collaboration.* Translated by Georgette Chatinet. Paris: Fayard, 1969.

Wormser, Georges. "Allocution." *Journal des Communautés* 40 (2 February 1968):4.

————. "Notre organisation après la défaite de 1940." *Journal des Communautés* 459 (24 April 1970).

Youdine, Albert. "Union—Die rumfule yiddishe vidershtant organizatsie." *Parizer Tsaitschrift* 33 (June 1964): 27–40.

Zalcman, Moshé. *Histoire véridique de Moshé. Ouvrier Juif et communiste au temps de Staline.* Translated by Halina Edelstein. Paris: Encres. Editions Recherches, 1977.

Periodicals

Le Monde Juif
YIVO Bleter
Yad Vashem Studies
Journal des Communatés

Interviews and Discussions

(With the names of the organizations, and positions of responsibility, to which the interviewed individuals were affiliated, and, where significant, relevant biographical data.)

Borenstein, Bernard. Solidarity, youth section. Paris, 5 May 1978.

Bulawko, Henri. Hashomer Hatzair, Amelot Committee. Paris, 10 July 1978.

Diamant, David. Solidarity, trade-union activities. In 1978, archivist, Institut Maurice Thorez. Paris, 2–15 June 1978.

Endewelt, Robert. Solidarity, leadership youth section. In 1978, staff, Central Committee, PCF. Paris, 10 April 1978.

Ezerowicz, Broniek. Bundist, Amelot Committee. Melbourne, 15 November 1977.

Fridman, Joseph. Left-Poale Zion, leadership of CGD. In 1986, president, Association of the Former Immigrant Volunteers in the French Army. Paris, 10 August 1978.

Korman, Ydel. Solidarity, leadership. Paris, 15 March 1978.

Radzinski, André. Solidarity, youth section. Paris, 9 March 1978.

Radzinski, Samuel. Solidarity, youth section, leadership. Arrested July 1943, Auschwitz, escaped January 1944. Paris, 10 March 1978.

Rayski, Abraham. Solidarity, leadership. Paris, 17 June 1978.

Rozemblum, Albert. Nonaffiliated. Paris, 15 May 1978.

Schrager, F. Bund leadership, leadership CGD, former Communist. Paris, 2 May 1978.

Schwartz, Jean-Claude. Solidarity, youth section leadership. Paris, 5 April 1978.

Smolinski, Pierre. Solidarity, youth section, UGIF employee. Paris, 7 April 1978.

Somer, Emile. Solidarity, youth section, trade-union activities. Paris, 14 March 1978.

Szlamowicz, David. Communal activist, nonaffiliated. Melbourne, 15 March 1981.

Tachnoff, Georges. Solidarity, youth section, leadership. Paris, 2 July 1978.

Tancerman, Jean. UJRE, military commander of the milices patriotiques juives. Paris, 12 July 1978.

Waiszbrot, M. Bund. Director of the Medem Library. Paris, 2 March 1978.

Zaidov, Simon. Solidarity. Former member of the International Brigades in Spain. Deported from France in March 1942. Escaped from Auschwitz. Melbourne, 15 April 1982.

Index

Abetz, Otto, 56–59, 251*n*
Achenbach, Ernest, 57
Akerberg, Albert, 156, 218–19
Alexander II (czar, Russia), 5
Alliance Israélite Universelle (Universal
    Israelite Alliance; AIU), 4, 33, 54,
    241*n*
  funds held by, 91, 146–47
Alperine, Abraham, 137, 157, 203, 212,
    218
Alsace-Lorraine, 4
Amelot Committee, xiv–xv, 62–64
  beginning of functioning of, 167–69
  budget of, 76
  canteens of, 194, 205
  children aided by, 208
  clandestine newspaper publication
    rejected, 177
  closing of, 212
  contacts with Julien Weill, 168, 169
  Coordination Committee and, 68–72,
    79, 174–76, 178
  deportations and, 123
  on formation of CGQJ, 64–65
  founding of, 166–67
  illegal aid by, 199, 203–4
  Jewish Communists and, 169–70
  mass extermination reports not believed
    by, 202
  non-Jews approached by, 193, 200–201
  not consulted on UGIF, 104
  relief to detainees by, 187–88
  request for volunteers refused by, 181
  Resistance work refused by, 190
  resumption of activities of (July 1943),
    214
  strategy of, 227–29
  UGIF distrusted by, 116–17
  UGIF passes accepted by, 198
  unite with Solidarity, 182–83
  warned of mass arrests, 197
American Jewish Joint Distribution
    Committee, 142–45, 167

criticisms of, 144
Amitié Chrétienne (Christian Fellow-
    ship), 127
Antignac, Joseph, 26, 136
antisemitism
  attempts to combat, 55
  census of 1940 and, 11
  during early months of Occupation, 37
  immigrant Jews' experiences with, 165
  Jewish Communists on, 173
  Jewish economic basis and, 18
  mistakes in strategies to combat, 224
  in propaganda, 40, 187
  in Vichy government, 15, 56, 226
Arbeiter Ring (Workers' Alliance), 171
armed struggle, 188–92, 195, 200, 201,
    233–34. *See also* Resistance
  endorsed by CGD, 234–35
  losses in, 203
  by MOI, 217
  Paris uprising, 221
  by UJRE, 219–20
  in Vichy Zone, debate over, 215–16
  of Warsaw Ghetto Uprising, 211, 229
Armée Juive (Organisation Juive de
    Combat; AJ; OJC), 220
Armistice (June 1940), 34
arrests, 49, 133. *See also* internments
  of all remaining foreign-born Jews, 156
  of Baur, 151
  of Bund leaders, 179
  of children, 159
  Coordination Committee protection
    from, 78–79, 115, 263*n*
  to curb Resistance, 110
  of elderly, 136
  first, 11
  of foreign UGIF employees, 137
  by French police, 253*n*
  of immigrant Jews, 123–24, 175–76,
    206, 218
  of immigrant Jews, warnings of, 196–97
  of Jewish Resistance fighters, 217